D1592588

PICTURE BRIDE STORIES

PICTURE BRIDE STORIES

Barbara F. Kawakami

A Latitude 20 Book

UNIVERSITY OF HAWAI‘I PRESS

HONOLULU

21 20 19 18   6 5 4 3 2

Library of Congress Cataloging-in-Publication Data

Name: Kawakami, Barbara F., author.
Title: Picture bride stories / Barbara F. Kawakami.
Description: Honolulu : University of Hawai'i Press, [2016] | Includes index. |
  "A latitude 20 book."
Identifiers: LCCN 2015051278 | ISBN 9780824866242 hardcover : alk. paper
Subjects: LCSH: Mail order brides—Hawaii—Biography.
Classification: LCC HQ1032.K386 2016 | DDC 306.82—dc23 LC record available
  at http://lccn.loc.gov/2015051278

DESIGNED BY JULIE MATSUO-CHUN

In memory of my mentor and dear friend, Professor Dorothy Vella,

who encouraged me to keep on writing

CONTENTS

FOREWORD

Barbara Kawakami's research on Japanese immigrant clothing first came to my attention in 1988, while I was curating the inaugural exhibition at the Japanese American National Museum (JANM), "Issei Pioneers: Hawaii and the Mainland, 1885–1924." The exhibition was scheduled to open in 1990 at the Nishi Hongwanji Buddhist Temple, a historic cultural site in Los Angeles's Little Tokyo that would serve as the museum's first home.[1] We knew it was essential to start the exhibition in Hawaii, since this is where the issei first migrated to beginning in 1885 and where they had become permanent settlers by 1924, when the United States barred further immigration from Japan.

One of the greatest curatorial challenges I faced was how to experientially depict the world of the early issei, especially since the newly incorporated JANM did not have a permanent collection from which to draw. While Irene Hirano Inouye, then the chief executive officer of the museum, and the Board of Trustees worked to make known the mission and vision of the JANM, I spent much time reviewing the extensive literature on issei prior to World War II and consulted with numerous scholars who were known for their research on primary source materials and field-work with issei.[2] In the process, I discovered the important Japanese immigration collection at the Bishop Museum, from which a limited number of artifacts and numerous pre–World War II photographs were selected for display.[3] However, the issei story still remained far from complete.

During this initial phase of exhibition development, I made field visits to various Japanese American communities, primarily in California, where the greatest number of issei had settled before the war. While poring over my field notes, I received a call from a colleague, Professor Dennis Ogawa at the University of Hawaii, Manoa, who asked me whether I would be interested in reviewing a manuscript under consideration for publication by the University of Hawaii Press. My excitement grew as he described the author's unique approach to examining the issei immigrant experience through documentation of the clothing they wore for work, weddings, and funerals. I accepted Professor Ogawa's offer, and shortly after receiving and reading the manuscript, I booked a flight to Honolulu to meet with the writer/researcher, Barbara Kawakami.[4]

From the moment she welcomed me into her home, I knew Barbara would become a major force in shedding further light on the early issei experience in Hawaii. Her energy was boundless as she graciously showed me photographs and clothing, recounting in great detail and with much affection the unique histories of each of her interviewees. When I asked her about the work clothes worn by issei plantation workers, she told me about Mrs. Haruno Tazawa, a woman who had immigrated to Hawaii as a picture bride in 1917. At the time Mrs. Tazawa was in her nineties and still as sharp as the leaves she used to strip from the stalks of sugarcane. Barbara offered to introduce me to Mrs. Tazawa, and before long we were sitting in the living room of her neat, small one-bedroom plantation cottage at the Ewa sugar plantation.

After offering us some tea, Mrs. Tazawa disappeared into her bedroom and returned with a wicker basket, which she set before her on the floor. With her legs tucked neatly under her, she lifted the lid of the basket and carefully retrieved objects she had saved to remind her of the past. As she spoke of the grueling, backbreaking work in the cane fields of Hawaii, she explained how she had dressed herself from head to toe to protect herself from the searing sun, the razor-sharp sugarcane leaves, and the bites of poisonous insects.

The first thing she put on was a pair of long underpants (*momohiki*). Next came denim leggings (*kyahan*), a tie-dye (*kasuri*) jacket, a dirndl skirt (*koshimaki* style), and a rectangular cotton towel (*tenugui*) tied securely around her head to protect her face and hair from the sun and dust. She wrapped a black sash (*obi*) twice around her waist before she slipped hand coverings (*tesashi*) over her rough hands. Finally she put on a straw hat (*mugiwara bo*), which she secured with a hatpin and a bleached rice bag folded diagonally and placed over her hat and tied at the chin. After all of these work garments were assembled, the patchwork of fabrics and styles reflected the diversity of the Ewa plantation workforce, which comprised Hawaiians, Chinese, Japanese, Korean, Spanish, Puerto Rican, Filipino, and Portuguese.

With Barbara's assistance, Mrs. Tazawa agreed to have her story and her work clothes and lunch box (*bento bako*) displayed in the inaugural exhibition at the Japanese American National Museum and in a subsequent exhibition, "From *Bento* to Mixed Plate: Americans of Japanese Ancestry in Multicultural Hawaii," which traveled throughout the islands of Hawaii and to the Japanese American National Museum and the Smithsonian Institution on the mainland, as well as to four venues in Japan, including Hiroshima, Osaka, Okinawa, and Niigata. Many museum-goers were visibly moved when they learned about Mrs. Tazawa's hardships and saw the frayed and faded work clothes she had sewn and patched throughout her years as a plantation field hand. Mrs. Tazawa is featured in this book, along with the remarkable stories of fifteen other picture brides.

Throughout Barbara's thirty years of research on issei, she recorded a total of 250 tapes. Although she had "officially" started gathering their stories in 1979 as a class project in fashion design and merchandising at the University of Hawaii, Manoa, her curiosity and interest in the lives of those around her had its genesis in her childhood on a sugarcane plantation in Waipahu. Fluent in Japanese and familiar with the Pidgin English that had evolved from the multiethnic mixture of Hawaii's peoples, Barbara was able to understand and communicate with them as an insider, a woman raised in Hawaii. At times it was difficult for her to comprehend the various Okinawan and Japanese dialects and the Pidgin that had evolved on the plantations as a result of the different languages spoken by the mixture of ethnic groups. But her ability to establish rapport and gain the trust of her interviewees enabled her to elicit sensitive information rarely discussed with outside researchers regarding married life, husband-wife relations, pregnancy, childbirth, birth control, and child-rearing.

The issei interviewees made it abundantly clear that without a supportive network of parents and in-laws, childcare was a constant problem. Many mothers, such as Ushii Nakasone, had no choice but to take their infant to the cane fields, lay the baby on a straw mat, where the child was vulnerable to the blazing sun and pesky insects, and work while keeping one eye on the baby. After working ten hours in the field, Mrs. Nakasone returned home to cook, make a fire for the *furo* (tub), wash dishes, tend to the baby, and prepare the next day's lunch, before catching a little sleep and then rising to repeat the routine the following day.

Whether in Hawaii or on the U.S. mainland, issei women's labor was essential for survival, since few fathers and husbands made sufficient wages to support their households. To supplement the family income, women engaged in various enterprises, such as cooking, sewing, doing laundry for the large number of single men, raising chickens or pigs, or growing vegetables and flowers to be sold at local markets. In large families, the older children quite often had to drop out of school to support the household; the daughters helped with childcare and housework, while the boys labored in the fields. These adult responsibilities were onerous, and often fraught with guilt and peril. Such was the case for Mrs. Tatsuno Ogawa, who never forgave herself for the tragic accident that took the life of her twenty-month-old daughter, who drowned in a sugarcane irrigation ditch.

The picture brides that Barbara Kawakami interviewed in their eighties, nineties, and even hundreds concluded that despite the hardships and sufferings they experienced in America, they had found comfort in their children and pride and fulfillment in their own accomplishments. Separated from their families in Japan and thrust into new responsibilities and occupations, they developed unique modes of communication and devised ingenuous tools, skill sets, and systems for survival. In the process of making America their home, they raised families, established communities, and created and transmitted customs and cultures influenced by their Japanese and Okinawan heritage and the rich diversity of peoples in their new environments.

Mrs. Shizu Kaigo, a bridal consultant, kimono dresser, and teacher of Japanese arts featured in *Picture Bride Stories,* perhaps summarized the feelings of many issei women when she said, "In the beginning, I suffered because of the language barrier. Everything was so different from what I had expected. I cried and cried, and wondered why I ever came to Hawaii. . . . I kept reminding myself, '*Gambare! Gambare!* Have courage! Don't give up!' Now, I'm so happy I came. I'm moved to tears with gratitude."[5]

When I think back to 1988 and my first meeting with Barbara Kawakami, I feel full of gratitude for her spirit of *gambare* (perseverance) and her deep commitment to documenting, preserving, and sharing the issei's stories with wider audiences so that their accounts and legacy will live on in books, films, videos, exhibitions, and other educational platforms for future generations.

Dr. Akemi Kikumura Yano
November 15, 2015

Former president and chief executive officer and first curator of the Japanese American National Museum; currently visiting scholar at the Asian American Studies Center, University of California, Los Angeles, and affiliate graduate faculty at the University of Hawaii, Manoa

NOTES

1. Because of numerous unforeseen delays, the Japanese American National Museum and the inaugural exhibition, "Issei Pioneers: Hawaii and the Mainland, 1885–1924," finally opened on April 30, 1992, the day following the verdict in the Rodney King trial and the outbreak of civil unrest in Los Angeles.

2. A partial list of the research on prewar issei includes Evelyn Nakano Glenn, *Issei, Nisei, War Brides: Three Generations of Japanese American Women in Domestic Service* (Philadelphia, 1986); Toden Higa, *Uchinanchu: A History of Okinawans in Hawaii,* Ethnic Studies Oral History Project (Honolulu, 1981); Yuji Ishioka, *Issei: The World of the First Generation Japanese Immigrants, 1885–1924* (New York, 1988); Michiko Kodama-Nishimoto, Warren S. Nishimoto, and Cynthia A. Oshiro, eds., *Hanahana* (Honolulu, 1984); Alan Moriyama, "Imingaisha: Japanese Emigration Companies and Hawaii, 1894–1908," Ph.D. dissertation, University of California, Los Angeles, 1982; and Ronald Takaki, *Pau Hana: Plantation Life and Labor in Hawaii, 1835–1920* (Honolulu, 1983). The scholars working with primary source materials and doing fieldwork with issei include Harumi Befu (Stanford University), Lane Hirabayashi (University of Colorado, Boulder), Franklin Odo (University of Hawaii), Gail Nomura (University of Michigan), Gary Okihiro (Cornell University), Ron Takaki (University of California, Berkeley), Yuji Ichioka (University of California, Los Angeles), and Mitziko Sawada (Hampshire College); the educational affiliation for each scholar indicates the institution with which she or he was associated while work on the "Issei Pioneers" exhibition was under way.

3. Documented by Franklin Odo and Kazuko Sinoto in *A Pictorial History of the Japanese in Hawaii, 1885–1924* (Honolulu, 1985).

4. Barbara Kawakami's manuscript was subsequently published by the University of Hawaii Press as *Japanese Immigrant Clothing in Hawaii, 1885–1941* (Honolulu, 1993).

5. Mrs. Shizu Kaigo's three-layered wedding kimono was displayed at the Japanese Overseas Migration Museum in Yokohama in 2009, at the Japanese American National Museum in Los Angeles in 2010, and at the Bishop Museum in Honolulu in 2012.

PREFACE

People often ask me how I got started at age fifty-three in an academic career and how I came to research Japanese immigrant clothing and the lives of issei picture brides. An important turning point in my life came the night before my youngest son, Gary, left for a mainland college. He came into my sewing room to talk to me and asked, "Mom, didn't you have a dream when you were young, something you always wanted to do?" Of course I did!

At that instant, my mind flashed back to 1936 and to Ms. Shizue Kawamoto, my English teacher in eighth grade at Waipahu Intermediate School. A few weeks before graduation, she spoke to me after class and surprised me with some unexpected news: there was a teacher couple who wanted to pay my expenses to continue studying at McKinley High School in exchange for light household duties as a live-in maid. I ran home to tell my mother the good news. I thought she would be happy, but her reaction was quite unexpected. She said, "How can you think of yourself when you have four more siblings below you to help support? The day after graduation, you have to go to work."

Things were quite different when I was growing up on the Waipahu sugar plantation during the Depression years. My widowed mother had eight children to support. She didn't believe that education beyond the eighth grade was necessary for girls. She herself had had only a fourth-grade education in the village in Japan. During the Meiji (1868–1911) and Taisho (1912–1925) periods, women had virtually no freedom in the Confucian-influenced patriarchal society. It was believed that women didn't need higher education and that they had to strictly obey their husbands, their in-laws, and the elderly. Almost every picture bride I interviewed mentioned this in her interview when she discussed why she came to Hawaii. Even my mother practiced this in Hawaii.

I remember the meaningful words Ms. Kawamoto inscribed in my autograph book in 1936: "Although you may not be able to continue to high school, remember: education is a lifelong process. Keep on learning. Don't give up and keep on striving."

From then on, I never gave much thought to furthering my education. Years later, I realized how much Ms. Kawamoto had been concerned about her students' future. She came from Honolulu on Saturdays to teach her students to type, to prepare for work or for high school. She did not charge her students for the class, but they had to pay two dollars for the paper and equipment. I tagged along with a friend who had plans to continue to high school. For my mother, who had eight mouths to feed, two dollars was a huge amount, and so I was there only to keep my friend company, but Ms. Kawamoto was so kind—she told me to go ahead and join the others on the type-writers. Somehow I didn't think it was right for me to learn for free when the others were paying for it, so I declined. Much later, when I started my education at the university, I had so many papers to write, and I paid a dollar per page to have them typed; how I wished then that I had learned to type!

Most of us who grew up on a sugar plantation simply accepted the fact that any education beyond the eighth grade was impossible. We didn't have a high school in Waipahu then. The few dollars it would cost for books and transportation to Honolulu was beyond our means. The majority of students began working immediately after graduating from grammar school. Most girls worked either in the sugarcane or pineapple fields or as domestics for *haole* (Caucasian) families on the plantation; some entered an apprenticeship program to learn a more lucrative trade or skill. Only about six boys and five girls out of my class of forty were fortunate enough to continue to high school.

The day after graduating from eighth grade, I enrolled in a sewing school in Waipahu. We learned the basics of apparel designing through the flat-pattern method. For each garment, we learned to draft the pattern on paper—infant wear, boys' and girls' outfits, men's trousers, men's tailored long-sleeved shirts. I graduated in ten months and continued to Keister's Tailoring College in Honolulu. In the advanced course we were required to complete a woman's tailored suit and a tailored coat. Some of the interesting things I learned were to create floral bouquets out of leather and to make roses out of silk organza; the most difficult to learn were the intricate smocking techniques. After earning my instructor's certificate in 1938, I taught sewing and continued sewing in Waipahu. One day the Singer sewing machine salesman told me of a position at the Fashion Dressmaker in Wahiawa, which seemed exciting. The owner, Mrs. Kiyomi Furukawa, was known for her expertise and excellent skills in dressmaking, and among her customers were the wives of many military officers from nearby Schofield Barracks and Wheeler Air Force Base. I knew I would have the opportunity to sew fancier dresses and gowns while working with her. The progress I made during the year I worked for this talented and gifted woman was remarkable.

I then began a thirty-eight-year career as a professional dressmaker. When World War II came, I married Douglas Kawakami, a clerk at the plantation store. Five months later he was inducted into the army, serving in the Army 1399th Engineer Construction Battalion. I lived with my widowed mother-in-law and other members of his family while he was in the army, and I continued sewing at home. Our first son, Steve, was born in 1944. When the war ended and my husband completed his military service, I opened a dressmaking shop in Waipahu, near Hawaii Plantation Village. The location was ideal, and the timing was great. It was during General Douglas MacArthur's command of the occupying forces in Japan, and officers brought back from their Asian deployments unique kimonos and obis that had been Japanese family heirlooms sold in desperate times, fabrics from Thailand and India, and exquisite Chinese brocaded silks as presents for their wives. The military wives going to the

Marine Corps base, the naval station, and Iroquois Point in Ewa stopped by my shop. I began designing cocktail dresses using these incredible fabrics. I designed a ball gown made of Chinese tribute silk that was worn by an admiral's wife at President Harry Truman's inaugural ball. While sewing for the military wives I learned so much from them. Many of them had traveled throughout the world and eagerly shared their experiences. Our conversations covered geography, history, culture, fashion, and many other topics. Later, during my college days, I was able to better understand and relate to the subject matter I was studying because I had had all these vicarious experiences. Learning has always been a part of my life.

Many nisei girls who went into dressmaking did well during World War II. When my second child, a daughter we named Fay, was born in 1949, I closed the shop and moved into our new home in Wahiawa, near Leilehua High School. My final child, Gary, came four years later. I continued sewing, designing the cheerleaders' uniforms for Leilehua High School and sewing more wedding gowns.

While working as a seamstress, I took evening adult education classes, and I became a naturalized American citizen in 1955. At that time, Mr. Paul Shimizu, principal of the adult education program, advised me to take the GED placement test. I took one semester of algebra, then took the ten-hour GED exam at McKinley High School. Thanks to Mr. Shimizu, I earned my high school equivalency diploma in 1959.

When my older son, Steve, returned from his second year at the University of Oregon, I became aware of the changes his advanced education had inspired in him. I was fascinated by my children's expanding knowledge in the academic world. Watching them progress through high school and into college, I could see the value of a good education, a world unknown to my husband and me. I did not want to be left behind.

In 1973, two weeks after my son Gary left for college, I enrolled at Leeward Community College at the age of fifty-three. My husband was opposed to the idea of my quitting sewing and going back to school; however, my three children were very supportive. After gaining an associate's degree at Leeward Community College, I transferred to the University of Hawaii at Manoa and earned my bachelor of science in fashion design and merchandising in 1979, and a master's in Asian studies in 1983. What started as a class project in my fashion design and merchandising program in my senior year in 1979 became my lifelong work: studying Japanese immigrant clothing in Hawaii, beginning with the *kanyaku imin,* the first official contract laborers who came to Hawaii in 1885. It was clear that my primary sources of information would have to be the issei themselves.

Again the timing was right. In 1978, after years of toiling in the fields, many issei had moved out of their plantation homes into the newly constructed senior housing provided by the plantation for their retirement; their old termite-ravaged houses were demolished to make way for new development. These issei were in their eighties and early nineties, their memories were still intact, their children were away, and they were alone. They were eager to pour out their hearts about their struggles and hard lives.

When I began interviewing the issei women I had known during my childhood on an Oahu sugar plantation, I learned that they had come as picture brides from villages in Hiroshima, Yamaguchi, Kumamoto, Fukuoka, Okinawa, Fukushima, Niigata, and other places. Since I had grown up among people from these areas of Japan, I could understand the various dialects, although I could not speak them. The fact that I grew up on the plantation, had experienced similar hardships, was bilingual, and had thirty-eight years of professional dressmaking experience made it easier for us to communicate and share intimate stories. I am eternally grateful for their generous willingness to share their stories with me.

After those initial twenty interviews, I continued taping oral history interviews for thirty years, amassing a total of 250 tapes. As I conducted these interviews, the scope of my studies became broader. The interviews unearthed valuable information not only about clothing but also about many other aspects of the Japanese immigrant experience.

The focus of my master's thesis, "The Role and Position of Farm Women in Suye Mura," gave me the opportunity to study the daily life of women in a village in Kumamoto, Japan, two and a half hours by train from my ancestral home. I was struck by the similarities between village life in Japan and plantation camp life in the 1920s and 1930s in Hawaii. The clothing, food, mannerisms, and customs were so similar. This experience provided a better understanding and appreciation of the village culture my parents and other issei from various regions of Japan had brought to Hawaii. I didn't realize it at that time, but I unconsciously must have been laying the groundwork for my first book on Japanese immigrant clothing (1993), which eventually led to this book on picture brides.

If I hadn't pursued my study of issei men's and women's plantation work clothing, I never could have obtained the rich material about the lives of the Japanese immigrants who wore those clothes. When I started interviewing people about their clothing, I learned about their experiences as immigrants and about the clothing worn in Japanese villages. The immigrants also talked about their work experience. When I brought up the subject of wedding costumes, I heard many stories, some funny, others sad. When I asked about funeral costumes, they talked about the grief of losing their babies because of poor living conditions and neglect, and of their husbands who died so young because of the strenuous conditions and poor nutrition.

The issei women who came as picture brides recognized the advantages of the traditional kimono; however, it was too cumbersome to wear for fieldwork. Many of the picture brides were expected to work in the field starting just a day or two after they reached their new home. They were fortunate to have other issei share the type of clothing they needed. Working alongside women of diverse ethnic groups, they took some ideas from each group and designed a composite fashion that was similar to the Gibson girl look with a straw boater hat. The straw boater hat was the fashion in Paris in the 1890s, then spread to the eastern part of the United States, and was introduced to Hawaii by missionary women. My professor in fashion design was surprised when I showed her the photos of picture brides dressed in such fashionable work clothes. For the issei working woman, no other garments combined so many practical attributes: the carryall, the large *bento* (lunch) bag of denim, a large kerchief to protect her delicate skin from the tropical heat, accessories to protect her from the stings of poisonous insects in the fields, and, most important, the black cummerbund-like sash tightly wound around the waist to help her overcome hunger pangs. I marvel at how these picture brides who came from farming villages and had no knowledge of Western sewing could have put together a composite fashion that was the envy of the women of other ethnic groups. Back in Japan, their kimonos were all hand-dyed, hand-woven, and hand-sewn, stitch by stitch. Most women had never seen a sewing machine until they came to Hawaii.

Each story in this book was carefully selected for its uniqueness and because it conveyed substantial information. Many of the women died in the years following my interviews with them, and in many cases I contacted surviving family members to do further research, which took considerable time and effort. The family members often said I knew more about their parents than they did, as issei parents often did not share their experiences of immigration and work with their children.

Many of these picture brides were widows when I interviewed them, living lives largely confined within the boundaries of the plantation camps. Quite a number had raised their children as single parents, courageously carrying out man-sized jobs to supplement the small pension provided by the plantation. The stories of the picture brides exemplified the importance of friendships and familial networks in coping with hardships and poverty. I was moved by their inner strength, innovativeness, adaptability, and ability to improvise with their minimal resources. Despite the language barriers and a foreign environment, the issei women were able to overcome tremendous adversity and managed to instill in their children the solid values of their own upbringing.

The personal experiences documented in this book often led my thoughts back to my childhood days of growing up on a sugar plantation as an immigrant child. I recall my early memories of the old Buddhist temple, two blocks away from our home in Camp One, also known as the Japanese camp. This temple was a haven for the many poor and lonely immigrant workers struggling to keep their families alive on meager earnings. When I began my immigrant clothing research, I stumbled onto the fact that my father was one of the twenty-four issei pioneers who built the original Soto Zen temple in Waipahu in 1903. At the memorial service commemorating the fiftieth anniversary of my father's death, the priest pointed out that my father had handcrafted the *osaisen bako* (offering box) out of heavy wood. He said the bold calligraphy strokes of the word *osaisen* had also been written by my father. In those bleak years of the Depression, the offering was a nickel or ten cents at the most. When I mentioned that my father had died young, at the age of sixty-three, the priest said that had been considered a long life in the early period. He noted that, according to temple records, the median age of men dying during that period was between thirty and forty, largely because of the long hours of manual labor and the poor nutrition that was a consequence of the meager pay.

A multitude of discoveries sprouted from my late education. This passion to learn shaped my future, setting me on an exciting journey that became my lifelong work. Little did I dream when I began my research in 1979 that today I'd be sitting here writing my second book, this time about the picture brides. This book vividly symbolizes the life experiences of the courageous young women who traveled across the Pacific to marry men they had never met, and illustrates their transformation and many contributions to American culture and history. Although I had a late start in higher education and research, I certainly feel blessed to have come this far. My only regret is that so many of the issei, the older nisei, and people of many other diverse ethnic groups who so unselfishly gave their valuable time and information for my research are not here today to enjoy the fruition of our work. This dream never could have materialized without their help. I offer my heartfelt thanks to each and every individual I encountered during this long journey.

Like the exquisite splashed-pattern designs of the *kasuri* cloth the picture brides brought with them, the life journeys of these women were filled with twists and turns, playing out amid the knots and crimps of struggles and circumstances. The resulting pattern of their lives, revealed in this collection, is a marvel to behold, like the brilliant hues of the rainbow as it forms an arc across the blue Hawaiian sky.

ACKNOWLEDGMENTS

This book is dedicated to the issei picture brides who came to Hawaii during the period from 1908 to 1924 to marry laborers working on the sugarcane and pineapple plantations. This book was made possible because they shared their extraordinary life stories with me. These women opened their hearts and souls to me and entrusted me with their priceless stories. I promised to include their stories in a book along with their photos. I could never forget how their tired eyes sparkled! Although they are not here to share the fruition of our work, I am profoundly grateful for their patience and for the endless hours they have shared with me.

I owe a special debt of gratitude to the nisei men and women who remembered things that their parents forgot to mention. Children and grandchildren who were scattered throughout the United States, Japan, and Hawaii became interested in these stories and assisted in finding missing family documents and long-forgotten photos. I also want to thank the people of many other ethnic groups who worked alongside the issei men and women and provided their own valuable perspective.

Many people read the initial manuscript or portions of it at various stages and gave me helpful suggestions and encouragement. I particularly wish to thank Marie Hara, author and retired teacher of English at the University of Hawaii, Manoa, who helped in editing some of the earlier stories and provided valuable comments and recommendations, and Dr. Chieko Tachihata, emeritus librarian of the Hawaiian Collection at the University of Hawaii, Manoa, who has been a consultant and advisor throughout this project and assisted in editing some of the stories.

I am most grateful to John W. Conner, emeritus professor of literature at Leeward Community College and the University of Hawaii at Manoa, who has been of tremendous help from beginning to end. He took care in editing my stories to keep them as authentic as possible, and served as a valuable advisor and consultant.

Special thanks to Jeff Gere, "talk story" genius with a superb memory, who infused me with his enthusiasm and passion to do this book. He helped to bring these quiet issei characters to life in their own unique ways.

Velma Yoshitake has been my indispensable personal assistant. She revised and tracked the edited manuscript and organized the photos with the text. Without her patience, understanding, and abiding friendship throughout the years, I never could have completed this book.

John Esaki, director of the Frank Watase Media Art Center at the Japanese American National Museum in Los Angeles, helped with every aspect of my book, from editing to offering warm words of encouragement. JANM's staff earns my thanks for their continuing expert care and preservation of the immigrant clothing given to me by the issei. Special thanks to Audrey Kaneko for her excellent contribution while working at JANM, digitizing my extensive photo collection and carefully organizing and documenting the photos for publication.

I also want to thank the Bishop Museum, especially Betty Kam of the archives collection; Carole Hayashino, president and executive director of the Japanese Cultural Center of Hawaii; Jeff Higa, executive director (retired) of Hawaii's Plantation Village; Dr. Margaret Oda and the Oda Foundation; and the Hiroaki, Elaine, and Lawrence Kono Foundation for their continuous support in perpetuating interest in Japanese culture for future generations. I am also grateful to the staff at the Hawaii State Library, the Hawaii and Pacific Reference Collection staff, and the Consulate General of Japan in Honolulu, which provided important historical information.

My sincere gratitude to Corey Johnson, great-grandson of picture bride Tei Saito, who helped in the early part of the editing, and made structural suggestions that were helpful. Tei's second-eldest son, Masaharu, third-eldest daughter, Hiroko Saito Yamaki, and youngest daughter, Edith Saito Gima, all helped in editing and checking on the dates and events that took place in their mother's story.

Robert Castro, secretary of the Portuguese Genealogical and Historical Society of Hawaii and an expert on plantation immigration history of every ethnic group, provided a wealth of firsthand knowledge. My profound gratitude goes to him for all his hard work and patience in discovering some of the more complicated data involving the early issei arrivals and location of the plantations first settled.

Carolyn Uchiyama, granddaughter of Kishi Tsujimura, was of tremendous help in loaning me six cassette tapes in Japanese recorded in 1985 by Mrs. Reiko Yano. Carolyn also made a timeline of her grandparents' story after coming to Hawaii.

Gary Smith, a historian and scholar with many fascinating stories about every immigrant ethnic group who settled in Kilauea, Kauai, was of enormous help with information on Soto Kimura's story.

I would especially like to thank Michael and Barbara Ritchie for their generous support and the endless hours they spent transferring and upgrading the photos for this book. My deep appreciation to Kaede Yanagihara, Matt Maeda, and Nicholas Arakawa, who contributed valuable comments and editing as representatives of the younger generation.

My final and greatest thanks go to members of my family, especially to my late husband, Douglas, for valuable insights and for introducing me to several of these extraordinary people through his Wahiawa Farm and Feed Store. I am most grateful to my three children, Steven, Fay, and Gary, for their love, constant encouragement, and generous support. My older son, Steve, in South Carolina, called me every weekend to give me moral support and proved to be a wonderful consultant and editor. In spite of her busy schedule, I depend greatly on my daughter, Fay, who lives nearby. I can never thank her enough for the tremendous help, guidance, and support she has given me since I entered the academic field at age fifty-three. Without her valuable assistance every step of the way, I never could have completed this book. I am especially grateful to my younger son, Gary, for finding time in his busy schedule to assist me with the complicated revisions and, more important, for helping me turn my life around. If not for his encouragement to pursue my personal and academic goals, I would not have had the determination to publish these stories.

I am most appreciative of the late Sally Yamanaka, my dearest friend since grade school, who provided laughter and lifted my spirit through tough times. I have been fortunate to have the support of so many people throughout my life's journey, and I will be forever indebted to them.

Tamara Zielinski, who did the final editing, deserves the greatest recognition for what was indeed an awesome task. She has been an especially patient and understanding editor, working closely with me to preserve the language and image of the picture brides. Her dedication to seek clarity has resulted in an accurate portrayal of the lives of these women.

My sincerest thanks go to the three manuscript readers assigned by the University of Hawaii Press for their evaluations, insightful comments, and suggestions. I will be forever grateful to Nadine Little, former acquisition manager, and the University of Hawaii Press for invaluable editorial guidance, advice, and assistance as we started the publication process. Special thanks go to Emma Ching and Dr. Masako Ikeda for following up on the work through completion. Julie Matsuo-Chun patiently worked on the book's cover, which incorporated the visual essence of a picture bride, and on the photo layout in the text. My heartfelt thanks go to Maggie Yanko, from Westchester Publishing Services, for her help as I worked on the final stages of publication. Everyone's encouragement and commitment are endless, and I truly appreciate their unrelenting support. The responsibility for any remaining errors or misrepresentations is mine.

Introduction

THE EARLY IMMIGRATION PERIOD TO HAWAII

My first book, *Japanese Immigrant Clothing in Hawaii, 1885–1941,* documented the early arrival of Japanese in the Hawaiian Islands, offering insights into the exodus of immigrants from certain regions of Japan and Okinawa. In this book, I am pleased to focus on the personal stories of the picture brides themselves, whose open and honest revelations to me during my interviews provided a compelling human side to this history. So that the reader may better understand the lives and experiences of these women, it will be helpful if I briefly lay out the chronology from my earlier work.

The unofficial migration of Japanese to Hawaii began in 1868, a time of social and political unrest during Japan's transition from the Tokugawa shogunate to the Meiji oligarchy (1856–1911). The sugar industry in the Hawaiian Islands sent recruiters to Japan in search of cheap labor. People who lived in the Tokyo and Yokohama areas were the first to hear about the search, and they responded eagerly. These immigrants were known as the *gannen mono,* or "first-year people," because they left Japan in the first year of the Meiji era, the beginning of the rule of the new emperor. There were 153 immigrants aboard the British ship *Scioto,* including five women who ranged in age from nineteen to forty. Two of the women were pregnant at the time, and a baby boy was born during the voyage. However, since one man died en route, the total number of passengers remained the same. The first group included people of diverse backgrounds: skilled workers, craftsmen, a few displaced samurai, a few farmers, and some vagabonds, coolies, and unruly adventurers more concerned with drinking and gambling than with working. Upon arriving in Hawaii, however, they worked very hard from dawn to dusk, an average of twelve hours a day under the tropical sun, for a wage of $4.00 a month. Forty-three people from this group returned to Japan at the first available opportunity; the rest remained in Hawaii.

The second group of Japanese immigrants came during the years 1885–1894, known as the government contract period. During this time, a total of 28,691 Japanese laborers and members of their families came to Hawaii on three-year government contracts. During this period, average wages ranged from $9.00 to $12.50 per month for men for ten hours of work a day, while women were paid less than men for the same type of work. Almost all of the immigrants who came during this period stayed in Hawaii, and today many Hawaiians of Japanese ancestry are descended from this group. Most of these immigrants came from the southwestern region of Japan, including the prefectures of Hiroshima, Yamaguchi, Kumamoto, and Fukuoka. One of the major factors contributing to this large-scale immigration was the severe economic conditions in this region. Geographic factors were another significant element, since there were similarities between the subtropical climate of their respective prefectures and that of Hawaii. And, given the Japanese fondness for fishing, many immigrants likely were attracted by the promised abundance of seafood in the Hawaiian waters.

A third period of Japanese immigration began in April 1894, when the Japanese government licensed private companies to oversee the immigration process. This period, which lasted until 1900, is called the private contract period, during which 57,000 immigrants came to Hawaii. This group encountered more problems than the immigrants who came before them, since these private companies frequently exploited their fellow countrymen through complicated financial arrangements that made it necessary for a laborer to spend his initial contract period working to pay off debts to the contracting company for the start-up materials required for employment on the plantation.

In the years from 1900 to 1908, the importation of contract labor was prohibited by U.S. law. During these years, known as the free immigration period, a great number of Japanese, about 71,000 all told, immigrated to Hawaii. Many of them were subsequently attracted to the higher wages offered on the U.S. mainland. Resentment against cheap labor on the West Coast of the United States led to the so-called Gentlemen's Agreement of 1907–1908, whereby Japan voluntarily placed severe restrictions on immigration to the United States.

However, the Gentlemen's Agreement also opened the door for picture brides to immigrate to Hawaii, as it soon became apparent that the single men who had come to labor on the plantations were being paid wages so low that they could not save enough money to return to Japan as quickly as they had hoped. The Hawaiian government reluctantly allowed Asian women to come as picture brides because it was believed that the women could provide a stable family life for the male workers. This period, from 1908 to 1924, was called the restricted immigration period, when only returning former immigrants and immediate relatives of immigrants were permitted entry. Nevertheless, 61,000 arrivals were recorded. The issei refer to this period as the *yobi-yose jidai,* or "summoned by relatives period." It was also popularly known as the *shashin hana-yome jidai,* or "picture bride period."

More than 20,000 so-called picture brides, whom Japanese men had married in absentia, arrived during this period. The majority of the women were from Japan, but the group also included 900 from Korea who were listed as Japanese nationals. The young girls from Korea came as picture brides of Korean men who worked on the sugar and pineapple plantations. At that time, Korea was under the control of the Japanese government, so most of the Korean people could read and speak Japanese.

Between 1885 and 1924, some men came with families, while some left their wives and children with their parents, grandparents, or relatives in Japan. Some sent children born in Hawaii back to Japan to be raised by relatives there. When these children became old enough to work, the father summoned them as *yobi-yose.*

These children who later returned to live with their parents in Hawaii are called *kibei*. Because of the long years of separation from their parents, there are many sad stories about the *kibei* son or daughter who felt unloved and treated like an outsider, even among once-familiar siblings.

Of course, the greatest number of those recruited as plantation laborers were single young men, many from Hiroshima and Yamaguchi prefectures. They became an important part of the Hawaiian plantation labor force, aspiring to make their fortunes within the three-year contract period and then return triumphantly to their villages.

A few men worked hard enough to attain their goal of returning home with enough money to invest in new ventures. For the great majority, however, it was an impossible dream, as they struggled through hard times and had difficulty merely making ends meet. As the years went by, these men made new friends and found fellow villagers who had successfully adopted the lifestyle taken on by the early settlers. As their standard of living improved along with the work experience and methods of communication, they gained confidence and a sense of pride in being part of the new frontier. Rather than returning to Japan as failures, they chose to put down roots in Hawaii.

In some cases, bachelors who had decided it was time to settle down wrote home to ask their parents or other relatives to find them suitable young women as wives. However, in most cases, it was those back home who initiated the process of finding a bride to help a bachelor settle down in Hawaii. This was the beginning of a long series of picture bride marriages arranged by a go-between (*nakoodo,* also *baishaku nin* or *shinpai nin*) through an exchange of photos across 4,000 miles of ocean.

The commonality of such marriages has led to a misconception about picture brides. Within the descendant communities of the early twentieth-century East Asian diaspora, it is usually believed that the exchange of pictures was a proxy for the marriage itself. In fact, initially picture exchange occurred between the families of prospective brides and grooms living in the same area of Japan because gender segregation before marriage was the norm in certain social classes. Later, an exchange of pictures was useful in marriages involving a laborer working in an industrial city such as Osaka, Nagoya, Hiroshima, or Tokyo and a woman from his rural hometown.

In 1900, out of the total population of 24,326 Japanese immigrants in the United States, there were only 985 females (twenty-four males for every female). By 1910, the female population had climbed to 9,087, and by 1920, there were 22,193 women.

Before 1900, all of the Japanese immigrants to Hawaii had come from the four main islands of Japan, but in 1900, for the first time, the immigrants included Okinawans. The first group of twenty-six Okinawan immigrants arrived in Hawaii on January 8, 1900. Like the *naichi* (main-island Japanese), the Okinawans also dreamed of making a fortune and helping their loved ones in the homeland. They came to Hawaii to escape poverty and corrupt tax collection practices. As a consequence of peasant uprisings in the late 1800s, Okinawa lost its political independence and was incorporated into the Japanese prefecture system in 1889. Many of the peasants had to sell their land and become tenants, while others migrated to foreign lands to search for a better life. Between 1900 and 1924, approximately 25,000 men, women, and children came to Hawaii from Okinawa.

On June 30, 1924, the U.S. Congress passed the Immigration Act of 1924 (called the Japanese Exclusion Act by the Japanese). This act prohibited the entry of all aliens who were ineligible for citizenship, thus virtually ending Japanese immigration to the United States. Under this law, only "non-quota immigrants," such as government officials, ministers of religion, professors, students, and merchants, were allowed entry. Travelers were admitted, but only for brief visits—and of course, even these visits came to an end with the outbreak of war between the United States and Japan on December 7, 1941.

Historically, picture bride marriages were a continuation of the system of arranged marriages that had had its origin in the feudal period during the later part of the Tokugawa period (1603–1868) in Japan and which had become accepted even among peasants in rural communities. The exchange of photographs was an obvious way of introducing a couple to each other when a face-to-face meeting was difficult or impossible. Because photographs were a luxury item, the exchange of such images lent a formality to the matchmaking process. And if one of the parties did not like the look of the other's photograph, the rejection was less embarrassing (especially for a young woman) than if it had occurred after a face-to-face meeting, and the matter could be quietly forgotten.

The *nakoodo* had to be carefully selected because of the importance of the task and the difficulties that might be involved in arranging such marriages. The *nakoodo* could be a man or woman, or occasionally a couple. He or she had to have great intelligence and social sensitivity and be someone who was highly respected in the community. A conscientious and sincere *nakoodo* would try to find an ideal match. Preferably the man had slightly more education than the woman, as well as higher social status, so that the woman would respect her husband and be willing to obey him; at a minimum, the man and woman should be of equal educational background and socioeconomic status. A thorough investigation into the families on both sides was conducted for most of the picture bride marriages between plantation bachelors in Hawaii and women in villages back home. In fact, until World War II the practice was often followed in Hawaii even for marriages among nisei (second-generation Japanese in Hawaii). For example, my older sister was married in 1936 through matchmaking, and the *nakoodo* came from the same prefecture as my mother and the groom's family. Both sides asked family friends to conduct a thorough search of the other family's background, and especially to check for insanity and leprosy. I remember how relieved my mother was when she heard that the water in her prospective son-in-law's village was pure, which, according to the beliefs of the time, was a sign that a family's bloodline was healthy.

While the *nakoodo* set out with a particular match in mind, an experienced go-between would bring extra photographs along. After meeting and talking with the intended bride or groom, the *nakoodo* might decide that someone else would make a better match; in such cases, the new match's photo could be presented instead.

Another type of arranged marriage negotiated by the *nakoodo* for the plantation laborers involved a *kari fufu* (temporary or borrowed spouse). To come as a temporary spouse with a worker who had previously immigrated was one way for a young woman to gain entry into the United States during the restricted immigration period. After the couple entered Hawaii, they applied for a divorce; after the required one-year waiting period, both were free to remarry. Some of the women who came as *kari fufu* are included among the approximately 20,000 women who were picture brides. One issei woman I interviewed said, almost in a whisper, "You ask me if I came as a picture bride? Not really. I came to Hawaii as a *kari fufu.* So actually, this is my second marriage. Even my family doesn't know this. But I hardly knew the man I came to Hawaii with. I do not even remember his name. We parted as soon as we got here." Sometimes, though, the "borrowed spouses" might actually fall in love during their ten-day Pacific voyage, in which case the unlucky prospective groom waiting in Hawaii would have to arrange for another bride.

Of course, in the Japan-Hawaii matches, the exchange of photographs also proved to be very useful in identifying mates when they met for the first time at the immigration center in Hawaii. There are humorous anecdotes about grooms who had borrowed photos from someone younger and better-looking, resulting in a bride shocked to be claimed by a man old enough to be her father. It comes as no surprise to hear that a few of the arriving women became runaway brides.

Quite a number of the couples brought together through the picture bride system were married twice: once in Japan and again in Hawaii. For the ceremony in Japan, the marriage ritual was performed in the presence of both families, even though the groom remained in Hawaii. The essence of the marriage ceremony is the *san san kudo,* or the exchange of nuptial cups. The bride and groom take turns sipping sake three times from each of three cups. This ritual seals their marriage vows. In some of the picture bride marriages, a proxy was chosen to play the role of the groom; in other cases, brides did the *san san kudo* in front of the groom's picture.

The bride's name was legally entered into the groom's *koseki,* or family register, in the village office in Japan. But, in accordance with U.S. government regulations in effect during the restricted immigration period, she had to wait six months before she could join her husband in Hawaii. If her in-laws were not satisfied with her character or her performance as a bride during that period, they could have her name removed from the *koseki.* Thus this waiting period was an important time for the bride to please her mother-in-law in every way. For some brides, being under the scrutiny of their mother-in-law was the most difficult part of the experience. However, one picture bride, who was from Fukushima prefecture and who was marrying a man whose parents lived in Niigata prefecture, recalled that the period she spent with her mother-in-law was the happiest and most memorable time of her life.

Once the visa came through from the government office, the bride usually returned to her natal home to bid farewell to her parents, relatives, and friends before departing for Hawaii. This was probably the most heartbreaking part for a young girl, maybe only sixteen or eighteen years old, who perhaps had traveled to only a handful of nearby villages and who was now about to journey alone across the Pacific to marry a man she had never met. Many of these young women would never see their family or village again.

Upon arrival in Hawaii, these young brides encountered another problem. Up until 1917, they had to go through another marriage ceremony before they were recognized as legal wives by the territorial government. All of them had to go through a group Christian ceremony, sometimes including twenty or more couples, at the immigration station before they could be granted the right to enter the Territory of Hawaii. But after 1917, when the picture brides were recognized as legal wives, they could be claimed by their husbands without going through such a ceremony. However, many men continued to take their brides to either a Shinto shrine, a Japanese-owned hotel in Honolulu, a minister's residence, or a plantation home to have a religious marriage ceremony.

The issei weddings that took place in Hawaii varied from traditional and elaborate to nontraditional and simple. Some men sent the bride's family a monetary betrothal gift large enough to enable the bride to have a set of formal bridal wear. Usually, however, the issei groom made barely enough money to pay for his bride's passage to Hawaii, and in such cases the bride's parents sometimes provided the wedding costume for their daughter. Many of the prospective picture brides were eager to come to Hawaii. From what they had heard, it was truly a paradise where their life would be much better than the life of hard work and struggles they could expect as a farmer's wife in Japan. However, many were shocked at the sight of their first home on the plantation: as some of the women recalled, the house reminded them of a "chicken coop" or "horse barn" back in their home village.

Many husbands were deeply in debt from gambling, and quite a few drank away their earnings, so brides often began working in the fields immediately, spending ten hours a day in the sugarcane or pineapple fields. Wives had to learn new ways of providing food for their husbands, such as preparing lunch in double-decker *bento* cans to take to the fields. They were also tasked with doing the laundry, and some women took in laundry soiled with hard-to-remove red dirt from fieldwork to pay off the debt. New wives learned to sew work clothing for themselves and their husbands, including making raincoats for their husband out of muslin, applying linseed oil and turpentine to the fabric to make it water repellent. Many sewed not only for their own families but also for the bachelors in the camp to supplement their meager income. All told, it was the wife that in any number of instances paid off her husband's debt. Some husbands participated in the *tanomoshi,* a mutual financial system into which many issei put half their monthly pay. In some cases they used the *tanomoshi* to improve their lives, but in others the money went for drink, adding to their woes.

EARLY PLANTATION WEDDINGS

Not all the issei women who were married to issei men in Hawaii were summoned as picture brides. Some of them had come earlier as *yobi-yose* and were already working on the plantations. The wedding of Yasu Abe and Soshichi Sato is an example. Yasu was born in Shimizu village, Fukushima prefecture, in 1893. Her father died when she was four years old, so she never attended grade school. Instead, she helped her mother raise silkworms. She was also trained from an early age to weave tatami (straw mats), which she sold to buyers who came from the next village. Then her older brother summoned her to come to Hawaii.

Yasu left Japan on the *Shinyo Maru* during an eventful time in Japan's history: the transition from the Meiji era to the Taisho era. Yasu had vivid memories of the day she left. There was much commotion and excitement in the port city of Yokohama after the Meiji emperor's death, and the passengers were not sure whether the ship would be allowed to leave. When the ship finally got under way, the winter sea was rough, and the ship rocked back and forth like a *buranko* (swing); Yasu was seasick and miserable during the twelve-day voyage across the

Pacific. She was greatly relieved when the ship finally anchored in Honolulu on December 21, 1912.

Yasu was detained at the immigration station for three days, spent one night at the Yamashiro Hotel, then took the train from Iwilei station to Waipahu. From there, she rode in a horse and buggy to her first home, a whitewashed longhouse in Camp One, near the old Soto Zen mission temple.

A few days later she was sent to work in the sugarcane fields for Oahu Sugar Company, working a ten-hour day for 75 cents. Life in her Japanese village had been difficult enough, but it was even harder working in the cane fields. She continued working until she got married at twenty-three, which in those days was considered an advanced age—most girls were married by the time they were seventeen or eighteen years old.

Yasu's marriage was arranged by a *nakoodo* who came from her village in Fukushima. The *nakoodo* sold dry goods and Singer sewing machines, and as he traveled through the plantation towns he did a lot of matchmaking—it was a way of making extra money. When the matchmaking resulted in a marriage, he would be given a gratuity. The wedding ceremony was held at Yasu's home in one of the plantation longhouses. She wore a formal black *montsuki* (a kimono featuring five crests) with the Sato family crest that her husband-to-be had given her as a betrothal gift. Yasu's *montsuki* had no design on the bottom, and her brocaded obi was not of the finest silk because Soshichi was still struggling and sent half his monthly pay of $15 to his parents in Fukushima. Without anyone to help her, Yasu combed her hair into a pompadour hairstyle herself and arranged a white bow in the back of her hairdo.

Soshichi wore a black wool suit, long-sleeved white shirt, and necktie. The *nakoodo* officiated at the *san san kudo* ritual. He also sang the *sansa shigure,* a ceremonial song performed at weddings in Yasu's village in Japan. Reminiscing about the song moved Yasu to tears. She added, "We did not have much of a feast, just simple food, but there was plenty of sake. We were so poor we could not afford to have a formal portrait taken. I still have the black *montsuki,* but I sent the rest of the kimonos back to Japan after World War II. I felt that the relatives back home could make better use of the kimonos."

The wedding of Kaichi Abe and Miki Takahashi is another example of a marriage between an issei man and woman who were both already working on the plantations. The wedding and reception, which were conducted in traditional Japanese style, took place in 1923, a time when issei who could afford to do so began reviving the old village marriage customs and turning receptions into community celebrations.

Kaichi Abe had come from Fukushima prefecture when he was fifteen years old. He soon began working in a *konpan* (a group of people who formed a partnership to farm a designated area of land). He worked very hard and was able to send large sums of money to Japan to his older brother, who was taking care of the family farm and their widowed mother back in their village.

Miki Takahashi was also from Fukushima prefecture. She came to Hawaii as a girl of nineteen, summoned by her father, who worked at Waialua Agricultural Company on Oahu. She arrived in Honolulu on June 11, 1917, when people were celebrating Kamehameha Day. After a few days of rest, she began working in the rubber tree fields in Kawailoa, where her family lived. Two or three years later, she moved to the Ewa sugar plantation, where her older sister's husband was the leader of a *konpan* gang; Miki worked hard alongside the men. After the historic Oahu Sugar Strike of 1920, she moved to the Waipahu plantation to live with an older brother and his family.

Miki's brother-in-law in Ewa told a friend of his, Kaichi Abe, who lived in a nearby camp, that he thought his wife's younger sister would make an ideal match for Kaichi, and he arranged an opportunity for Kaichi to get a good look at Miki without her knowledge. Kaichi told me, "My friend took me to a home with a hibiscus hedge and told me to look over it. Beyond the bush, Miki was working in the yard. I thought, although she was not an outstanding beauty, I liked her quiet and gentle ways. I felt that she would not be a domineering type of wife and felt safe enough to marry her. I feel that I made the right choice; we've been married sixty-one years, she's never talked back to me, and we've never had a fight!"

The marriage was agreed upon, with Miki's older brother giving his consent in place of her father, who had returned to Japan by then. Miki didn't even see Kaichi until the day the betrothal gift was brought to her home.

Kaichi told me the details about the betrothal gift. "I went to purchase the bride's *montsuki* and accessories at the Nagao Gofukuten in Honolulu, and there I saw my bride-to-be shopping for her trousseau with her family. It was very embarrassing for both sides. At that time, a *montsuki* of fairly good quality cost about $40. The store carried *mizuhiki* [colorful red, white, and gold paper cords used to create fancy gift wrappers], on level wooden trays with legs, so everything could be presented properly. The betrothal gift consisted of a complete set of *montsuki* with my family crest, formal gold-brocaded obi, and accessories, and fresh sea bream, cuttlefish, dried laver, and sake, all symbolic of long life and happiness."

The Abes were married at the Kato Jinja shrine in Honolulu. The bride wore a Hawaiian muumuu, which was popular at that time, and the groom wore a dark wool suit custom-made for $20 (the suit is preserved at Hawaii's Plantation Village).

The Abes' reception was held a few months after the marriage ceremony, in December 1923, at the groom's brother's home. More than eighty guests were invited, a large number in those days. A cook was hired from the boardinghouse to supervise the preparation of the feast. Among the foods served were a large sea bream, sashimi (thinly sliced raw fish), *nishime* (a dish of meat or poultry with vegetables seasoned with sugar and *shoyu*), a traditional assortment of delicacies known as *mori mono,* and plenty of sake. All this cost about $580, a sum that in those days took months to pay off. (The usual monetary wedding gift at that time was $2 or $3.) The bride first wore a black *montsuki* given to her by her own family that bore her father's family crest. The *nakoodo*'s wife served as the bride's attendant. The *nakoodo* made all the formal speeches and also sang the *takasago,* a wedding song traditionally sung in Japanese villages.

Gijun Funakoshi told me how his marriage was arranged while his father and cousins from Okinawa were working in the cane fields in Wahiawa, at the McBryde sugar plantation on the island of Kauai. They were both doing *ho hana* (digging weeds) when Gijun's father asked his friend Goro Taba, *"Oi, yuukata ni aaei girlu oruka?"* (By the way, you have a nice girl for my son?) The friend told him, "Oh, my seventeen-year-old niece recently came from Okinawa and is living with me. She is of marrying age." Gijun's father replied happily, "Ooh, just right for my son, he's twenty-eight years old!"

Thus the marriage arrangement was made without consulting the young couple, and they were married on August 12, 1930. When I saw the wedding photo much later, I could see that Gijun's wife, Tsuruko, had been a beautiful girl, and Gijun was certainly fortunate to have his father and good friend arrange the marriage. According to their daughters when they were planning a fiftieth-anniversary celebration, Tsuruko had strongly opposed the celebration at first because of their age difference, and she was too embarrassed to tell her children and grandchildren about how their marriage had been arranged. Gijun Funakoshi was a very handsome scholar and looked much younger than his age. He had received many awards from the Okinawan government for his outstanding contributions to the Okinawan community, and despite Tsuruko's initial reservations, I thought they made a wonderful couple. It's amazing how these marriages arranged by parents or relatives often turned out very well and lasted a lifetime, producing much happiness and many children.

The origins of my research into plantation history began with my interest in the sugar plantations on the island of Kauai. During my adolescence, I learned that my father, Torasaku Oyama, arrived in Hawaii on April 3, 1890, to work for the Kekaha sugar plantation with his first wife, Une. Until then, he had worked at the village office as a clerk in Kumamoto, Japan. At that time, his uncle served as the chief recruiting official in the Kumamoto area, finding young men to work as contract laborers for Hawaiian plantations. My father's adventurous spirit led him to join the other young men to come to Hawaii to do some exploring and to begin a new life. With Une they settled at the Kekaha plantation. Their eldest son, Shigeru, was born there, followed by twin sisters. When Father's three-year contract was over, he returned to Kumamoto. After his first wife passed away in Japan, he returned with his son, Shigeru, to Hawaii. There my father met and married my mother, who came from Fukushima prefecture. This was very unusual, as most of the arranged issei marriages were between people who came from the same prefecture. After my father passed away in 1928, my mother never talked about him. It was only after I started interviewing issei for my book on clothing that I learned about my parents' history.

I was the only one among my eight siblings to be born in my father's ancestral home, in Kumamoto, Japan, and in the course of pursuing higher education I decided to learn about my family's history and to focus on our own history in Hawaii. There was much to learn about my father's past. As I began to retrace his footsteps, I visited the Kekaha sugar plantation to see what it must have been like for him when he arrived in 1890. Not much appeared to have changed; it still seemed like a desolate, lonely community. I could imagine how difficult it must have been for my father and his first family to live here.

Although I was able to interview some issei women who had come as picture brides, I was sad to learn that no one in Kekaha had ever heard of my father, as too many years had passed. I was curious to know what kind of work he had engaged in in this isolated plantation town. After the plantation closed down, its personnel records had been moved to various locations on Oahu, and finally to the University of Hawaii Hamilton Library. There I did further research on the files from Kekaha, where I discovered that no specific information or mention of my father appeared in the plantation files.

While I was on Kauai, I also visited the Koloa sugar plantation, which was the first and oldest sugar plantation in the Territory of Hawaii. I was invited in 1985 for the celebration marking the 150th anniversary of its opening. It was a memorable event, and turned out to be one of the turning points in my research on plantation history and clothing.

By the time of the sesquicentennial celebration, the sugar mill had been closed for quite some time, and most of the old-timers were gone. But while there, I was fortunate to meet Mabel Kawakami Hashisaka (no relation), who later provided me with a rich source of photographs from the *kanyaku imin,* the issei who had come in 1885 as the first official contract laborers on the island. Hisa Kawakami's story in this volume helps readers understand what life was like for the early Japanese immigrants—and also for the members of the many other ethnic groups who had arrived in Koloa before 1885 and who must have endured just as much.

These photographs provided a visual trail of the lives of the people who had immigrated to these islands from other islands far away. While researching some of these photographs, I found some of these people, mostly issei women, and was later able to meet and interview many of them. Though their photographs may have faded, their memories had not. My hope with this book is to preserve their stories for future generations, so that they can understand how the picture brides adapted to living in a new land with someone they knew only through a photograph, overcoming many challenges and establishing families who have contributed to Hawaii's legacy.

METHODOLOGY

In the course of writing my first book, on immigrant clothing, I became very interested in the lives of the people who shared their personal experiences on the plantation. I would take a tablet and pen anywhere I thought I might meet someone with a story—to *kenjinkai* (prefectural club) parties, senior centers, and other places. I would take down names and phone numbers, and follow up with in-person interviews and subsequent phone interviews to verify and clarify information.

During the face-to-face interview, I would record our conversation on tape, and later transcribe the interviews. I collected about 250 interviews, including some chance interviews that were brief but informative. After publication of my first book, I realized that I had many stories yet to be printed, and I embarked on another journey to tell about the women who came to Hawaii through arranged marriages, some of their own volition and others in obedience to their parents. The women spoke in a mixture of their village dialect and the Pidgin English that they had learned on the plantation while working alongside people of various ethnic groups; I have translated the Japanese into English, leaving some of the Pidgin English intact. In all cases, I aimed to keep their voices as authentic as possible. To fill in the details of their stories after these immigrants had passed away, I contacted their children and grandchildren, who recalled information and provided original documents.

While interviewing the picture brides, I noticed patterns indicating that their Pidgin evolved in different ways depending on the plantations in which they settled and the village dialect that they brought with them. For example, in Kohala, there may have been more Chinese and Hawaiians in the early period, and when the Japanese immigrants combined what they heard from co-workers with their own village dialect, a unique Pidgin English developed. Similarly, when I interviewed women on the Waipahu and Ewa plantations, there seemed to be more Portuguese and Filipinos, fewer Hawaiians, and some Koreans. When the Japanese immigrants settled in Waipahu and Ewa, their village dialect combined with the languages of their co-workers, and another unique Pidgin English evolved. Pidgin is characterized not only by its words and sentence structures but also by the speaker's accent, intonation, body language, and gestures. Some may simply refer to this as ethnic, linguistic, or cultural identity, but Pidgin in all its variations developed in the workplace.

Incorporating Pidgin components in their communication seemed to help the immigrants in breaking down cultural barriers and defusing hostilities in everyday activities. I had the great advantage of growing up on a sugar plantation, observing and experiencing firsthand the daily life of immigrants, so I was familiar with their patterns of speech. Among themselves, issei men and women would spontaneously drop into their regional dialects. In their interviews, we hear the colloquial ease and directness and the lack of formality that we associate with oral expression. And we hear the unique linguistic flavor of Pidgin, which exists in Hawaii to this day.

A last note: The Japanese consider a baby a year old when born. For that reason, there may be some discrepancies between a person's age as stated in these narratives and his or her age as it is commonly rendered in the American system.

THE BRIDES

Kaku Kumasaka
STOLEN *KAKI* AND THE MOTORBIKE SANTA

October 24, 1899–December 5, 1987
Born in Mugiwa, Yuno-mura, Date-gun, Fukushima-ken
Arrived in Hawaii March 16, 1922

Kaku Kumasaka was the first issei woman I interviewed for my research on plantation work clothing, for a 1979 class assignment at the University of Hawaii, Manoa.
At that time, there was hardly any information on plantation work clothing to be
found, whether at the University of Hawaii library or in public libraries, museums,
or archives. My mother suggested I talk to Kaku, who originally came from a nearby
village back in Fukushima prefecture. Kaku had been working for the Oahu Sugar
Company at Waipahu since arriving as a picture bride in 1922, and she was one of
the last issei woman to retire from the plantation, at age sixty-five. Since I knew
Kaku and her daughter, Yaeko, I felt comfortable beginning my interviews with her.

Kaku and her husband, Sashichi, now retired after their long years of hard work
in the sugarcane fields, were finally beginning to enjoy their retirement years. Aside
from traveling to Japan and Los Angeles to visit their children and grandchildren,
much of their time was spent at the Waipahu Senior Center. There they learned to
sing, dance, and play games with people of other ethnic groups who also had worked
in the fields for Oahu Sugar Company.

I met them at the Waipahu Senior Center for the interview. Kaku was seventy-
nine years old at the time. The modern senior housing is located next to the Hans
L'Orange ballpark, where the plantation community gathers to relax and enjoy various athletic interests. It was a far cry from Pump Four Camp at the plantation, where
Sashichi brought his new bride in 1922. Now she had a modern metal dinette set
where they ate their meals instead of the makeshift table and stools constructed
from discarded crates that had served them in their early years. Instead of cooking
rice outdoors over an open fire, she used an electric range, and she had a nice refrig-
erator to store fresh food, instead of using a block of ice.

Kaku was well known among the issei as a hardworking woman with talents in
sewing, quilting, and patchwork. She was petite, just four feet ten inches tall, a bit
stocky and sturdy in her build. Looking at her, no one would believe that she was the
only *wahine* (Hawaiian for "woman") to work alongside the men, day after day,

equal to them in doing all the heavy work. Her hair was silver gray, rolled neatly into a bun at the back of her head and held in place with a simple ivory comb.

Having come from Fukushima prefecture in northern Japan, known for winters with as much as eleven feet of snow, she must have had a beautiful porcelain-like complexion when she arrived in Hawaii. Although she would wear a wide-brimmed straw hat and kerchief in the fields, her skin was now ruddy and deeply tanned from years of being exposed to the hot sun. At age seventy-nine, she complained of severe back pain, but otherwise she was the picture of good health. She was an adorable *obaachan* (grandmother) with a warm, engaging personality and a uniquely Fukushima lilt to her words, the rhythmic *zu zu ben* cadence of the region's dialect. It is a difficult dialect to understand, but my mother was from Fukushima, so I was exposed to it from a very young age; I cannot speak it, but I am able to understand it. During the interview, Kaku spoke in this dialect and Pidgin English. When she was working in the cane fields with individuals from other ethnic groups, she spoke Pidgin English. To make the interview understandable to the reader, I have translated the Japanese, while keeping some of the Pidgin English commonly used by the early immigrants.

VILLAGE CHILDHOOD

Kaku Konno was born on October 24, 1899, in the isolated mountain region of Mugiwa, Yuno village, Date district, Fukushima prefecture, Japan, to Rijjyu Konno and Fuku (Watanabe) Konno. Her parents had ten children, eight girls and two boys. When they had three girls in succession, they were quite disappointed; finally, the fourth was a baby boy. Kaku was the fifth, followed by two more girls, then another boy, and two more girls. According to Japanese tradition, it was important to have sons to continue the family lineage, so her parents were overjoyed and pampered the boys. In contrast, the girls had to work very hard on the farm and had the responsibility of raising the silkworms. Four of the girls died young, leaving six children still living when Kaku left for Hawaii in her early twenties.

"Grandfather died when I was born in 1899, so Grandmother came to live with us. I was the naughty one in the middle, but Obaachan was very good to me. She was spry and still worked on the farm, weeding and going around picking up horse manure for her garden. She even delivered babies and dressed brides in formal traditional attire, although her style may not have had the elegance of the city people. Women in the country learned to do these things out of necessity, because we lived in such an isolated region. Whenever we girls went out, Obaachan would sit us down, scrub our faces. She'd say, 'Look this way, look that way,' and scrub and comb out our hair, too. During the Obon festival [the Buddhist custom to honor the deceased spirits of one's ancestors], most of the village girls participated in the dancing, but Obaachan was so strict, she didn't allow us girls to go out at night. If we did, she followed us wherever we went. People of the village used to say, 'There goes Grandma Oharu following the girls around!'

"Our favorite snack during my childhood was dried pickled *kaki* [persimmon] skin. In Japan back then, you didn't have much else for snacks, except rice crackers. No matter how good the snack is, when you eat it every day, you get tired of eating the same thing. We also used to get up before dawn to pick *kuri* [chestnuts]. We had to separate the good ones from the ones eaten by worms. The good ones we would roast, pickle, or dry in the shell for snacks. The good persimmons were precious. We would put those aside to serve with tea to guests. Our guests would rave about it. The spoiled nuts we would clean, chop up, and use to make steamed *kuri gohan* [chestnut rice], which was quite a treat!

"My parents belonged to the Tendaishu Buddhist sect in the village. They didn't attend temple services regularly, because they were too busy. However, when a person died, the priest came to the home to offer prayers and also officiated at the burial. In the village, they observed a certain custom. The first thing they did when a person died was to fold the legs into a sitting position, to make sure the body would fit into the coffin before the bones could get too stiff. The women who were close friends of the family gathered and sewed the shroud for the deceased using white muslin. They were careful not to make a knot or make a backward stitch: this was to make sure the deceased would not return. It is also a superstition that scissors are not used in making the kimono for the deceased. Nothing sharp can be used, since that may cut into the spirit. The last time I went to Japan in 1984, I heard there's hardly anyone left to sew the shroud anymore, so my older sister gets called for every funeral in the village. She's now ninety-two or ninety-three years old. She might die anytime. Who will sew the shroud for her?"

Kaku's story brought back memories. When I was a child, I recall seeing the neighborhood women in Waipahu following these same practices: no scissors, no backstitching. Clearly the tradition had continued in Hawaii.

Kaku continued, "As for our education, my oldest sister is the only one who graduated from the sixth grade. The rest of us girls went as far as the fourth grade. At that time, compulsory education was extended to the sixth grade, but I couldn't go because my parents were too poor. They needed my help for farming and raising silkworms. In those days, a sixth-grade education was considered a luxury for a farm girl.

"You would be surprised at how we dressed for school. I wore *monpei* [pantaloons] and *waraji* [sandals] woven from rice stalks. We were taught to weave the *waraji* at a very young age, as soon as our fingers were nimble enough to twist the rice stalks. Our *monpei* was made of handwoven *kasuri* [ikat] cloth that my mother and the older girls, including myself, wove on our handloom. Every home in the village had their own handloom. Some of the *monpei* were made of *yo-jima* [cloth woven in a design of horizontal stripes], which was sturdy and kept us warm. These were the *monpei* we wore underneath our skirts for work during the early period. In those days, we were embarrassed to mention that we brought to Hawaii these kimonos that were hand-dyed and handwoven in the village. Today, those things are rare and difficult to get and considered valuable."

The farmers used indigo dye a lot, because it was colorfast and made the fiber stronger. The farm women wore the indigo-dyed *kasuri* work clothes while laboring in the fields. Since ancient times, indigo leaves and seeds have been used to treat snake and insect bites. So farmers believed that because work clothes dyed with indigo had a strong smell, the dye would protect them from snakes and insects in the fields. That is the reason issei women working in the sugar and pineapple plantations in Hawaii took apart their indigo-dyed *kasuri* kimonos and made them into work clothing. In Hawaii's tropical climate, centipedes, scorpions, yellow jackets, and red ants were everywhere in the fields, and the workers were always fearful of the stings.

RAISING SILKWORMS

"My parents were poor farmers who didn't have any rice fields, only a vegetable garden. They raised mostly silkworms. With my mother's poor health, it was very difficult for her. Today it's much easier to raise silkworms, but in those days it was tedious work; everything was done manually. The *tane* [seed eggs] had to be bought and carefully put in a large room, where they were carefully watched. The room had to be heated at the right temperature to warm the eggs until they were ready to hatch. When they hatched, hundreds of tiny silkworms, the size of ants, crawled out. Then, with a chicken feather, the silkworms were brushed off onto a straw pad on which rice bran had been spread. Then they were brought back to the heated room. I cannot remember at what degree the temperature was set for the incubation period. A week later, the silkworms were put into a container for their sleep. They didn't eat mulberry leaves for one or two days. So we began gathering the young, tender mulberry leaves to get ready to feed them.

"We raised our own mulberry trees in the fields. Our family was about the last to give up raising silkworms. It's time-consuming work and most of the villagers gave up. Today, in Fukushima, instead of mulberry fields, they have lots of apple, twentieth-century pear, and peach orchards. When the flowers are in bloom, it is a sight to behold." Kaku's eyes were lively with the memory.

"In between the busy seasons with the silkworms, I was sent away to other farm families to do babysitting. You know, I did everything, even gathered firewood in the mountains to make charcoal. Fukushima is known for the heavy snow in winter, and preparation begins early. The menfolk burn wood to make charcoal; women then gather the charcoal to store in the shed. In winter, the *irori* [sunken hearth] in the main room becomes the center of the household. Most of the work was done around the *irori*. It kept us warm during the severe winter. The girls in the family used to strip the bark of the *mada* tree to make fiber for weaving cloth. We let it rot or ferment in the well. Then we *hai wo irete* [put the ashes] in a large pot and we simmered the mass of fiber for a long time. The *zenmai* [fern shoots] and other useful things gathered from nearby mountains were cooked together in the ashes to make the fiber. After that, it was ready to be strained in water until the water became clear. Finally we stripped the fiber, spun it into thread, and wove it into cloth. The short strips were all joined together. And that was sold to outsiders. This was all done by the young girls during the winter months. After the weaving was done, we sat around the *irori*. That was a happy pastime for us." Kaku smiled.

"We also hand-spun *tsumugi* [spun silk], joining the fibers and spinning them into thread and weaving the threads into cloth on the floor loom. This is how it was done with our feet," she explained, going through the motions. "Weaving *tsumugi* is done on a seated loom. It is called *jibata*. Also, I learned to do *ito-tori* [picking the thread], an important skill. I was trained to do it since I was thirteen years old. If you don't wind the silk thread from the cocoon correctly, it breaks. I still remember getting scolded by my mother for not winding the thread correctly. She was very strict. The thread has to be smooth and flat to produce fine silk cloth. I'll tell you a funny story about that. You see, to spin the thread, the white, egg-shaped cocoons are placed in a big pot of water and it takes a long time for the water to boil. So, in the meantime, I went swimming in the river. When I returned the water had evaporated. Did I get scolded then!" She had spoiled the whole batch of *mayu* (cocoons)— no fine strong thread would be unreeled from the gummy mass.

Kaku patiently described the intricate process. "You see, when you boil the cocoon and steam it for a while, the thread just comes off the cocoon. It's fascinating, really, how the thread is formed. Then that thread is carefully lined in a small frame. It has to be done right; otherwise, when the silk thread is reset on a larger frame, it will break."

The unique quality of the *tsumugi* was that the entire process of spinning the thread, weaving the cloth, and sewing was done by one person. This made the kimono particularly precious to the wearer. The issei women always spoke with nostalgia when they mentioned the *tsumugi-gasuri*. The thread produced for *tsumugi* was strong, elastic, and glossy, and it was usually woven in stripes, checks, and *kasuri* designs. Many of the issei women I interviewed confirmed this information. It is also mentioned in Norio Yamanaka's *Book of Kimono*.

It's amazing how Kaku remembered these minute details of raising silkworms and producing the silk for weaving after so many years. Throughout this interview, Kaku kept on saying that she was very ignorant because she had only a fourth-grade education. I could not help but imagine what she could have accomplished if she had had the opportunity to continue her education.

"Yes, even with so many sisters, we did get along quite well. I must have been the naughty one among us. I had a younger sister who was so spoiled that I used to scold her. My mother, who was a soft-spoken woman, often came after me, saying, 'Kaku, I brought up ten children without ever using one harsh word, so please don't scold her. After all, she is the youngest, you know.' I remember once my mother threw me out into the snow. She was a quiet person, never the kind to spank, but I must have done something terrible for her to give me such harsh punishment! She once rolled my sister and me inside a futon because we fought with each other. She tied both of us up in the futon and tossed us out in the snow! She shouted, '*Soo-reh, suki na dake kenka-seh!*' [There, fight all you want!] That taught us a good lesson," Kaku happily reminisced.

PICTURE BRIDE MARRIAGE

"My husband, Sashichi Kumasaka, is from Yuno-mura, a few villages away, kind of more advanced in many ways than our isolated village. He came to Hawaii in 1912 on the *Tenyo Maru,* when he was sixteen years old. His father had come a year earlier with plans to send for the rest of the family later as *yobi-yose*. In their village, rumors were spreading that you could make a fortune working in the sugarcane and pineapple fields in the islands. People said, 'Hawaii is *rakuen* [paradise]!' I thought so, too, from what my older sister told me. She was married to my future husband's older brother. I always had a yearning to come here, because my sister talked about it all the time. But no matter how badly she wanted to come, my parents wouldn't let her. They kept telling her, 'Why do you want to go to a foreign country?' Because she couldn't fulfill her dream, she kept reminding me, 'You're not going to get anywhere marrying a small-time farmer in this village! You go to Hawaii!' If not for her, I would have ended up being a farmer's wife back in the village.

"Sadly, my mother died three years before I left for Hawaii. This was after my oldest sister got married to my husband's older brother. I served as *oyagawari* [substitute mother] for my siblings, so I had more responsibilities. Of course, relatives tried to matchmake a spouse for me, but my father refused, saying that he would be lost without my help. That's why I didn't get married until I was twenty-one years old. My husband's auntie acted as the go-between for us, but actually it was my sister who made the arrangements for me to marry her brother-in-law."

Kaku shyly handed me a photo. "Here's the photo taken in 1920 used for the photo exchange. I don't think I ever saw this photo of Sashichi back then. Even if I did, it wouldn't have mattered whether I liked him or not. My father made all the decisions. Nobody even asked for my opinion. I had no choice! That's the way it was in those days. Oh, I saw him once when I was very young. That's all."

Kaku mentioned the great concern of her eighty-three-year-old *obaachan*, who had followed the girls around when they were kids. Kaku said, "She kept asking, 'Why do you want to go to Hawaii? Don't go!'" One of Kaku's younger sisters had died a few years before, so her *obaachan* must have been lonely. It was also a custom in Fukushima to return to the natal home to have your baby. "Obaachan opposed my going to the very end. She'd say, 'All this time, your sisters come home to have their babies—who's going to take care of you when you are so far away?' She cried out that no one would be nearby to care for me and my baby."

Kaku Kono's exchange photograph, 1920. Photo courtesy of the Kumasaka family.

Kaku came to Hawaii in 1922, and hoped that eventually she would be able to send for her younger sisters. Then on June 30, 1924, the U.S. Congress passed the Immigration Act of 1924, called the Japanese Exclusion Act. This act prohibited the entry of all aliens who were ineligible for citizenship. Under this law, only non-quota immigrants such as government officials, ministers of religion, professors, students, merchants, and travelers were admitted, and only for brief visits. This virtually ended Japanese immigration to the United States. In 1941, even non-quota immigrant visits came to an end. Thus, Kaku was never able to send for her sisters, who never left the farming village in Fukushima.

Kaku explained, "After both sides of our families decided on our marriage, my name was crossed off from my *koseki*, as they do for the deceased. Then my name was entered into my husband's *koseki*. That made our marriage official under Japanese law. It required six months for the visa to come through for me to be able enter the Territory of Hawaii. So altogether I stayed almost a year at my husband's parents' home, working for them. There was no marriage ceremony or party, not even a *san san kudo* ritual, because my husband was already here working for Oahu Sugar on the plantation. Many years later, when I returned to my village, I told my siblings, 'Out of ten of us, you all had a wedding party or something in the way of a dowry, but I'm the only one who didn't have anything done when I got married. All I received was one set of purple *montsuki* with *suso-moyo* [designs on the hemline] and a *yuino kin* [betrothal gift] of only *juyen* [10 yen, about $5].' Since I was going to a foreign land, everybody told me that I'd probably get $50 and I could buy anything I wanted. Nothing doing! It was only 10 yen from my husband's family. An informal marriage ceremony was performed in absentia, and my family sent for my aunt from the *honke* [main family] to be a witness. They had some kind of feast then." So even though Kaku thought that nothing had been done to celebrate the occasion, her in-laws seem to have prepared a feast to mark her marriage and departure for the islands.

"My marriage was a bit unusual," Kaku said. "Most brides return home during the six-month waiting period, but I lived with my in-laws and worked for a whole year on the farm. Of course, my father-in-law had remarried and got himself a young wife. My stepmother-in-law was a bit spoiled. She would buy fresh fish, cook it to her liking, and eat it all by herself, not sharing with her stepchildren, not even with her husband. Imagine that! She went to the *onsen*, the hot-spring spa, every day after lunch, and she didn't return until dark. In the past, such things would never be allowed. But my father-in-law was in his sixties and she was much younger. The first wife had died after giving birth to my husband's younger sister, who lived on the Ewa plantation.

"Before leaving Japan, I wanted to visit my family once more. I had a feeling I would not see them for a long time. So I had my hair done in *maru-mage,* or married women's coiffure, to surprise them. While I was taking a bath someone stole my purse at the bathhouse! I begged my sister-in-law not to mention it to anyone, as I'd get scolded for sure. The next day, before I left for my natal home, my father-in-law gave me a mere *gojyusen* [50 sen, about 25 cents in American money]. It was the custom to take a fairly decent gift for my first visit home as a bride, but since my purse had been stolen, I couldn't buy a gift. I was so embarrassed, but I went empty-handed to my parents' home. You can imagine how terrible I felt. But being my family, they overlooked the matter," she said sadly.

"The visit to my home was during the autumn, my favorite time of year, with the spectacular sight of the persimmon orchards filled with bright orange, mouth-watering fruits. The villagers take delight in stringing the ripe *kaki* on strong bamboo stalks to dry in the autumn sun, until each one turns a nice brown. It's a wonderful way of preserving the fruit." During this visit with her father, stepmother, and siblings, Kaku was happy when her stepmother told her to pick *kaki* to dry them to take to her husband in Hawaii. Every day she carefully picked the nicest ones and dried them on bamboo stalks out of doors. Kaku was looking forward to surprising her husband with something special from her village.

"You can't believe what happened!" Kaku said, remembering the incident as if it happened yesterday. Her eyes glared in anger and she gestured furiously with her hands. "She took them all one day when I was gone!" Everything still remained so vivid to her. "To think that I worked so hard trying to get the dried *kaki* ready so I could bring it to Hawaii. I didn't have any money to buy a gift, but those persimmons were something you couldn't get in Hawaii in those days. Can you believe it? Not a trace of them left. I didn't get to taste even one dried *kaki*. She didn't even leave some for me to take as a gift for my husband! I was never so disappointed in all my life. My stepmother sold all the dried persimmons. Ah, *akireta* [disgusting]! I was stunned!" Kaku was near tears as she recalled that incident. After all these years, one could feel the emotion she must have experienced that day. "I wondered whether I would ever care to set foot there again. Things were not the same anymore without the kind and comforting words I would have heard from my dear mother before I left for a foreign land. My father held back from doing things for me, and I understood his feelings. All I could do was kneel before my mother's grave and clasp my hands in prayer. Deep in my heart, I knew she would wish me well."

Kaku's selfish stepmother acted in ways that were contrary to traditional Japanese Confucian ethics, which emphasize cooperation and harmony. Selfishness is incompatible with the strong Japanese spirit of sharing. Thus Kaku still felt the shock, hurt, and outrage some sixty years later.

"It was the eve of leaving my husband's village home, and my father-in-law told me, 'I'd like to tell you to come home in two or three years, but I know it's impossible to save money that quickly.' He made a strange remark as we stood before the large field in front of the home: 'You both work hard and come back in ten years.' He said convincingly, 'Don't worry. Someday this is going to be your land and residence, so work hard and come home.'" Kaku raised her voice and told me, "Nothing doing! Ten years stretched to twenty, then to sixty years! Half our pay was sent home every month to pay for that land. All the time, we sacrificed so much, going without many things. How many times did I work overtime, just to make the 10 cents to save for that land! My father-in-law had been in Hawaii before. He had arranged to send for his two sons and daughter to come as *yobi-yose* to work on the plantations. He then returned home to Japan to retire while his sons supported him. Later he even found himself a young wife." She took a moment and looked out the window to compose herself. "If I told you the whole sad story, you could write a novel and win a prize."

On June 24, 2011, decades after this interview, I spoke on the phone to her son, Toshimi, who was living in Los Angeles. He recalled a trip he had made to Fukushima when his parents' health was failing, to see the land they had worked so hard to purchase. He said he was amazed at how large the property was. He looked over acres and acres of rich land and the mountain covered with bamboo and cedar trees.

Toshimi added, "On my mother's side, the Konno lineage goes back hundreds of years, with valuable timber. Also on my father's side, we were surprised that one of our uncles owned the popular Iizaka *onsen,* the hot spring in Yuno-mura. We also saw rows of weather-beaten tombstones with the Kumasaka name. There were so many generations that even today they are all strangers." But his parents had not been aware that all of this existed.

Kaku continued the tale of her journey. "My father-in-law accompanied me on the train to Yokohama and left me at a hotel where I met other picture brides headed for Honolulu. It would have been too expensive for him to stay at a hotel in Yokohama, so he stayed with a friend in Tokyo. I stayed there with other picture brides for about three days in the hotel. The hotel staff took care of taking us back and forth to all kinds of physical exams before departing to Hawaii. During that time, the officials told us to learn to speak English, since we were going to a foreign country. They tried to teach us some English, but I couldn't make heads or tails of what they were saying. All I can remember is they taught us how to say *guru moningu* [good morning] and *guru ebuningu* [good evening]. How could we learn a language in such a short time?" Kaku broke out in laughter as she recalled the terrible ordeal of trying to master a foreign language.

"In between our busy schedule in Yokohama, I was brave enough to take the train to Tokyo to meet my father-in-law. I guess I was younger then, so I had the courage to go alone by train. While in Tokyo, I heard rumors that the Tokyo Expo was going to open in ten days. How exciting, I thought. If that was today, I would have the guts to stay behind to enjoy it. But I had to go to Hawaii. I went to Uyeno station, where I was supposed to meet my father-in-law, but he was nowhere around. Finally, after a long wait, I decided I'd better take the train back to Yokohama, so I began walking. Then I heard a loud 'Ooooee!' I turned around, and there was my father-in-law. Imagine, right in the heart of Tokyo, yelling so loud! Plenty of heads turned. Only a country bumpkin would behave like that.

"In Yokohama the night before we left for Hawaii, many of the other picture brides cried and cried. They couldn't stand the thought of saying goodbye to their parents, who had come from the villages to see their daughters off." But Kaku was amused at the behavior of the weeping picture brides. "I thought, 'If they feel so miserable, they shouldn't go to Hawaii.' I didn't feel lonesome. I couldn't wait to see the paradise island I had been yearning to see for a long time.

"I shall never forget our farewell in Yokohama. Just before I boarded the *Korea Maru,* my father-in-law, who was the only one to see me off, said, 'Even if people say Hawaii is a nice place, be prepared to work hard. It won't be easy. And when you get to the sugar plantation, you have many siblings on your husband's side, so please, try to get along with them and don't fight. Save your money and come home quickly.' Then to my surprise, after I appeared on deck, my father-in-law threw bright-colored streamers to me from the pier to the boat. One after another, everybody was throwing streamers; it was so beautiful! I had never seen anything like that in all my life. I wished I could have shared this with my sisters. I held on to the tapes as the boat slowly pulled away from the pier, until the colorful streamers tore away, drifting

Immigrants leaving for Hawaii from the port of Yokohama on the *Tatsuta Maru*, having a memorable send-off, ca. 1920s. Photo courtesy of Masaki Tabusa. Barbara Kawakami Collection.

along with the waves. I should be grateful to my father-in-law for giving me such a memorable send-off."

Kaku Kumasaka came to Hawaii during the latter part of the restricted immigration period, which began in 1908 and lasted until 1924, and picture brides who came earlier seem not to have experienced this exciting, colorful farewell, as none of them mentioned it.

ARRIVAL IN PARADISE

"As much as I looked forward to coming to Hawaii, I was too seasick to notice anything. The voyage took about ten days, and I couldn't eat a thing. I threw up everything I ate. I just stayed in my room. The *Korea Maru* finally docked in Honolulu harbor on March 16, 1922. I got married at age twenty-one, but lived with my in-laws for a year, so by the time I came to Hawaii, I had turned twenty-two in October of that year. After we disembarked, we were taken to the immigration station. I was dressed in my striped cotton kimono and wore a pompadour hairdo."

Kaku continued. "At the immigration station they served us *takuwan* [pickled turnips] and *ume* [pickled plum] with rice and tea for breakfast. After being seasick for ten days and hardly eating anything, the simple rice and *takuwan* tasted so good. Even today, I can never forget how delicious my first meal in Hawaii was.

"There were several picture brides who received *sashi-ire* [food sent by relatives]. The brides had so much food, they couldn't eat all of it, so they shared some with me. I was the only one not receiving *sashi-ire*. It seems strange that no one came to see me when my husband had two brothers and a sister in Hawaii. Not one of them came to see me. I was lonely. I did not know anyone in this strange place. I noticed that some wives had already met their husbands, and they didn't appear to be too happy. Not having seen my husband's picture, I had some anxiety about what he would look like."

In Honolulu Kaku was happy to meet Dr. Tomizo Katsunuma, the inspector at the immigration station for the incoming immigrants from Japan. Katsunuma-san had left Japan to study to be a veterinarian at the University of Utah, intending to return to Japan to begin his practice. On the way home to Japan he stopped in Hawaii, where the immigrant officials noticed his fluency in English and Japanese and offered him the position of inspector. He was perfectly suited for the position because of his wonderful personality and sense of humor, which put the immigrants at ease.

He was also able to help them in many ways. In those days, the issei didn't have telephones, and letters took a long time to arrive by ship from Japan. Many of the men did not know their brides' arrival date, and there were times when the picture brides were left stranded and even unclaimed by the groom. Dr. Katsunuma, being a compassionate man, felt sorry for the unclaimed brides. If no one had claimed a woman after two weeks, he would take her home to his family, and eventually do some matchmaking to find the woman a husband. Katsunuma and his family were known to have helped many early immigrants in distress. Every issei I interviewed mentioned Katsunuma-san with much affection.

Kaku recalled, "There was a funny incident that happened at the immigration station on the day of my arrival. Katsunuma-san lined up all the picture brides who had come as *yobi-yose*. He cautioned us not to talk. He said to remain silent, for he was going to guess where each bride came from. He began correctly guessing the provincial background of each woman, one after the other, from the way they were dressed and behaved. The brides from Hiroshima and Yamaguchi prefecture were more *hokano* [Hawaiian for "well dressed"], and they were polished in speaking also. Not an *inaka-pe* [country bumpkin] like me. Some brides were just as poorly dressed as I was. I must have been wearing a *yukata* [kimono made from cotton fabric]. Some women had brought a *tansu* [cabinet] and other nice things, but all I had was one *yanagi gori* [basket trunk] with a few belongings. He finally came over where I was and paused awhile. 'You're the only one I can't guess. Where are you from?' I giggled and replied, 'I'm from Fukushima.' He said, 'I'm from Fukushima, too,' and we burst out laughing. How funny that he could not guess where I was from." We laughed together at this story.

"I'll tell you another funny thing that occurred at the immigration station," said Kaku. "I went looking around for the women's restroom. Not familiar with Western ways, and not being able to read the signs, I entered the men's restroom. You see, in Japan, we have only outside *benjo* [toilets] where you have to squat. The white porcelain looked more like a washbasin to me, so I washed my face with the water flowing in the white urinal. The water looked so clean, but that was where men's urine flowed down! Yeah, I heard that later," Kaku laughed. "Ah, that was a culture shock!

"We also took a short test at the immigration station. Mine was, 'Take out your *koseki tohon*' [family register]. I was worried because I didn't have it with me. When Katsunuma-san came by, I told him I didn't have it. He said, 'Okay.' And I passed. Some of the brides took so long to answer the questions. Some couldn't answer at all. Many couldn't speak or understand the standard Japanese [because they spoke a regional dialect]. There was one couple, an old husband with a young wife. During those days, some men who had money went to Japan and brought back a wife, as in this case. She passed the exam quickly and was allowed to go out. The poor old man couldn't answer the official's questions, so somebody whispered to the group, 'Why don't you just teach him how to answer?' We all laughed.

"The other picture brides, including myself, whose husbands didn't show up to claim their brides right away slept at the immigration station on a bed that looked like silkworm shelves back in the village. I was relieved when my husband finally came to pick me up two days later. He was twenty-eight years old then, and I was twenty-two years old. I never did receive his picture, so I didn't know whom to look for, but he had my picture.

"My first impression of him? I don't know what we said. I don't think we said anything. We were both too shy meeting each other for the first time. My husband hired a taxi to take us to Waipahu. In Yokohama, that's when I rode in an automobile for the first time. In the village where I grew up there were no cars. The most modern means of transportation was a bicycle. I think I was about eight years old when I saw a bicycle for the first time. One day, while standing in front of my home, at a distance, I saw a man moving very fast along the road. I wondered how he could run so fast at such speed! Then as he got closer, I saw he was riding a bicycle. Yes, we lived in a remote village, so I never saw an automobile until I went to Yokohama.

"From the immigration station, we went directly to my husband's older brother's house in Waipahu. They lived in a small house with a parlor, one bedroom, and a kitchen. His brother shared one bedroom with his wife and two children. We stayed there for a night and then went to my husband's bachelor quarters. Back home, we were poor, but we had a large house because we raised silkworms. My husband lived in a longhouse whitewashed with lime, not painted. Several bachelors lived in this longhouse, one room per person. Until our living quarters were available, we stayed in the one-room bachelor quarters."

Kaku was happy to know that her husband's boss was also from Fukushima prefecture and spoke the same dialect, so she could communicate with him and his wife. Bungoro Kimura was the boss of Pump Four Camp, also called Camp Seventeen. He was the *luna* (foreman) and ditchman, in charge of five cane fields that required irrigation, and he had a horse. His wife, Hatsu, ran the boardinghouse and did all the cooking and laundry for the single men who worked under him. Until they were assigned their own house, Sashichi and Kaku had their meals with the single men in the big kitchen.

Konpan is the Japanese pronunciation of the English word "company," but it also means "partnership." It was used to refer to a group of people who formed a partnership with one of them as the leader. The *konpan* men worked in a designated area of a cane or pineapple field for a few years until the plants matured and were ready to be harvested. The plantation paid the leader for the work they did at the end of the two or three years in one lump sum. The leader of the *konpan* distributed the profit to the men, usually about $400 or $500, depending on the success of the crop; the leader took more because he had greater responsibilities.

The Kimuras were very warm and generous and took good care of the *konpan* men who worked under Bungoro. They hosted a wedding party for the newlyweds; assisted by the other women in the camp, Mrs. Kimura prepared a feast. The reception was held in humble surroundings: there were no chairs, and the guests all sat on *zabuton* (cushions). Kaku wore the purple *montsuki* her father had given her as part of her dowry. All the men who worked under Kimura-san were invited. Kaku noticed that the men all came dressed in black suits, with white shirts and bow ties. She learned later that no matter how poor the issei men were, the first thing they invested in was a black suit. The suit cost about $20, an entire month's pay. It lasted them a lifetime and was often used for the final journey into the next world. The dark suit was worn at all special occasions, such as weddings, funerals, formal activities at the Japanese school, and community functions. In Japan, to show respect, they were accustomed to wearing the formal black kimono with the family crest, a long pleated skirt, and a *haori* coat for formal occasions. The one black suit served that purpose in Hawaii.

The women did not participate in the merrymaking, but helped serve the food and sake. There was lots of sake being passed around, accompanied by singing and dancing. The highlight of the marriage celebration was the *utai* (chanting) of the Takasago, a Noh drama text, a very difficult piece to sing. A long time ago, a poem was written about the grandeur and beauty of two pine trees on the shores of Takasago on Kyushu island. The ancient black and red pines stood with their branches entwined together, appearing to be a single tree. The pine trees were widely worshiped as a symbol of long life and wedded bliss. The drama was recited by Bungoro Kimura in his rich baritone voice. It was his specialty. Two decades later, during World War II, I was married, and although it was a small wedding, Bungoro, who was related to my mother and looked like Napoleon Bonaparte, sang the Takasago, much to everyone's delight. It sounded so romantic.

For wedding gifts, Kaku received many *yukata tan-mono* (rolls of cotton kimono fabric). In those days, each roll of fabric cost $1. Kaku was happy, and she didn't have to buy kimono fabric for a long time. Until World War II, issei women wore cotton kimonos for casual wear, shopping, and visiting friends. When a kimono became faded, it was used as *nemaki,* or sleepwear. Finally, when that got faded and torn, the nicer part was saved to make babies' diapers. Nothing was wasted!

"I know you well enough, so I'm going to share this with you," Kaku confided. "This might help you to understand what I went through as a picture bride. Mine may be an exception. Yes, I am embarrassed to even tell you about it. When I left Japan in 1922, my father-in-law paid for everything, so I thought the things I got were given to me as gifts. Nothing doing! When I got here, I started sorting out some things that I had brought from Japan. I found a *kakizuke* [list of items] of all the things he gave me: the *toko-tokin* [traveling expenses], the *yuino kin* [betrothal gift], even the *zori* [slippers] I wore to Hawaii. I was shocked! Even the kimono I brought from Japan I had to send back because it was on loan to me. Also the *toko-tokin* and the *yuino kin* of $5. So that's the way it was. I didn't get a thing from either my family or my in-laws. My real mother was long gone, and I took care of the household until I got married. My family was very poor, so I didn't have the heart to ask my father for anything."

EARLY PLANTATION LIFE IN WAIPAHU

When Kaku first came as a bride, she didn't have any relatives or friends nearby, except her husband. She said, "One day, I was so homesick and lonely I wanted to visit my husband's younger sister, who lived on the Ewa plantation." She walked from Pump Four Camp in Waipahu down to Depot Road, below the Arakawa store, where the Oahu Railway train stopped to pick up passengers. When Kaku found out she had missed the train, she followed the train tracks along the shoreline to visit her sister-in-law, not even realizing how far that would be. This was in the 1920s, when hardly any issei families on the plantation owned a car. Only the plantation manager, assistant manager, and camp police were seen driving cars around the plantation. Later, a few issei men started running taxis from Waipahu to Honolulu. She must have been desperately lonely to have walked more than five miles from Pump Four Camp to Ewa that day.

"I was so lonely at first. I had come with high hopes and dreams of a life of luxury, but when I arrived, ahhh . . . *tamageta,* I was shocked! Because my husband had been a bachelor for a long time, living in a *konpan* camp, everything was so neglected."

A few months later, they were assigned their own small house, whitewashed with lime. "The first thing I did as a housewife was complete a good general cleaning of the shabby plantation house. It was really pitiful, you know. I noticed the *tanzen* [cotton padded kimono] he had brought from Fukushima had never been washed. I took the kimono apart, washed it, aired the cotton in the hot sun to fluff it, and resewed the kimono again. Then I took apart the futon, washed it, and put it back together. The kitchen had an earthen floor—no chairs, no table, not one piece of furniture. So we got empty crates from the store and used them as a table to eat our meals. With crates we also made a safe, the cabinet for food with a screen door to keep flies out. I cooked rice in a large *kama,* a cast-iron cooking pot, so it tasted good. We had no electricity, so we used a kerosene lantern for light. With that dim light, I sewed at night and did ironing. I subscribed to the Japanese paper so I could educate myself, but I had no time to read.

"Mrs. Kimura, the lady who ran the boardinghouse where my husband had his meals before I arrived, sewed me a complete fieldwork outfit of *kasuri* fabric, and all the accessories. As soon as I put the house in order, I went to work in the cane fields in the *pula pula* [Hawaiian for "seedlings"] gang. That was three weeks after I arrived from Japan.

"We sharpened the cut-cane knife at the workplace ourselves, you know. Yes, women sharpened their own knives. We had different kinds of cut-cane knives for certain kinds of work. The knife is wide at first, but each time we sharpened it, the blade gradually became narrower. Men and women both used the same type and size of cut-cane knife. The cane knife with the hook on the tip was handy to use to pick up cane stalks from the ground. You don't have to bend too low each time. When I first came in 1922 and started working for the Oahu sugar plantation, the pay was 45 cents for ten hours a day for women, $1 a day for men."

Young women from the Oahu sugar plantation marched down Depot Road to catch the train to Honolulu to participate in the 1920 strike parade. Ruth Nobuku Maki Collection.

Waipahu Train Depot. Barbara Kawakami Collection.

The Kumasakas showing the *dotera* (cotton-padded kimono) brought from Fukushima. Barbara Kawakami Collection.

When I asked if she had been acquainted with any of my relatives, she told me, "Yes, I knew your auntie Sawa. She was a neighbor of ours at Pump Four Camp. She used to babysit our two children when they were babies. I left my children with your aunt Sawa, then rushed to catch the early train by 5:30 a.m. I had to pass the wooden bridge [near Hawaii's Plantation Village in Waipahu] every morning. Once there was a *pakesan,* a Chinese man, hanging from the kiawe tree near the bridge." Here she switched into Pidgin. "Lucky I no see, but the man behind me see. Oh . . . real scary, he cannot sleep nighttime! He tell me, lucky I no see." Switching back to Japanese, she went on, "I get the chills even now when I think about that. That man who saw the Chinese man hanging told me he could never pass that same road again. There was another Chinese man who committed suicide where the group of Japanese stores once stood, across the bridge." Hearing of this incident reminded me of the cruelty and prejudice Chinese people suffered on the plantation during the early years. They came as single men and were very lonely, so it was much more difficult for them. "I think it was worse for them than the Japanese—very sad," Kaku said quietly.

"You ask me if I work with my husband? No, my husband work in the *konpan* group under *luna* Bungoro Kimura. His work location was some distance in an isolated area where they had to carry their equipment—cut-cane knife, *kappa,* and of course *bento.*" The *kappa,* or raincoat, was one of the most important accessories, one that no worker should ever forget. Because plantation workers labored in isolated fields where there was no place to find shelter from a heavy downpour, the humble homemade *kappa* was a lifesaver. Purchasing a rubber raincoat from the store would have cost them $5, five days' pay, so they learned to make their own *kappa* at half the cost.

"I worked with the *wahine* fieldworkers. I got up at three in the morning, made breakfast, and packed our double-decker *bento* can. I had to walk about a mile and a half every morning to get to the warehouse to grab the burlap bags. It was really hectic. Everybody was so desperate to get enough burlap bags for the *pula pula*. The old-timers were smart. They went early to grab the smaller burlap bags. The larger bags would require more time to fill up. We were paid by the bags, not the weight. So as I got wiser, I went earlier to get the smaller bags. As soon as we got the bags, we jumped on the train by 5:30 a.m. Then we were taken to distant fields to work for ten hours.

"I can't forget that incident that happened during the early days, not long after I came from Japan. There was a black [meaning "dark-skinned"] *kanaka* [Hawaiian] *luna*—really black, his teeth so white. He came over to give me instructions on how to cut the cane stalks to make *pula pula*. Only the tips of the good cane stalks are used for cane seedlings. I no understand, so I cut the cane stalk from the base. The *ookina* [big] *kanaka luna* come over, tell me what to do, but I don't know one word, what he say. No matter how many times he yell at me, with his eyes glaring, I no understand! I scared, all I could do was stare at him blankly. Then he get more mad. He take my cane knife from me, then throw that at me, and yell, 'Getta lale heah!' [Get the hell out of here!] Oh, he so angry, I still donno why. I sure thought he was going to kill me! I sat down on the rock and cried and cried and wonder why I ever come Hawaii. I think later, somebody talk to him. Then he slowly come toward me, his voice more kind. I still no understand what he say. But I can tell by hand sign. He feel bad, yelling so loud at me, throwing cut-cane knife at me. Then he come over, and show me how to cut the cane stalks, to make *pula pula*. The man—big, strong— easy for him. He chop the cane straight across. No matter how hard I try, holding heavy cane knife hard, no can cut the cane stalk right. Every time, I cut slant, no good. Even though I used to doing farm work in Japan, this much harder, cutting the *pula pula*. Really, working in the cane fields was harder than farming in Japan. It's real different. You work under big *luna* who tell you what to do, how to do it. In Japan, family work together, no stress. Well, in time I get used to it, but first time was really terrible.

"When I work with my husband in the *konpan* group, I did all kinds of work. We work by contract. I did everything what the men did. I even sprayed chemicals in the field, carrying one heavy tank on my back. Had twelve people in the *konpan* group. I was the only *wahine*. There were many Filipinos. They very hard workers!"

HOLE HOLE (STRIPPING LEAVES)

"When we did the irrigation in the cane fields, we irrigated two rows at a time. Besides that, we had to hoe the weeds out of the field. It was hard work, because we had to stay ahead of the water flowing down. We hardly took time for lunch. As the cane grew taller, we had to *hole hole* [strip the cane leaves], tie them in bundles, and put the bundles in rows to stop the flow of water. We had to work fast to get the bundles ready. Kimura-san, the water *luna,* told me I remind him of a chicken, scurrying around to do the work. We had to control the speed of the water flow, and shut off the water supply before it reached the end. Now, when I think back about those days, I don't know how I did it.

"For us *konpan* workers, our everyday pay was small. But once in two years when we harvested our fields, we get paid a lump sum. I still remember the first harvest when we got paid $400 for both of us. When the *okanjo* [big pay] came, you could see all the store clerks waiting outside to collect the debt the workers owed!

"I was very careful with my purse strings, so I never had any debts, even if I had to send half our pay to Japan. We put the entire amount into the Japanese banks, the Shokin Ginko [Yokohama Bank] and the Sumitomo Bank. In those days, the exchange was $1 to 2 yen. When World War II ended, Sumitomo Bank did not plan to give the money back to overseas people, so I went to Japan myself to get it. At that time, I had saved 70,000 yen. Oh, the bank teller felt so sorry for me. At the old rate we would have had a substantial return. 'I am sorry for you. You must have really worked hard to save this amount.' The exchange rate had become $1 to 369 yen. I hardly had anything left, so I spent whatever was left in Japan. At least, from Shokin Ginko, we managed to get few hundred dollars back. To think of the supreme sacrifice we made, going without things, letting the children cry at the baby home [the plantation day care center] waiting for me, working overtime, only because we intended to return to Japan. Instead, if only we had been wiser and decided from the beginning to make Hawaii our home! At that time, we could have bought a place in Pearl City for 10 cents a square foot, land was so cheap. Even when I delivered laundry to the people who lived in Ota Camp, Waipahu, they encouraged us to buy land, because it was so cheap. We were really mistaken. All I remember was my father-in-law's voice: 'You must return.' Look at us now. We don't have anything. We'll probably end our lives here."

CHRISTMAS AT PUMP FOUR CAMP

There was not much to look forward to, living in an isolated place like Pump Four Camp. It was too far to go to see the free Japanese movies shown at the Waipahu Social Club on Saturday nights. And even though there was no electricity, Kaku always did her sewing late at night, making *tabi,* the heavy work socks made of denim, and *bento* bags to sell to the single men. One quiet night—it was Christmas Eve, but for Kaku and her family it was just another night, as nobody there ever thought about Christmas anyway—she suddenly heard a loud rumbling sound. Her husband and children were already sound asleep. The noise stopped in front of her house. Kaku was unsure whether to wake her husband. Suddenly there was the sound of heavy footsteps . . . then someone knocked at the door. Wondering who would come this late at night, Kaku slowly opened the door. There was a big *haole* (white) man, very kind-looking and friendly. He was dressed in a red Santa outfit. He handed her a huge bag and greeted her with a cheery "Merry Christmas!" She was taken by surprise and didn't know what to think. All she could say was, "*Arigato, arigato!* Thank you, thank you!" and bowed her head many times. Later, she found out that this was

Hans L'Orange, the field supervisor for the plantation at that time. L'Orange was loved and respected by every ethnic group.

"Every year, the Oahu Sugar Company invited all the families—Hawaiian, Chinese, Spanish, Portuguese, Japanese, Puerto Rican, Filipino, and Korean, all of them—to the huge warehouse for a Christmas party, right across the railroad tracks from where we lived. All the families walked to the huge warehouse to celebrate Christmas. Most of the Japanese were Buddhists, but it didn't matter. What a treat it was! That's the only time I ate ice cream, once a year at Christmas. I remember the sound of 'Jingle Berus' [bells], and a big fat man dressed in a Santa outfit merrily passing around bags of goodies."

For people who lived in isolated *konpan* camps, there was no way to come to the Christmas party. However, every family received a generous package of apples, oranges, nuts, and candy canes. Mr. Hans L'Orange, who was a compassionate man, wanted to bring some cheer to the lonely families living in the *konpan* camps. Every year he loaded his Harley-Davidson motorcycle with bags of goodies and made many trips through the *konpan* camps, zooming through clouds of red dust and hopping over railroad tracks, to spread Christmas cheer to the hardworking plantation families. After all these years, Kaku Kumasaka still remembered the love and generosity L'Orange had for the plantation people.

SEWING MACHINE

Kaku continued, "In Japan, I learned to sew kimonos by hand during the winter, when it snowed and we could not work outside. Usually there was no time for farm children to have the luxury to learn *shugei* [handicrafts] and other feminine skills to prepare for their marriage. I sewed all our clothes. I never really learned to sew, of course. Sewing Western-type clothing was new for me. My husband bought me a Singer sewing machine that year, 1922, for $100, a treadle type, and to this day I am still using it. I borrowed patterns from Mrs. Kimura at first and learned to sew myself. I never thought it was easy nor hard—I just had to learn, to save money. I sewed all my children's clothing, and now, when I think of it, how did I ever let them wear such funny-looking clothes to school? If now, I could probably dress them mo' betta. My boy even wore the same thing as his older sister. Only for my dressy dress, I took to the village seamstress. When I was young, I used to do lots of sewing, even after working ten hours in the field. I sewed *tabi* and all my husband's work clothes myself because I didn't want to pay for sewing. I even made his *konpan* hat, made of heavy white canvas fabric worn by people who worked in a contract gang, and also his Sunday outfit, khaki pants and a white shirt. The richer members of the community wore blue serge trousers." She donated her 1922 *tabi* pattern to my collection for my immigrant clothing book. "You know," Kaku said, smiling, "that sewing machine still works today, except for a little trouble with the bobbin winder. It's amazing to me that it still works, even after sewing the thick layers of the *tabi* sole with that old machine!"

For some time, this sewing machine was in Haleiwa at the home of Walter Yamada, whose mother is Sashichi's cousin. Kaku's son, Toshimi, took his mother's *toronko* [trunk] and *tansu* [chest of drawers] to California to his home. Today, Kaku's sewing machine is at the Japanese American National Museum in Los Angeles.

Kaku with her Singer sewing machine
purchased in 1922 for $100. Barbara
Kawakami Collection.

FIELDWORK

"You know, when I was young, I used to work ten hours a day in the fields, take in
laundry from Filipino bachelors, and sew *tabi* for workmen. People used to say,
'Anybody who works hard like you must have plenty of money.' So I would tell them,
'I don't have money.' All our hard-earned money, we sent home to save our land. I
told you. It's a heartbreaking story. Someday, when you have time, you come back
and I tell you the whole story. You can write a best seller on it." She laughs. "All that
pain is almost forgotten now, thanks to my Christian faith. It has given me strength
to see me through a terrible time."

RAISING A FAMILY

"I came to Hawaii in March and I had my first baby the next year in February. I had
intended to work the full month of January, although I was pretty big then. At the
time, I thought, 'I really shouldn't work anymore,' and I quit the next day. And oh,

Kumasaka family photo with oldest
daughter, Yaeko, and infant son, Robert
Toshimi, 1929. Barbara Kawakami
Collection.

the first baby was really hard. It was a girl, Yaeko. Ishikawa-san was my midwife.
She helped with my second child, too; that was Toshimi, born in 1929. She was really patient, really kind. I wonder how much we used to give for a gratuity. They
didn't quote a fee, but we made *orei* [offerings of gratitude]. When my oldest daughter was born, I took care of her for six months. Then I let your aunt Sawa babysit for
me, and I went back to work until I got pregnant with my second one. Was a boy this
time. She took care of them both for about a year. Then we got a house at New Camp,
or Nishi Camp, by the wooden bridge by Waipahu Elementary School. Our neighbors
were the Koizumi, Inokuchi, Furoyama, Hishinuma, and Kaneshiro families. There
were a mix of Japanese from different prefectures and a few Koreans. After we
moved to Nishi Camp, I left the children at the baby home."

WORKING CONDITIONS DURING WORLD WAR II

"During World War II, work conditions really changed. Even the attitudes of other
ethnic groups changed toward us. It was so sad. While working, if we sang Japanese
songs, we got scolded, 'Japanese talking. No talking.' The *luna* were all *gaijin* [foreign-
ers, in this case referring to Portuguese and Spanish], but had a few Japanese, too.

"I left my children at the baby home run by the plantation when they were very
young. My girl used to cry and cry. Even now when I think about it, it makes me

teary." The child care facility was established by the plantation after many horrible accidents occurred while mothers who had taken their children to the fields were busy: more than one toddler wandered off to a nearby ditch and drowned, and babies left to rest on straw matting would get stung by centipedes, scorpions, or red ants. The nursery charged $2.50 a month to care for a child from 5:00 a.m. to 3:30 p.m. five days a week. "Every morning when I took my baby girl to the baby home and leave her, she cry after me. I used to wonder if I should go home today or quit my job when she cry after me. How often I walked as far as Nii-san's house and pondered because her crying bothered me so." Nii-san was the sugar company's accountant, who lived two houses away from the nursery. "I had to remind myself that I would miss the train if I didn't hurry up. Then I run for the train. I felt *nasa ke nai* [just miserable]."

"My husband used to pick up the children when I worked overtime in the fields. When he went to the baby home, all the other children were gone except for our two. My boy used to get so angry to be kept waiting that he didn't want to come home. My husband was at a loss. Oh, my boy, so young at the time, maybe two or three years old. Once, when I came home late from work and nobody was home, I found my children sleeping outside on the huge pipe high above the ground. When the days are short, it's dark by 6:30 p.m. After I got off the train, I had to walk a long way from the train, about a mile and a half. Really, the kids were pitiful. When I think about it now, I wonder how the two children walked to school together. The oldest, being a girl, was afraid to go in the kitchen in the morning when it was dark." In the plantation houses, the kitchen was built a few yards away from the main house. "She sent her little brother, Toshi, into the kitchen first. When I think about it now, I really feel sorry for what the children had to go through, because we had to send half our pay to Japan."

"When Toshimi was four years old, Kimura-san was promoted and moved to the big house on Waipahu Street. He recommended to the manager that the Kumasakas take over his house. This was to be our home for the next fifty years!"

Kaku gave a deep sigh as she said how much she regretted sending Yaeko, her daughter, to Japan to study. "When she graduated from the eighth grade in Hawaii, I wanted her to attend high school here, but she insisted on going to Japan. So with the help of our Christian minister, she got accepted to a good school in Tokyo." She stayed with her grandparents, who were eager for her to have a better education. Kaku felt that her own lack of education didn't give her any choice in pursuing a better life, and she wanted her daughter to have better opportunities. "But after she went, Yaeko suffered deeply, because the Japanese education in Hawaii was so backward, and she couldn't follow the students who were trained in the Japanese language. In Hawaii, during this period, the nisei children attended Japanese school for only forty-five minutes a day. Besides that, there were young girls from well-to-do families who were mean to her. She didn't know too much about city ways, so they picked on her. They used to fight sometimes, and she made one of the girls cry. After that they became good friends. She warned us not to send our son to Japan to study. My son didn't even finish high school here. That's the reason we're still in Hawaii. We were planning to move back to Japan as soon as he finished school." I heard that he went to a business school.

"I worried so much about my daughter in Japan that I even dreamed about her. This dream seemed so real, it scared me, you know. She appeared in my dream and said, 'Mama, I came home. I came on a boat and I can stay only one night and I have to go back tomorrow, so let's stay up and talk all night.' I even dreamed that I saw her off the next day and we walked down the long pier. And when I said, 'When shall we meet again?' she answered in the dream, 'Let's meet in China.' At the pier, she kept looking back and looking back. I heard that when a person is dead and appears in a dream, they never look back. Because of that weird dream, I was beside myself. The only thing that comforted me was that dead people don't look back. Gosh, how a mother worries when the children are far away.

"Then Yaeko went to Niigata prefecture as a teacher, but she became ill due to a poor diet and returned to Fukushima. Both my grandparents were already dead, and my stepmother favored her own daughter. Yaeko thought her uncle and aunt had left a *musubi* [rice ball] for her lunch, but this stepmother took it. She really suffered. When she finally got married, she didn't give us any warning, just a note from my brother saying that he was a nice man. So he gave her permission to marry. I was worried that she might have married a soldier from Hawaii of another ethnic group. Later, my daughter wrote and signed her last name, Kasahara, so I was relieved.

"Yes, today she's happily married to a judo instructor, and he specializes in mending bones. I go to Japan to see them, to see my grandchildren. She has two. One daughter is taking after her father's profession." Kaku showed me many photos of her grandchildren. "Oh, I went in 1937. Since then, she's only been home once. She writes often, and she telephones sometimes."

"My son, Robert Toshimi, and his family live on the mainland. He comes home quite often to see us. Someday, after his children all finish college, they're coming back to look after us. We have a good daughter-in-law and she always sends us things. We're probably the only ones here in the senior center without relatives. My daughter-in-law has no relatives, and my daughter doesn't have any relatives there either; only Papa's side has brothers and a sister here. His brother in Ewa doesn't have any children, too, so we hardly have any relatives around. His younger brother comes once in a while. My son says when his children graduate from college he'll come home and look after us. He's sixty now and has three children."

KAKU DESCRIBES HER HUSBAND, SASHICHI

As I learned more about Kaku's life as a picture bride, I wondered whether her husband was like some of the husbands who drank a lot, gambled, and beat their wives, or whether he was nice and helpful. Her immediate reply was, "Oh, no, he was never sweet and thoughtful. He was never gentle, either. He never helped around the house. Typical Japan style. Men were not supposed to do anything to help. No, no, no. Even now, if I should die first, I don't know how he's going to manage. He'll be sent to the children, but they will have a rough time. They'd go crazy. He's ninety now. He can't even turn off the stove. He never did anything by himself. I've been married to him for more than sixty years, but only once, when I had stomach pain, did he get up and cook for himself. Other than that he never did a thing. Oh, when I had the baby, the first time, he tried to cook for himself. He tried for one week to make *bento,* then went to work. He had brothers and a sister, but none of them came to help."

RELIGION

"When I came in 1922, my husband was already baptized as a Christian, but he never went to church. When the children came, we sent them to church, so that's when I began going to the Christian church. My husband told the children to go to church, but he himself never did go. I felt it wouldn't do any good to send only the children, so I myself began going. How time has swiftly gone by. . . . I've been here sixty-three years now. Papa has been here seventy-three years. It's such a shame, we've been here so long, and we still can't speak English. It's a shame we're so ignorant about so many things."

END OF CAREER

Kaku Kumasaka and Kama Asato were the two last survivors in their work gang. Kaku worked until 1964. "I worked until I was sixty-five years old, and Kama Asato worked until sixty-two years old. I worked the longest; the others quit along the way. At times, my thighs used to hurt so much, I could barely walk home after *pau hana* [Hawaiian for "finish working"] time. But those days I was young, so once I had my rest, the pain went away. Then the next day, I'd go to work again. Later, just before I took my pension, the pain got so bad on the thighs, but because I thought I would be retiring soon, I endured the pain. Then one day, a Filipino worker said, 'Mama, wassamata you? Quickee makule natta zo!' [Mama, what happened to you? You became old fast!] Now the pay is good, but in those days, there was no choice, so I thought, 'Gee, how long do I have to go on like this?' I really felt miserable. And then I finally quit."

RETIREMENT

"Here at the senior center, we don't get lonesome, and we don't have to worry about vandalism. Everybody's really good to us. Even in my younger days, I never gossiped with other women in camp, because I always was busy.

"My husband and I, we celebrated our golden wedding anniversary in 1972 in Japan, and we're about the only healthy couple here at the senior center. Most of them are widows or widowers, or have strokes and are too sick to take part in the activities. My husband is slowing down with age, but we're thankful both of us are able to go to the senior center every day. They send buses to pick us up, we have lunch there, and have a chance to learn new things every day.

"It's more than sixty-three years now since I came to Hawaii! When I first came in 1922, I used to cry and wonder why I ever came to this lonely place where I hardly had any friends. But now I think different. The climate is so wonderful, I'm glad I came. Actually, my daughter has built us a modest *inkyo-beya* [a house to live in after retirement] in Fukushima—we could go back and live there anytime. But it's so cold that we don't want to live there. Most of my friends and family are gone now. All our friends are here at the senior center; they are like family. Everybody exchanges vegetables we grow in our garden. You know, we were the last ones to move into the senior center, but everybody treats us so nice. When we go to lunch at the center, the Filipinos and other nationalities all come to talk to us, I feel so grateful. It keeps us from getting lonely. Yeah, yeah, Hawaii *ni ite yokatta yo* [I'm glad we stayed in Hawaii]."

MILESTONE IN LIFE'S JOURNEY

On January 6, 1985, Governor George Ariyoshi proclaimed 1985 as the Centennial Year of the Japanese Immigration to Hawaii. Sashichi and Kaku were among the hundreds of issei honored by the governor and the State of Hawaii. Sashichi at eighty-eight and Kaku at eighty-five had never dreamed that someday they would be stepping into the Hawaii Ballroom of the Sheraton Waikiki Hotel for such a cere-mony. They had never been to a fancy place like this before. Everyone was dressed so beautifully in their very best. They were filled with awe at the splendor and elegance of the spacious ballroom, decorated with huge, breathtaking floral arrangements. All the anxiety was a bit overwhelming. Their legs felt a bit unsteady. Unconsciously they held hands tightly, something they had never done before. Out of all the guests, they were among the very few couples; most had already lost their spouse.

What a journey this proved to be for Sashichi and Kaku, as they reflected on their long years of struggle together. They never did return to live in the home in Japan they had sent money for every month. Today, according to their son, Toshimi, the rich farmlands and mountains they had struggled to help pay for, Kaku even working overtime for years to earn a mere 10 cents extra, are worth a fortune. As Kaku noted, their daughter, Yaeko, had a retirement home built for them in beauti-ful Fukushima, but after living all those years in a warm climate, just the thought of the harsh winters in Fukushima made them shudder. Besides, in Hawaii they were surrounded by lifelong friends who had worked together, played together, and now enjoyed their twilight years together.

Kaku died at age eighty-eight, and Sashichi died a month later at age ninety-two. Their weary bones now rest in Westminster Memorial Park on a peaceful hillside in Orange County in Southern California, near where their son and his family live.

Hisa Kawakami
ISSEI PIONEERS WHO PAVED THE WAY
February 6, 1889–October 7, 1978
Born in Choja-machi, Asakura-gun, Fukuoka-ken
Arrived in Hawaii 1909

As I was preparing the final section for this book in January 2014, I received a twenty-minute tape recording from a friend in Kauai, Mabel Kawakami Hashisaka (no relation). Mabel's family owns the Kauai Cookie Company. For more than twenty years Mabel has expressed her support for my work, often donating cookies to my openings and special events, including the opening of the "Textured Lives" exhibition at the Japanese American National Museum in 2010 in Los Angeles, as well as the opening of a traveling exhibition in collaboration with the Bishop Museum in Honolulu in 2012.

I was always fascinated with her parents' stories about how her father came from Fukuoka, Japan, in his youth to work on the sugar plantation and started a small business that eventually expanded to eight stores. Until recently I hadn't known that Mabel's mother had come to Hawaii as a picture bride, but I always felt that a man who had attained such success and had overcome so many obstacles and hardships must have had a very special woman for a wife.

When I found out that Mabel's mother had been a picture bride from Fukuoka, I wanted to include her story, and I contacted Mabel for information. After we'd talked for a while, she suddenly remembered an interview recorded with her mother in 1976. Perhaps because she could not bear to hear her mother's voice after she had passed away, Mabel had completely forgotten about this recording until I started asking questions. The tape had been passed on to her older brother Norito, who also couldn't bear to listen to his mother's voice. When Mabel told him of my interest, Norito gave the cassette tape to his nephew James, who digitized it and then brought it back to Kauai. In 2014, then, for the very first time, Mabel listened to her mother's words. This serendipitous recording provided a vivid picture of what life was like in the early plantation days on Kauai, and I was excited to hear the frail voice of Mabel's mother, Hisa, then eighty-seven, tell her story. I'd also recently received a photo of Hisa, her silvery gray hair pushed back from her slim face, and from her expression, one could imagine that she was a very kind, thoughtful, and happy

The early Koloa plantation and the sugar mill, ca. 1895. Photo courtesy of Mabel Hashisaka Collection.

person. She appeared to be petite, but she must have been strong in order to work in the fields with her husband. In the months that followed, Mabel filled in her mother's words.

HISA OKABE, PICTURE BRIDE

In a soft voice, speaking in the Fukuoka dialect, mixed with some Pidgin English and some *kanaka go,* or Hawaiian words, Hisa Okabe Kawakami began her story.

"I was born in Fukuoka-ken, Asakura-gun, Choja-machi, on Meiji *nijyu ninen, nigatsu, muika* [February 6, 1889]. I came as *shashin-hana yome* [picture bride] to Fukutaro Kawakami, in Meiji *yonjyu ninen* [1909] to Wahiawa on Kauai *shima* [island of Kauai].

"Coming to this unfamiliar, strange place, I was worried and filled with anxiety, but I immediately met some *tokoro no hito* [people from Soneda village] who had come earlier as picture brides . . . Hoashi-san, Miyabara-san, and others. They were very kind to me and helped me get adjusted to my new home. They helped me get my fieldwork clothing ready, so I went to work right away. I started *kibi shigoto* [work in canefields] get pay $13 per month. Because *zeni ga sukunai ke* [pay was small] I join Oto-san [Japanese women referred to their husband as *oto-san,* or "father"] in *hapai ko* gang. We worked as couple. I work *paila* [piler], *kibi atsu*

Fukutaro and Hisa Kawakami wedding photo taken in Wahiawa, Kauai, 1909. Photo courtesy of Mabel Hashisaka Collection.

meru [gather the harvested sugarcane in piles], then Oto-san *hapai* [carry] as many sugarcane on shoulders, then walk up the plank to load into cane car. Oto-san was strong man and fast worker, so *isshoni* [together] we did well. We get paid $70 a month, was good money at the time. Then I got pregnant with first son, Norito, and worked until ready to give birth, then stay home for little while. As soon as I felt strong enough and Norito was few months old, I went back to work. I get up early when still dark, make *bento* for Oto-san and me, then *oppa* Norito [carry baby on back with sash] and went to work in cane fields. Those days, nobody to watch baby for us. No relatives around to ask for help. All the mothers *oppa* their babies and *hana hana* in fields, was hard time for mothers."

Hisa explained, "*Soo shite yari yotte* [that's how we went to work]. *Kondo* [then] Oto-san hear about other job at Port Allen wharf. At Port Allen, close to Eleele, the ships load raw sugar. If he work job, he get 25 cents one hour, good pay."

At this point Mabel stopped the tape to elaborate: "Father was a stevedore, and he drove the winch . . . in those days, they called the worker on a winch 'donkey.'"

Hisa's voice continued, "Twelve men in gang, work on boat. Oto-san wanted to make more money so he can send for Papa [grandfather Fukujiro] from Japan. As soon as he made enough money, he sent for Papa from Soneda village." Then Mabel added, "Grandfather's wife suffered from severe vertigo and couldn't stand to travel on a ship, so she stayed behind." The government had changed the law so that at least

Koloa Landing, one of the major ports on Kauai, 1910. Photo courtesy of Mabel Hashisaka Collection.

one parent had to be in Hawaii to send for one's children from Japan as *yobi-yose*. Mabel mentioned that her father's dream was to bring his father and siblings to Hawaii. We continued listening to Hisa on the tape. "After his father, Fukujiro, was in Hawaii, and as soon as Fukutaro had saved enough, he sent for his second brother, Sakuichi, and got a job for him as a watchman at Port Allen. As soon as Sakuichi was doing well on his job, Fukutaro arranged to matchmake a picture bride for Sakuichi and sent for a lovely girl, named Tomo-san, from a nearby village in Japan. She was an intelligent young lady, a hard worker, and started working in the cane fields. Later one of the bosses working at Port Allen got her a job as a maid at a *haole* home. That was much better than toiling in the cane fields, and she could learn a lot while working as a *hooko-nin* [domestic]."

Fukutaro, being the oldest son and always thinking of others, wanted then to bring a third brother, Saburo, to Hawaii. Saburo (later known as H. S. Kawakami, after he had taken the English name Harvey) was just twelve years old when he came in 1912. Fukutaro wanted to give his brother a good education in America so he could have a better life in the future. Fukutaro himself had hardly finished grade school, instead staying home to help his parents, who, like many in the farming villages of Japan, were having a difficult time financially. He continued, however, with a program of self-education, taking correspondence courses from Japan after he came to the islands in 1904. He felt Saburo was still young enough to attend English school and gain an opportunity for a better life than his. Hisa mentioned in the recording that if Saburo had stayed with them, he would never learn to speak English because they only spoke Fukuoka dialect, Pidgin English, and *kanaka go*. Saburo attended Eleele School for one year and must have felt very out of place, being placed in first grade at age twelve. Fukutaro and Hisa decided to send Saburo to the Mills School, a private school that later became the Mid-Pacific Institute, in Honolulu. Public school would have been too difficult for Saburo because he couldn't speak any English, and he was so much older than the other children. To send his younger brother to a private school in Honolulu required a lot of money. During the period of poor economic conditions after World War I, when everyone was putting family members to work, Fukutaro was called "stupid" for spending his money on something so seemingly unproductive as his brother's education.

When Fukutaro got the stevedore job around 1911, the family moved to Port Allen, near the shore, and their new house was located nearby on a cliff. From there they could see the ships arrive; the vessels had to anchor offshore, and the passengers were transported to land on a smaller boat. This was a busy place. Port Allen had replaced Koloa Landing as one of the major ports for shipping goods in and out of Kauai. It was also the third-largest whaling port in Hawaii at the time. The waters off Koloa were treacherous, and a number of shipwrecks occurred in the area after the port was established in the 1850s. By 1912, all major shipping transactions began to take place through Port Allen, and Koloa Landing was closed in 1928.* Fukutaro, at this early stage, had the foresight to realize that finding a better-paying job could help him give his children and his brother Saburo a good education. He always believed that a good education was necessary as a stepping-stone to success. Hisa herself was never able to attend even grade school in the village, and that lack made her keenly aware of the importance of a fine education.

Hisa had been really concerned about Saburo's future. "To send Saburo to a private school," she said, "Fukutaro wanted to earn more money to pay for the tuition. Port Allen was an ideal place to raise hogs. Raising hogs was a tough job, besides working ten hours a day as stevedore. Here Oto-san could get the pig slop from the ships that anchored at the wharf. He would carry the five-gallon cans of pig slop from the ship to the pigpen near a boathouse by his home. On Saturday, after *pau hana* [the work was done], he would go to the fields to cut *hono hono* by the light of the moon." Hisa mentioned that in those days, she would use *hono hono* grass in place of taro leaves to make *lau lau* [pork wrapped in leaves], and it tasted just as good! Hisa learned to improvise with *hono hono* grass, which grew in abundance in the pastures. "On Sunday, Fukutaro cooked the *hono hono* grass in a big can to feed the pigs," she added.

Hisa pointed out in her tape that because they lived near the ocean, the pigs could be carried away if strong storm waves swept into the pigpen, so Fukutaro always tied the hogs to the boathouse when there was a storm warning. Hisa described how hard he worked all those extra hours to make enough money to send his younger brother to Mills School. And while Saburo was much older than the regular students and it must have been awkward for him there, he appreciated his brother's great support and studied very hard. Hisa added that Fukutaro sent Saburo to Mills School an extra year, for a total of nine years, with the money made from the hogs. In those days, few issei families could afford to send their children even to public high school, but

---

* Friends of the Koloa Community/School Library, *Historic Koloa: A Guide,* ed. Martha Hoverson (Koloa, Kauai, Hawaii, 1985), 23.

All the plantation families gathered at the park to celebrate the Fourth of July. Photo courtesy of Mabel Hashisaka Collection.

Fukutaro believed that good education always stayed with you and was important in achieving a successful future.

Hisa continued, "On weekends, *mee ra* [us women] *oppa* our babies and went to park nearby to watch our boys play baseball. I ask Oto-san, 'Why not come with us and watch boys play?' He tell me, 'Oh, you go, have *guru* [good] time. Maybe next time I go.' Oto-san always only think of work, day and night. He never rest. Raising hogs kept him busy seven days a week, *butto* that's how he sent Saburo to Mills School. He never *monku* [complain] how tired he was, *butto* he happy to see Saburo study."

FUKUTARO AND HISA

Both Hisa and Fukutaro had to struggle to rise above daunting circumstances. Between Hisa's own words on tape and Mabel's reminiscences of conversations with her parents, a story emerged of how both these remarkable people had been willing to sacrifice and persevere through difficult times, and their resilience and resourcefulness in the face of tragedy.

Fukutaro Kawakami had left Japan with an adventurous spirit and a big dream of coming to Hawaii, the land of opportunity. Fukutaro's aspiration was to make some money and then send for his father and siblings. His parents, like many other farmers in southwestern Japan, had endured numerous hardships. Foremost in his mind was to relieve his parents of the heavy debt imposed upon his father, Fukujiro, because Fukujiro's eldest brother had lost the family fortune to gambling. Fukujiro once had belonged to the fairly well-to-do Shinagawa family in Fukuoka, but after the family went bankrupt, he was given as a *muko-yoshi* (adopted son-in-law) to the Kawakami family. Fukutaro wanted to provide a better life for his parents. He responded readily when he heard of the call for plantation laborers to work in the sugarcane fields in Hawaii.

Fukutaro came from Soneda, Yasu-mura, Asakura-gun, in Fukuoka, Japan, the firstborn son of Fukujiro and his wife, Kiyo, followed by siblings Sakuichi, Saburo, and Chuyoshi. Fukutaro immigrated to Hawaii in 1904 at age nineteen to work as a contract laborer at the Paauilo sugar plantation near Honokaa, on the Big Island. The *luna* was cruel and mistreated the immigrant laborers, so Fukutaro took off for the island of Kauai and found work at the McBryde Sugar Company in Wahiawa. There he was happy to find many friends, *tokoro mono* (fellow villagers) from Soneda. Fukutaro, who was five feet four inches and of stocky build, had the physical attributes to handle any type of heavy work on the plantation. Besides, he had been a sumo wrestler back in Fukuoka, so he must have had tremendous strength and energy.

Fukutaro worked in the *hapai ko* gang, one of the more strenuous types of work done by men in the cane fields. Years later, while talking about the early days, he told his daughter Mabel that it was about this time that the late Senator Daniel Inouye's father, Hyotaro, was working in the same gang as a water boy. He had been brought to Hawaii by his parents as an infant, and they also settled in Wahiawa. Mabel did not know how old Hyotaro had been at the time, but he was too young to do any of the heavy fieldwork. Still, water boys had to carry water to the fieldworkers in heavy pails on both ends of a pole balanced on their shoulders, so it was just as demanding on a young boy. Fukutaro said Hyotaro was a good worker and their families became lifelong friends.

In 1909, Fukutaro's father, who lived in Yasu-mura, thought it was about time for his son to settle down. He knew of a lovely girl in nearby Choja-machi, Asakura-gun, also in Fukuoka prefecture, and sent her photo to Fukutaro in Hawaii. Photos were exchanged by mail. Both young people accepted their parents' decision and consented to get married.

The young girl that Fukutaro's father thought would be an ideal wife for his son was Hisa Okabe. According to Mabel, her mother had had a difficult childhood, losing her father at a very young age. When her mother remarried, Hisa was completely under the dominance of her stepfather, who would not allow her to attend grade school in the village. Hisa envied her friends who were able to attend school, and tried to learn on her own, but she couldn't afford to buy a tablet and pencil. So she practiced writing the basic "a i u e o," the alphabet in Japanese, in the sand on the temple grounds. Her parents raised silkworms, so Hisa, from a very young age, worked from dawn to dusk picking mulberry leaves to feed the silkworms and taking care of them indoors, which was an exacting and time-consuming task. Heat from warm lamps had to be maintained to regulate the temperature for the silkworms to thrive. Other times she was sent to babysit for mothers who were busy working on the farms. She hardly had time to play with friends. One day one of the lamps used in the silkworm room fell over, setting a terrible blaze. The house burned down and her parents lost everything, with the family escaping with only the clothes on their backs.

PICTURE BRIDE MARRIAGE

Hisa remembered how miserable her existence was after that fire, with the stepfather who had always been so unkind to her. In addition to babysitting, Hisa was sent out to do farm work and to weave cotton kimono fabric to earn some money. "I think my mother suffered as much, watching her little girl not being able to attend school or have any playtime with her friends. She couldn't help me much, for my stepfather was our only means of survival." Typical of the Meiji women of that period, her mother quietly obeyed her husband's wishes.

A few years later, something unexpected happened. A close friend of Fukujiro Kawakami paid the family a visit. He wanted to do a matchmaking by exchange of photos between Hisa and Fukujiro's son Fukutaro, who was working on a sugar plantation on the island of Kauai. For Hisa, who had never ventured farther away than the nearby villages, this meant she could begin a new life. Yes, it would be in a foreign country and with a man she had never met, but she was told he was quite an outstanding young man. When Hisa was shown the photo, she thought he looked very nice. In the village, boys and girls were not allowed to socialize together, so for Hisa this was altogether a new experience. And she had heard many exciting stories about this beautiful garden island called Kauai.

Issei man's funeral attended by close friends and neighbors in Koloa, Kauai, ca. 1920s. Photo given to Mabel Hashisaka by Reverend Motoyoshi of Koloa Hongwanji. Photo courtesy of Mabel Hashisaka Collection.

To arrange Fukutaro and Hisa's marriage, Grandfather Fukujiro must have appointed a close friend in the village to act as go-between to approach Hisa's parents, which was the proper traditional procedure to ask for a daughter's hand in marriage.

Hisa told this story to Mabel: "Once the talk of marriage was decided, I waited the six-month period for the visa to come through. We were married in absentia with someone acting as proxy for Fukutaro, who was in Hawaii. We went through the marriage ritual with the *san san kudo*." Hisa Okabe's name was removed from her family's *koseki* and registered into Fukutaro Kawakami's *koseki*. Under the laws of the Japanese government, they were now legally husband and wife, even if her husband was in Hawaii.

As part of her dowry (part of which was provided by her father-in-law, because her family was of such humble background), she brought with her a very ornate *toronko,* a trunk embellished with gold trimmings. It is still in fairly good condition and treasured by Mabel as a *katami* (keepsake) from her mother. Mabel showed me the elegant *montsuki* and the many silk kimonos and obis her mother had brought with her in 1909. Among the keepsakes was a *furoshiki* (wrapping cloth) made by Hisa, with a hand-dyed design in indigo and the Kawakami name written in calligraphy in one corner. Mabel showed me some of Hisa's beautiful *nihon shishu,* Japanese embroidery in satin stitch, which she had done during her relaxed moments.

UNEXPECTED TRAGEDY

Fukutaro and Hisa began their life in Hawaii and arranged to bring Fukutaro's father and brothers to the islands. Then came an event that changed their lives.

"Six months after Fukutaro had arranged the marriage of his brother Sakuichi and Tomo-san, Tomo-san's aunt died suddenly of Spanish flu. It was highly contagious and many died during the epidemic. People even dreaded attending the funeral service for fear of catching it. Grandfather Fukujiro volunteered to go because he said he was the oldest, so it didn't matter as much if he caught it. Fukutaro said no, he would go, but Sakuichi said Fukutaro had too much work to do, so he made up his mind to attend the funeral himself. After all, it was his wife's aunt who had died, so Sakuichi felt he should be the one to go.

"At the funeral, fellow villagers from Soneda asked why his wife, Tomo-san, didn't come, since it was her aunt. The funeral was on March 2, and two days later Sakuichi got sick and was rushed to the hospital. He died on March 10 of Spanish flu." I could hear Hisa's voice quavering amid her sobs as she recalled hearing the news from Fukutaro.

Hisa explained, "I just gave birth to Keiji, second son [born January 2, 1919], so I cannot attend services. The work gang from Port Allen wharf come, *horu puka* [dig grave], then all take off. Everybody scared after what happened to Sakuichi. Only Fukutaro and Papa Fukujiro stayed to cover *haka* [grave]."

Hisa remembered the day when Fukutaro came home from the burial service. "Oto-san tell me, 'This was most loneliest funeral I've ever seen . . . so *samishii* [very sad], with hardly anyone to offer prayer of *namu amida butsu* for Sakuichi to enter nirvana.'" Hisa's voice faltered as she repeated Fukutaro's words. "At that time, Oto-san told me, 'When I die, be sure to bury me beside my brother Sakuichi.'" And so, Hisa said, when Fukutaro died at the relatively young age of sixty-eight, "I made sure I followed his wishes and buried him beside his brother Sakuichi. Until the very end of life, Oto-san always thought about his family and *kyodai* [siblings]."

After the tragic incident, the Kawakami family wanted to send Sakuichi's widow, Tomo-san, back to Japan. It had been only six months since they were married, but Tomo-san didn't want to return to her village. She was very fond of the Kawakami family and begged them to let her stay, adding that she would be willing to do any kind of work for them. Hisa mentioned in her tape that Tomo-san was very pretty, smart, and hardworking, so there were many men who asked for her hand in marriage. But Tomo-san refused all of them.

In the meantime, Tsubaki-san, a *tokoro mono* from Soneda village, made a proposition: "Since Tomo-san wants to stay here, why not matchmake her and Saburo?" Tomo-san and Saburo, who was still studying at Mills School, were the same age. Thus the family friend wrote an agreement that when Saburo graduated from Mills School, the two would be married. "Until then," said Hisa, "Tomo-san lived with us. She was a big help to our family."

She added, "Tomo-san, *totemo guru girlu datta yo* [such a very good girl]. Norito, my oldest son, was about two years old at that time, and Tomo-san practically raised him. I was busy working in the fields, so Tomo-san took good care of Norito. I still remember when Norito was nine years old, the plantation hired nine-year-olds during summer vacation. Norito was the only boy going to work in the cane fields from Port Allen. Tomo-san got up early every morning to cook rice out of doors over open fire, make *bento* for Norito, and walk to the Eleele train stop, which was near the plantation store. It was quite a walk from our house, but Tomo-san made sure Norito caught the train on time. Even now, when I think of Tomo-san, it brings tears to my eyes. If she was living now [in 1976], she would be seventy-five years old, same as Saburo." One could sense Hisa's emotion as she spoke fondly of Tomo-san.

A FATEFUL STEP

"Norito graduate grammar school one year early. You see, when he was five years old, he follow his six-year-old friend to first-grade class. Teacher let them study together. Since he could keep up with the studies, teacher allowed him to stay in class. So Norito saved one year, he graduate when he was thirteen years old, a year younger than his classmates," Hisa chuckled.

Fukutaro, ever a proponent of learning and bettering oneself, was determined to give Norito a good education, so when Norito was ready for high school, Fukutaro moved the family from Wahiawa to Ahukini, which was closer to Kauai High School, the only high school on the island, and Norito graduated in 1929.

Hisa said, "Fukutaro bought him an old car to commute to high school. He was only thirteen years old then, but he lied about his age that he was fifteen. He got his driver's license and gave his siblings and other students who lived in Ahukini rides to Lihue Grammar School and Kauai High School. Although the car was so old, it was our only means of transportation. I never forgot the time, on one of our visits to the Waimea store, when coming back to Ahukini our car always got stuck going past Wahiawa on the way to Kalaheo, the old car no go up hill, car stuck!

Everybody got out of car, and push and push . . . *whoo da!* [my goodness!] When I think of before days, what we went through!" Hisa burst out in laughter.

Saburo graduated from Mills School in 1921. Now equipped with a higher education, he was ready to embark on a new career. He first went to Kona, on the Big Island, to work. Fukutaro advised Saburo at that time, "Even if you have to carry heavy goods on your back, you should start a business on your own, be independent."

Later, in 1925, a man who operated a small store in Waimea, across from the Old Waimea Landing, died in a car accident, and the store was put up for sale. That was when Fukutaro saw the opportunity for Saburo to start his own business. Fukutaro thought that Saburo had prepared well with his studies and could handle it.

So Saburo took Fukutaro's advice and decided to open his own store. He didn't have any money at that time, so Fukutaro gave him money from his savings. Tomo-san, Sakuichi's widow, was now married to Saburo, and offered Fukutaro and Saburo her savings, which might have been $200 or $300—it was hard for Hisa to remember. This was surprising and unexpected. In all the years Tomo-san had stayed with them, Hisa said, they never charged her for room and board, and they let her keep whatever she earned working in the cane fields and later as a maid for a *haole* home, because Tomo-san had helped the family so much, especially by taking such good care of Norito when Hisa was busy. But that unexpected blessing of Tomo-san's contribution at a critical time helped the Kawakami family to start their first independent business. Even with Tomo-san's gift, more capital was needed, so Fukutaro went around to his friends in Makaweli to raise money. He sold shares for $10 and finally raised enough to purchase the store for his younger brother.

When Fukutaro was fifty-three years old, he moved the family to Waimea so that he could work in Saburo's store and learn to become a businessman. About two or three months later, a friend, Mr. S. Hanki, visited him and asked him about his impressions since becoming a businessman. Fukutaro stated that recently he had been going to the Kekaha area to take orders and was not able to have his meals on time. For lunch he would have something from the store and eat it while traveling in the car. The friend commented that to remember the prices of goods, Fukutaro must have worked night and day, or *fumin-fukyu* (without sleep, without rest)—a term the friend had seen in books.

After two years in Waimea, and after Norito graduated from the University of Hawaii in 1933, Fukutaro moved the family to Hanapepe, where they started a grocery store in a small rented space. Fukutaro went into the surrounding camps to take orders, while Hisa was the saleswoman who took care of the customers. She also supervised the young girls who worked for them, making up the orders for Fukutaro and the sons to deliver.

According to Mabel, Hisa did not have any formal schooling, but she had a sharp memory and was an important asset to her husband's business in the years to come. It was amazing that even though Hisa couldn't write in English, she remembered every item purchased by each customer, and after school she would have Mabel record the purchases in the charge book. Her customers, most of whom were issei and who themselves did not know how to write in English, knew her memory was sharp and trusted her to keep accurate accounts.

Hisa's first son, Norito, handled the store's account books at night and worked as a University of Hawaii agricultural extension agent during the day. Keiji, the second son, was in the first class to graduate from Waimea High School in 1937, and he too went on to the University of Hawaii, graduating in 1941, after which he returned to Kauai to work in the store with Fukutaro.

Then came the war. After basic training at Camp Shelby, Mississippi, Norito was transferred to the Military Intelligence Service (MIS) because of his knowledge of the Japanese language. Following further training at Camp Savage in Minnesota, he was assigned to serve under Gen. Douglas MacArthur in the southwest Pacific. Keiji volunteered for the army and was assigned to the 442nd Regimental Combat Team, serving in Italy and France. The third son, Toru, who by then was attending the University of Hawaii, became part of the Territorial Guard. When the unit was disbanded, he wanted to volunteer but came back to Kauai to help Fukutaro run the store because he had two brothers already serving in the military.

When the older boys returned safely from the war, Toru was drafted and served in the MIS in Presidio, California, while Daniel, the youngest boy in the family, also served in the U.S. Army. Hisa was Buddhist, but there were no Buddhist churches to attend during World War II because all of the ministers had been interned, so she went to a Christian church to pray for her sons. When the war ended, Hisa was very happy that all of the boys came home safely.

The entire family played their part during the war. After graduating from business school in Honolulu, Hisa's older daughter, Yukie, returned home to serve as treasurer of the family business while her husband, Tsukasa Murakami, served with Keiji in Italy and France. Mabel's husband, Norman Hashisaka, also served with the MIS, trained at Camp Savage, fought in the Philippines, then served as an interpreter at the Yokohama war crimes trial in occupied Japan.

All of Hisa's children furthered their education. Norito went to the University of Colorado Law School using the proceeds from Oto-san's charcoal-making venture and the GI Bill, and later became a judge; Keiji went to New York University for his MBA in textiles and business, later opening Iolani Sportwear; and Toru also went to NYU to finish college. Mabel attended the Indiana University and earned a master's degree in education. As an entrepreneur, Fukutaro believed that even girls should have a solid education, as it would come in handy in case something unexpected should happen.

Had he lived long enough, Fukutaro would have been happy and proud to see his daughter Mabel selected as one of the Outstanding Business Women of the Twentieth Century in Hawaii. When she started off to college, Fukutaro told her, "You can study whatever you're interested in, but be sure to take economics and Japanese language." True to her father's advice, economics and Japanese language proved to be valuable assets in her career as a businesswoman.

After Hisa's children finished their education, all of them returned to Kauai. With Keiji managing the store, they leased the parcel of land next door and built a larger building with more general merchandise. In 1950 the business was incorporated as N. F. Kawakami Ltd.

During his time at NYU, Keiji became familiar with large discount supermarkets in the New York–New Jersey area and learned about trends in store operation and merchandising. It was really by happenstance that he met the manager of the McBryde sugar plantation, Mr. Sanderson, on the plane going to Kauai. Mr. Sanderson told Keiji that McBryde's parent company, Alexander & Baldwin, was planning to develop some land formerly used as cane fields and housing into a retail shopping center, and he invited the Kawakami family to start a supermarket in Eleele. This supermarket, which Keiji named Big Save, was the first cash-and-carry store on Kauai. Its presence caused the plantations to change their payroll schedule, first from once a month to every two weeks, and then to every week, so that employees could make purchases at the store.

With a big sigh, Hisa said at the end of the tape, "Starting that small store in Hanapepe *ga ichi ban yokkata. Are kara tsugi kara tsugie to dan dan bisunesu ga hiro gatta* [was the best thing Fukutaro did. After that, gradually they expanded the chain of stores]." She added thankfully, "Oto-san worked very *hardo, butto* we were very *shiawase* [lucky] to have such good children to help us during a tough time. They must have been tempted to play with friends, but not once they complain."

With emotion choking her voice, Hisa recalled, "My children, all good children. They were so small and they couldn't go out to play because they had to help Oto-san and me at the store. *Jyaken me ga honto ni lucky data* [reason why I'm so lucky] because Norito and Keiji really work hard small time, never complain, *guru boy datta* [very good boys]. They work hard to help. *Kon toni raku dekin data yo* [I could not have had this good life now if not for the boys working so hard]. Now I'm enjoying my retirement like this. My grandchildren come see me all the time, they think of me and scold me sometime not to do certain things. You [Mabel] come every day to visit me. Norito come every Saturday. Me, *honto ni lucky yo* [how lucky I am to be at peace and enjoy my retirement]." She sounded very happy.

Though Fukutaro died in 1954, he established a solid foundation for the store, and with the children all working together, it became a great success, with Big Save expanding all over the island of Kauai. It remains one of the most successful stores on Kauai and has since been acquired by an off-island chain.

My friend Mabel was also the source of a treasure trove of rare photos from the early plantation era. This amazing collection of photos started when she decided to open a snack bar in one of the Big Save stores in Koloa. She was looking for special photos of past plantation days to put up on the wall for the customers to enjoy, thinking it might get them to reminisce about the good old days. One day a police officer named Ernest Almeida came in, and Mabel told him about her search for old photographs. Miraculously, he had boxes of old photos of many different ethnic groups dating back to the early immigration period, collected from the families who had settled in Koloa.

In addition, Mabel mentioned that during World War II, an issei photographer had hidden a couple of boxes of photographs when Pearl Harbor was attacked by the Japanese, as there were many rumors going around then that if anything Japanese—such as rising-sun flags, photos, kimonos, and artifacts—were found in homes, the inhabitants would be arrested. These photos were mostly of individuals from various ethnic groups who worked for the Koloa sugar plantation. Mabel had kindly told the families who came to the store that if they could identify the people in the photos, they could have them; the rest of the rare collection she kept in the basement of her home. Fortunately, in 1985, when I attended the Koloa sesquicentennial celebration, I met Mabel and got permission to make copies of rare issei family photos, which became so valuable for my research on immigrant clothing and for which I am so grateful. Kauai is rich in historical artifacts and photographs because Hawaii's sugar plantations had their beginnings on that island, in Koloa; Kilauea Sugar, on the other side of the island, is the second-oldest plantation. Tragically, however, most of the photos that Mabel kept were damaged during Hurricane Iniki in 1992.

When the grandchildren gathered around Hisa, they asked her if she was glad she had come to Hawaii as a picture bride to marry a man she had never seen. Hisa replied, "I was very lucky, because your grandpa was all your great-grandpa said he was, and more . . . kind, generous, and a hardworking man."

Soto Kimura

TRAGEDY AND TRIUMPH

June 29, 1892–May 23, 1990
Born in Fuju-machi, Iwakuni-shi, Kuga-gun, Yamaguchi-ken
Arrived in Hawaii November 10, 1911

Back in 1979, I saw a photo that really caught my attention. It was taken at the Kilauea sugar plantation on Kauai and showed the many ethnic groups from which the women laborers came. In this photo, the women were all dressed in their native costumes. There were Hawaiians, Chinese, Norwegians, Germans, Japanese, Koreans, Portuguese, and Puerto Ricans, and the black women seated in the front row were known to have come from the U.S. South. I noticed the Japanese women in the back row, wearing cotton kimonos with their long sleeves tapered off, holding their hoes. It was this photo that inspired my study of plantation clothing, a study that became my lifelong work.

Kilauea, the second-oldest sugar plantation in Hawaii, situated next to the town of Koloa, celebrated its sesquicentennial in 1985, and I was fortunate to be asked to participate in the commemoration. Unfortunately, there were hardly any old-timers around to talk to. However, the Koloa sugar mill was still standing, and we were given a guided tour (though certain areas were off-limits because they weren't safe). At the conference held at the Koloa library, I saw an amazing collection of original photographs of early immigrants of every ethnic background. This rare collection came from Mabel Kawakami Hashisaka of Eleele, Kauai. These photos were perfect for my book on Japanese immigrant clothing, and later for this book on picture bride stories. Only a few of the issei women who came as picture brides had ever had formal photos taken, so these early ones were an invaluable asset for my research.

Although the sugar mill closed in 1971, the people who worked their entire lives on the Kilauea plantation had their hearts and souls rooted in this community. They were content to live out their remaining days on the site of the former plantation. Over many long years of laboring together in the cane fields and sugar mill, they shared customs and traditions from the villages they had left behind. There seemed to be a unique melting pot of diverse ethnic groups still living in this old plantation community.

Women of various ethnic groups at Kilauea plantation on Kauai. The Hawaiians were the first laborers, followed by the Chinese, Norwegians, Germans, Japanese, Spanish, Okinawans, Puerto Ricans, Portuguese, Koreans, and blacks from the U.S. South. Photo courtesy of Hawaii State Archives.

PICTURE BRIDE: SOTO KIMURA

In 1985, I visited the Kilauea Senior Center to interview the issei women who had come to Hawaii as picture brides during the period from 1908 to 1924. I talked with several especially interesting women. They greeted me warmly, seeming happy that I could speak Japanese fluently and understand their various provincial dialects. Among them was Soto Kimura, one of the earliest picture brides, who had arrived in 1911. She had quite a remarkable memory for someone ninety-three years old.

When I asked her what part of Japan she came from, she looked at me and let out a deep sigh. Her dark brown eyes grew wistful as she said, "You know, it's hard to believe that seventy-three years have gone by since I left Japan. The years have gone by too quickly."

Soto Kimura was distinctively tall for an issei woman. She said she had been five feet three inches when they measured her at the immigration station on arrival. In Japan, measured by the Japanese *mono sashi,* the bamboo ruler used for kimono sewing, she was five feet two and a half inches. She must have been a striking figure in her younger days with her long nose, dark eyes, and wide forehead, which in Japan was traditionally considered a sign of high intelligence. Her darker, weathered skin indicated much time spent out of doors. She was in perfect health, with good vision and good hearing in addition to that remarkable memory. Soto seemed to be having a good time at the senior center.

At the center, I observed men and women from different ethnic groups sharing and learning new things, even at their advanced ages. They seemed to be communicating well with each other in their unique Pidgin English mixed with their own native dialects. Now I could see how the issei generation picked up words from other ethnic groups to effectively communicate with them. Words combined with comic gestures increased their understanding. When they spoke in Japanese, all of these words adopted from other languages came into play, so when relatives and friends would visit from Japan, they could not understand the locally spoken Japanese. The local nisei could not understand it, either.

Soto Kimura was very kind to invite me to interview her in her quiet home. She still lived in the modest, comfortable house where she and her husband had raised their family; after her husband died, the plantation allowed the family to stay in the house. (As a general practice, the plantation allowed retired employees to remain in their residences.) Her spacious yard was filled with all kinds of fruit trees and a garden with many varieties of neatly planted vegetables. Yukio, her second son, lived with her. Soto chuckled as she told me, "Yeah, he's still a bachelor, so even if I'm ninety-three years old, I still cook for him and do his laundry." Yukio had just come home and was surprised to see a stranger in his home. He was as friendly as his mother, and didn't seem to mind that I had come to interview her. He agreed that his mother was very sharp for her age and kept very busy. After a friendly chat, he left us alone for the interview.

Soto offered me some of her homemade green tea with toasted rice. It had a special aroma and was very refreshing. I shared with Soto that my mother used to make this, too, with leftover cold rice that she would dry in the sun before toasting it. We both sat comfortably on the sofa, my cassette recorder on the coffee table, placed closer to her for recording clarity.

Soto told me, "My hobby is to crochet all kinds of decorative things. My bedroom looks more like a *mono oki* [storeroom]. I have about a hundred items, including bedspreads made of popcorn stitch, cushions, shawls, and so on." She gladly took them out to show them to me, adding, "I don't need written directions. I can copy just by looking at the samples and counting the threads. I learned to crochet all these fancy things by watching the people at the senior center. There are many women of other ethnic groups. They are so good in making all these fancy things."

CHILDHOOD MEMORIES

Soto spoke reflectively about her childhood days in the village of Fuju.

"I was born in Yamaguchi-ken, Kuga-gun, Iwakuni-shi, Fuju-machi, on June 29, 1892. I was one of ten children, six boys and four girls, born to Kisaku Shigehiro and Toki Fujioka. My family did not have any samurai background. They were simple farmers, but we lived in a fairly comfortable home. We grew everything, from *ine* [rice] and *mugi* [barley] to *awa* [millet] used for *awa mochi* [cake], and raised all kinds of vegetables, which we sold at the market. My parents worked very hard all year round, like the other families in the village.

"Today, it's a big city," she said. "During the Meiji period [1868–1911], compulsory education was extended from *jinjo ka* [fourth grade] to *koto ninen* [sixth grade]. Our parents made sure we studied hard because it was impossible for them to let us continue to high school. Having six boys, my parents didn't let us girls work on the farm. My brothers all worked hard on the farm while the girls were sent to various training classes such as kimono sewing, *ikebana* [flower arrangement], *nihon shishu* [Japanese embroidery, which is a fine satin stitch], *reigi saho* [etiquette], and tea ceremony classes conducted by individual instructors in the village. For fun, like most girls, we played *ojyame* [bean bag toss], jump rope, hide-and-seek, and many other games. On New Year's, we get dressed in our finest kimonos and after going around visiting relatives and close friends with New Year greetings, we play our favorite *karuta* [game of cards] and *hagoita*," a traditional game similar to badminton, played with paddles but no net. Soto's eyes sparkled when she thought about the innocent and carefree days of her childhood.

According to Meiji-era tradition, Confucian ethics were strongly emphasized in schools and at home. A mother's responsibility was to train her daughters in various creative skills, the arts, and etiquette in preparation for marriage, so as not to embarrass the family. "This training began while we were in grade school and continued through our teen years until marriage. My teenage days were carefree, and my sisters and I enjoyed many girls' sports and games."

MARRIAGE ARRANGED BY PARENTS

Soto continued, "In the meantime, a *tokoro mono,* a fellow villager who knew both families, just came back from Kilauea plantation on the island of Kauai. He talked to my parents and wanted to *shimpai* [matchmake] Kuniyoshi and me. He said, 'It's about time Kuniyoshi, the Kimura boy, get married.'"

Kuniyoshi Kimura was born on November 3, 1887, in the same village as Soto. Like many other young men, he caught the *netsu* (fever, craze) and joined the group of young farmers who went to Hawaii to work on the sugar plantations. They were sure they could make a bundle of money and return after their three-year contract was up. In his case, he was the only son in the family, the *ato tori* (heir who would continue the family name), so it was a bit unusual that his parents allowed him to go abroad. He left in 1903, when he was sixteen years old (though according to the Japanese way of calculating age, he was still fifteen). After his three-year contract was over, he did not come back and his family hardly heard from him; his mother was beginning to get concerned about his well-being.

When Kuniyoshi came to Kilauea in 1903, it was still a desolate wilderness of kiawe trees, and the living conditions were very poor. Toiling under the intense tropical heat for ten hours a day was quite an adjustment. His mother could never have imagined that her only son was going through such extreme hardship. At home, everything had been done for him. Life in Kilauea was altogether a different experience from working at one's own pace in the rice fields back home with family. The only pleasure the men found after ten hours of backbreaking labor came from gambling and drinking. It somehow helped them to overcome the loneliness of being away from loved ones, and allowed them to temporarily forget the struggle to survive on their meager earnings.

Kuniyoshi's mother liked Soto and was impressed with her upbringing. She wanted her as a wife for her only son, now in faraway Hawaii. She felt she would make a fine daughter-in-law to help perpetuate the family name.

Although they grew up in the same village, Soto and Kuniyoshi were not well acquainted, as Japanese boys and girls were not allowed to socialize or be friendly with each other. Even at the elementary school, the girls and boys weren't allowed to speak to each other or sit close to each other. So it wasn't strange that Soto hardly knew this young man who had left the village a few years before, when she was only eleven years old. She had no romantic notions about him. She didn't even understand the real meaning of marriage. Now that she was nineteen and had begun to "blossom," however, she heard many stories about matchmaking and whom she might be matched with. One in particular was a man in Hawaii. "All I knew was that his mother wanted me to go to Hawaii as his picture bride and bring him back to the village." A family friend served as *nakoodo* or *baishaku nin* and started the procedure by first sending photos to the families of the prospective bride and groom. Once the match was agreed upon, the bride had to be registered in the groom's family's *koseki* in the village office, and the paperwork for her visa needed to be completed. In the meantime, the bride's family was busy preparing the dowry.

Soto smilingly recalled, "You know, before this matchmaking with Kuniyoshi in Hawaii, my mother was trying to arrange a picture bride marriage with a man who left the village to work as *dekasegi* [immigrant worker] on the U.S. mainland. But I didn't want to go because I knew I would get too seasick traveling that far. In those days, girls did whatever our parents wanted us to do. Imagine what kind of life I would have had if I married someone on the mainland! During World War II, the mainland Japanese really suffered even if they had nothing to do with the bombing of Pearl Harbor. Japanese in Hawaii were lucky, though some issei were interned. I'm glad I didn't go to the mainland United States."

THE JOURNEY

On November 1, 1911, nineteen-year-old Soto Shigehiro left Japan for Hawaii to become the picture bride of Kuniyoshi Kimura. The families had made the decision for the young couple; all she knew was the exciting rumors she had heard about this *tengoku* (paradise) from villagers who had returned from Hawaii.

"I left from the port of Kobe. Saying goodbye was very hard. Growing up in a large, close-knit family, this was my first experience of traveling to a distant land that I had no knowledge of. . . . The sea was choppy and rough in November, and the boat rocked and rocked. My *kori* [wicker trunk] went *koron, koron* [clunk, clunk] on the deck; even the fishes leaped onboard when the strong waves hit the ship! Ahh . . . I got so seasick on the boat. I couldn't eat anything . . . never felt so miserable," she recalled of her first journey crossing the Pacific.

"What type of kimonos did you bring for your dowry?" I asked.

"Well, my relatives told me not to bring any good clothes to Hawaii. 'Just bring some dressy *kasuri* kimonos and casual *yukata,* that's enough! You're going to work in the cane fields right away.' So I left my *montsuki* at home. I brought a few *meisen* and *omeshi* dressy silk kimonos and brocaded obis and accessories."

Soto continued, "After being seasick for nine days, ahh . . . what a relief, when the ship finally docked in Honolulu harbor. The passengers were fascinated with the breathtaking view of Daiyamondo Heto [Diamond Head] as we gathered on deck. So different in shape from our majestic Mt. Fuji. To the picture brides who came from isolated mountain villages, everything seemed so *aka rui* [bright] and beautiful. To see the *ki rei na awoi sora* [beautiful blue sky]! In Japanese, *awoi* means 'green color,' but Japanese call the sky blue [*awoi*]. For the first time, we saw the dark-skinned Hawaiian people. The young girls had big, round eyes, long hair, very pretty, little *momona* [chubby]. They swayed and danced for us. We learned they were called *kanaka*. It was easy to learn that word—sounds like *kata kana* in Japanese."

Before leaving the ship, Soto put on the dressy *meisen* kimono that she had sewn herself. She wanted to look her best, although she hardly knew her husband-to-be, except through the photo sent to her parents from Hawaii. At five feet three inches in height, Soto stood out among the other picture brides, who averaged about four feet ten inches tall. They all wore their hair in the fashionable pompadour hairdo. Soto told me, "I didn't comb my pompadour too high because I was so much taller than the other brides. I wore a wide white ribbon in the back."

ARRIVAL IN HAWAII

Arriving in Honolulu harbor, "I was surprised there was no one at the immigration depot to greet me. There was Katsunuma-san dressed in a dark suit and a white cap. I heard he was the inspector. He was very kind and helpful to us, the newly arrived immigrants who could not speak nor understand the English language. We spoke our provincial dialect, and did not understand the standard Japanese language unless we had finished the sixth grade in the village school. He made funny jokes to put us at ease. He poked fun at the pompadour hairdo worn by the picture brides. He said, 'It looks like a bird's nest!' I passed all the requirements for the exams and inspection. Sadly, some brides who didn't have much schooling could not understand the standard Japanese questions at all, so they were detained. I sensed their feeling of fear and uncertainty . . . no one to turn to, but we could not help them. The majority of the picture brides who came on the same ship were claimed by their husbands and left. There seemed to be some awkward moments and disappointments when the couples first met. The husbands or the wives didn't seem to look like the photos they brought with them. But it was too late to make a fuss and each couple went their way.

"As I watched the other women being claimed by their husbands and my husband never showed up, my anxiety grew. I kept looking at his picture and wondered if he couldn't identify me. I didn't know a single soul in Hawaii, nor did I have a return fare for Japan. I waited and waited, crying at night out of fear and loneliness in a strange place. Those days, no telephone, come to a foreign land, I only know my Yamaguchi-ken dialect, nobody can understand. If now, I talk some Pidgin, maybe help a little bit," she laughed gently.

"At last . . . after two weeks of waiting at the immigration station, my husband finally came. The boat from Kauai took five hours to reach Honolulu. When my husband went through the official procedures and claimed me, there were two other couples who were also delayed. A Christian minister asked us three couples to stand together. The minister was mumbling something, but we couldn't understand what

Kuniyoshi and Soto Kimura wedding
photo, 1911. Barbara Kawakami
Collection.

he said. I found out later that it was probably a brief Christian ceremony given in English. After the ceremony, he asked each of the newlywed couples to shake hands with each other. That was all," she said. "My husband hired a *hakku* [hack, a horse-drawn carriage], and he took me to see his sister who lived in Honolulu. We stayed there one night. Then he took me to the interisland pier to get on a boat to the island of Kauai."

"What were the first words you said to each other?" I asked.

"Funny, I can't remember. Waiting two weeks . . . was too much worry for me. I think I just felt relief to see him. I can't even remember the first words we spoke to each other!" she said with a chuckle.

KOLOA LANDING

When Soto came in 1911, Koloa Landing was still one of the major ports on Kauai, and the third-largest whaling port in Hawaii at that time. Koloa Landing also served as the port of entry for foreign goods coming into Kauai. Depending on the wind and surf conditions, the water off Koloa could be treacherous.

"My husband and I finally headed for Kauai on a small freighter, the *Kinau*, which was loaded with bags of sugar. When the sea was rough, the bags of sugar would roll on the people seated on deck. There were many Hawaiian people on

Soto Kimura's ship was anchored offshore and the passengers were brought by a smaller boat to Koloa Landing, ca. 1907–1915. Photo courtesy of Mabel Hashisaka Collection.

board, friendly, playing nice music. When we reached Kauai, the *Kinau* was anchored offshore. All of us were put on a small boat and taken to the landing dock in Koloa. There, we were told to jump onto the landing when the waves swelled high. The Japanese brides, all dressed in their tightly wrapped kimonos and obis, did as they were told without any effort. I was the only one, much taller than them . . . and too scared to jump!" With eyes wide and gesturing with her hands, she told me, "Ahh, one big wave come, big *kanaka* man lifted me off the boat and put me on the landing! That's the first time I was ever held by a man! You know, in Japan that would be terrible for a young girl to be held by a man!" she exclaimed.

Soto also remembered, "You know, getting on the landing was rough and scary, but climbing up the steep hill in my tightly wrapped kimono and sandals was just as hard. I carried a *gassai bukuro* [big traveling bag for personal belongings] and I somehow climbed up the hill. That hill is still there!" she reminded me.

A NEW HOME

"During the long ride to the Kilauea sugar plantation I saw nothing but kiawe trees for the first time. We don't have that kind of tree in Japan. It seemed like the car was going to an isolated mountain area with strange-looking shacks surrounded by sugarcane fields. When we finally stopped, my husband showed me my new home. I could not believe what I saw! It reminded me of a *hoito beya* [beggar's house] back in the village. It even had a piggery built next to it. Even a beggar lived in a better home than that!" Soto exclaimed.

"There was only one room, with everything combined. The sleeping area was higher, with strong boards, and laid with *goza* [straw matting], with a futon placed over the straw matting. When not in use, it was neatly folded and put away. His futon was in bad shape, so as soon as I settled in, I took it apart, washed the cover, and sewed it back together. Most brides brought a set of handwoven cotton- or silk-covered comforters as part of their dowry. The fabrics used for the futon covers were specially ordered for the bride's dowry.

"The kitchen was an earthen floor, and cooking was done on an open fire in one corner. Empty apple boxes from the plantation store served as a table. I thought, 'Oh my, if his mother knew how her one son was living in this miserable place, she would cry her heart out.' They were not rich farmers, but they had a big, comfortable home."

The people of the small plantation camp in Kilauea were excited at the arrival of a picture bride from Japan. As Soto described it, "Those days, every time issei man's bride come from Japan, the manager give the workers time off. My husband lived in Chinese camp. Those days, many Chinese single men. Sometimes they intermarry Hawaiian *wahine* [women]. They never intermarry with Japanese. So many Hawaiians in Kilauea at that time. My husband made big party, and many friends of every ethnic group came, too. The celebration lasted for three days with feasting, singing, and lots of sake."

ADJUSTING TO PLANTATION LIFE

Soto continued, "I found out my husband worked at the Kilauea sugar mill nearby."

I asked, "So you heard from the go-between that your husband was a wealthy man?"

She broke out in laughter. "Nothing doing! He was deep in debt from gambling, and that was the reason he could not go home to Japan." Although Soto had never worked on the farm back home, she made up her mind to work in the sugarcane fields to help pay her husband's gambling debt.

One of the first things Soto noticed in her new home was a strange-looking object in the corner. Her husband explained that it was a Singer sewing machine, and showed her how to use it. She had never seen anything like that in her village. In Japan, kimonos were all hand-sewn. With no women around, the men must have learned to sew so that they could patch torn work clothes and make simple things. Her husband and his friends had invested in a sewing machine with money from a *tanomoshi,* a mutual financing system.

"When I came in 1911, the issei women were already wearing *holoku* [muumuu with a train] for home and for special occasions. The styles were the same as the ones we wear today." Showing me a photograph, Soto pointed out, "I am wearing a white *holoku* I sewed myself, taken in 1912, in front of the plantation slaughterhouse. That photo was taken at the farewell party when someone was returning to Japan. Some of the women are wearing their kimonos. During those days, the issei women called the long Hawaiian dress *holoku* even if there was no train. Maybe it was easier for us to say it. The high yoke and gathered bodice was popular. Today, we call it the *tutu muu*. I took apart my *kasuri* kimonos to make them into *tutu muu*. There were lots of Chinese and Hawaiians in Kilauea those days. Today, I am finally learning to sew properly at the senior citizens center. I'm ninety-three years old now but still sew all my own dresses without using eyeglasses."

Soto continued her story. "I came in November and made arrangements to work right away. My kind neighbors said I needed to rest from the long sea voyage and get my work clothes ready. They helped me, and loaned me clothes patterns to get started with my work clothes immediately. I copied the patterns on old Japanese newspapers my husband kept. I took apart my *kasuri* kimonos to make into work clothes. Then I work on the *kappa* [raincoat], so important for the rainy weather on Kauai.

"The *kappa* was hard to make. The ladies showed me how to make out of heavy muslin cloth. After the muslin coat was sewn into a loose coat, they taught me how to make it water-repellent. First, they showed me how to apply *kaki shibu* [astringent juice of persimmon that came from Japan in small bottles]. Then let it dry a few days to tighten the fabric. The ladies taught me how to boil turpentine and linseed oil, slowly, in a large can outdoors, over an open fire. The mixed oil is so thick you cannot use a brush to put it on the muslin coat that was treated with *kaki shibu*. So I use old rag to rub the thick, gluey mixture on the muslin coat. Then the coat put on hanger and hang in shade to dry. You do it two more times. We make nice raincoat without spending much money," Soto said with pride, adding, "Lucky my husband had sewing machine.

"Without taking sewing lessons, I borrowed patterns from friends and I've been sewing all my husband's work clothes and children's clothes. I used to sew my own dresses. Only the dressy silk dresses someone sewed for me. Today [1985], we learn to sew at the senior citizens center. Mrs. Harada comes to teach the seniors. Now when I think about it, the clothes I sewed a long time ago for my children must have looked very funny!" She broke out in laughter.

Another thing she was surprised to find was that her husband had been trying to sew a *hino maru no hata,* a Japanese flag with the rising sun. He had bought red and white cloth for a dollar, sewed it halfway, then put it aside. "So I learned to pedal the machine and finished sewing the flag. That was the first thing I learned to sew on the Singer machine."

In Hawaii until World War II, every Japanese home kept a Japanese flag to display on the emperor's birthday. It touched Soto deeply to think how difficult it must have been for these single men to survive in this isolated camp without the comfort of things so dear to their heart. In those days, there was no electricity, so a kerosene lamp was used to provide dim lighting. All cooking was done over an open fire, and the ceiling would get all *makkuroke* (black from soot). Rice was cooked in a *hagama,* a cast-iron pot, out of doors over an open fire of kiawe wood. Rice cooked in a *hagama* was delicious—even the burnt part was good. Sweet potatoes and yams were roasted in the hot ashes. The issei made charcoal out of kiawe wood and used it in their hibachis for cooking. In those days with no electricity, to do the family ironing, women of all ethnic groups used a heavy device made of cast iron that they filled with hot charcoal from the hibachi.

WORKING IN THE CANE FIELDS

"My husband worked at the sugar mill, and I started working in cane fields with the *wahine* group until I had my children. That was the first time I work in the fields. I work very hard and kept up with the other women. The other workers worry my hands too small—they didn't think I could handle the heavy work—but I did fine. The roughest time I had was when we had to walk for miles to work in the cane fields near the mountains. At times we rode the cane car, to take us through the fields! Only thing, I cannot jump off cane cars like the other *wahines*. I was too scared. We all walked a lot in the hot sun! No trucks like they have now.

"To think that every morning, I get up at three-thirty, make *miso* soup for breakfast, make *bento* lunch for husband and me. Fieldworkers had to catch the train at 5:00 a.m. I cook rice outdoors night before. Next morning, I get up at 3:30 am to pack the double-decker *bento* can, fill rice on bottom can and put *ume* [salted plum] on top the rice. We call *hino maru bento* [rice with red pickled plum in the center]. *Ume* gives you energy when tired. I cook on *seki tan* [kerosene stove] in the kitchen. For *okazu* [main dish], I bring *nishime* [cooked vegetables] from night before, dried fish, *sakuranbo,* imported from Japan—the sardines were dried and seasoned with teriyaki sauce, with the fish laid out in a row; the package sold for 50 cents, and lasted for months without refrigeration. Also we have *tara* [codfish], and a small piece of *shio shake* [salt salmon] was a treat for *bento*. Canned deviled ham was cheap in those days, and I split with my husband and put half portion in his *bento*. We lived frugally. Fresh fish was plentiful in the waters in Kilauea. My husband was good fisherman. When he caught plenty small *akule,* I salted them and dried them in the sun. They tasted good for *bento,*" she recalled happily. "That's how we got by and we stayed healthy.

"When I first came in 1911, I work ten hours a day and got paid 45 cents a day. For *pula pula* [cane seedling] contract work, by myself, I made 60 cents a day. *Hole hole* work was hard, stripping the *iga mabure* [leaves full of sharp edges]. The pay for that was 45 cents for ten hours a day. We really work hard for so little pay. The women sang 'Hole Hole Bushi' while stripping the cane leaves, but I couldn't sing at all. Some of the songs were sad and made the ladies think of loved ones at home."

RAISING A FAMILY

"After I came to Hawaii I work three years, then had first baby in 1913. I was twenty-two years old. The firstborn son, Kiyoshi, died when he was about one year old. He was the only baby delivered by a midwife [*tokoro no hito*] who came from same village in Japan. She didn't charge regular fees for delivering the babies. She usually helped for a week, bathe the newborn, wash the *omutsu* [diapers], and sometimes make *okai* [rice gruel] for the new mother so she would have more milk. I gave breast milk to my first four children. The others, no breast milk, so I gave them bottled milk. People made *orei* [offerings of gratitude] with whatever they could afford. The midwife knew everyone was struggling. For diapers, I ripped my faded *yukata* or bleached rice bags. For diaper cover, I took apart my kimono obi made of *mosu* [wool fiber] that made it water repellent." It's amazing how the issei women learned to be so frugal to survive.

"When I was pregnant with my second son, Yukio, I was twenty-three years old. I work until the eighth month in the cane fields. People surprise, I work until July when I expecting baby in August. The weather so hot! Everybody worry, but I needed money so I worked. When labor pain start, somebody ran to sugar mill to get my husband. He helped me deliver the baby. He learned to cut the *heso* [umbilical cord]. I was lucky I didn't suffer like some ladies. I had easy time in giving birth and the babies were healthy. My husband help deliver all the six babies.

"As soon as Yukio was few months old, I used to *oppa* him and went back to work. I would lay him down on *goza* matting while I did the fieldwork. I give him toy to play. But one time when he started crawling around and I busy working, he play with the double-decker *bento* can and spill the food. So when lunchtime come, I look in *bento* can, I see rice all cover with dirt and sand. My stomach was growling with hunger, not having anything since early breakfast. I work all day, without eating anything. When I think about those days, I wonder how I manage to do it. It was tough in those days with no family nearby to ask for help," Soto said sadly. "How many times I cried myself to sleep. I thought . . . I should have stayed in Japan. Those days, my husband gambled and drank a lot. No money. I wanted to go home. No place to go, so I *gaman* [persevere, endure]. I *gaman*.

"Third child, I had boy again. We name him Tadayoshi. Then fourth son, Takayuki, was born, and then fifth son, Seiki, was born. Finally, the sixth child was a baby girl. We named her Michiko. We were very happy. The seventh child was a boy again, James. He was born in 1931."

Out of sheer necessity, many immigrants from all ethnic groups learned to give birth by themselves because they lived in such isolated areas and no doctors were available. Soto said, "In those days, we had no knowledge of birth control, and had one baby after another. You had as many babies as they came along. Some women did have abortion but if found out, they went *kara boshi* [jail]. People were so poor they did it out of desperation."

A TRAGIC ACCIDENT

When I interviewed Soto Kimura in 1985, all she told me was that she had lost her husband when she was young. Gary Smith of Kilauea, who knew the Kimura boys, was kind enough to share the story. He wrote me that in 1937 Soto's husband, Kuniyoshi, had been *ulua* fishing with a fellow mill worker named Lucas at the point of land that is the western flank of Crater Hill, east of Kilauea Lighthouse. It is a dangerous area, steep and crumbly. No one had fished there in many years. According to Takayuki (who is nicknamed "Taxi"), his father was standing on the ledge, lifting an *ulua,* when he lost his balance and fell to the rocks below. His partner saw it happen but could not do anything, as the fall probably killed him instantly; the waves then washed his body away. His friend hurried to summon Taxi and three friends, who rushed to the cliff site. All that was left of Kuniyoshi was his pack of Lucky Strike cigarettes on the ledge. Taxi was only thirteen years old when the tragic accident occurred, yet he also was working in the mill part-time while going to school, since his father had wanted him to get an education. After his father's death he began to work full-time in the mill. When federal law changed to require mill workers to be at least eighteen years old, he was sent out in the field as a tractor operator.

Kuniyoshi Kimura's favorite fishing spot was near the Kilauea Lighthouse overlooking a rocky ledge where he slipped and drowned. On April 4, 2013, it was rededicated as the Daniel K. Inouye Kilauea Point Lighthouse in the National Register of Historical Places. Photo courtesy of Kauai Museum.

When Soto Kimura's youngest son, James, and his wife, Sandra, returned to Kauai for a visit, Taxi's wife, Sally, called me, and James and I shared a long phone conversation. James recalled the sad incident of his father's death. "I was about six years old. I remembered it so well. It was October 31, Halloween night. My friends and I, we were trick-or-treating around the camp when someone came running and told us about Father having an accident while fishing near the Kilauea Lighthouse." James and his friends rushed to the scene. Everybody helped search for his father for days, but his body was never found. For young James, who had enjoyed many happy days fishing with his father, it was a devastating blow. One fond memory James shared of his father was this: "When Father came home from a hard day's work at the sugar mill, he enjoyed his sake, then soaked himself in a hot steaming *furo* [wooden tub]. Sometimes he fell asleep. I often worried about Father drowning in the hot tub, and would check on him."

Soto recalled sadly, "After my husband died, our lives changed completely. We were already struggling with our growing family, and now it became more difficult. I became a young widow with six children to support."

Yukio and Takayuki both had to go to work immediately after graduating from the eighth grade. Yukio later went to vocational school on the Big Island and became a skilled carpenter. Seiki, who was born on September 13, 1924, later served in the military and was killed in the Korean War on October 3, 1951.

James was also serving in Korea, but after his brother's tragic death, the army reassigned him.

In 2013, the Kilauea Lighthouse was dedicated in honor of the late Senator Daniel Inouye, who had been awarded a Medal of Honor for his bravery and courage in World War II, where he lost his right arm serving in northern Italy. He went on to have a distinguished career in the U.S. Senate, rising to become its president pro tempore. With the rechristening, Kilauea Lighthouse may attract even more visitors to this beautiful yet dangerous spot. Japanese Buddhists believe that the spirits of the deceased return to earth during the Obon festival. Perhaps during that season the spirit of Kuniyoshi Kimura returns to the spot where he drowned in 1937. I wonder if he—along with countless others who died in similar accidents at this prominent point—smiles down on the lighthouse's many visitors. Whatever the case, I hope that all their memories are honored by this favored but treacherous fishing ground, now dedicated in remembrance of Senator Daniel Inouye, one of America's most accomplished nisei.

SOTO IN WIDOWHOOD

It was Sally Kimura, who was married to Soto's fourth son, Takayuki, who introduced me to Gary Smith, lifelong resident and historian in the Kilauea area. He knew the Kimura family well and was just the person I needed to provide more information about what occurred during Soto's lifetime. Gary Smith remembered that when he was a young boy he saw Soto taking care of her large number of potted plants, as well as her collection of lovely anthuriums. She also had some white sweet pea flowers, a guava, and a *kaki* (persimmon) tree.

She had a large plot in the Japanese garden that the plantation supplied for its employees' families. She grew the typical vegetable crops for home use, such as green onion, cabbage, *gobo* (burdock root), green beans, tea plants, carrots, small onions to make *rankyo* (pickled onions), and daikon. Like many other elderly Japanese women, she also raised Easter lilies, which were sold to the Yoshida store in Kapaa.

Gary mentioned that after Soto Kimura lost her husband, she did laundry for the Lung family, who owned the Kong Lung store, still a landmark building in Kilauea today. Mrs. Lung was a schoolteacher who taught second grade. Soto also did laundry for some plantation supervisors, such as the Riola family, George Akana, and a single man, Andres Gonzalez. She was a very hard worker.

Soto was a devoted member of the Kapaa Hongwanji Buddhist temple and attended their monthly service. As she got older and it became difficult for her and the other older folks to travel to Kapaa, the minister made monthly visits to Kilauea to conduct Buddhist services at the Kilauea Gym. This continued after the war until the 1960s. In the 1980s, the minister came from Kapaa once a month and conducted services in members' homes. The Mitsui, Sawada, and Motoyama families took turns opening their homes for the service. In this old plantation community, the families gathered to share their joy of the *nembutsu,* or Buddhist teachings, and found peace in their retirement years.

In 2013, I spoke on the phone to Rev. Shinkai Murakami of the Wailuku Hongwanji. He had been the resident minister at the Kapaa Hongwanji from 1988 until 1995, and remembered Soto Kimura as a very dedicated member and a very *kichomeina* (respectful and kind) person. He recalled performing her funeral service in 1990.

RECONNECTING WITH SOTO'S CHILDREN IN 2013

For six years, I tried calling Soto's home periodically to get more information from Yukio about his mother, but never got an answer. I was surprised one day in April 2013 when a male voice at the other end answered the phone. I asked, "Is this Yukio?"

The voice on the other end replied, "No, this is Joe."

"What happened to Yukio? I have been calling him for the past six years and he never answered, so I thought maybe he passed away."

Joe answered, "Oh, he is still living, but he is stone deaf. Even if he is at home, he can't hear the phone. Yeah . . . Yukio not in good health. He is bedridden and cannot come to the phone. I'm his caregiver." I explained to Joe that I had met Yukio about thirty years ago when I had interviewed his mother. There were still so many things I wanted to find out about his mother that I had failed to ask in the first interview.

Yukio, nicknamed "Yonkie," remained a bachelor and lived with his mother until her death at age ninety-seven. Gary Smith said Yukio led a happy, productive life hunting for wild chickens, pheasants, other birds such as plovers and doves, and wild pigs. Most of all, he enjoyed fishing with his friends well into his nineties. His mother was a very good cook and used her culinary skills to prepare the fish and wild game he caught. The meat must have been tough, but she knew how to turn it into delicious, hearty meals. Between Yukio and his mother, the family was able to economize and stay healthy. Gary described Yonkie's delight in his old jalopy, a Ford Model A. He always brought something home from his hunting expeditions, even if it was just *warabi* (tender ferns) or bamboo shoots from the mountains. Soto was always able to turn whatever he brought home into a gourmet treat. Maybe this was part of the reason for their long and healthy lives. Yukio passed away in 2013, at ninety-seven.

I asked Joe if there was anyone else in the Kimura family who could help me complete my research. The patient and courteous Joe gave me the number of Soto's daughter-in-law Sally. What a wonderful miracle it turned out to be that Joe introduced Sally to me. She was so knowledgeable about her mother-in-law's activities and her many outstanding talents, which otherwise would have been forgotten.

Takayuki and Sally had a happy family, with seven children, nineteen grandchildren, and twelve great-grandchildren. They were selected as Hawaii's Grandparents of the Year for 2013 and were honored at the Ala Moana Center. Takayuki, who like Yukio had quit school after the eighth grade to help support his siblings and had worked hard all his life at the Kilauea plantation, was ninety-one in 2013 and had been in poor health, but Sally was taking good care of him. Their children came every day to help her. In spite of her busy schedule, Sally was also helping care for her grandchildren and great-grandchildren, and found time to take ukulele lessons. No matter when I called, she was always so cheerful, and she was a tremendous help in completing this portrait of her mother-in-law, Soto Kimura. Takayuki died in October of that year.

Soto had only one daughter, Michiko. After Kuniyoshi's death, his parents urged Soto to return to Japan with the six children. She visited them with four of

Soto Kimura and family. She had to give her only daughter to her husband's family in Japan. Photo courtesy of Sally Kimura.

the children—three sons and Michiko. Her in-laws wanted Michiko to stay with them so that they could adopt a son-in-law to continue the family name. Michiko cried and cried and hung on to her mother. Soto felt bad leaving her young daughter behind, but she had to respect her in-laws' wishes. In 1985, Soto told me that Michiko by that time had three children, three grandchildren, and six great-grandchildren, and had returned to Hawaii twice to see her family.

James, the youngest son, was eighty-two in 2013. Under the GI Bill, he attended Washington State University and became a teacher. He met his wife, Sandra, at college, and both had successful careers in education.

SOTO, AN INSPIRATION

Soto Kimura died in 1990 at the age of ninety-seven. She had always been very healthy and enjoyed a productive life until she had a bad fall and hit her head. After falling a second time, near the Buddhist altar in her home, she was hospitalized. The doctor said she would not be able to walk again; however, she was always a determined person and tried very hard. She was a fighter until the very end, when she died of pneumonia.

Soto was a wonderful mother, mother-in-law, great-grandmother, and great-great-grandmother. She was always fun to be with, and was well liked by everyone.

Everyone called her *obaachan* in an affectionate manner, and so did I when I interviewed her.

Sally mentioned what a wonderful cook Soto was. The roast chicken she cooked on the stovetop was delicious and enjoyed by all. Sally never forgot her mother-in-law's kindness during the early years of her marriage to Takayuki. When they first got married, they lived for a year with Soto and always had an excellent relationship.

After they set up their new home, Soto would prepare special food to share with them. Sally could never forget the time she was too sick with fever and couldn't get up. Soto made her Japanese *okai* (rice gruel) and brought it for her. "It tasted so good and it made me feel so much better. I'm Portuguese, but she accepted me as part of her family. When our first son was born, she was so excited. She adored him and spoiled him. Such a wonderful mother-in-law."

Sally talked about Soto's beautiful crocheted bedspreads, cushion covers, and shawls, all those lovely things I'd seen years ago. But when I asked what had happened to all those fancy crocheted things, Sally said she didn't know.

DOTING GRANDMOTHER

James's wife, Sandra, sent me a note. "You asked me about remembrances of Obaachan—I can share these with you. It was a wonderful walk through the years! We were married in late 1967 and so we made our first Kauai visit as a married couple in the summer of 1968. Obaachan was very welcoming even though I think she would have preferred a Japanese daughter-in-law. She made me feel very comfortable

Tadayuki and Sally Kimura with three generations of her family. Honored as Grandparents of the Year in 2013. Photo courtesy of Sally Kimura.

during that visit and took me to her community garden plot to meet her friends. The following year, she came to visit us. That was the summer we put a man on the moon, and even though she did not speak English, she was absolutely mesmerized by the television coverage of that event. While it was a nice visit for Jim and her, not being able to speak the language made her a bit lonely. One of the big highlights of her visit was being able to visit with the owners of the Japanese grocery store we frequented. She loved our adopted children—our son, Tim, who is Korean/Caucasian, and daughter, Naomi, who is Japanese/Caucasian—equally as her other grandchildren. Whenever the grandchildren visited, she would open her oven door and share with them whatever goodies she had stored there. She never cooked in her oven! Whenever we would visit, the first night was always our favorite dinner prepared by her: frog legs, rice, and a multitude of wonderful garden vegetables. She also prepared lots of fishcakes (adored by the children) from the fish that Yukio had caught. I can remember her making her own tea. She would harvest the leaves and dry them outside on screens, roast the rice inside, and then mix the two together. Whenever we would visit, she would make a muumuu for Naomi. She sewed with a treadle machine! She always made her own patterns out of newspaper with the help of a ruler. At one time, she had purchased a new electric portable Singer sewing machine but didn't know how to use it. I did spend some time with her showing her the basics of the new machine and from that time on the treadle was retired!"

The photo of Takayuki and Sally with their children and grandchildren captures the beautiful, cosmopolitan melting pot of races that is Hawaii. When Soto Kimura came as a picture bride from Yamaguchi prefecture, she could never have dreamed that someday she would have such an exquisite potpourri of races in her family.

GAMAN

Soto Kimura's story is typical of the stories of early issei women. They arrived in Hawaii unprepared for the harsh realities that confronted them. The majority of them came with only a fourth-grade education from rural villages. Yet no matter what the situation was, somehow they had the physical strength and moral courage to survive under tremendous adversity, and the ingenuity to learn new skills in adapting to a new environment. They labored beside their husbands and raised their children as best as they could within the framework of their traditional beliefs and values. Issei mothers never failed to instill in their children an appreciation for the value of good education, hard work, perseverance, and honesty, all keys to elevating the quality of their lives. Soto Kimura is an example of a life lived in this spirit of *gaman*.

Tatsuno Ogawa
FROM HIROSHIMA TO THE PUPUKEA PINEAPPLE FIELDS

November 20, 1892–December 22, 1991
Born in Sanman-machi, Jinseki-gun, Hiroshima-ken
Arrived in Hawaii July 26, 1913

Tatsuno Ogawa was ninety-two years old in 1985 when I interviewed her in the modest little house she and her husband had bought for $3,500 in 1933, using money obtained through a *tanomoshi,* a mutual financing system formed among friends. Their house, painted in salmon pink, stood out among the rows of other homes on Olive Avenue in Wahiawa. It was unusual for an issei couple, who tended to prefer subdued grays or neutral tones. This modest little home was Tatsuno's pride and joy.

Tatsuno welcomed me in her Hiroshima dialect into her cozy little kitchen. There was a long wooden table with benches on each side the length of the table. It reminded me of growing up on the plantation, where the entire family sat down together to eat supper and "talk story" about the day's events. I explained to her the reason for the tape recorder and set it in front of her on the table. At ninety-two, she was still very spry and in good health, with good vision. She did her own gardening and raised quite a number of Rhode Island Red chickens in her spacious backyard; she sold the "red eggs" (the name issei used to refer to the hens' dark brown eggs) with their rich yellow yolks to her Filipino customers, who also bought the chickens for their moist, tasty meat once the birds were no longer productive layers. I was surprised to hear that at her age she still did her own sewing as well as lots of fancy patchwork for bed coverings. In fact, the dark floral-print cotton dress she was wearing was one that she had sewn herself. A denim apron covered the dress. Her gray hair was combed back in a bun and neatly held in place with a black hairnet. Her favorite pastime was to have her children, grandchildren, and great-grandchildren all gather in her backyard for the chicken *hekka* (sukiyaki) she made on weekends.

Tatsuno still had vivid memories of her childhood and the fascinating events that took place in her early years in Hawaii, times of struggle when she had to adjust to a new life on foreign soil. She was happy to reminisce about her past as she spread out some old photos brought from Japan.

"Look at this photo taken when I was nineteen years old," she said in her Hiroshima dialect. "*Shosha ga no, kore minsai ya!* Look at my *oshare* [fancy] style. You

Tatsuno Ogawa standing in front of the home she purchased with money earned in the *tanomoshi* system. Barbara Kawakami Collection.

know what my uncle said when he saw this picture? '*Anta no kao wa hyotan ni me kuchi wo tsuketa yo na* [Your face looks like a round squash with two eyes and a mouth stuck in it]!' So I replied, '*Umaretsuki dakara shikata ga nai* [I can't help it, because I was born with this face]!'" She broke out in laughter.

Tatsuno closed her eyes as if she were trying to envision what had happened the day she left her farming village. "I had an uncle and an aunt from the *honke*, the main branch of the family, who had been very affectionate with me. They came at two o'clock in the morning to bid me goodbye. I can never forget the last words my uncle said to me, in Hiroshima dialect, '*Tatsuno, yoo mito kinsai yo, moh . . . kore ga ito ma goe dakara . . . , iki wakare dakara. Honto ni iki wakare ni nari ma shita.*' [Tatsuno, take a good last look at your home—this may well be a lifelong separation. We may never meet again.] And that was truly the last time I ever saw them." Tears were streaming down her cheeks as she solemnly recalled those words. It made me cry, too. Tatsuno remembered every word her uncle had told her seventy-two years ago in parting.

CHILDHOOD DAYS

Tatsuno Aoyama was born on November 20, 1892, to Seishiro and Tsuchi Aoyama, in Sanman-cho, Jinseki-gun, Hiroshima prefecture. When I asked about her childhood, Tatsuno's face lit up and the stories seemed to flow from her memory, clear

Tatsuno Ogawa wearing a *kasuri* kimono. She wove the fabric on her hand loom and sewed the kimono in 1912. Barbara Kawakami Collection.

and strong, in her rhythmical dialect. At times she gestured with her hands to emphasize her point. She was a born storyteller.

"I was the eldest of ten children, so from a very young age I was trained to prepare family meals while taking care of my seven brothers and two sisters, because both my parents were too busy. My mother did most of the farming and kept busy raising *ine, awa, azuki* beans, *mugi, daizu,* and whatever vegetables that grew seasonally. In the village, everyone made their own miso; it was so delicious! My father was an *okeya,* a tub maker, in partnership with his brother. During holidays, such as New Year, Father took orders from *shoyu* and sake brewers, usually with a contract for three hundred to five hundred tubs. I started school when I was eight, and as soon as I came home from school, I had to help my mother in the fields, besides helping with all the household chores. I had to work, work, work, morning and night, no time to play. I think my body was made to work." She said this with a sigh.

Tatsuno spoke fondly of her father. "My father was a gentle person, and very religious. He belonged to the Nichiren sect, memorized the prayers by heart, and knew the sutra of the Soto Shu sect. He was an intelligent man. All he had to do was listen once, and he could memorize it. He was called *man nen goyomi* [literally, remarkable memory worth 10,000 words]. That was the *shikona* [nickname] given to him, because he had such a good memory. He also knew the *kagura* [sacred Shinto music and dance] used at festivals. He knew all of them. Many young men from the village came to learn from him. He studied at the *tera goya* [temple school] in the village. In those days, the parents didn't have money to send their children to school. So, on a tray, they spread *nuka* [rice bran] and students were taught to write with a chopstick on that. That is how my father learned to write. Also, to learn calligraphy, they used thick paper and reused it many times. They did not spend any money for learning, but it was done with the strictest discipline." Tatsuno seemed very impressed with the way her father had mastered all this knowledge.

"We were so poor, I went to school only until the fourth grade. In those days, our parents could not send us beyond that grade level. At the age of fifteen, I was sent away to another village to learn *kasuri* weaving."

Tatsuno explained, "*Kasuri* weaving requires a lot of skill. I began as an apprentice and had to live in with that family to learn. The girls received room and board but no pay. I stayed there from when I was fifteen to eighteen years old. Then I began *chin-ori* [piecework] and for two years I lived with a different family. This time, I got paid 30 *sen* for *jittan* [ten rolls] of cloth that took twelve days to weave. I received *hobi* [reward] many times for being a fast weaver. I always worked hard and earned some money, from when I was eighteen to twenty years of age, by weaving cloth." I could see the pride in her face as she told her story.

YEARS OF MARRIAGE

"My grandfather suffered a stroke," Tatsuno told me. "My grandmother, being a tiny person, could not care for him. The family needed someone to help out, so I was called to take care of Grandfather. It was about this time, in 1912, that talk of marriage came up. Hiroji was my first cousin, and we grew up in the same village, but we hardly knew each other. Hiroji was leaving for Hawaii to work in the pineapple fields to help earn money to pay the family debt."

During the early Meiji era, a great number of peasants were struggling under the economic pressure from landowners; the annual yield from their land was not enough to provide a decent living for these families. Small landowning farmers, obligated to continue paying the fixed land tax, were forced into debt and eventually reduced to tenants. That was why Hiroji went to Hawaii with the desire to earn big money quickly, to help pay down his family debt.

"We got married in Japan with the marriage ritual, the *san san kudo*. We were legally married, but the marriage was not recorded in the Ogawa *koseki* in the village office, since everything was done in such haste. So when I came to Hawaii, I was categorized as a picture bride." Hiroji left for Hawaii in 1912 thinking that he would return in a few years, while Tatsuno would remain behind to take care of her grandfather.

"I stayed with my in-laws for a year and helped our grandfather until he passed away. Then I went back to my parents to bid them farewell and soon left for Hawaii. So, actually, I got married in 1912 but didn't come to Hawaii until a year later." It was difficult for Tatsuno to comprehend the distance she had to travel to come to Hawaii, never having traveled beyond the neighboring villages except for the years she worked as a live-in apprentice weaver.

Tatsuno's family in Sanman-cho, Jinseki-gun, Hiroshima-ken, Japan. Barbara Kawakami Collection.

"I left the village with one *kori* packed with a couple of sturdy, handwoven cotton kimonos, and an intricately woven *kasuri* kimono for dressy wear that I had woven myself. My parents were so poor, they couldn't afford even a plain *montsuki* with the family crest," she said sadly. She remembers trudging through several miles of rough terrain, dragging the *kori* and *shingen bukuro* (a large pouch), from her remote mountain village to catch the only train to Yokohama. "I still don't know how I did that in the dark, on a treacherous mountain road. In Yokohama, I met many picture brides bound for Hawaii. They were all lonely and full of anxiety, unsure of themselves and the future," she said.

"At that time, there was a large group of picture brides on board the ship, and that may have been another reason why I was included in the picture bride category. They were married in Japan by proxy through exchange of photos and had to wait six months for their visas to come through. In my case, my photo was taken earlier, because of the urgency of the situation." Since the olden days in Japan, the matchmaker, or *nakoodo,* would show photos of the prospective bride and groom to both sides of the families. The parents would make the final decision. In Tatsuno's case, she did not really know Hiroji, and that may have been another reason she and others felt that she was in the same category as the picture brides who came to Hawaii.

"I was so seasick during the ten-day voyage, I couldn't get up to eat anything. I envied the lady who slept next to me in steerage who didn't get seasick at all. Every morning, she got up early, put on her makeup, got dressed in a nice kimono, and went up on deck. Then she found a boyfriend, one of the passengers! I don't know what happened to her. After we left the ship, we all went our separate ways and never saw each other again."

ARRIVAL IN HAWAII

"After being seasick throughout the voyage," Tatsuno continued, "we finally arrived in the port of Honolulu on July 26, 1913, at ten o'clock in the morning, a beautiful blue, blue sky above. Because I had hardly eaten anything during the voyage and threw up whatever I ate, my legs were so *hyoro hyoro* [weak and unsteady] I could barely walk down the gangplank. At the immigration station we were served white rice and it was so delicious that even to this day I can't forget how good it tasted! I can't remember what kind of side dish they served but I ate four bowls of rice! Back in the village, we only ate *mugi meshi* [barley rice] and *awa meshi* [millet], so it was indeed a luxury!" Today, barley and millet are priced much higher than white rice.

Then she chuckled as she remembered something else that occurred on the day she arrived. "I remember Katsunuma-san, the inspector at the immigration station. I guess I was lucky compared to some picture brides, whose husbands never showed up to claim them. I was detained at the immigration station for three days, until I passed the required exams and tests. During the waiting period, I met a woman whose husband was a *nani wa bushi katari* [reciter of stories]. She traveled first-class because of his professional status. She had oranges, food, and drinks sent in every day. Her husband was staying at the Komeya Hotel. There were hotels for each prefecture where they spoke the local dialect. The Komeya Hotel was run by and for people from Hiroshima prefecture. That's where I was supposed to go. I asked this woman to deliver a message to my husband, through her husband, and that's how I got to know her. I'd never tasted a navel orange before. Oh, it was so juicy and delicious! She shared the rare treat with me, so I was very lucky," she said.

"My husband came to pick me up in a *hakku* on July 29. We went straight to the *daijingu* [Shinto shrine] in Honolulu to get married in accordance with the laws of the Territory of Hawaii. There was no time to change! I was married in the *kasuri* kimono I was wearing. The marriage ceremony was very brief. The Shinto priest gave us *omiki* [sacred sake] and waved the *gohei* [sacred cut-out paper] over our heads for good luck!"

SETTLING IN PUPUKEA HIGHLANDS, ON THE NORTH SHORE

"That night we stayed at the Komeya Hotel. The next day, we had to find a *tokoro mono* to give him a *kotozuke* [gift] sent by a friend back in the village. We found him in Moiliili, so we spent the night there, catching up on stories about family and friends. The next day we finally headed toward Pupukea by train. There was a funny incident at that time. Hiroji was not familiar with the train route since he had taken the train only once, when he came the year before. We got off at Haleiwa. From there, a Mr. Doi drove us in a *hakku* to Pupukea. That turned out to be quite a bumpy ride along the rugged coastline. It seems to have taken us forever, until it finally stopped in front of the Bailey store, where a friend was waiting for us. He said he'd waited and waited and we never showed up! Hiroji didn't know that the train went all the way to Pupukea. "*Ojya ni natta* [everything got mixed up]*! Misu teki yo* [it was a mistake] my husband made!"

I asked her how long it had taken to go to Pupukea. She replied, "I don't know, because I didn't have a watch." I should have known that even issei men often were not lucky enough to own a dollar pocket watch in those days.

Tatsuno's memory was amazing. She recalled, "When I came in 1913, I remember passing a wooden bridge, and then we went further into the mountains, to an isolated camp. It was just a wilderness of kiawe trees with a few Japanese immigrants engaged as independent pineapple growers. Mr. Taketa was the leader of the *konpan* managing two hundred acres of pineapple fields. Growing pineapple was still at its pioneering stage. Hiroji's older sister was married to Taketa-san, who also had come to Hawaii to make his fortune to pay off the family debt."

"What was your impression of the pineapple plantation camp?" I asked.

"Well," she answered, "it was a desolate-looking camp, quite a distance from the nearest town. There was a married couple living on one side, a bachelor in the middle house, and the Taketas on the other side. They gave us a small room to sleep in. We also cooked for the thirteen bachelors who worked for Taketa-san. The arrangement for food expenses was called *wari-gokku* [split expenses], which was deducted from the monthly pay."

"So you had to help with the cooking?" I asked.

"Yes. In the beginning, my sister in-law taught me to cook, and after that I was left to do all the work myself. I got up at 3:00 a.m. every day to make breakfast, hot rice cooked out of doors, miso soup, and pickles, for the thirteen men. Besides breakfast, I had to prepare their lunch in double-decker *bento* cans to eat in the fields. In the lunch can, rice was put on the lower deck, with an *ume* in the middle. We bought *ume* by the *taru* [tub]. We used *shio shake* [salt salmon] for *okazu* [side dish] because it was cheaper and tasted good. Just a little piece was put into the *bento*. In the olden days, tea was put into *shi go bin* [green glass bottles used for vinegar]. If the tea was too hot, the bottles would crack . . . and they did! Try and imagine, putting hot tea into thirteen bottles for the workmen! I always kept extra bottles handy in case the bottles cracked!" Then she went to work at 5:00 a.m.

When I asked how they obtained their food while living in such an isolated area, Tatsuno continued, "In Pupukea, we had lots of fresh fish from the sea, so we had fish almost every day. A Chinese peddler came once a week from Haleiwa. I didn't have any idea what cut of meat it was, but he sold meat for 15 cents a pound. Two pounds cost 25 cents, so I usually bought two pounds.

"To think that at that time, in 1913, after only two days of rest from my long sea voyage from Japan, I started working in the pineapple fields. Imagine! Going to work the day after I arrived in Pupukea! I did *hoe hana*, weeding, which I had done back in the village. However, for the first time I learned to strip the sharp, spiny leaves of the pineapple plant. That was rough. The razor-sharp leaves used to cut through my gloves, so I had to wrap a piece of *ahina* [denim] around my hands before I put on the gloves.

"Look at my hands—they're all scarred and gnarled from years of twisting those tough, spiny pineapple leaves. I worked ten hours a day for 65 cents. Hiroji drove the mule to till the land, and his pay was 75 cents a day for ten hours of work. It's hard to imagine we worked so hard for so little pay," she sighed sadly. "Farming back in the village was hard work, but we did it at our own pace. The long hours of strenuous, backbreaking labor under the scorching heat, and being stung by insects, made it so much harder in Hawaii."

In Pupukea, there still was no plumbing. Water had to be carried in buckets from a nearby stream. "I had to climb up the hill to get the purest water for cooking. People didn't go upstream. I first washed the rice and saved the water to clean the vegetables. That water was also used to wash the rice bowls after supper, and finally used to scrub the pots and pans. Even that water didn't go to waste," she chuckled. "From the wooden sink, a pipe was installed so the soapy water flowed outside, on the eggplants and green onions planted alongside the kitchen wall. I raised the most luscious and best-tasting eggplants that you can imagine!" Her eyes beamed with pride as she described the ingenious methods she devised while living under such primitive conditions. She further added, "To scrub the pots and pans, I used ashes from the burned kiawe firewood and the pans turned out sparkling clean! There was no such thing as Dutch cleanser in those days." Tatsuno laughed.

"The Japanese could never go without a *furo*. A large wooden tub was built and placed in the open. Rainwater was used to fill the tub. The bottom of the tub was reinforced with copper, and racks of thick wooden planks were built a few inches above to protect the bather. The water was heated using an open fire of kiawe wood, which was plentiful and produced the best charcoal. Men bathed first, then women and children. Five families shared the tub, so everyone scrubbed the soil off their bodies and rinsed well before soaking in the tub. How soothing and relaxing to soak in the steaming bath after a hard day's work," she said. When asked how it felt bathing outdoors, she replied nonchalantly, "Oh, there was hardly anybody around except a few Hawaiian hunters passing by, only during the day, and lots of rabbits running here and there."

Tatsuno could hardly believe the changes that had taken place since she arrived in 1913. "Today, it's a community of wealthy landowners living on fancy estates overlooking the cliff. They are able to enjoy the scenic beauty of the coastline, where we once traveled with difficulty by horse and buggy. There's no trace of the vast acres of pineapple fields. Not even a kiawe tree remains in the place where we once worked so hard for such cheap pay." She sighed in disbelief.

As Tatsuno gradually adapted to her new life in this isolated camp, she realized that she needed a sewing machine. In Japan, she had never seen a Western-type dress being worn in her village. The kimono was their everyday garment, and they were all sewn by hand. She bought an old hand-crank sewing machine for $2.50 from her sister-in-law. She borrowed patterns traced on old Japanese newspapers and started sewing her husband's work clothes, *tabi* (split-toe socks), and other accessories. She made many errors at first, and spent lots of time ripping apart the seams, but she never gave up. There was no electricity in Pupukea in 1913. Imagine sewing late at night under the dim light of a kerosene lamp! On rainy days when she couldn't work in the pineapple fields, she kept busy sewing *tabi* out of heavy denim. The sole of the *tabi* was several layers thick and very difficult to stitch together with the hand-crank machine. She always kept a hundred pairs of *tabi* in stock, to sell to schoolchildren who came to work in the pineapple fields during the summer. She sold them for 50 cents a pair.

"It wasn't until 1919, when my first son, Toshimi, was born, that I was finally able to buy a Singer sewing machine for $60. I also bought a large scissors for cutting fabrics, and one buttonhole scissors. Both were made in Germany. In those days when buttonhole machines were unheard of, we used the special scissors designed to cut a slit to fit the buttons. The slit was then neatly bound in blanket stitches. Thus the issei called it 'buttonhole scissors.'"

When it came to doing the laundry, she said, "the soiled clothing was taken to the nearby stream to be washed. First the red soil had to be scrubbed off and [the clothes] pounded on rocks to remove the stubborn dirt. My hands used to bleed from the cuts until I learned to do the washing properly."

Tatsuno had been accustomed to hard work and heavy responsibilities since she was young, but life in Pupukea was filled with new struggles and anxiety. She said, "The manager's wife, Hiroji's's older sister, made things very difficult for me. From the day I came as a young bride, she left all the heavy work to me and didn't try to help. She lashed out with harsh words at me, but I learned to endure. After all, she was my husband's older sister. Even on days when I went to pick up my husband's pay, she would lash out at me, saying that it wasn't a woman's place to pick up her husband's pay. She hit me a few times in anger, but I didn't say a word. Hiroji was very thin—whenever she got angry at him she used to call him *haibyo* [tuberculosis]. That really hurt. In those days, it was a stigma to be associated with tuberculosis or leprosy, and the family was ostracized if someone had that illness. Hiroji felt miserable to be called that openly. He tried to gain weight by drinking one gallon of *yomeishu* [wine] a month, but that didn't seem to help." Tatsuno shook her head as she recalled her earlier years.

RAISING A FAMILY

When Tatsuno gave birth to her second child, a daughter, Ayako, on May 4, 1914, she stayed home for thirty-three days. According to traditional belief, it was important for the new mother to rest so she would have lots of milk and take care of her newborn. Then, on the thirty-fourth day, she took her baby to work with her, to the pineapple fields. "I made a tent of denim cloth, to protect the baby from the strong tropical sun. But the salt air and the scorching heat proved too much for my baby's tender skin. It turned red and started to peel. The poor baby broke out in a fever. I still feel guilty for exposing my newborn to such a harsh environment." She cried as she told me the story. "I had to breastfeed her when she was hungry, so I had no choice. It was the most difficult thing to endure as a new mother. How often I thought of my family back in the village. They would surely have come to help me.

"One day when I went to give Ayako my breast milk at lunchtime, she wasn't there! I found her sleeping on the ground, where it was very hot. As the months went by the baby grew stronger and started crawling out of her sleeping bag into the fields. The pineapple fields were infested with centipedes, scorpions, yellow jackets, and red ants everywhere; even the adults were afraid. I cried when I saw how red and swollen she was from the insect bites.

"My husband was a good man and a good father. He never drank or smoked. He was very *oyakoko* [expressive of filial piety]. His parents in Hiroshima had a big debt, so he worked hard to help pay the debt. With our growing family, we were struggling to survive, too. I never argued about sending half our earnings to his parents in Japan." Tatsuno lowered her voice as she tried to explain why she never opposed her husband for doing this. "Well, when I was still in Japan, a young man from our village came to Hawaii to work on a plantation. He never sent money to his parents, so his father used to go around the village, begging for food. Of course, there were rumors that their son lost his money gambling. His grandmother, who was partially blind, often came begging to our house. After we gave her something, we would escort her to the neighbor next door. Because I witnessed such things, I didn't want the same thing to happen to Hiroji's parents," she said sadly.

Her face became grave as she whispered, "I can never forget that horrible day when I was busy preparing lunch for the fieldworkers." Tatsuno sighed. "You see, every day I took the children with me to work in the pineapple fields. It was lunchtime, so I came back to the house. The children were hungry, so I fed them first and they all went down to the irrigation ditch to wash their hands. Then all of a sudden, there was the sound of running footsteps and someone yelled, 'Oba-san, Oba-san, please come quick!' Akemi, my twenty-month-old daughter, had fallen into the ditch and drowned! It happened so suddenly—I couldn't believe what I heard. The kids always took care of each other and I had relied on them. I stood there pale and motionless. My body was numb and I couldn't even utter a single word. It was such a traumatic experience. After I saw my dear Akemi's lifeless body, I couldn't forgive myself for not taking better care of the little ones. Never did I miss my family in Japan more than at that instant, and oh, I so wished they were here to comfort me." Endless tears streamed down her cheeks as she recalled this tragic accident, still vivid in her memory. "My husband and I were both so busy trying so hard to help his parents pay the debt for the land that at times we neglected our children." Tatsuno wiped away her tears.

After a few minutes, she continued, "As a whole, they were all good children. When I took them to the fields, they looked out for each other. It's strange how they somehow had the intuition about whether it was going to rain or not. The daughter who drowned in the ditch at twenty months was very intuitive. She could sense when it was going to rain, because one day she urged her older sister to take her home, and right after that, there was a heavy downpour. That's when I realized that no matter how young a child is, they can sense the change of weather."

While Tatsuno was working for the Taketas, the price of pineapple dropped drastically, and the company went bankrupt. The Taketas lost everything in the venture. This happened to many issei who had invested all their savings in a business, and even borrowed money for it.

"So, after four years of trying to adjust to the difficult and demanding work conditions, we moved to Kawela, over in Kahuku, to work for Izumi-san, another independent pineapple grower. He was a nice man. He opened a new field and we stayed there for four years. Living conditions were similar to Pupukea, undeveloped land with no water pipelines. Water was limited to five gallons a day for use in the kitchen. I followed the same routines as I did in Pupukea. I was a little wiser by then," she said thoughtfully.

"A huge tank was installed to catch the rainwater. There was no stream nearby. We did our laundry when the tank was filled. When there was no rain, we took our wash to where the Boys' Reformatory School, *kara boshi* [jail for boys], in Kahuku used to be. Later, it was moved to the windward side. A Hawaiian man used to live there and he made sure there was enough water preserved in the large tank." Tatsuno's memory was amazing.

PLANTING ROOTS IN PARADISE

"We finally moved to Wahiawa, near the bridge, the entryway to Wahiawa town. The bridge was called 'airplane bridge' by locals because it rumbles like an airplane when a car passes through. There was a Filipino camp there. My husband went into the taxi business. At first he drove only locally, but later bought the route to Honolulu. There were only two issei drivers, so each took turns going to Honolulu. With Schofield Barracks nearby, Hiroji made good money in the taxi business. Of course, he couldn't read the street names in English, so Toshimi, our son, went with him and directed the way," she said.

The ties that bound the issei to the community were based on an emotional feeling of cooperativeness and also on economic self-interest. One example of ethnically based economic dependence was the *tanomoshi,* a mutual financing group. Anywhere between six and twenty friends joined in a *tanomoshi* as a means to raise money to help one of the members or to make a long-term investment. Members agreed to put up a specific amount of money each month, usually $5 or $10. The promoter or leader of the group kept a record of the account. During the early years, issei used the *tanomoshi* system to finance the cost of their nisei children's weddings, a bride's dowry, investments in business, assistance in time of illness, return trips to Japan, and so forth.

Tatsuno continued, "At this time, I started doing laundry and sewing for the bachelors. I combined the earnings and invested $200 into *tanomoshi,* putting $50 into four *tanomoshi* groups a month, a small fortune. If you took the money out of the fund early, you lost the interest earned. I made $8 on every $50 invested. I always waited until the very end and made good profit on the *tanomoshi* system. With the *tanomoshi* money, we were able to buy this house for $3,500 in 1933. That was during the Depression years, when everybody was having a hard time, and the prices on houses were very low." In spite of her limited education, Tatsuno proved to be a self-made entrepreneur and was able to provide a good education for her eight children. Her only son eventually attended a mainland college and became an optometrist. Her hard work and keen business sense paid off.

Tatsuno explained, "My son first studied agriculture at the University of Hawaii, in Honolulu, and graduated in 1941. Then he worked at Pearl Harbor as a timekeeper. When World War II broke out, my husband was forced to quit his taxi business, because he was considered an 'enemy alien.' He was banned from entering Schofield Barracks or any other military establishments. My husband asked our son to take over his business. So Toshimi resigned his job at Pearl Harbor and took over the taxi service. After the war was over, my husband was able to get his taxi license back, and Toshimi left for Chicago to study to become an optometrist. There he met a Japanese girl from Nebraska, got married, and came home. She was a nurse at Wahiawa General Hospital for six years. At that time, Tripler Army Hospital did not hire outsiders [civilians]. As soon as Tripler started hiring civilians, she applied and got hired. She was a good nurse and had the opportunity to travel to Italy and other places."

"*Okage sama de.* I feel thankful for my good health. It will be seventy-two years since I came to Hawaii, and I have never been sick, nor have I been hospitalized for illness. Even at home, I have never been in bed for more than three days from any

Hiroji and Tatsuno Ogawa standing in front of his taxi in Wahiawa. Photo courtesy of Patricia Ogawa Sakata.

kind of illness," Tatsuno said gratefully. "Only once I was sent to Kuakini Hospital for a check-up and kept for a week, but nothing was wrong with me," she said.

"Then about five years ago, while visiting my married daughter, her dog playfully jumped on me, and I fell on the concrete pavement and fractured my thigh bone. The doctor put in some kind of metal and joined it together. I was confined in the hospital for two months. I went twice to the hospital after I came home because my leg got infected. I didn't notice it until my daughter in-law, who was a nurse, walked in when I was having dinner with a teacher friend. I had filled a bowl of rice for my friend, and I was just filling my rice bowl, when she said, excitedly, 'Mom, your leg is badly infected! You have to go to the hospital!' But I told her, 'I have to *kau kau* first,' and she said, 'Never mind about eating! What if they have to amputate your leg? What are you going to do?' So she rushed me to the hospital, and I stayed for a week. Other than the accident, I have never been sick until now," she sighed gratefully.

Fifteen years after Hiroji came to Hawaii, he was finally able to return to Hiro-shima to deliver to his parents three-fourths of the amount of their debt. He came with the dream of making a large sum of money in a few years, but with his eight children and many setbacks, he could not completely pull up his roots here. He still needed $500 more to send to his parents.

Tatsuno spent forty-five years in this foreign land before she was finally able to return to Hiroshima in 1958. She took the remaining $500 for her in-laws to finish payment for the debt on the land tax.

In the late 1980s Hiroji's two nephews came from Hiroshima to see Hawaii. The Ogawa family brought them to my home for a visit. They revealed then that the hard-earned money Hiroji and Tatsuno had sacrificed so much for to send to Japan had been squandered by one of Hiroji's brothers. He had used the money to build his own luxurious home and fulfill his own selfish needs.

After moving to Olive Avenue, Tatsuno started raising a lot of chickens, about a hundred at a time. My husband, Douglas, opened his farm and feed store on Olive Avenue, where Tatsuno Ogawa was one of his favorite customers. She had a wonderful attitude about life and always displayed a happy smile. Douglas made sure to put the bags of chicken feed, one hundred pounds apiece, in a convenient and safe place for her to reach. Even for that little service, she was so appreciative. She paid in cash and never purchased anything if she didn't have the money to pay for it. It was her philosophy in life that because she had suffered from being poor, she never bought anything unless she could afford it.

Tatsuno celebrating her ninety-ninth birthday with her family. Photo courtesy of Patricia Ogawa Sakata.

I said to Tatsuno, "You are very traditional, a subservient wife, and you followed your in-laws' and your husband's wishes throughout your marriage. Today, in Japan, there is a saying that women are stronger than men. What do you think?"

She replied immediately, "That reminds me of my daughter Helen, who gives an allowance every month to her mother-in-law and me. Whenever her mother-in-law meets me, she says, 'Please say thank you to Helen!' So I tell her, 'The money is not from Helen but from your son, Kunso.' Then she says, 'No. In Hawaii woman is the boss, so even if my son wanted to give me money, if his wife said no, he could not give me, so please say thank you to Helen for me!'" She laughed.

"How sweet of Helen's mother-in-law," I said.

She agreed, "Yeah, she's very *yasashi*. My daughter is very lucky!"

Tatsuno Ogawa led a very productive life and spent many happy days in this house with the unusual salmon-colored paint. The highlight of her twilight years was "talking story" with Mrs. Murakoshi about village life in Japan. When this dear friend passed away, Tatsuno spent more time with Mrs. Hayashi, a fellow villager from Hiroshima, who lived a few doors away. They would reminisce about their childhood days, talking for hours and hours, enjoying the same stories over and over. It kept them both happy.

Tatsuno continued in a reflective manner, "When I close my eyes and think back to all the things that happened to us in the past, it makes me wonder how I had the strength, *gaman,* and courage to endure all those crises. We had no choice. The money we earned went to pay the debt for Hiroji's parents. Our children went without a lot of things because of that. Yeah, but we somehow managed to survive. When I left my village, my uncle said to me, 'Tatsuno, you're the oldest, so you come back in ten years.' But it took me forty-five years to finally return. Sadly, my parents, my uncle, aunt, and all my relatives were gone by then. I guess my uncle knew. I am ninety-two years old now. *Okage sama de,* I am still healthy. It's seventy-two years since I came here and I've never been sick in my life, except for the accident I had when the huge dog jumped on me! I still feel that I enjoyed a very productive life and was able to give my children a better education."

At the age of ninety-nine, surrounded by her family, Tatsuno Ogawa passed away on December 22, 1991, in Wahiawa. The memorial service was held six days later at Calvary Independent Church in Wahiawa. The church was overflowing with family and friends who had loved, admired, and respected her. Tatsuno's children and grandchildren wanted to do something special for her. They spliced together a three-minute video from the television special *Plantation Weddings,* produced by the local PBS station, KHET-TV, in which Tatsuno was interviewed by me about being a picture bride. The children and grandchildren all agreed that it was wonderful to hear her telling the story of her hardships during the early years in her own voice. Her grandson gave a heartwarming eulogy with excerpts taken from transcripts of our interviews, which touched everyone's heart. It was a beautiful and fulfilling celebration of the life of a very remarkable woman.

Tei Saito
STRONG AND RESILIENT LIKE THE BAMBOO

October 16, 1896–August 25, 1989
Born in Kamata-mura, Shinobu-gun, Fukushima-ken
Arrived in Hawaii September 21, 1913

My search to find issei women who had come as picture brides from Japan began with Tei Saito. I found, to my amazement, that there were many ways in which these marriages were arranged for issei men who had immigrated to Hawaii to work on the sugar and pineapple plantations. I was told that Tei Saito had an unusual story to recount: how she had unknowingly replaced an original picture bride.

At age eighty-four, Tei was spry and still quite sharp, with a wonderful sense of humor. The interview turned out to be a fascinating firsthand account of the early immigration period and of the childhood of a young girl growing up during the Meiji period (1868–1911) in Japan. It was a time when Japan was ending the feudal and military regime that had lasted seven hundred years and the country was being transformed under Western influence. The clarity of Tei's recollections, the specific details she told me, and her thoughtful, carefully chosen words took me on a vicarious journey into the past.

As Tei Saito welcomed me into her living room, I noticed an exquisitely shaped bonsai plant in one corner, a beautiful floral arrangement, and an elegant *sumi-e* brush painting on the wall. I immediately sensed that this was a woman who was very committed to traditional Japanese culture and the arts. In addition to all these "hobbies," as she modestly called them, she raised beautiful and rare anthuriums, such as the huge *obake*—the name literally means "ghost"—with flowers that transform into a variety of sizes and colors depending on the skill of the grower. One could see the loving care she gave to her beautiful garden.

Tei was brought up in the Buddhist and Shinto traditions, but through her children, she had converted to the Christian faith. She attended church regularly and studied the English language so that she could have a better understanding of the Bible. Indeed, her Sunday school ladies called her *iki jibiki,* "living dictionary," for her knowledge of the Japanese language, traditional culture, and history. If she were still alive today, I feel sure she would be honored as a living treasure.

CHILDHOOD IN FUKUSHIMA

Tei was born to Sadashichi and Mine Shida on October 16, 1896. Tei had five brothers and a sister: the brothers were Masao, Yoshichi, Toshie (who died in infancy), Mitsugi (later director of Chu-o Keiba Jyo [Central Horse Race Track] in Tokyo), and, much later, Toshi. "Sadly, Masao, my oldest brother, died just before he was to graduate from medical school. He unknowingly lived in a room previously occupied by someone who had died from tuberculosis, and he contracted the disease. Yoshichi died in Osaka of typhoid, which was traced to someone selling shaved ice. So, so sad.

"The youngest brother, Toshi, was born in August 1918. Toshi graduated from Tendai University and worked at Toshiba Company until he was called to military service. I was told that while he was running an errand with a buddy, he was gunned down by a Chinese pilot. When he died, Nobuko [Mitsugi's wife] heard the heavy footsteps of soldiers outside, but no one was there. She was convinced that the heavy footsteps were Toshi's spirit coming home to tell her that he had died." The family received word later that he had been killed on September 9, 1944. He was twenty-six years old. Toshi was the brother Tei had never seen, since he was born five years after she left for Hawaii.

Tei's mother, Mine, had inherited the family property and was the matriarch of the Shida family. "Her oldest brother, a doctor, didn't want to assume the responsibility

Tei Shida and family in Japan before she came to Hawaii. Her uncle, Dr. Tsutou Shida, is in the black suit on the left in the back row; her grandfather Reizo Shida has the long beard; Tei (sixteen years old) is on his right; her mother, Mine Shida, is seated in the left foreground. Tei Saito Collection.

of taking care of the farm. My mother was a refined and well-educated woman." Sadashichi, her husband, was a *muko-yoshi* (adopted son-in-law). He worked hard taking care of the rice paddies and vegetable garden with hired help. They were also engaged in *kaiko,* or sericulture. Much of the work involved in raising the silkworms was done by the women in the family and with the help of hired hands, Tei explained.

After World War II, the only children who remained from Mine and Sadashichi were Tei and Mitsugi. Mine's mother was an *ojosan,* a lady, and so she didn't do much work; a man was hired to work with the silkworms. Mulberry leaves were fed to the silkworms in flat baskets. When the caterpillars turned to cocoons, they were boiled and the silk thread was unwound. Tei learned that each cocoon would have one continuous strand of silk, about 600–900 meters (2,000–3,000 feet). Cocoons that had two silkworms were imperfect and were made into *mawata* (silk floss), which was used in the making of futons: the *mawata* was stretched over the cotton and kept it in place. Many times *mawata* was sent from Japan and Tei would use it when she made *zabuton* (cushions) or futons. It was amazing that after all these years, Tei still remembered every detail about raising silkworms and spinning the silk.

Tei had fond memories of her grandfather Reizo. Not only was he a learned physician, but he was also an excellent calligrapher, using brushes he made himself. With a brush about five inches in diameter he would write the banner that was placed in front of the *jinja,* the Shinto shrine. Tei would have to *suru* (rub) the *sumi* (charcoal), to make the ink rich and dark, until her arm ached. The *kannushi,* the priest of the Ishimori *jinja,* would say, "Dr. Shida is always writing on the *hata* [banner], so I will, too." However, the priest's calligraphy was not as bold as Tei's grandfather's work. Grandfather Reizo also excelled in playing the *shakuhachi,* a five-holed bamboo flute.

EARLY CHILDHOOD

Tei recalled a happy childhood, one in which she flourished without experiencing much hardship. "I was sort of a tomboy, growing up among my brothers." She was athletically inclined and even won a 300-meter race when she was fifteen years old. Tei's father took care of the rice paddies, where *unagi* (eels) thrived in the water. Eels are considered a special treat in Japan and were used to make *unagi kaba yaki,* or barbecued eel; even today it is considered a gourmet dish. She remembered how the eels could sometimes be seen slithering across their path.

Between her studies, she often helped her mother care for the silkworms, which was a time-consuming task. Tei's eyes lit up as she recalled fond memories of her childhood collecting caterpillars that were three or four inches long. The caterpillars would be kept in large flat baskets and fed on mulberry leaves. Tei would grab a long caterpillar and break its "back" in half, revealing a long, thick length of silk that would be put into vinegar to harden. The end result of this process was a fishing line.

Another incident that came to Tei's mind was a story she shared with her children, who in turn shared it with me on May 13, 1980. Her great-grandfather Denjuro was very ill with stomach cancer. Everyone was gathered in his sickroom. "I had just come home from playing with friends and as usual washed my hands in the *ike,* the pond for the *koi* fish, before going into the house. Suddenly I looked up and saw Great-grandfather walking down the road. I yelled, 'Ojichan is walking away!'

Everybody came running out and someone asked, 'Which way did he go?' There was a fork in the lane. One path went *nishi* [west] to a cousin's home, the other went *higashi* [east] to the cemetery. Great-grandfather was going east. But before I could reply, the family rushed back to his room. Ojichan had just died."

Although Tei spent much time studying, she had time for pleasure, and she recalled her favorite games: *ojyame* (tossing the bean bag), *mari tsuki* (hitting the ball), and *ito tori* (doing tricks with string using both hands). As nisei growing up on the plantations here in Hawaii, we were experts in playing these same games.

During the Meiji period in the early 1900s, *gimu kyoiku* (compulsory education) stopped at the fourth grade. The curriculum included courses in *kokugo* (Japanese language), *sanjitsu* (mathematics), *saiho* (sewing), *taiso* (physical education), *uta* or *shoka* (singing), *shushin* (morals, ethics), and *shuji* (calligraphy). As a young girl, Tei attended the Kamada *sonritsu sho gakko,* the village elementary school. The classes ran from 8:00 a.m. to 3:00 p.m., and she spent a good part of her time walking back and forth to school.

After the fourth grade, most of the boys and girls helped their parents on the farm or found work elsewhere, but Tei was determined to continue toward higher education. During this period, the educational system went through a change and compulsory education was extended to the sixth grade. The extended grades were called *jinjo sho gakko* (fifth and sixth grade) and classes were held in the next village, Senouye.

Tei took a *keibin,* or jitney train, to the next village to continue her education. While riding in the *keibin,* she had to be very careful not to sit too close to a male student or even talk to one. If someone reported such an incident, the student would be expelled from school. In Japan, boys and girls were segregated as they reached the upper grades. Boys attended the *chyu gakko,* or boys' school, and girls attended the *jyo gakko,* girls' school. The students were not allowed to date or even speak to the opposite sex in public. "Things were very strict in those days," she added. Tei felt it was faster to walk miles through the desolate countryside than to ride the *keibin.* She didn't mind. When the days were short, she left home while it was still dark and returned after dark.

Tei graduated with top honors, valedictorian of her graduating class of fifty students. Because of the change in the educational system, she actually graduated twice—once at the end of fourth grade and then again at the end of sixth grade—and was valedictorian in both of her graduating classes. Tei's goal was to go to medical school.

After the sixth grade, Tei took another test, and because of her high scores she was allowed to enroll in the Fukushima *kenritsu jyoshi koto gakko,* the girls' upper secondary school in the prefecture, without going through the seventh, eighth, and ninth grades. She graduated from high school in March 1913, at age sixteen. Tei's performance and hard work proved that she was an exceptional student. Her grandfather and uncle were also inspirational in encouraging her toward a medical career.

TURNING POINT IN LIFE

Walking home from grade school one day, Tei Shida encountered a group of young men carrying their meager belongings on their shoulders. She never forgot this incident. They were walking toward the train station to go to Yokohama. Tei over-heard the village people saying that the men were going to Hawaii to work in the sugarcane and pineapple fields. "Although I was just a little child, I felt sorry for them. I had heard that only the poor, the farmers, the uneducated were recruited by the Hawaiian government. They would be going across the ocean to a strange country, so far from Japan." As Tei watched their figures disappearing over the landscape, she wondered if they would ever be able to come back to see their parents.

Tei continued, "My maternal grandparents lived in Osaka and I was supposed to go there to fulfill their plan for my future to be a doctor. Grandfather Reizo wanted me to follow in his footsteps. An older brother, Masao, was supposed to be a doctor, but he died just before he was to graduate from medical school. A younger brother became a pharmacist and the four of us were to open a clinic."

TALES OF PARADISE

"It so happened that when my mother went to Osaka to visit my grandfather Reizo, he gave her a glowing account about the beautiful tropical islands in the Pacific. He had heard that it was truly a paradise." Tei's mother also heard about Masanari Saito, who had struck it rich and owned a pineapple plantation in Hawaii. Masanari had recently returned to his village to claim his picture bride, with the match arranged by a *nakoodo* after an exchange of photos. He was one of the few issei men who could afford to return to his village to claim his wife. However, when he arrived and met her in person, he noticed that while she was very pretty, she appeared too frail to withstand any kind of hard work in the fields, and so he changed his mind about her. This young girl happened to be Tei's cousin on her mother's side.

"After returning from Osaka," Tei continued, "my mother heard that my cousin's marriage arrangement didn't turn out. She saw Masanari Saito as a successful businessman with a promising future."

Although her mother had always had great aspirations for Tei to become a medi-cal doctor, following in the footsteps of her grandfather and uncle, she now felt that here was a great opportunity for her daughter to find true happiness. She thought that Tei, with her fine education and upbringing, could surely live like an *ohime sama*, a princess, with such a wealthy man. Thus Tei's mother decided that, rather than enduring years of study in medical school, Tei should get married to this enter-prising young man. Mine must have had a family friend act as a go-between to talk to Masanari Saito about Tei and show him her picture, for without his approval, a *miai* (matchmaking meeting) could not be arranged. Like other picture brides, Tei had her marriage planned by her mother without her consent, but with good intentions for a better life in Hawaii.

MOTHER DECIDES TEI'S FUTURE

Mine forced Tei to meet with Masanari Saito, the pineapple grower from Hawaii, though she assured Tei that it did not mean she had to marry him. Of course, Mine was quite impressed when she caught a glimpse of Masanari. He looked quite dap-per, dressed in a dark suit, a white shirt with a debonair collar, and a black bow tie. That was a rare sight in the village. Masanari seemed to have liked Tei at the

Tei Shida's graduation photo from high school as valedictorian. Tei Saito Collection.

miai. Otherwise, her mother wouldn't have sent her away to proceed with wedding plans.

"Do you know, that was the only meeting I had with Masanari Saito? After that, I was sent away to my aunt in another village, supposedly to help with her new baby, while the marriage plans were being arranged by my mother. In those days, Confucian ethics were strongly emphasized and children were taught to obey their parents," Tei said sadly. She looked for a long moment at the beautiful *obake* anthuriums.

"So after I graduated from *jyo gakko,* my mother sent me to help an aunt who had just had a baby. My aunt was married to a Shinto priest in another village. Upon my return, I was told by my mother, 'Tei, you have been promised as a bride to a successful pineapple grower in Hawaii.' I was so shocked, I could not speak! During my absence, she had arranged this marriage to this man without my knowledge or consent, and told me that I was going to Hawaii as his bride. My heart sank. I remembered those rows of men leaving for Hawaii a long time ago, and they never came back to the village again. I thought only those who didn't have much schooling were sent overseas to work. After all, I had graduated from high school, and I was supposed to attend a medical school in Osaka. I didn't want to go.

"I begged my aunt to persuade my mother not to send me to Hawaii, but my mother had already made up her mind. My mother was the matriarch of the family. Because my father was a *yoshi,* neither my father nor my grandparents had a say in my mother's decision to marry me to Masanari Saito. It was entirely my mother's decision." With great reluctance, Tei made her plans to leave home and travel to Hawaii with her husband.

"I remember the tall bamboo grove that was growing at the far end of our property. Bamboo bears flowers every hundred years or so, and then it dies." When she left her home to come to Hawaii, she noticed the flowers were in bloom, which added to her sadness. She wondered, "Was that an ill omen?"

THE WEALTHY BRIDEGROOM

Masanari Saito had come to Hawaii earlier, in 1906, as a *yobi-yose* summoned by his older brother, who was already in Naalehu, on the Big Island. While working with his brother, Masanari read in the Japanese newspaper about the thriving pineapple business on Oahu, and decided to move. First he bought three acres of land near the present location of the middle school in Wahiawa. He collected and planted the pineapple double tops, the crowns that were discarded by the Dole Company trucks. Later he sold this land and moved to Kunia, where the community gym is now. There he planted twenty-five acres of pineapples and sold the fruit to the predecessor of California Packing Corporation at a high price. Through his hard work, sweat, and determination, the plantation became quite profitable. Masanari got ambitious and wanted to move to Leilehua, the present site of the Schofield Barracks military base, where there was not even a road developed yet. Masanari, his friend and partner Mr. Tamotsu Ono, and others cleared a path several miles long that is still used by the Del Monte Corporation today. They cleared the land by day and slept in horse-drawn buggies at night. At Leilehua, Masanari became well known as a successful pineapple grower, and eventually a big company from the mainland bought the twenty-five acres.

Masanari Saito and other workers in a Wahiawa pineapple field. Tei Saito Collection.

Money from the sale of this property enabled him to finally think of settling down to have a family. So he enlisted help from a close friend to be his *nakoodo* and focused his attention on building a home on his Leilehua pineapple fields. The first thing he built was the chicken coop, in which he and Mr. Ono slept. Then he built a kitchen and used that as sleeping quarters, and finally he erected the main room. In the vast wilderness of kiawe trees, it was quite an undertaking. The men then put up a huge water tank and planted pineapple seedlings in the fields. This was all complete before Masanari returned to Japan to claim his intended picture bride. The *nakoodo* who had conducted the photo exchange with the parents of the first prospective picture bride made the arrangements for Masanari's return to Japan.

Against Tei's wishes, a big, traditional wedding was planned. Masanari Saito and Tei Shida were married in June 1913 in an elaborate ceremony in Tei's village. Tei wore the formal five-crested gray *iro tome sode montsuki* with an exquisite hand-drawn *suso-moyo* (design on the hemline) and a gold brocaded obi. The traditional marriage ceremony was conducted with the exchange of nuptial cups of sake. For the family members who gathered for the auspicious occasion, beautifully arranged dishes were served in individual *ozen,* little black lacquered trays. When asked about her wedding photo, Tei said that because she was forced into marriage, she didn't want to have a wedding photo taken. "I was fresh out of high school and barely sixteen years old then. I was still so much a child." Her wedding kimono has been on exhibit at the

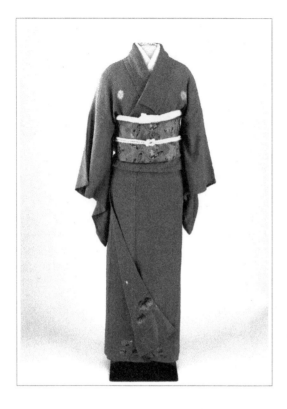

Tei Saito was dressed in her *montsuki* when she arrived in Hawaii. Photo courtesy of Smithsonian Asian Pacific American Collection.

Smithsonian's National Museum of American History, in the Asian American Heritage Collection, since April 2009.

Masanari's father had died earlier, and everyone said he had been a very nice man. But when remembering Masanari's mother, Tei's face grew sullen. "To this day, I can never forget the cruel words Masanari's mother told me before we left Japan. She said, 'If you ever leave Masanari, I will pray for your death.'" Tei's eyes got misty as she continued. "Imagine! Her daughter also told me the same thing! His mother had a *kitsui* [harsh] face, and I sensed that she was a cold and unfeeling person to even say such things to a new daughter-in-law. It would have been nice if she gave us her blessings and wished us a happy life together," she said wistfully.

VOYAGE ACROSS THE PACIFIC

Three months after the wedding, on September 13, 1913, they sailed from the port of Yokohama on the *Tenyo Maru* for Hawaii. Since Masanari could afford to travel first-class, they had a nice stateroom. "In fact, we could have gone to the dining room to have our meals, but because we were not familiar with the Western type of table etiquette in using the knife and fork, we had our meals in the room. The cabin boy served us three meals a day. We had a choice of American and Japanese dishes and the food was well prepared. We were both young and naive, not understanding the culture or the English language. We didn't take advantage of first-class travel at all and stayed in our room. Looking back, I can laugh at how inexperienced we were. I heard we were the only issei couple traveling first-class on the ship." She chuckled.

Finally, after nine days at sea, the newlywed couple arrived in the port of Honolulu on September 21, 1913. Tei was proud and happy to be wearing her elegant gray *tome sode,* much to the envy of the other picture brides who had come in steerage class, wearing their simple cotton kimonos or their handwoven *kasuri* kimonos. Because Tei's family raised silkworms, they could well afford to provide exquisite silk kimonos for their daughter's dowry.

Tei remembered that Masanari wore a Western-style business suit of dark navy blue, and a white shirt with a debonair collar, which was fashionable at that time. Having traveled first-class, they didn't have to go through a strict inspection like the other immigrants who came in steerage. Because Tei traveled by ship, she was able to bring a *kiri-dansu,* a chest of drawers made of paulownia wood, as part of her dowry. Remarkably, the *kiri-dansu* has withstood the constant rainfall and damp weather in the Wahiawa highlands and is still in perfect condition; it is carefully preserved by Tei's youngest daughter, Edith Saito Gima, as a treasured *katami,* or keepsake, from her mother.

Tei recalled a funny incident that occurred when the other immigrants were going through passport identification. A fellow villager from Fukushima prefecture in Japan was being detained. The man's passport and identification specified that he had a flat nose, but actually he had a long nose. Dr. Katsunuma, the inspector at the immigration station, asked Masanari for help. Masanari verified his identity, and the man was finally able to go on to the island of Maui.

Tei chuckled as she talked about the confusion among the picture brides. "Some of the pictures sent to the prospective bride didn't match the man's face when they met. Some men were twenty years older than their picture, for they had sent photos taken when they were much younger. Some even borrowed photos of their friends who were younger and better-looking. There were stories that some women ran away in disappointment or disgust."

Masanari and Tei stayed overnight at the Onomichi-Ya hotel, located on Beretania Street. The next day, Masanari hired a horse and buggy and took his bride to their home in Leilehua.

TEI'S NEW HOME

After traveling first-class across the Pacific Ocean for nine days, Tei was more than disillusioned when she first got a look at her new home. With tears in her eyes, she said, "Imagine, the house looked like our chicken coop back in the village!" It was indeed a shock for Tei to see the shabby dwelling in an isolated area near the mountains, a far cry from the comfortable village home she had left behind. It was a typical plantation house, crudely put together with the help of friends. For Masanari, it had been hard work to build that first home. There was another couple, Mr. and Mrs. Tamotsu Ono, and their three children, who lived in a separate house nearby. This was a rough start for this bright, well-educated new bride who had planned to be a doctor.

Until then, Tei had led a carefree and comfortable life, with everything done for her so that she would have time to pursue her studies. She had never been trained to cook or expected to do any domestic chores. It was a great adjustment for her. Mrs. Ono, who had come as a picture bride from Fukushima a few years earlier, did the cooking for the workmen, and Tei took care of her children. It was a rough and miserable experience until Tei got accustomed to doing the cooking and the heavy laundry. The first six months were the loneliest. She could never forgive her mother for forcing her into this marriage and sending her to such a harsh, desolate environment. She said, "When nightfall came, I cried and cried out of loneliness, not knowing a single soul or even a relative I could depend on or talk to." Tei never wrote a letter to her mother after she was sent to Hawaii. Tei's mother, thinking that she was living a life of luxury as the wife of a wealthy man, wondered why she never heard from her. Whenever her mother met someone who came from the islands, she asked about her daughter: had anyone seen Tei or heard about her?

Tei's husband was a very ambitious independent pineapple grower. After their marriage, he continued to lease land from the railroad company to expand his business. During the harvest season, he hired extra help to work in the fields.

"At that time, we had a small house, so we built another house, almost as large as a schoolhouse, to accommodate all the workmen," Tei said. "Masanari himself worked very hard in the fields among the workmen. At first we had only Japanese workers but gradually added Okinawan and Filipino workers. So Mrs. Ono had her hands full, cooking and washing for the workers while raising her own family."

Tei eventually learned to cook and do the laundry while helping Mrs. Ono. "I started cooking for twenty men, sometimes forty, depending on the pineapple season,

Pupukea pineapple plantation *konpan* gang, led by Masanari Saito, December 12, 1919. Fred Haley, the only Caucasian, on the left, is the landowner. Tei Saito Collection.

and I was still only barely out of my teens. I had to cook everything over an open fire. It was rough for someone who had led a good life in the village. There was a cook before me, and I had to learn fast because when our income was less, we could not pay his salary. I got up at 3:00 a.m. to do all the food preparations and make *bento* for the workers. Fortunately, water was piped into the kitchen. However, the bathhouse was up on the hill, and I had to carry water up the hill in buckets. I never had to carry water before in my life! Often, by the time I reached the top, half the water had spilled out." Tei's brow creased as she recalled the hard times. How could she even think of writing to her mother about all the misery she was experiencing?

During this time, Tei got busy raising her own family, as she started having one child after another. While living in Leilehua, she had seven children, in addition to taking over the cooking and doing the laundry for the many workers. To supplement the family's income, Tei started sewing men's work clothing: *kappa,* the treated muslin raincoats that were such a time-consuming project, along with accessories such as *ahina* (denim) *tabi* (split-toed socks), *tesashi* (hand mittens), and *kyahan* (leggings).

While the family was living in Leilehua, the children went to school in Wahiawa by train at first, until Masanari was able to purchase a car. They attended Wahiawa Elementary School, on the site where Wahiawa General Hospital is located today. During the 1920s, most of the immigrant children on the plantations were not able to go beyond the eighth grade, though some quit earlier and started working in the fields to assist with family finances.

"After my eldest daughter, Ayako, graduated from eighth grade," Tei mentioned, "she attended the newly built Leilehua High School on Wilikina Drive and was in the first group of students to graduate. After World War II, it became Schofield Elementary School, and later was renamed Wheeler Elementary School."

During the war, the military took over the Leilehua High School property, which was located near Schofield Barracks. The Department of Public Instruction, today known as the Department of Education, moved the high school campus to various locations in lower Wahiawa town. Today Leilehua High School is located on a beautiful campus in the upper Wahiawa highlands. According to Tei, it was easier for the children to commute to the high school when it was in the lower area of Wahiawa. In those days, most issei parents couldn't afford cars, so the children walked for miles to attend school.

Until Tei came to Hawaii, she had never seen or used a sewing machine. In Japan, kimonos were always hand-sewn; now, however, with her growing family, she had to learn quickly. Her newfound friends taught her how to use the sewing machine, and she figured out how to sew her children's clothing by borrowing patterns and learning by trial and error. Tei said, "Many garments were ripped apart at the seams and resewn so many times." It was a frustrating experience until she mastered the techniques of Western sewing.

Tei made good use of the fine education she had received in Japan. She observed how her husband, Masanari, carried out the business transactions necessary to buy heavy equipment from Theo. H. Davies and Company in Honolulu. Davies was one of the big companies known for importing from Europe and the mainland United States machinery that was used in the fields. Davies also provided all the plantation stores with a complete line of dry goods and other necessities.

Tei was smart enough to conduct some business of her own to economize on the family budget. Since Tei had many girls, she got Masanari to purchase dress fabric by the bolt at wholesale prices from Davies. He would purchase the entire bolt for $3, which would average out to less than 10 cents a yard. "All you need is about two yards to make a little girl's dress. Of course, my two older daughters wore identical dresses in the same print and styles to school. I was happy to be able to economize, but the two girls weren't so happy wearing identical-looking dresses to school every day. They used to come home from school and complain that because the dresses were identical, they were teased that they looked like twins."

During the early 1900s, Tei let the children wear cotton kimonos at home after school. Kimonos were easier to cut and sew because of the straight lines. They could easily be handed down from one child to another because they were wraparound garments with a loose fit. When children were little, mothers often dressed boys and girls in the same kimonos. This was a practical way of economizing with a large family.

The family lived in Leilehua until 1927, then moved temporarily to a rented house on Walker Avenue in Wahiawa. Edith, her youngest daughter, was born there.

MR. TAMOTSU ONO

Masanari and his partner Tamotsu Ono, known as Tamo-san, were the best of friends, although no one who saw them when they fought, especially when they were inebriated, would have imagined it. Both men were heavy drinkers who often drank until they were in a stupor, but they fought even when they were sober. They would taunt each other, saying things like, "The line is crooked," or "You work too slow!" However, when they fought, they both worked harder, perhaps to let off steam.

When the family moved to Kunia, they rented a house behind where the community gym is now. Land was included in the lease, and they raised *fuki*, daikon, cabbage, and pineapples. They took the produce to Waialua and Ewa in their horse and buggy. Asked whether the pineapples were *sui* (which means "sour" in Japanese), Tamo-san would answer, "Yes, sweet."

A PIONEER IN THE PINEAPPLE VENTURE

Masanari's business venture was going well because he had made a favorable arrangement with the cannery. Because it cost a lot to can pineapple, the first crop of pineapples was given as a *kei-hin* (gift or premium) to the cannery. Then if the second crop was good, the grower made a profit. This was a convenient and profitable arrangement for the pineapple growers, so everybody wanted to get into this venture. Masanari prospered and leased 50 acres more, then an additional 250 acres.

When I asked how the pineapples were sent to the cannery in Honolulu, Tei explained, "At first the pineapples would be weighed at the railroad station on a large scale before being sent. Later, as my husband increased the production, he put the pineapples on the freight train and sent them to the cannery in town, sometimes as many as ten freight cars per day. By 1915, there were too many people growing pineapples, and the canneries refused to take them. This created a grave problem for the growers, but Dole continued to buy our fruit longer because of our prior dealings."

Tei continued her vivid recollections. "Later, Masanari developed one hundred acres in the Dowsett Tract to grow pineapples. The area was close to the Nuuanu Pali, so there were often strong winds that hampered the growth of the fruit. He built a beautiful home there with a $3,000 bridge that crossed the Nuuanu Stream." Tei remembered the big sugar plantation strike in 1920 when about ninety people who had been evicted from the plantation came to live in their warehouse. After the strike was over, Tei and Masanari received only a certificate of appreciation for housing all those people!

Eventually the land in the Dowsett Tract dried out, partly because of a drought and partly because the patented paper mulch used to retain moisture for the pineapples was very costly. The family moved back to Walker Avenue in Wahiawa on the day before Christmas in 1927. Masanari lost $20,000 because of the Dowsett disaster, and they returned to Wahiawa really poor. After that, they tried raising silkworms, but that didn't work, either. Tei couldn't believe that life could be so harsh.

"We became *maruhadaka* [bankrupt] and completely lost everything in the investment. It was sad that we couldn't even bring the big house we had built to accommodate the workmen, because the land belonged to the railroad company and we were not allowed to move it from the property." To hear Tei say the word *maruhadaka* tore my heart and brought me to tears. I could imagine how devastating it was to lose everything after they had put their heart and soul into this huge undertaking. Masanari and Tei already had eight children. "The children all worked so hard before and after school to help us out," she recalled. "That was probably the most difficult period of our lives." Having no marketable skills except determination and hard work, they went into the laundry business, rising early in the morning and working until late at night, trying to make ends meet.

PLANNING A NEW START

An unusual thing happened one day while Tei was hanging up the laundry. Some sparrows perched on the clothesline close to Tei and chirped in unison, as if to tell her something. She felt a strange premonition and stood still for a while. A few days later, a letter arrived from Japan to notify Tei that her mother had passed away. "The incident of the birds chirping on the clothesline had occurred that same day." A lock of her mother's hair, still black, was enclosed in that letter from Fukushima. "My father died of a stroke. I don't remember the year, and then my mother died of a heart attack while taking care of her granddaughter Michiko, who was then about two years old. My mother suddenly felt tired while carrying Michiko. She set her down, collapsed, and died."

Tei had never quite forgiven her mother for all the hardships she had forced Tei to endure. Still, it was heartbreaking to think that she had never seen her parents again after moving to Hawaii in 1913. She was sad that she could not be at either of her parents' funerals.

Tei thought about the bamboo flowers that had been blooming the year she left her village in Fukushima. According to Mock Joya in *Things Japanese,* the ancient Chinese first noticed the bamboo's rare blossoming. Because the bamboo flowers bloom only every hundred years or so and then die, various meanings have come to be attached to the phenomenon, including the belief that something bad is going to happen.

Tei said that she worked together with her husband washing, ironing, and even chopping kiawe trees for firewood, as the laundry had to be boiled in a large can to remove the ever-present red soil from the clothes. The children all helped with the chores after school and never complained. "In spite of the hard times, we were fortunate to have such good children. They were all so obedient and well-disciplined that they never gave us any problems. The education methods were different in those days, much stricter, so the children behaved much better than today's children. In this way we got back on our feet and all our children were able to graduate from high school."

When Ayako, the eldest, graduated from Leilehua High School, she went to Chicago and worked her way through business college. Tei's second daughter, Itsuko, went to Baylor University in Texas, also working her way through college. Her third daughter, Nobuko, attended the University of Hawaii, financing her college tuition by working as a live-in maid for a Caucasian family, and later worked for Dole as a personnel manager. After high school the oldest son, Masaaki, went to work for Dole Pineapple Company, where he was a computer technician until his retirement. Tei's third son graduated from the University of Hawaii, then went to the University of Wisconsin and earned a master's degree in chemistry. All the children went to either college or business school. Tei beamed with pride, saying, "We couldn't help them at all, but each one worked their way through school." Clearly, they all had absorbed the high value Tei put on education.

WORLD WAR II: SENDING A SON TO WAR

Tei's second son, Masaharu, graduated from high school during World War II and was inducted into the armed forces within the year. At the 13th Replacement Depot in Wahiawa, the army didn't have enough men to fill the 100th Battalion Unit quota, so Masaharu was inducted into that outfit and sent to Italy in 1943. Tei could not control her tears as she recalled the first time Masaharu left home to serve his country. "He was so young, barely a year out of high school, and he was going off to war," Tei said sadly.

"In Texas, when he was in training, he had to do his own laundry for the first time. I still remember when he wrote to me, how he wished his mother could be there to do his laundry. For the first time, he must have realized *oyano on* [gratitude for parental love]," she said wistfully.

"When the war finally came to an end, the boys started coming home. There was a great celebration at Iolani Palace for the 100th Battalion and 442nd soldiers, for their outstanding heroic deeds. The families were thrilled to see their sons home again," Tei recalled. "All the anxiety of waiting for my son Masaharu was released when I saw him. Our entire family was so excited when we went to greet him at Iolani Palace. After worrying about him all these years, instead of even saying 'How are you?' to us, his first words were, 'Okaasan, did you bring *musubi* filled with *ume?*' He must have really missed his *nori* [seaweed] *musubi* while he was away. Luckily, I got up early and made *sushi* for him. We all sat down on the palace grounds to have lunch, and he was very happy to see his family again. I guess nothing tasted so good like the simple taste of rice after being away from his mother's cooking." As Tei lovingly told this story, she seemed to be crying and laughing at the same time. It was an emotional moment for her. "He was a boy, inducted right after high school, and now he returned a twenty-three-year-old man." He was finally home.

IN RETIREMENT

Masanari retired from the laundry business and worked as a custodian at the local bank to keep busy. One of his sons said he would dress in a suit when he left for work, change into his work clothes for his job, then change again into his suit at the end of the workday. Perhaps it was a way to remind himself of his successful days as an entrepreneur, or perhaps it was his pride. He passed away in 1958 at the age of seventy-six.

Tei seemed happy in her retirement, busy with her many hobbies. "I joined the anthurium club, the bonsai club, and the *ikebana* [floral arrangement] class." She studied flower arranging for twenty years under Reverend Oda and received her instructor's certificate. She is also noted for her outstanding *sumi-e* brush painting, which has been presented in many local exhibits. The aesthetic quality of her *sumi-e* has been much admired and recognized, and its skill reflects years of training in calligraphic writing.

RETURN TO JAPAN

Tei returned to Japan in 1959 for the first time since coming to Hawaii in 1913, long after World War II was over. Tei's mother and father had already passed away, and four of her brothers and her sister were gone; only one younger brother still lived in Tokyo. He was seventy-three years old then and retired, but he still retained his position as director of the horse racing track in Tokyo.

Visit to Alma Mater

"I visited my alma mater to get my *meibo* [the membership list of graduates], so I could get in touch with my old classmates. I met a former graduate of the girls' high school who was then the alumni president in charge of the *dosokai* [class reunion]. She asked me how many years it had been since I left school and was surprised when I replied forty-six years. My return to my alma mater made big news in the school paper! They gave me a copy of that paper and I still have it with me."

Tei also found out that she had been in the school's tenth graduating class. That year the students had planned a strike to protest a teacher they didn't like. "This teacher I met remembered that incident well and said, 'Imagine, that strike was discovered before it occurred.' I still remembered that. It was so embarrassing," Tei recalled.

"At that reunion, I met many of my old classmates, although some had died during World War II. I had two other very good friends and we corresponded regularly until recently. One of them still lives in Fukushima city, and she writes often. The other friend got married to someone in Chicago and had left Japan a little earlier, before I came to Hawaii. Her daughter recently wrote that her mother had gotten absentminded and was finding it difficult to write anymore. So for the first time since we graduated in 1913, I didn't send her a *nenshijo* [New Year greeting].

"When the three of us got together during that visit in 1959, my friend in Fukushima said that I hadn't changed much and that she found it easier to talk to me now. The other classmate who got married and moved to Chicago had become so Americanized in her mannerisms, her speaking, and her way of dressing that my friend felt that she was a changed person. Nevertheless, it was wonderful to discover that the bond of our friendship remained so strong through the years."

Paying Respects to the Ancestors

"One of the reasons for going home for a visit was to *ohaka mairi* [pay respects to the ancestral grave]. My sister-in-law from Tokyo accompanied me. That was one of my most delightful memories of that trip.

"The village roads are so narrow. It's easy to meet someone along the way. That was how we met an old friend who happened to be taking care of her grandchild. She invited us to stop by, but we excused ourselves and went to the cemetery. When we returned, there she was, waiting for us on the roadside. So we sat down to have tea with her on the porch. She was anxious to hear stories about Hawaii.

"As we hurriedly left there to be on our way, there were five children playing along the path. At the sight of us, they ran into the house, yelling, 'Here they come!' Probably the lady was afraid that we wouldn't stop by and had the children on the lookout for us. It seems that while we were at the cemetery and paying our respects, the news spread quickly of the rare visitor from Hawaii. That was big news! Every home we stopped by served us *monaka manju*," a tea cake with a wafer-thin crust filled with sweet beans. It was quite a treat in those days, and Tei realized the trouble all these friends had gone through to purchase the tea cakes, because there were no stores nearby. The nearest store was in town, near the *kokudo* (highway).

"One elderly woman remembered my wedding day and regretted not being able to see me in my traditional wedding attire. There was so much warmth and friendship, and life was still so simple in the village, I was overwhelmed with gratitude. That was one of my happier experiences from my visit. In a way, I felt thankful that I had been able to enjoy so much more freedom than my friends back in the village. I was able to pursue whatever hobbies or leisure activities interested me in Hawaii.

"After visiting my classmates, friends, and relatives whom I hadn't seen for forty-six years, I realized the tremendous suffering they must have endured during World War II. I felt so thankful then that I had come to Hawaii. My children have earned a good education and are Americanized in every way. They have greater opportunities and challenges in America. They were able to grow and to participate in the community as worthy citizens."

Until she was eighty-four years old, Tei still ran the household and prepared the meals for herself and her bachelor son, Masaaki. She also babysat Masaharu's twin grandsons. Whenever I visited her, she seemed so happy pushing the boys, Ben and Corey, in their twin carriage. Today, Ben and Corey Johnson are completing their doctoral programs at prestigious universities. All her grandchildren have done exceptionally well in their chosen careers.

Although she was forced against her will to get married and was sent away to a strange land, Tei had the courage and determination to help her husband during difficult times, and together they built a happy family. The children were all devoted to her, and one could see the love, respect, and admiration they had for their mother. If her life had been different, Tei would have become an outstanding doctor. However, as I reflect on Tei's strength and courage, it is clear that her *gaman* (perseverance, endurance) and her attitude of *shikata ga nai* (it's fate, it can't be helped) helped her to overcome many obstacles throughout the difficult times. Because of her wonderful guidance and teachings, all of her children were motivated to work their way through college. Today they are all very successful in their chosen fields, and one can easily see the pride and happiness Tei feels for her children, grandchildren, and great-grandchildren. Unlike most immigrant brides, Tei did not have a farming background and was one of the very few women with a fine education. Still, Tei was not afraid to work as hard as the other issei mothers, and she proved to be a great asset to her husband.

Just as the bamboo grove was dying before she left Japan, only to grow strong again, so Tei began her life anew in a strange land with the strength of a determined woman. She had the resiliency of the bamboo, which can withstand wind and rain to bear the storms of life with a can-do philosophy. Tei Saito exemplifies the true spirit of the Meiji woman.

Ushii Nakasone

SONGS OF ENDURANCE AND PERSEVERANCE

September 9, 1897–November 19, 1990
Born in Misato-mura, Nakagumi-ken, Okinawa
Arrived in Hawaii 1914

Human beings should cry when they cry.
You laugh when you laugh.
You suffer when you suffer.
The daily attitude is important.
If you *kuyo kuyo* [be fretful, mope one's life away]
you will only shorten your life.
If we learn to overcome the hardships
and maintain a happy self,
a person will live a long life.

This is Ushii Nakasone's philosophy about life. She made up her own creed. Perhaps her optimistic attitude toward life gave her the spiritual lift that sustained her during the most difficult times. Ushii Shimabukuro was eighteen years old when she came to Hawaii as the picture bride of Matsukichi Nakasone in 1914. This interview took place on August 9, 1985, at her home in Wahiawa. She was eighty-eight years old.

I met Ushii Nakasone through my husband, Douglas, who owned the Wahiawa Farm and Feed Store. She was a special customer who always bought her garden supplies from his store. She lived nearby and would walk over, and whenever she bought heavy bags of fertilizer, Douglas would deliver them for her. For the elderly, Douglas always delivered the hundred-pound bags of fertilizer and livestock feed. The elderly issei who could no longer drive a car or lift the heavy bags appreciated this extra service. Ushii was happy for the kindness and always had a sack full of delicious *satsuma imo,* or purple sweet potato, and fresh vegetables from her garden for Douglas. It was also a time to share stories with each other. Douglas found out that Ushii had come as a picture bride from Okinawa. He told me, "What she experienced throughout her long journey sounded more like a movie drama." When I contacted her, she was more than happy to grant an interview. In fact, Ushii even laughingly told me at the first interview, "Kawakami-san, you bettah watch out, or I take your *hansamu* husband, yeah!" Ushii, at the ripe old age of eighty-eight, was spry, full of life, and bursting with funny anecdotes.

That first interview was full of surprises. The Nakasone family had ten children, five boys and five girls. In order of age, they were Matsue, Edward Matsuzen, Kay Kimiko, Nancy Shigeko, Edwin Masanobu, Jeannette Kinue, Walter Masahira, Marian Masako, Edgar Masayuki, and James Shinkichi. One of her daughters, Kay, was there to provide any additional information I needed, and it turned out that Kay and I both had taken the ten-hour GED exam at McKinley High School in 1959 and earned our equivalency diplomas. As sharp as Ushii was, I was asking questions about events dating back to her childhood, and it was impossible for her to recall every detail. Kay remembered the stories that Ushii had told them during their childhood, and so she was able to fill in many of the gaps. It turned out to be a rich and meaningful two hours filled with laughter.

I could see and feel that Ushii seemed very content with her life, surrounded as she was by a loving family. Her husband, Matsukichi, had passed away on June 17, 1963. He had suffered a stroke in 1953 and lived for ten years at home. Caring for him had taken a toll on Ushii. She was now living in the cool, lush highlands of Wahiawa, in a comfortable three-bedroom home with her youngest son, Jimmy, his wife, Norma, and their three daughters. Matsukichi had made sure that whoever took care of them in their old age would have the house he bought.

Ushii's favorite pastime was tending to the garden, raising a variety of vegetables. She had *satsuma imo* growing in her garden all year round, as her family had done in Okinawa. She had a healthy suntan from working in the garden every day and wrinkles deeply etched in her skin from all the years of toiling in the hot sun. Her big eyes sparkled with delight, at times mischievous, as she reminisced about her past. Her long gray hair was combed back and held in place with a black hair net, typical of issei women. What caught my attention was the fashionable two-piece gray knit pants outfit that she was wearing, as I was used to seeing issei women in muumuus. Ushii sat on the floor, one leg stretched out and her left knee bent as she leaned comfortably against a folded chair.

Once the interview started, she was so much at ease that all I needed to do was ask a few questions. She was a wonderful storyteller, unfolding the almost forgotten stories from her childhood in an isolated village in Okinawa to her life in Hawaii. I was spellbound by her remarkable account, told amid bouts of hilarious laughter. Even her daughter Kay, who was standing by to assist, was hearing some of the exciting stories for the first time. Many issei never had the opportunity to talk about their own stories to their children.

Ushii's speech was a mixture of Okinawan, Japanese, Pidgin English, Portuguese, Chinese, and Hawaiian. She easily switched it around to fit into her story. It was a bit difficult to translate into writing and make it understandable for people who are not familiar with the local type of Pidgin, which varies among different ethnic groups.

CHILDHOOD IN OKINAWA

Ushii was born on September 9, 1897, the second-to-last child in a family of one boy and six girls. "My parents had a farm in small village of Misato, Nakagumi province, in Okinawa. It was far from the city. When I was seven years old, they give me to my uncle and aunt who had no children. I was the only one they give away. But I go back and forth to old home and was close to brother and sisters. I was not cut off from my brother and sisters, so it was *guru* [good] while growing up.

"I started school when I was seven and *sotsugyo* [graduate] at sixth grade. Back then, compulsory education was only to fourth grade. During my time, they extended it to sixth grade. Those days, few girls could even finish fourth grade because the parents badly needed the children's help on the farm, and help with housework and cooking. Only my oldest sister and younger sister get to go to sixth grade. *Oji san no okagede* [thanks to uncle], I *sotsugyo* from sixth grade."

"Did you like school?" I asked.

"Yes, I like it. I like singing best, though, and got ten points for that."

"Do you remember the song? Could you sing it for me now?"

"You want me to sing it now?" she said, and I noticed the sparkle in her eyes. Ushii proudly began singing her school song:

Watakushi domo wa Misato-son
Na mo uruwashiki Ritoo Ko no
Seito wa mai nichi sensei no
Oshie wo ukete okonai wo
Tsutsu shimi mamori yoki hito ni
Nari masho.

We, the children of Misato village
Every day, we learn from teachers
At Ritoo School . . . a beautiful name
Where we study hard and behave well,
To become a good person.

I exclaimed, "Oh, you are really good! In what grade did you learn to sing that song?"

"I think fourth grade," she recalled.

"No wonder you got a good grade in singing!"

Ushii laughed, "*Guru* grade, ha, ha, ha! *Chiri* [geography], *rekishi* [history], *sanjitsu* [arithmetic], *wa totemo hardo deshita* [those subjects were too hard for me]! Even now, *zeni no kanjo* [counting money] I'm *ton chin kan* [hopeless]!"

"Were the teachers hired from Okinawa?" I inquired.

"Yes," she responded. "One teacher was my cousin, his last name not *samu* [same] like me. It was Shimabukuro. He come from Yogi village. There's one more teacher, Agena *sensei*. He was mean, we all scared of him!"

"What kind of games did you play with your siblings or friends, between going to school and doing chores?" I asked.

"No time to play. Everybody busy, work *hardo*. But my second-oldest sister *guru* in *mari tsuki* [hitting the ball]. We play New Year's time. The ball is wound with lots of bright color thread, very pretty. My sister was *guru* in making the ball." She smiled with fondness at the memory.

"My uncle [foster father] was nice to me, but his wife like cats more. She always feed the cat *guru* food first, and give me the leftovers. I come *hagayui* [angry] and wish the cat no stay around," she said, bursting with laughter. "My youngest granddaughter living here love cats, so now I like cats a little bit, yeah. So, morning time, I feed cat; my daughter-in-law feed him evening time. As I come *makule* [Hawaiian, meaning "older"], *chikusho mo kawai rashi* [even animals can be adorable]. Yeah. Now I even think cats are *cuuto* [cute]!"

Ushii continued, "I always love to sing from young time. Yeah, until I was fifteen years old, I was *guru* singer. Back in the village, after hard day's work and all housework *pau* [finished], the young girls get together for *moasobi* [night play] when parents work nighttime. When I no show up, girlfriends used to say no fun if I no come for *moasobi*. They say my singing make them happy!

"Back in those days, no had such things as bed to sleep on. Japanese style, we all sleep on futon, spread on straw matting on floor. My uncle, aunt, and me all sleep in one room. My aunt sleep on one side of futon, my uncle on other end. I sleep in middle. Lots of times, after I go sleep, my girlfriends come and wake me up. My aunty say, 'Our *kamigwa* [also *kamigawa,* an affectionate term used for girls and close friends] sleeping, so you girls go and play.' Of course, when I hear the voices calling in the dark, '*Kamigwa! Kamigwa!*' I jump out of futon and ran to them! I love to sing so the girls like that."

DOING ROAD WORK

"By the time I *sotsugyo* from sixth grade, there was road work going on in village, so I began work for them," she told me.

"What kind of work clothing did you wear for road work?" I asked. "You mentioned wearing a kimono to work. Did you weave your own cloth?"

Ushii answered, "No, I never did. My aunt used to weave the plain cloth, not the fancy kind with *dezainu* [design]." Ushii was referring to the intricate *kasuri,* the splashed-pattern weave that Okinawa is famous for. The plain cloth was for summer because it is very hot in Okinawa. "You know about the banana plant? The *ito* fiber taken from outer layer of the bark of plant. The banana plantain in Okinawa is shorter, and no have banana fruit like tall banana plants we have in Hawaii. Many picture brides who come Hawaii wear kimono made of *bashofu*. They weave cloth themselves. Everybody wear kimono made of *bashofu* summertime in Okinawa. It keep you cool, *guru* feeling, easy to take care," Ushii added. "You just wash and wear.

"So for road work, I wear kimono length this short," she said, pointing high up the ankles, "then tie narrow *obi* around waist. Then I tie *tenugui* [towel] around my head so hair no catch too much dust. When we fill dirt into *torakku* [truck], large crate box with wheels, we no wear *papale* [Hawaiian for "hat"]. While pushing the *torakku,* then we wear *papale* and sang songs, so kind of fun," Ushii recalled happily.

"You know, we had to fill up big *galo* [gallon] bucket with dirt and carry on our head. The village women and young girls know how to carry *omotai* [heavy] things on the head and learn to balance it well. We had two *naichi* [Japanese from the main islands of Japan] who was our boss. They stand by and tell us what to do.

"When road work *pau,* we work on family farm. We take turn and help each other on farm. We no can pay for workers. When we really young, the girls work hard in the sugarcane field, clean roots of cane plants and pull weeds. Work on farm take all our time till we ready to marry."

"How much did you get paid then?" I inquired.

"Oh . . . only *chi bitto* [very little]! When we get pay, our parents so happy and would say, 'Oh, *mo kete kita ka* [you earned some money]?' We gave them every bit!

"We work hard during day, but we go out to play at night, *moasobi,* I say before. The boys and girls used to get together while parents *yo nabe* [work all night]. Of course, the girls older now and want to look nice for the boys. Girls would go to *mizu tamari* [water well] to wash faces, because they going see the boys. Even to buy one skin soap was *hardo,* but we bought one soap to scrub our faces so we can look pretty. Other than that, we never use makeup. Then, we went out to play and sing songs. Many boys came out from our village and also from nearby village of Toguchi. The boys and girls come by roadside and we sing with lively *sanshin* music. Living in small village like ours, no more any kind thing to do."

Looking at her photo, I said to Ushii, "You were very pretty. You must have had a boyfriend, then?"

She laughed, "Yeah, I was beautiful. Everybody is *beppin* [pretty] when you young!"

PICTURE BRIDE MARRIAGE

"One day when I was eighteen years old, something happen. We had surprise guest. This couple had son, Matsukichi. He work on sugar plantation in Hawaii and they come talk about marriage between their son and me, exchanging pictures with each other. That was when I first saw my husband's picture. I thought he look very *hansamu,* so I said, 'Okay.' Just like that!

"Ever since I was young girl, I always dream of going Hawaii. When people come back Okinawa I hear many *guru* stories about island paradise where people go make big money. They come show us pictures they bring back from Hawaii. I think, how pretty the Okinawan girls look, dress in beautiful kimono, wearing them the way *naichi* girls wear them. In the village, the Okinawan girls wear the kimono short, few inches up the ankles, their obi sash tied and come down the front like a courtesan." For this reason, many picture brides from Okinawa who were on the same ship as the picture brides from mainland Japan were ridiculed by the *naichi* brides. Glancing at the photos sent from Hawaii, Ushii thought the girls from her village appeared more *oshare* (stylish) and seemed to enjoy life in Hawaii. "How I want to live in wonderful place," she thought. "So right away, I say yes to marry and go to Hawaii.

"At that time, my mother was very worried because I give fast answer. She asked me, 'Ushii, you sure you want to marry this man, eleven years older than you? If you go to Hawaii and marry this man, you no can get divorce no matter how hard time you might have. All your sisters, marry only once, live with one husband, you know.

Once you marry, no can get divorce.' These words stay with me all my life. Well, I fall in love with my husband's picture, so my mind made up. And maybe because I really want to go to this paradise island I dream so much about.

"I remember long time ago seeing Matsukichi in village first time he left Okinawa to go Hawaii. I was too young to notice boys or even think about boyfriends. But I know he did have a girlfriend in the village, long time ago.

"Things start happening fast after we give each other the picture and I say yes to marry him. I start getting ready for my trip. Then the unexpected happened. Matsukichi's stepmother get Spanish flu and die, so he hurry home to Okinawa.

"This was first time I meet him face-to-face, when he came to our house to see me. I thought his face was *handsamu,* just like his picture, but his feet so small, I get little turned off," she laughed. "But since I promise his parents, no can do anything, so I make up mind and go ahead with wedding.

"One day my mother told me, 'Ushii, today is your wedding day.' So I wear my kimono, more dressy than the one I usually wear at home. A *chitto bitto* better than the ones I wear to the fields for work. I comb the *kampu* [Okinawan hairdo] with a fancy *jifua* [hairpin]."

What was supposed to have been a photo exchange marriage in absentia, with the groom in Hawaii and bride in Okinawa, turned out to be a small, informal wedding. About thirty relatives and friends attended. Because of Matsukichi's unexpected return home, both sets of parents decided to rush the wedding. They were worried because Matsukichi already was twenty-nine years old. If he stayed too long in Okinawa, he would be recruited into military service. There was lots of feasting and celebrating with *awamori,* or sake.

"Wedding food in Okinawa not same as here, very simple," she told me. "There was lots of good food and fun with *awamori*. Food for wedding was *nishime,* pork, tofu, *kamaboko* [steamed fish cake], and that's about it. Soon after the party *pau,* my husband left for Hawaii.

"I cannot go to Hawaii with Matsukichi, because my father-in-law was alone by himself and nobody to help him on the farm. Husband's half sister want to find him wife, but he say over and over, 'I'm too old to marry one more time, and I no care to marry.' He keep on worrying about me and keep tell me go to husband so we can start a family. 'No worry, I can stay by myself,' he tell me. Husband's half sister live in another village, that make it hard to let him stay by himself. But father-in-law keep tell me over and over, 'You go Hawaii.' So I finally joined my husband in Hawaii, three months later.

"Few months after I live in new house in Hawaii, we get letter from father-in-law. He wrote that he planted many things in fields but nobody to help take care and bring them into house. 'It was too much for me so I finally get myself a wife,' he wrote. Ah, we were so happy to hear that."

Ushii took out a photo. "See, this father-in-law's second wife. She is beautiful. When he was young, my father-in-law was in love with husband real mother and want to marry her but his parents opposed, even when she *hapai* [pregnant]. So when Matsukichi was born, his father and stepmother took him as a *yoshi*. In the meantime, his birth mother married someone else and had several children."

JOURNEY TO HAWAII

Ushii recalled her departure from her village. "I was eighteen years old when I leave Misato village. That was 1914, all my friends and family come say goodbye. I can hear my friends yelling, '*Kamigwa! Kamigwa!* You take care and stay well! When you get to Hawaii, you be sure to write us right away so we no worry!'

"My eyes get tears when I see them wave goodbye with *tenugui* and their hands, and they keep calling, '*Kamigwa! Kamigwa!*' My mother keep telling me, 'Be *guru girlu,* save money, so you can come home as soon as you can.' My father die before, so it was only mother, sisters, brother, uncles, and aunts. Our ship went to Kobe, and we meet large group of picture brides on the *Shinyo Maru.* I wear the stripe silk kimono that I wear in family picture. Some girls too seasick, but I was lucky. I never get seasick. I did not feel lonely at all, because there was many girlfriends who come from the same village. I cannot wait to come to Hawaii. I know my husband waiting for me."

ARRIVAL IN PARADISE

Ushii had a vague memory of her arrival in Honolulu. "After I come to immigration station, someone send in some food for me, so I know my husband come for me. I feel so happy! I think I take my physical exam and written test, but I cannot remember, it was long time ago.

"The first words my husband greeting with me was, 'Oh, you *kita ka* [came]?' That's all. Not like today young people, no *lavu lavu* [hugs and kisses], you know. If our meeting was more romantic, then I would have something exciting to tell you. Too bad!" She burst out laughing.

ADJUSTING TO PLANTATION LIFE

"From immigration place, husband call *hakku* and we went to train station. We took train and headed straight to Mokuleia, near Waialua, one drab and lonely pineapple town. When I come in 1914, no more job for women, so I stay home for a while. Then one day my husband come home and say that Waianae sugar plantation give women work. He hear that women can take their babies to work. So we decide to move to Waianae. It must have been 1915.

"At Waianae sugar plantation, we had big surprise. They have big *imo-mushi* [potato worms] in cane fields. Ugh! I hate that so much. They come down with rainwater from mountains into cane fields where I *hanawai* [Hawaiian for "water the fields"]. Times like that, I used to wonder why I ever come to Hawaii. Of course, husband help me cut grass. I think many times about the picture I used to see back in Okinawa, how the issei work so hard on plantation, but it more bad than I think. How I want to go back to Okinawa . . . but my mother's words rang in my ears: 'Once you marry, you can never come back.'

"I work with husband for two planting seasons, even when I was *hapai*. After first baby come, I stay home for one year. But I still work. I do laundry for three single men and make *bento* for them to take to work. At least I make extra money." She sighed when she recalled the hardships back then.

PREGNANCY AND CHILDBEARING

Ushii continued, "In them days in 1914, nobody ever hear of how no get *hapai* [i.e., birth control]. We keep getting one baby after another. We no see the doctor [for prenatal care] even when months go by. I had no problem while being *hapai,* so every day I go work until last minute. To *mukaeru* [give birth], midwife come to help. My oldest daughter, Matsue, was born when I was twenty years old. That was after I work in sugarcane field two years.

"Those days, no more babysitter. Everybody have hard time. So when first baby one year old, I take her to cane field with me. I make tent with *ahina* cloth to keep hot sun off baby . . . make me feel real bad, but all mamas have to do that. I no can *oppa* baby and work, so I put baby on straw mat, and when baby cry, I go see if baby hungry or make *shishi*. We make the *mutsu* [diaper] from the old cotton kimono. It was soft for baby, you know. Feeding time, I open my *chichi* [breast], the nipple full of dust, so I wipe it with my saliva before I give my milk to baby. The cane field very dusty place, really sad for baby . . . I no can say any more, too much pain." Tears filled her eyes as she recalled those early days.

"I work ten hours in hot sun with one eye on baby, then I fold the tent and all my things and go home. For me, no time for rest. When I go home, I make fire for *furo* and make *yuhan* [dinner]. I let baby sleep on porch when I cook in kitchen. When husband come home, he say, 'You let baby sleep out here, what you going do if bird come and bite her?' He scold me like that. Yeah, mother with baby have hard time. We work hard all day with husband, get up early, make *asa gohan* [breakfast], make *bento* for both of us, work, then we go home, I hurry make fire for *furo* so husband can soak in hot tub, relax. Meantime, I make *yuhan,* then clean up dishes and take care of baby. I prepare rice for next day to make lunch for husband and myself. Papa tired. He go to sleep. But Mama stay up all night when baby cry. Still, next morning when baby cry, I get up early and go work with Papa and do same kind work. Yeah, issei *wahine* all work *hardo*."

ECONOMIC STRATEGIES: DECISION TO MOVE

"Papa not happy making so little money, so from Waianae, we move to Kaneohe. Those days, buying and selling *pinapuru* [pineapple] was *guru* business. One day, my husband go see his cousin off to Okinawa. He not come home for three days, so I worry, worry! Then one friend say my husband go *pinapuru* place, so I stop worry. My husband invest in some *pinapuru* land. This time, we work harder, but by time *pinapuru* ready for market, the price go down, cannot make money. So, we move again to another place!

"This time, again, husband and me, work, work, work. We cut trees and make mountain land *guru* to plant *pinapuru*. But no can make money again. Now we so poor, no money to buy food. This time in Kaneohe, such hard time, Papa go from one relative to another, one friend to another to try and *kariru* [borrow] money. Oh, I suffer plenty heartache by myself because husband neva stay home. One time was really sad, I had only one last bunch of *somen* noodle to feed children. I use only half a bunch, and make soup to stretch the meal, until Papa can borrow some money and come home.

"Sometimes I don't have no kerosene when Papa gone for days, not knowing where he was. I used to bring empty ketchup bottle to *kariru* some kerosene from couple with no children who live down the road. I ask if I can *kariru* some kerosene till husband come home. I have to have kerosene to start firewood and light lamp at night. No more electricity in Kaneohe yet. I was *hapai* with second girl when we move again, this time, to Heeia.

"My daughters Kay and Nancy was born in Heeia. Husband start one more *pinapuru shigoto* [business] and that neva go well, too. This time, we move to Moiliili in Honolulu. Ohh . . . really hard time . . . no money. This time, husband *guru* friend give us money. We raised hogs and make *chitto* money. We give back the money we *kariru* to friend. Even now, I no can forget his kindness. That man is gone now and bury in Okinawa, so whenever I go back to Okinawa, I offer *senko* [a stick of incense] and clasp my hands in prayer at his grave . . . to say thank you from my heart. In olden days, everybody help each other.

"In Moiliili, there was one nice *kanaka* [Hawaiian] man, where we no have to pay to stay in house. We live there, and I work in kitchen, my husband go here and there and do yard work. He very rich Hawaiian man, let me keep my children while I busy work in kitchen. Not too long afterward, we move again.

"One thing happen after another. Maybe I should not say this, but Papa and his friend start to make *shochu* [wine]. They get caught by police, and had to give that up too. After that, he do yard boy job. Then, plenty people make *okolehao* [alcoholic beverage] out of root of ti leaf plant. Husband dig hole under kitchen floor, to bury the stuff. He did that by himself.

"Next we move to Wahiawa and Papa work as strawberry farmer. After so many times, try hard to make living on our own, we move out to Poamoho, near Wahiawa town. Over there I work in *pinapuru batake* [pineapple fields]. I take the *poki* [sharp, poking] leaves off the pineapple top. *Hardo* job, hands get cut and bruised, but all the *wahines* keep working. Papa work as hard, planting, weeding, and peeling off leaves. We struggled four more years at Poamoho. By then, we have four more children! Four or five years later, Papa go back to strawberry farm. He think he can make better money this time." Ushii sighed again, recalling the bad times.

FROM FIELDWORKER TO DOMESTIC WORKER

"I have to tell you a little about my *hokoo* job. I used to wash clothes for the *pinapuru* boss. I no sure if they pay me or not, maybe I get some money. Husband no more work again, so I worry, maybe suffer like the last time when he lose everything when he try grow *pinapuru*. So this time, I look for housemaid job. One day, army lieutenant and his wife come ask me to work for them. I say, 'I no can speak *haole*.' They say no worry, they teach me. Then I say, 'I have to take my little girl to work too' and the Mrs. say okay to bring her.

"So I start work for them, but I no understand what they say. I get so mad at myself! So I buy me one tablet and pen and write down every word they say. When the Mrs. hold the broom and say 'broom,' I write down *burumu* in Japanese so I can remember. Still more problems when I try to cook. I no can read the English words on the cans. The lieutenant come in and show me the can, point to the picture, and tell me what's inside. Then I write down in Japanese again. That's how I learn my English.

"I was live-in maid, and had own room. But my girl no like stay with me. She stay only three days with me and like go home. She lonely and miss her sisters and brothers. So I stay by myself and work. Every night, I think about my little girl. I cry and cry until my pillow all wet." Tears streamed down her cheeks as she recalled those heartbreaking experiences. Those days were very hard with no family or relatives to help. It was the language barrier that was the most difficult for her; it must have been just as difficult and frustrating for the *haole* bosses, but most seemed to have lots of patience and were kind and understanding to these issei women.

"My eldest daughter, Matsue, really suffer, too. . . . When she was fifth grade, she only went halfway, I let her quit school because I work as live-in maid and I let her take care her younger brothers and sisters. One day the police come and say she too young, she have to go back school. So she went to sixth grade. Halfway I got her to quit again. The policeman never come after that so I let her watch all the young children. She did the cooking and laundry, too. She never complain, not once. Oh, it broke my heart to let her do that." Tears flowed as her voice broke. One could feel the pain she had to endure. I *morainaki* (cried along with her). "When the youngest one no like stay with me at the *haole* house, I cry myself to sleep every night. I miss my children so much. Even now, I feel the terrible pain in my heart when I think about my children. Somehow I stay as live-in maid until the lieutenant go to mainland. I lucky they really nice people."

Ushii Nakasone when she worked as a domestic for a military family at the Schofield Barracks. Ushii managed to have her two youngest children live with her in the maid's quarters. Ushii Nakasone Collection.

"The next place I work for was captain house. Again I ask if I can keep child with me. They say all right. While I work for them, I was *hapai* [pregnant] with numba six child. By then, I can speak some English," she chuckled. "Because I keep baby with me, I work for them until last minute. That night, I hurry make dinner, wash all the dishes, and then go home to my family.

"Before I go home, boss ask me when I can come back to work. So I say one *monsu* [month]. That night, baby born. I work until nine months! The numba six baby was few months old when I let my oldest girl take care of her and the younger ones, so I can go back work for the captain's family. When I start work for them, they pay me $40 a month. In 1920, this was two times what women working in fieldwork get, so it was *guru*. I clean the house, cook, wash clothes, and iron. I was *guru cooku*." She smiled with pride. "Because I *oppa* my girl when I work for them, I can keep her with me when I go back to work. There was small yard outside the kitchen. I put baby in playpen. Then I do my work. The boss's mama live with them. Every time baby cry, she give me the eye. Oh . . . times like that, I suffer inside, every time she look at me like that. It break my heart, even now, when I think about it." Ushii grew very silent and sad.

"The next place I work for was colonel and his wife. They had no children. When I got *hapai* with numba seven baby, he feel sorry and say, 'Seven children enough!' He like teach me to stop, no make baby, but I no understand what he say. No Japanese country women talk about birth control. The colonel was very nice man, *guru* to my little girl, and he took her around with him. My girl very happy riding in car, seeing places her siblings never got to see." Ushii smiled as she thought about the pleasant times working as a maid.

Matsukichi and Ushii Nakasone with their family. Ushii Nakasone Collection.

Matsue and Takeo Shimabukuro on their
wedding day, 1935. Photo courtesy of
Takeo and Matsue Shimabukuro.

   "I work as maid for twenty years to help Papa pay back money he borrowed and
to make money for family. The most hard time I had was when I work as live-in
maid and let my oldest daughter take care of younger children. She never *monku*
[complain], but she suffer too. She no can go school with her friends. That time,
Papa worked for the *pinapuru* company, Camp Nine. He *kariru* money from plenty
people. Too much *tanomoshi* to keep up. His pay not enough to pay all the people, so
I had to take the live-in maid job.
   "My oldest daughter even wash clothes for single man. If not for her, I no can
work outside. When she was eighteen years old, one relative like matchmake with
friend's son, who was nineteen. She big help to me all these years and I want her to
be happy so I give her away. I bought her a beautiful *montsuki, kuro tome sode* with
five crests. I put aside from *tanomoshi* money. She was a beautiful bride dressed in
traditional formal attire. She live with in-laws, but mother-in-law die young. Her
husband had seven brothers and sisters. They all very young, so she was like mother
to them. She clean the house, cook, wash clothes, sew their clothes, and take care of
father-in-law. Poor thing, I feel sorry for her. She sacrifice so much from young time,
and even after she marry, she still have to suffer. Today, her husband's brothers and
sisters all so good to her, you know, because she take good care of them. They treat
her like real mother. The children always bring presents for her birthday, Mother's
Day and Christmas time. Her husband good to her, too. After my oldest daughter
marry, my second-oldest daughter, Kay Kimiko, help me, too. My children, all good

children, always help, no grumble, and work hard. I feel so *arigatai* [very grateful]. Thanks to my children, I can *naga iki* [enjoy this long life]!"

BACK TO WAIANAE

Around 1932, Matsukichi returned to Waianae to work on the sugar plantation. There was no piped water in the house, and the children remembered walking a long distance to get water in a pail. They also remembered picking kiawe beans that they sold to supplement the family income. Matsue recalled, "Father used to make illegal rice sake, and once he was apprehended by the authorities."

RAISING HOGS

"In 1936, when I was two months *hapai* with numba nine child," Ushii told me, "Papa find *guru* job at the *pinapuru* place, the Pineapple Experimental Station, where they try grow sweet and different kind *pinapuru* and strawberry. We move back to Wahiawa and found a home where Leilehua High School is now.

"Papa started to raise pigs on the side, so I take care of hogs for first time. When I work as maid at Schofield Barracks, I always wear nice cotton dress that I make myself, *tabi,* and slippas. After working in clean *haole* house for twenty years, uhhh . . . no can stand working in dirty pigpen, you know, so I buy boots to wear in pigpen. About then, World War II end in Italy."

As the piggery grew, it became the family's full-time occupation. In those days, the pig slop from Schofield Barracks was delivered to the farm by commercial vendors. Everyone in the family had to help with the chores. They cut *hono hono* grass to add to the slop, tended the wood fire to cook the slop, fed the pigs, cleaned the pigpen, and more. "Just before my numba three boy *pau* high school, Papa buy small pickup truck. My boy used to pick up *buta kau kau* [pig slop] from homes and restaurants, early in morning before go to English school. After son graduate from high school, he supposed to go army, but because he say he farmer, he no have to go army. My numba three boy help right through with taking care of hogs. If not for him, we cannot keep piggery."

In 1947, the Department of Education decided to build a new campus for Leilehua High School and Intermediate School. All the farmers living in this area were evicted. Matsukichi bought property on Makaweo Avenue and built their home.

"We lease land in Waipio which belong to military during World War II. Papa stay there by himself and watch animals. He give hogs food two times a day. Papa clean the hogs, clean place they live, and cook the *buta kau kau.* I do housework. My son do outside work and take care hogs, so he busy, too. Everyone in family help and do work at home.

"Them days, Papa love to drink, so when he cook the slop, he used to drink. He buy Japanese *sake* from Toda store in Waipio and hide the drink in field. You can imagine, by *pau hana* time, he too drunk! Oh, my boy, he get so angry, he throw the empty cans around. No, no, he no aim at his father, but that was *ate ko suri* [insinuating dislike] at Papa being so drunk.

"I used to tell Papa, 'Oto-san, the heat so bad daytime, the sake going burn your insides, *abunai* [dangerous].' But Oto-san love sake, and no can quit! He was drunk all the time, no can help, you know. But one thing I tell you, no matter how much he drank, no matter how sound sleep he was, when the *buta kai* [hog buyer] come by, he just jump up and go into action! Those days he cook the *buta kau kau,* and he get up early to cut the *hono hono* grass. Oto-san was very hard worker. He was *shimbo nin* [frugal man]. I never know how much money he had, because he never give me money. Only my children give me money from what they make. If I ask Papa for money, he may give, but I afraid to ask. I made *guru* money but that we pay husband's debt he owe to friends. The rest, all go for food. In those days, women pitiful, you know, they no can keep money the way young people today keep checkbook, no such thing. All we know was to work, work. Only thing we know was to *shinbo* [endure]."

Matsukichi suffered a stroke in 1953. Ushii cared for him with the help of her son Masahiro. He passed away ten years later, on June 17, 1963, at the age of seventy-seven. His children remembered him as a stern and strict father. James, the youngest son who took care of both parents until they passed away, reflected fondly, "He was a hard worker who was determined to provide the best for his family. He loved to drink, wine in particular. He would sing and dance at parties after having a few. He was smart. Without a pencil and paper, he could compute in his head how much a certain number of pigs, weighing so many pounds, priced at so many cents a pound, was worth. This was truly amazing for a man with only an elementary education."

RELIGION

Ushii leaned back against the sofa and closed her eyes. "Ahh . . . seem like *yume* [dream], such a long time ago, all we did was work, work, work. I cannot even believe I was strong enough to go through all that hard time. Now, *intai shite* [in retirement], I enjoy getting together with friends, especially on weekends when we go to Wahiawa Hongwanji temple together. Ever since we move to Wahiawa, we became active members. The church is part of my life. I go to *fujinkai* [women's association] meeting. What I learn from church sermons I can take to the next world. I no care to learn songs, but stories I like to hear. I can learn from other people. I go to church with Mrs. Kiyan. She from Okinawa, too. She go every Sunday for *oasaji* [morning service] at 7:00 a.m. She pass my house so they pick me up on the way. Tonight is Ohigan [equinoctial week, a time to follow the Buddhist path and attain enlightenment], so I go to church. But Mrs. Kiyan not going, so I ask my son and daughter-in-law to take me. I look forward to attend the temple services. Whenever the church has special activities, *fujinkai* ladies help with cooking and cleaning. The issei women always clean the temple and lavatory. Gradually, the young *fujinkai* members will take over." Ushii's face lit up as she talked about her church activities and friends.

RETIREMENT AND REFLECTION

"All my children come visit me all the time. Even my son Edwin Masanobu, in Minnesota, he come home often. I have twenty-seven grandchildren and fifteen great-grandchildren. I hope I can live till great-great-grandchildren come! All my children have love marriage. I think that better than matchmake kind like us." She chuckled.

"At night, I watch TV in bedroom. I no like Japanese show, because all in series and you have to watch all the time. I watch *haole* kind. I no understand English too well but I watch faces of actors, hands too. I try to think what they say, make up my own word, and enjoy. I was born like this. When I stay with young people, I try to speak English even if I no can speak *guru* English. If I make mistake, I ask them, 'What you say?' I hate to *kuyo kuyo* [be fretful]. I cannot stand that.

"I like going football game with my daughter and son-in-law James Iha, principal at Leilehua High School, when the season come around. I never miss one game. I go with them everywhere Leilehua High School play. They no ask me anymore if I want to go, they just come and pick me up.

"Not too long ago, at *kojukai* [retiree] party, Mr. Taira look at me and say, 'Nakasone *oba-san* really spry, she never miss one football game for Leilehua High School!' Everybody burst out in laughter! Me, the only issei woman in Wahiawa who go to football game.

"My younger son Jimmy and daughter-in-law, grandchildren all live with me now. Husband die few years ago from stroke. When he was well, he make clear that whoever take care of us in old age get the house and lot. My son know this. Daughter-in-law work in office all day, but she do most of the housework and cooking. When daughter-in-law want to cook something special, she cook. Son love to cook, so he cook all the time, too. I no have to worry anything about food. I not *guru* cook. During younger days, I only feed my children *udon* or *somen*. I still do plenty work in garden, but I never *monku* that I tired. Daughter-in-law feel bad if I *monku* all the time. When I *pau* work in garden, I come in house, take hot *botcha* [bath], and rest on couch. I getting old so my back hurt sometime. I no can wait to eat dinner with them.

"I always feel *kansha* [grateful] to them and say, 'Thank you, thank you.' We have to show appreciation. Garden is my place, and when I *pau* work and come in the house, dinner is all ready. When some food get cold, they heat it again for me. It is really *gokuraku* [paradise] for me. Every night, I eat my dinner in thankfulness.

"So anything they serve, I tell them how *oishi* [delicious] it is, because it really tastes *guru*. Should be that way. Not like my young time days, when I come as young bride of eighteen and marry someone my parents want. My son and daughter-in-law not the same. Theirs is love marriage. They no do things like me, because they born not same time like me. If I try to let my daughter-in-law do things like when I was young bride, I make big mistake. Our young time days, we live the way we had to, we have to please our in-laws, but now it is young people time, so we have to follow daughter-in-law way. That how I feel. Whether it's about food or anything to do with decoration for house, young people not think same like us, time change, so I have to change, too. Yeah, so I say, 'Okay, okay' to everything. Daughter-in-law, she very young. She teach me many new things and that is the right way. When she tell me how she does something, I think about it quietly, and think how right she is."

"How do you feel about your life now?"

"All the suffering I had my young time days is nothing. Now when I think back, I feel that all the *kuro* [troubles, hardship] we endured taught us a lot of *daiji na koto* [important things] in life. Now I am happy and free to do what I like to do. No more worry, just work in garden. Now *anshin* [found peace of mind]."

"Are you glad you came to Hawaii?" I asked.

Ushii replied without hesitation, "Yeah, yeah. Hawaii *kite yokkata!*"

"Can you say that in English?" I inquired.

"I so happy now. Before, young time days, no understand English but now little bit I understand, very, very *guru*. I so glad I come Hawaii, very, very happy."

Ushii was always proud of her children. Even if her first three children did not graduate from high school, they all became outstanding members of their community. Matsue Nakasone Shimabukuro, born in 1915, did not attend high school. She finished fifth grade and then quit because she had to take care of her siblings. She married Takeo Shimabukuro at a young age and, after her mother-in-law's untimely death, raised a fine family. She is an active member of Aiea Hongwanji Mission. Edward Matsuzen Nakasone, born in 1918, did not attend high school. He died of tuberculosis at Leahi Hospital in 1941. Kay Kimiko Nakasone, born in 1920, did not attend high school, but earned her GED diploma later, as an adult. She was the cafeteria manager at Kunia School when she retired. Nancy Shigeko Blalock, born in 1922, graduated from Leilehua High School and got her bachelor's in education from the University of Denver. She retired as a teacher with the Department of Education. Edwin Masanobu Nakasone was born in 1927. He graduated from Leilehua High School and received his bachelor's and master's degrees in history from the University of Minnesota. He retired as a history professor at Century College, White Bear Lake, Minnesota. Jeanette Kinue Matsukawa was born in 1928. She graduated from Leilehua High School and Honolulu Business College. She was a homemaker and farmer's wife, and passed away in 1992. Walter Masahiro Nakasone, born in 1931, graduated from Leilehua High School. He operated a pig farm and an express trucking service and retired as a concrete delivery truck driver. Marian Masako Iha, born in 1933, graduated from Leilehua High School and Cannon's School of Business. She is a homemaker and housewife. Edgar Masayuki Nakasone, born in 1936, graduated from Leilehua High School. He retired as a United States Air Force master sergeant. He passed away in 1984. James Shinkichi Nakasone, born in 1938, graduated from Leilehua High School. He received his bachelor's degree in mechanical engineering from the University of California. He retired as the chief technical engineer for the Corps of Engineers, Pacific Ocean Division.

Ushii lived a life of contentment, finally finding the paradise she had dreamed of before coming to Hawaii. The hardships and dire poverty she endured as her husband struggled as a pineapple grower, the loneliness and guilt she felt working as a live-in maid without her children beside her, are memories of her past. Cooking, gardening, and attending football games are now her simple pleasures.

Ushii was fortunate that she did not have any serious illnesses or health problems. She died in her sleep at home on November 19, 1990, at the age of ninety-three.

Ushii's son Jimmy shared his memories: "Mother was a special person. She endured many years of hardships and misfortunes but yet maintained her joy and happiness for living. She embraced her faith in the Buddhist religion. She loved to sing and dance and would be among the first to volunteer to perform at parties. She had clever ideas and was very resourceful. When she was working as a maid and trying to learn English, she kept a log and entered every new word she learned, translated in Japanese. When she had trouble pulling out the daikon that she grew, she would run water from a hose down along the daikon root to make the ground soft and was able to easily pull out the daikon. When her eyesight began to fade, she was able to make the distinction between a penny and dime and between a nickel and quarter by feeling the edge of the coin. She would say, 'The dime and quarter had *giji giji* [serrations] and the edges of the penny and nickel were smooth.' She was a confidante to many a troubled wife who came to see her for comfort and advice. Even today, after so many years have passed by, we get comments like, 'Your mother was a wonderful person,' 'I really miss seeing your mother,' or 'We can never forget your mother.'"

Fuyuno Sawai

THE SCENT OF GOLDEN PINEAPPLES

January 19, 1895–June 28, 1991
Born in Wada-mura, Futami-gun, Hiroshima-ken
Arrived in Hawaii February 16, 1915

Who would have ever imagined that Fuyuno Tani, a quiet, shy young girl who came to Hawaii as a picture bride of a pineapple fieldworker, would be such a valuable asset to a hardworking issei *luna*, even contributing effectively to his second career after he retired from the plantation? Facing many considerable challenges, she displayed exceptional qualities of compassion, perseverance, self-sacrifice, and determination as she grew into her own as a wife, partner, and mother, meeting all demands made on her and finding joy in keeping her large family healthy and happy.

This fascinating story unfolds from a photo I had sought for years for my book *Japanese Immigrant Clothing in Hawaii, 1885–1941*. Initially I had looked for an original *luna*'s outfit that had been worn in the fields, still with traces of the red dirt that is so impossible to remove. It was wishful thinking on my part that any issei woman might have kept her husband's old clothing for sentimental reasons.

Although I was not successful in finding an original *luna*'s outfit, I was able to finally find a photo of an issei man wearing the typical *luna*'s riding breeches made of khaki, with a black vest, a wide-brimmed felt hat, and leather boots. This man, I discovered, was Daikichi Sawai—Fuyuno's husband. In the photo he is standing in front of a Chevrolet truck before the Wahiawa Pineapple Stand, in its original location. Today it is world-renowned as the Dole Plantation, a great tourist attraction on the road from Wahiawa to Haleiwa.

Through a relative, I was fortunate to meet Daikichi Sawai's second-youngest daughter, Sumako. After retiring from the civil service, she had returned to live with her parents in Wahiawa, and she was the one who had the photo of her father in the *luna*'s outfit. When I asked Sumako about her parents, she said, she hardly knew anything about their personal experiences, their history, or their reason for immigrating to Hawaii. If I hadn't had the tenacious curiosity to pursue the research on the *luna*'s outfit, imagine what a significant story I would have missed! Sumako herself didn't think she had enough information to help write a story about

Daikichi Sawai in a *luna* outfit, standing beside his pickup truck. Photo courtesy of Sumako Sawai.

her parents. She had never written even a short story before, but much to her amazement, she started remembering many things about her parents.

In my interview with her, Sumako mentioned that her mother had come to Hawaii as a picture bride. This revelation made it all the more exciting, although this story has an unusual twist in that Daikichi, the issei husband, plays a prominent role. Of course, behind many successful men there is often a strong woman, quietly serving her husband without taking any credit or complaining about all of her responsibilities.

I thank Sumako for sharing her parents' story, and for her patience and hard work in assisting me with the telling of this remarkable life journey of an issei couple who served as role models in their community and left such a deep imprint on the red soil in Pineapple Town in Wahiawa. This is a story of a very humble and modest issei man who reached the pinnacle of success in partnership with his picture bride wife, who proved equally accomplished at raising a wonderful family of ten children.

After her parents passed away, Sumako moved to the Olaloa Senior Center. This center is built where Pineapple Camp Five once was located, the site of her birthplace and upbringing. I first interviewed Sumako in 1995, when she still had some of her parents' artifacts, though she mentioned that many precious photos had been lost in the process of moving.

THE *LUNA* AND HIS OUTFIT

Plantation managers wore these outfits because they rode horses to effectively supervise the vast expanse of sugarcane or pineapple fields. For that reason, breeches were specially tailored to make them comfortable when riding a horse. The Caucasians, referred to as *haoles,* were usually given the position of *luna;* occasionally Portuguese, Hawaiians, and some issei men who did well were promoted to that position. To be a *luna,* an issei man needed intelligence, knowledge of field operations and procedures, and the respect of the workers. So I knew Daikichi was not an ordinary person. I learned that he first started working for Hawaiian Pineapple Company, which later became Dole, in Wahiawa.

Sumako mentioned that she had not been close to her father as a young girl. "He was always too busy working. I got closer to my mother after I moved in with them. Those were wonderful days. I enjoyed hearing about Mother's younger days. Her village in Japan was in walking distance to Father's village, but in those days, boys and girls were not allowed to even talk to each other, so she never knew him." Sumako recalled her mother saying that she was a rascal as a young girl, and that she used to "cut class and go swimming with her friends."

DAIKICHI SAWAI

Daikichi Sawai was born December 25, 1883, on a remote farm in Wada Son village, Futami district, in Hiroshima prefecture, the eldest son of Tagoro and Kato Sawai. The family was very poor, like many families in Hiroshima hit by the famine during that time. Compulsory education ended at the fourth grade, and all the children worked on the family farm. Daikichi also served in the Japanese army for eight months during the Russo-Japanese War, from June 15, 1905, to February 15, 1906. Perhaps this experience serving in the military during a historic period contributed to the strong character and determination he exhibited later in life.

After the U.S. government signed a treaty with Japan that allowed Japanese men to work on the pineapple and sugar plantations in Hawaii, it was Daikichi's dream to come to Hawaii like other young men from the village to try to strike it rich. Perhaps he could save $1,000 and make a triumphant return home as a hero. Daikichi left home with his father at the age of twenty-four and crossed the vast Pacific Ocean on a small ship, the *China Maru.* The seas were rough and everyone was seasick. They arrived in Honolulu in the Territory of Hawaii on February 12, 1907.

They were first sent to a camp in Waipahu and worked for Hawaiian Pineapple Company. After ten days they were transferred to a pineapple plantation in the Wahiawa district and were assigned to work at Kipapa Five Camp, which was located about four or five miles from the little town of Wahiawa. They must have done well. Daikichi gave all his earnings to his father, which was the proper thing for the eldest son to do. Within a few years, his father saved the grand sum of $1,000 and returned to Hiroshima. During that period, this was a nearly impossible task for most immigrant families.

Daikichi toiled daily in the pineapple fields, in heavy rains and in the hot, humid summer heat. Having come from a farming village, where the families all worked together at their own pace and where they did not have to work under a *luna,* it was a challenge to learn how to work under the strict rules of the pineapple fields, but nevertheless they gradually adjusted. Daikichi learned all phases of field operations: plowing the rough terrain, planting pineapple slips, fertilizing, spraying, weeding, and finally harvesting the fruits. He worked diligently and gained knowledge of all aspects of growing the luscious pineapples.

Sumako once wrote down a conversation with her parents that revealed their thoughts about the distant past. She remembered her father saying, "I didn't intend to get married until I was thirty. I needed to save money first, before thinking of settling down. You needed guaranteed income to enter into marriage. Being the oldest son, I had to send $1,000 or $2,000 back to Japan to help my parents. Also, you needed big money to send for a bride from Japan." Daikichi told his daughter, "Plenty of local-born nisei in Hawaii, eighteen, nineteen years old, but I didn't want to marry a Hawaii-born girl." He preferred the traditional cultured women of the Meiji period.

PICTURE BRIDE MARRIAGE

After Daikichi's father, Tagoro, returned to Japan, he and his wife decided to find a bride for Daikichi. They wanted to make sure they found a good wife for him, since it was supposed that, as their eldest son, he would someday return to take care of the farm and continue the Sawai lineage. A girl named Fuyuno, twelve years younger than Daikichi, lived in a nearby village, and the families were acquainted. His parents knew Fuyuno well and felt confident she would be a good wife. Fuyuno's parents also were impressed by all the good things they had heard about Daikichi, who was very *oyakoko* (demonstrative of filial piety) in sending money home to his parents regularly.

Fuyuno was born on January 19, 1895. Because she was born in the winter (*fuyu*), she was named Fuyuno. Both families agreed she would be a good match for Daikichi. Fuyuno recalled that Daikichi's father had walked to her remote village to show her Daikichi's photo. With the exchange of photos, they were married in the summer of 1914 with Daikichi's younger brother, Ryoichi, acting as proxy for Daikichi. The priest, who was also the go-between, performed the *san san kudo* ritual exchange of sake cups. In the eyes of the authorities, Daikichi and Fuyuno were now husband and wife, even though the marriage ritual had been performed in absentia. The bride's name was then registered in the Sawai *koseki* in the village office.

TO HAWAII *RAKUEN* (PARADISE)

After several months during which Fuyuno worked on the farm and lived with her in-laws, her visa came through. Through many interviews with picture brides, I learned that this is a "trial period" for the bride, to gain the approval of the in-laws. If the mother-in-law disapproved of the daughter-in-law, she would be sent home. Apparently everything went well in this case. Having spent a pleasant time with her in-laws, Fuyuno learned much during the brief period in preparation to begin a life with a man she had never met. She felt thankful to be marrying into a family that seemed to have a special bond and respect for one another.

So Fuyuno looked forward to beginning a new life with Daikichi, whom she felt she had gotten to know somewhat through his parents. She vowed to herself that she would work very hard to be a good wife and be worthy of the eldest son. With a group of other picture brides, she boarded the ship *Shinyu Maru* in Yokohama and arrived in Honolulu harbor on February 16, 1915. All passengers were taken to the immigration station for clearance, where the eager husbands and relatives were waiting.

Daikichi was nicely dressed up in his dark suit, white shirt, and bow tie. He had been anxiously waiting at the immigration station along with the other grooms, who were just as eager to see their picture brides for the first time. When he caught a glimpse of Fuyuno as the door opened, he thought, "Ah, she's my wife—she's pretty, just like her picture." Directly from the immigration station, Daikichi got a *hakku* and took Fuyuno to the Kotohira Shinto shrine to get properly married. Fuyuno recalled that upon seeing Daikichi for the first time in person, she thought he seemed like a nice man. "Many picture brides got divorced when they didn't like their husbands, but I never thought of those things." Sumako smiled as she recalled her mother's words about her arrival at the immigration station.

"After settling down in my new home, in Camp K-5, I worked in the pineapple fields, trimming the crowns of the pineapple, until my first baby was born. By the time I had our third and fourth child, I was too busy taking care of the children to work in the fields," Fuyuno told her daughter about these early days.

ISSEI *LUNA*

Daikichi was a hard worker. The manager, J. Dickson Pratt, who had recently graduated from Harvard, still had a lot to learn. He immediately noticed Daikichi's outstanding ability and knowledge of growing pineapples. He had the leadership ability, he knew exactly what to do, and the other issei workers did what he said. Sumako said, "Mr. Pratt offered Father the *luna* position three times, but he always refused." Any issei man would have been happy to take the position. I wondered why he didn't want it.

Sumako shared an incident that Daikichi had told her about, something that occurred during the early years of his marriage. "Father did not want to accept the position because of the language barrier. He could not speak, read, or write English, and if he became a *luna,* he would have to write reports in the daily log in English. Because he could not comfortably communicate with his supervisor, who was a Caucasian, Father was terrified. He could not converse with the many Filipino workmen who spoke only the Filipino language, either. There were also a few immigrant Chinese and Korean men. For him, it seemed like an awesome responsibility. Making a mistake meant failure. He did not want to fail." So, in spite of the boss's utmost confidence that Daikichi had the ability to be a *luna* and could efficiently supervise the work group, he refused.

"Eventually, it was getting harder to say no to Mr. Pratt. One night in desperation, he told his wife to pack whatever was important and necessary for survival. Fuyuno packed the essential items, the futon and clothing. They loaded everything into a pushcart. Then, in the darkness of the night, they began their escape from the camp.

"Now, issei women who were brought up during the Meiji era were taught to abide by the Confucian ethics. Once you're married, you honor and obey your husband, your elders and in-laws. It was difficult to leave their friends behind, especially for Fuyuno, who did not know what to do except to obey her husband. But she was an obedient wife and never talked back. With heavy hearts, Fuyuno and Daikichi pushed the loaded cart down the bumpy dirt road in the darkness, hoping to find their village friend who was farming five miles away in Kipapa Gulch. Fearful of what they were doing as they pushed their cart in the chill of the night, they were quite a ways from Camp K-5 when a car slowly gained on them from behind. The headlights flashed into their faces. Oh! It was the boss. Someone must have told him. Mr. Pratt seemed very relieved and kindly asked the couple to get into his car. He took them back to Camp K-5. Apparently he caught them just in time; otherwise this would be an entirely different story.

"Eventually, Father did become a *luna,* a most prestigious position for an issei. Now, the pay for one month was about $28. One day's pay was $1.10, and one hour's pay was 11 cents. As the years went by, he had a raise to $60 month, then to $100 a month. Along with the promotion, the boss gave him a horse. In those days, being a *luna,* astride a horse, denoted his high status. As camp boss, Father constantly surveyed the many acres of pineapples to determine the necessary work. Luckily he had experience in handling horses and mules from his service in the Japanese army. Still, until he mastered full control over the horse, he got thrown off to the ground and kicked several times." Sumako chuckled as she marveled at the way her father had the strong will not to fail and never gave up.

"Much later, the boss gave Father a car, an old Model T Ford," Sumako related. "The car was old and often wouldn't start in the morning, so Mother would wake up the three older boys at 3:00 a.m. and they had to push the car to get it started. The boys did that every morning without complaining. Once the old Model T got started, the car would jump and go backward, so the boys had to push from the back until it could go downhill on its own with Father at the wheel," Sumako said. "Later, I spoke to two of my older brothers, who were in their eighties. They still remembered those days and broke out in laughter," she chuckled.

Sumako recalled life in Camp K-5. "Oh, I remember lots and lots of kiawe trees, with thorns! The camp had three sections, five families in each part. There were five or six Filipino bachelors, too. There was a laundry area for everyone to share. Further away was the Filipino camp, where three families lived, all nice people. Father was picky. He would chase anyone out if they didn't behave or follow orders."

ILLNESS

Daikichi was dedicated to doing a good job running the myriad plantation operations. "He left home early, in the dark, and did not leave the office until seven o'clock or later each night. His office was in the camp near our home. When the children heard Father's footsteps nearing the house, they always grabbed a book or pretended to be reading or studying."

At supper, to relax, Daikichi began increasing his sake intake. He began to have stomach pains and eventually went to see his doctor in Waipahu. He was informed that he was suffering from stomach ulcers and was advised to ease up at work and to consume milk for his ulcers. The nearest market was in Wahiawa town, miles away from camp. He arranged for a milkman to drop off milk bottles in a wooden box in the pineapple fields along Kamehameha Highway. Then Daikichi would travel two or three miles to collect the milk.

Many years later, Daikichi resumed the habit of drinking his favorite sake, but this time he never consumed more than half a cup at suppertime. At times he indulged in a bottle of beer, but throughout the rest of his life he continued to drink milk.

"In 1918, Mother caught the Spanish flu," Sumako recalled. "There was an epidemic that spread around the world and many people lost their lives. She became severely ill and almost died, but, through a miracle, she recovered and lived to the ripe old age of ninety-six. Strangely, after that, she never even caught a cold," Sumako said. "She sure was a strong lady."

COMPASSION FOR WORKERS

Daikichi was good to the families who worked under his supervision. He was not only smart but also a very compassionate man. He understood how hard it was to live so far away from home and family, with no one to provide help. Fuyuno was always there when the bachelors had no one to care for them. When a bachelor got sick, Daikichi would ask Fuyuno to make *okai* (rice gruel) to help him get well. One *ume,* the salted pickled plum, in the *okai* was a perfect remedy. When three issei men on Daikichi's work crew got older and the fieldwork proved too much for them, Daikichi kept them on the payroll by assigning them to less strenuous jobs such as yard maintenance work. Fuyuno took good care of the older workers and prepared nourishing food for them.

Daikichi also hired an older Filipino man with a wife and a half dozen young children. When asked why, he replied, "Who is going to hire an old man who isn't strong enough to work in the hot fields? He can go from one camp to another but no one will hire him. Here he can work in our camp doing some yard work and cleaning up the neighborhood." Daikichi cared deeply about all his employees and families.

There was a man with a spouse and five young children. He was quiet, honest, and hardworking. His only vice was that after a hard day's work he enjoyed some sake, perhaps too much. Eventually he became addicted to alcohol. He could not start the day without drinking. Day after day he was drunk, and soon he was unable to report to work. His wife, a picture bride who had come to marry this man she had never seen, was distraught, with no income to buy food for the family. In those early pioneering days, wages were so low that no one was able to save money for emergencies.

During this period, the pineapple companies did not allow women to work on a permanent basis. The only time women were hired was during the summer months for *pula pula,* when men would gather pineapple shoots for replanting. Women would peel off the leaves at the bottom of the shoots and stack them in neat rows to dry in the sun. Fuyuno also worked among the other women during these summer months, doing *pula pula*. However, this woman, whose husband was an alcoholic, needed a full-time job to survive.

Daikichi had to do something to help the family. He pleaded persistently with Mr. Pratt for an exception for this woman. Ultimately the company officials gave in and allowed this one lady to work permanently in the fields. However, she was not allowed to work alongside the men. Daikichi drove around daily to look for fields overgrown with weeds and unwanted plants, and then he personally gave the woman a ride to the fields, where she worked alone. Alone amid the silent acres and acres of pineapple plants, with no one to talk to, she toiled all day long. At the close of the workday, Daikichi picked her up in his car. Her family was saved and remained in the protective environment of K-5 Camp, surrounded by friends. Noticing the struggles of other picture brides during the same period, Fuyuno felt very grateful indeed to have a good husband like Daikichi.

Daikichi was very generous. Many families worked hard but struggled to make ends meet and to stay afloat financially. When his workers or friends found themselves in dire straits, they conferred with Daikichi. They sometimes borrowed as much as $100—a huge amount back in those days. Many were able to repay their debt, but some never could.

HIROSHIMA CONNECTIONS AND CARS

Sumako recalled that Peter Fukunaga's father, who came from the same village in Hiroshima as Fuyuno, first opened a repair service in Waialua, then later moved to Wahiawa and started Service Motors Company, an automobile dealership today known as Servco. The elder Fukunaga, a *tokoro mono* from Hiroshima, was a good friend and visited the Sawais frequently. In 1930, Daikichi purchased a brand-new Chevy from Peter Fukunaga Sr. It was the talk of the town: a plantation worker was the proud owner of a brand-new auto. The interior was adorned with velvety curtains over the side windows. Sumako said, "Father was too busy working to enjoy driving his family around to show off his new acquisition. He asked a Filipino workman, whom we called 'Puka-Puka' because of pockmarks on his face from smallpox, to chauffeur his family to doctors' and dentists' appointments. In the early years Father was totally lost because he couldn't speak English. When he hired many Filipino men, he couldn't pronounce their names. He decided to apply nicknames until he could learn each man by their proper names. 'Puka-Puka' was the man with smallpox scars; 'Cigaretto' was a man who resembled the male picture on the pack of Camel cigarettes." Daikichi's sons were proud and overjoyed to be riding around in a nice new car, but his daughters were shy and embarrassed at being driven by a chauffeur.

FUYUNO'S MANY JOBS

Daikichi's son Satoru recalled, "Mr. Pratt was really good to my father, whom he designated as camp boss. Mr. Pratt was a humble and wonderful boss. He nicknamed Daikichi 'Doc' because of his intelligence and knowledge of the pineapple business, and for being a loyal employee." His children felt that perhaps Mr. Pratt might also have had trouble pronouncing Daikichi's long name. Sumako said, "Mother couldn't work in the fields because she had to take care of the many children, and also it was her responsibility to answer all the phone calls that came from Mr. Pratt, who called several times a day. He would say, 'Hello, Sawai stop [is Sawai at home]?' Then Mother replied, 'Sawai no stoppu [no, he's not home]!' That was all, and they understood what it meant." Daikichi had to arrange the work schedules for the workers, determining what fields they should be sent to and what tasks they would have to perform. Whenever Mr. Pratt wanted to contact Daikichi, he had to go through Fuyuno. Today she would be categorized as a receptionist because of the important functions she fulfilled.

Daikichi, being a supervisor, had the privilege of coming home to a hot lunch. That meant extra work for Fuyuno, but she never complained. Because he left for work very early, he took a nap after lunch. Then, after riding around in the fields all day for his supervisory job, he went to his office to do the day's report and worked until dark.

There were about fifteen families in the camp, along with some Filipino, Chinese, and Japanese single men who lived in a boardinghouse. "Mother cooked for all those men," continued Satoru. "She did their laundry, and made them *bento* to take to the fields. She got paid for that. There were two camps: upper camp and lower camp. The lower camp was a quarter mile away. Mother also ran the warehouse store herself, which opened in the 1930s for the convenience of the families. It was not the usual type of store, but more like a huge warehouse where she sold rice, shoyu, canned goods, and other everyday staple foods. The door was usually closed, so people had to call and let her know what they wanted. In those days, K-5 Camp was isolated by about two miles from the main town, and nobody had cars."

Satoru mentioned that his mother could carry a hundred-pound bag of rice on her shoulder when the customer ordered one from the warehouse. When the men offered to help, she would say, "No, no, I can carry." She also raised hogs. Satoru said, "My mother was a real tough lady! She never took time to rest. She was a good cook and everybody liked her cooking. Those days, rice was cooked out of doors in a big *kamado* [cast-iron pot] over an open fire, so it was very good. To think that she used to start the fire herself with kiawe wood! She was a small woman, barely five feet tall, but very strong." He marveled at all the things she took in stride.

Imagine Fuyuno, a short, slender woman, carrying out this multitude of tasks besides handling the phone calls and taking care of ten active children, disciplining them, and supervising their English and Japanese homework. Yet as Sumako said, "Except for catching the Spanish flu and almost losing her life, she never got sick after that, not even a cold. What a remarkable woman." Sumako continued, "I never heard my mother complain, or say how tired she was with her endless chores."

Fuyuno wore many hats and did everything efficiently. Her children all marveled at her remarkable *gambare* (never give up) spirit and energy and organization. The only thing she didn't do was sew for her husband and children, which was commonly done by the issei mothers, regardless of whether they were good seamstresses or not. Most had to do it out of necessity. Fuyuno was one of the few picture brides who had a seamstress sew for the entire family. Even Daikichi's *luna* outfit was sewn by Mrs. Morioka, who had a tailor shop in Wahiawa. Fuyuno did sew kimonos for her family, but never the Western style of clothing. (In fact, when Mr. Pratt's first son was born, Fuyuno made a kimono for the baby that was designed with all the traditional good-luck symbols for boys. Daikichi also gave the manager's family a big paper carp to fly over their roof. The Pratts were overjoyed!) Daikichi was a good provider, so Fuyuno and the children wore custom-made dresses. As Sumako recalled, "Most of the girls in camp had to wear underwear made of bleached rice bags, and poorly constructed homemade dresses that at times were ridiculed when worn to school. We were fortunate we never had to wear things made of bleached rice bags."

RELIGION

Among the many immigrants who came from Hiroshima prefecture, there were many Buddhist ministers who arrived in Hawaii to spread the teachings of Buddhism in the plantation community. One of them was the Rev. Yoshio Hino, who was assigned to the Wahiawa Hongwanji Mission in 1928, serving as its fourth minister. It was a joyous reunion to meet someone whose family lived near Daikichi's village in Japan. This connection led Daikichi to become more active with the Wahiawa Hongwanji. He served on the board of directors for many years. Fuyuno was also a member of the *fujinkai* (women's association) and actively participated with others in cleaning and polishing the interior of the temple. She enjoyed taking part in the religious and social events.

Buddhism was a way of life for Daikichi and Fuyuno Sawai. It showed in the way they conducted their lives. He was a unique, exceptional character, compassionate

Mrs. Fuyuno Sawai was an active member of Wahiawa Dai-Ichi Fujinkai (Wahiawa Hongwanji Mission Issei Women's Association). Mrs. Sawai is in the second row, first person on the left. Ayako Kikugawa, included in this book, is in the front row, third from the left. Photo taken in 1979. Photo courtesy of Wahiawa Hongwanji Mission.

and intelligent, who rose to the top with hard work, integrity, and determination. They both gave willingly and generously to the Wahiawa Hongwanji Mission and other charitable organizations. As Sumako laughingly said, "My father earned good money during that period. However he loaned money easily when people were in need, and donated generously, so that monetarily he wasn't wealthy in his later years, but rich in the most meaningful way." Daikichi and Fuyuno built a solid foundation of strong values and citizenship for their offspring. The core of their strength came from the rich Japanese cultural values of respect for authority, *gaman* (perseverance through adversity), and the importance of family.

EDUCATION FOR THE CHILDREN

Daikichi and Fuyuno were always interested in their children's education. Despite their busy work schedules, they supported the schools, both English and Japanese.

Once a month, after a hurried lunch, Daikichi drove Fuyuno to Kipapa Elementary School. Though Fuyuno did not speak either English or Pidgin English, she was always welcomed with open arms by the principal, Miss Cook. All the teachers appreciated her visits, too. An older teacher, Ms. Lina, took special delight in showing Fuyuno the vegetable and flower gardens the children had planted. Fuyuno spent the afternoons quietly visiting each class, standing in the back of the room, observing. All the children nervously behaved well and paid attention to the teacher. Even the naughtiest boys were quiet and respectful. After observing classes at the English-language school, she would do the same at the Japanese-language school nearby. She felt more at ease there because she could converse with the teachers. The teachers remembered her as a beautiful and gracious person. Her main focus was to educate herself, along with the children. At the close of the school day, Fuyuno and her children rode the school bus home. Fuyuno, with a limited grade-school education, took pride in her children's education.

Sumako remembered that during the prewar days, they all attended the Kipapa Japanese School, after English school. The principal was Mr. Fujii. At the outbreak of World War II, Mr. Fujii and all the teachers were picked up by FBI agents and sent to internment camps. It was shocking and sad to see how, without warning, the FBI burst into their homes in the middle of the night and took them away without any explanation, with only the clothes on their back. It was a heartbreaking experience, for the families, for the students, and for the close-knit community.

When Chieko, Fuyuno's eldest daughter, finished the ninth grade, her mother sent her to the Royal Sewing School in Honolulu. There she studied all the basics of dressmaking and learned to sew men's shirts and trousers. The nisei girls who learned sewing during this period became outstanding seamstresses because they were trained under the strictest regimen. Chieko began sewing for the entire family. Coincidentally, she happened to be working at the Fashion Dressmaker in Wahiawa, for Mrs. Kiyomi Furukawa, when I worked there in 1938. This was my first job after graduating that year from Keister's Tailoring College in Honolulu, at age fifteen. Chieko and I actually sat across from each other at work, but we never had the opportunity to get to know each other. To think how much I could have learned from her at that time about her parents' background!

RESPECT

The people in camp lived in peace. Everyone respected and helped one another. But children, being children, often got into little fights. Daikichi was a quiet, serious man whom people respected or even feared. He was the boss, and because he was a man of few words, people did not know how to approach him. His stern, unsmiling face scared all the kids in camp. Even the most rascally ones stood still and at attention whenever he passed. One day Daikichi was asked to intercede in a fight involving two teen boys. The boys were scared stiff and were ordered by their fathers to face the boss. They walked the long driveway to his big house, shaking. They were surprised, however, when they entered the spacious home. They were not questioned, scolded, or lectured. Instead Daikichi simply reminded the boys of the importance of getting along well with neighbors and friends. "We must try to live in peace in our camp," Daikichi said. Everyone agreed. Then, with peace and friendship restored, they enjoyed a simple but delicious supper prepared by Fuyuno.

LIBERTY HOUSE

Daikichi followed the traditional Japanese custom of making *orei* (offerings of gratitude) to the boss. However, instead of sake, he gave American whiskey. Since Daikichi held the position of *luna* and was a valued employee, every Christmas the Pratts gave the Sawai family gifts from Liberty House department store. Daikichi wanted to reciprocate their kindness and generosity with something of quality.

Sumako remembered her mother going to Liberty House in the 1930s to purchase fine linen handkerchiefs to give as a Christmas present to Mrs. Pratt. During that era, hardly any issei plantation families were wealthy enough to shop at Liberty House, even if they had heard of the prestigious store. All the workers knew was the plantation store, which provided them whatever necessities their families needed, on *bango* (credit). Without any cash, they could charge whatever they needed. The second-eldest son, Satoru, drove Fuyuno to Honolulu to Liberty House and was somewhat embarrassed to take his mother because she always wore her kimono and most of the shoppers were upper-class Caucasian women, stylishly dressed in hat and gloves. He was still a teenager and felt very conspicuous being there, especially since there were hardly any men around. Satoru was a dutiful son, though, and did whatever his mother asked of him, but he remembered that trip as the most unpleasant experience of his younger days. Compared to other picture brides, Fuyuno was very fortunate to be able to shop at Liberty House.

FIRST TRIP TO JAPAN

Their six children, ages seven years to one month, accompanied Daikichi and Fuyuno on their first trip to Hiroshima, from October 16, 1923, to January 31, 1924. When it came time to depart for Hawaii, the grandparents insisted on keeping the three eldest girls in Japan. The eldest, Chieko, age seven, was delegated to look after her younger sisters. Daikichi sent support, money, and clothing for his daughters.

Soon Daikichi's younger brother and family moved into their father's home and took over the family farmlands. Eventually Daikichi financed the building of a larger house to accommodate the huge clan. Chieko became frustrated with the added work and responsibilities. She begged her parents to let her return to Hawaii. She arrived home alone at age twelve.

Daikichi's father passed away at age seventy, on November 2, 1934. His mother died two years later, on November 20, 1936, at age seventy-five. The other two Sawai sisters returned to Hawaii separately, after each graduated from high school in Hiroshima. Fuyuno was relieved and elated to have all her children together once again.

WORLD WAR II

Prior to World War II, the Department of Education in Japan cited Daikichi for his support of the local Japanese school in Hawaii. One day in early 1942 Fuyuno and her children returned home from school and were surprised to see all the lights in the house turned on in broad daylight. Their cousin Robert was there, awaiting the family's return. He said three FBI agents were searching the house. No one was allowed to enter until the search was completed. Daikichi was with the agents as they searched thoroughly every closet, dresser drawer, and even personal belongings and papers. They found nothing suspicious. The agents came with complete information about the family, probably from records seized from the Japanese consulate in Honolulu. They knew all about Daikichi, Fuyuno, and their six children visiting their homeland in 1923. They questioned Daikichi about the purpose of the visit. Why had they left the three older girls with their grandparents in Hiroshima? Why had the girls returned to Hawaii? Where were the silver bowl and certificate the Japanese government had awarded Daikichi for his contributions to and support of the Japanese-language school?

The interrogation was long and comprehensive, but Daikichi prevailed because of his honesty. After the house search was over and the FBI agents told him that he was in the clear, Daikichi took the agents to the pineapple fields adjacent to his property and picked a couple of the sweet and juicy fruits for them.

Satoru Sawai volunteered at age eighteen for the army during World War II and served with the 442nd Regimental Combat Team, Company K. As a private first class, he bravely fought in Italy and France and was wounded. He earned the Purple Heart, Distinguished Unit Badge, and Combat Infantryman Badge.

FUYUNO'S MOTHER

The saddest memory Sumako shared about her mother involved money. Through the years of toil on the plantation, Daikichi, being the eldest son, regularly sent money to his parents in Hiroshima. Fuyuno held the purse strings and Daikichi gave his monthly salary to her, so she was the one who actually sent the money to Japan every month. She knew her parents were also suffering just as much, and yet she could not even suggest to her husband that he send support to her parents, too. Being a woman of the Meiji period, she could not ask. "He was a good man and probably would not have minded sending some money to my mother's parents, but she could not ask." Sumako realized the greatness and nobility in her mother's dutiful marriage to the eldest son. "She quietly made sacrifices and did not want to add any extra burden to her husband," Sumako remarked with a sense of pride and admiration. "When the war finally ended, and she found out how much suffering her parents had endured because of lack of money and food, she cried for a whole week." After World War II, when the children worked in the pineapple fields during the summer, they each handed their paychecks to their mother. "She was finally able to send money to her mother in Hiroshima. Fuyuno's mother was overwhelmed with emotion when she received the letter and money from her daughter and her grand-children. She cried in gratitude and was thankful for the kindness of these grand-children, who sent their hard-earned money." Sumako's eyes welled with tears as she shared this story.

BUSY RETIREMENT: THE PINEAPPLE STAND

After forty-three years, Daikichi retired from the pineapple industry in December 1949. He bought a piece of land in Wahiawa and built a four-bedroom home. After a year he got bored, since he was not interested in socializing all day with other retir-ees, nor did he have any hobbies. He did try to grow bonsai plants, but they could not keep his interest.

After years of tending to the pineapples, he could not get pineapples out of his mind. He visited several food markets but could not find any fresh pineapples. So, he thought, "Why not introduce this 'new' product to the local public?" Soon he asked his daughter Sumako to write a letter to his dear friend and former boss, Mr. J. Dick-son Pratt, now president of Dole Corporation. She wrote, "Father is getting restless in retirement and wants to start a small business by selling fresh pineapples on the road-side. With acres upon acres of pineapple fields surrounding us, he feels that maybe people will become interested in our golden fruits." The idea impressed Mr. Pratt, who immediately ordered the plantation carpenters to build a shed for Daikichi, with shelves to display the fruits. A huge sign that read "Dole Fresh Pineapples" was placed on the roof of the little shed.

Thus in the fall of 1951, a brand-new business started. His friends were leery about this new venture but faithfully congratulated him. At first business was very slow. Many cars sped by and ignored the prominent sign on the tiny shed. But Daikichi firmly believed the public would soon notice the pineapple stand on the roadside. One day a curious newspaper reporter stopped by to investigate. He had noticed the little shed in the middle of nowhere and wondered what was going on. When he heard Daikichi's story, he felt sorry for the old fellow. He spent some time talking and encouraging him, then bought a small pineapple. He and his family evi-dently enjoyed the juicy, delectable fruit. In the next issue of his monthly publica-tion, he wrote an intriguing article about his encounter with a lonely but spirited old man trying to sell pineapples in pineapple country. He praised the freshness and sweetness of this newfound delicacy and urged the public to stop by the highway shed.

Spurred by this unsolicited advertisement in the well-circulated free news-paper, curious people began to stop by the highway shed. Word spread all over re-garding the fruit, and skeptical customers wanted a taste, asking, "Is it really sweet?" Daikichi soon decided to sell sliced pineapples. So Fuyuno got busier and busier,

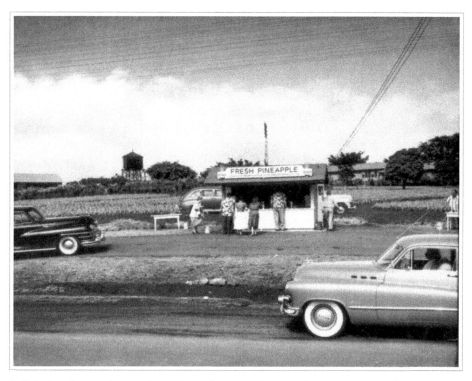

Daikichi Sawai's original pineapple stand in Helemano, Wahiawa, Oahu. Photo courtesy of Sumako Sawai.

rising early in the morning to prepare pineapple slices for the customers. Slicing so many pineapples was rough on the hands, and eventually the older children pitched in. Upon tasting the delicious morsels, customers soon began to buy the fruits for themselves—and for their neighbors, too.

Soon taxi drivers taking tour groups around Oahu made it a point to stop at the pineapple shed. Word got around fast. To Daikichi's delight, buses loaded with foreign sailors came. Local residents from faraway Honolulu and other towns crowded the shed. Summers, when people stopped on their way home from the North Shore beaches, were the busiest period.

Business was now great. Cars, taxicabs, and buses all converged, making Daikichi a bit dizzy. The fruits were handpicked daily by his older sons Kiyoto, Satoru, and Mamoru, so Daikichi could guarantee the freshness and sweetness of each fruit. Satoru said, "The sweetness of the pineapple depends on where it was picked. Dry places were the best—Kipapa One, K-5, Brody One and Two, and Whitmore. We would hit the pine with our fingers; if there was a hollow noise, no juice. We picked fifty pines a day. Mother did the cutting to sell. This was real hard work and required a lot of skill, slicing the pineapples quickly and evenly without losing the juice. Father bought the pine for 4 cents a pound and sold it for 6 cents a pound.

"When the Dole Company let the regular workers pick the pine to sell at the stand, the pineapple was not as sweet because they picked them from anywhere and they picked any kind," added Mamoru.

The children also helped with sales and arranged sliced pineapples on paper plates as Fuyuno cut them as fast as she could. In 1957 they sold a plate of sliced pineapple for 25 cents. The pineapple stand got so busy that Chieko, the oldest daughter, who was married by then, came from Waialua to help. As more pineapples were sold, getting rid of the rind became a problem. Again, Mr. Pratt sent workers to dig a large hole nearby to bury all the discarded parts.

The once stern-faced Daikichi underwent a complete personality change. Now he was full of smiles, and he freely conversed in his Pidgin English. He loved talking to the Caucasian tourists, and they seemed to find him amusing and fun.

UNEXPECTED HONOR

On April 6, 1953, Crown Prince Akihito of Japan spent twelve hours in Honolulu, with official greetings and sightseeing. It was the first visit to the United States for the nineteen-year-old future emperor, who was en route to London.

Mr. Pratt, president of Dole Corporation, was of course delighted to greet the young prince and introduced him to the pineapple plantation. After viewing the vast acres of pineapples, the imperial party made a short stop at the pineapple stand. The public was told of the prince's arrival at Helemano, so a large group of citizens drove down to the stand. The issei men all were dressed neatly in their white shirts, ties, and dark suits; Daikichi looked dapper with his bow tie. Daikichi's son Mamoru still remembers to this day how everybody shouted *"Banzai! Banzai! Banzai!"* as Prince Akihito appeared.

It was an exciting day for Daikichi and Fuyuno Sawai on October 10, 1953, when their manager, J. Dickson Pratt, introduced Prince Akihito of Japan to Daikichi. Akihito became the Emperor of Japan in 1989. Photo courtesy of *Waikiki Beach Press*.

Being an issei, Daikichi was well aware of protocol. In Japan, whenever the emperor passed, people had to kneel down and bow their head low; they were not allowed to look directly at the emperor. He stepped far away from the prince and Mr. Pratt, as well as a number of security officers. Mr. Pratt spotted Daikichi standing in the back of the crowd and called him forward. Daikichi hesitated at first, then slowly walked through the crowd, but still he held back from getting too close to Prince Akihito. Mr. Pratt introduced Daikichi to the honorable prince. To everyone's surprise, the prince extended his hand and shook Daikichi's hand. Daikichi immediately felt guilty, as though he had committed a crime. Touching royalty directly was unthinkable! Daikichi was so humbled and yet honored. His issei friends insisted he not wash his hand. They all wanted to shake the hand that had shaken hands with the prince. Fuyuno was just as excited and as proud as their friends. This would never have happened in Japan! Daikichi kept a low profile and would not talk about the remarkable incident. He was truly Japanese. Fuyuno, of course, never realized that she had played an important part in greeting the crown prince. She was the one who carefully sliced the specially selected golden fruit. Yes, she was probably the only picture bride who can say that she was honored to have the future emperor of Japan taste her delicious sliced pineapple.

SECOND TRIP TO JAPAN

In 1955, the Sawai family sailed back to visit postwar Japan. This time they booked passage on the SS *President Cleveland,* traveling first-class at their children's insistence. The liner departed Honolulu on March 25 and arrived in Yokohama on April 3. They joined a tour group and traveled to many cities and prefectures. They were shocked to witness the devastation caused by the atom bomb in Hiroshima city, and the extreme poverty all over the nation. After the tour, the couple visited their relatives again in the faraway Hiroshima countryside.

The return home to Hawaii was again via the SS *President Cleveland*. Daikichi and Fuyuno thoroughly enjoyed the luxurious voyage. The seas were fairly calm and the weather was fine. Daikichi made many friends aboard ship, probably telling tales about his wonderful, luscious pineapples. Fuyuno was quiet and demure as she listened to the other ladies' conversations. She enjoyed the time spent on the deck. All her life she had labored to serve her "master," her husband, as all Japanese women were expected to do. She was devoted to her children, too. Now she was in heaven—every day was a holiday, and she cherished every moment. She especially loved ice cream and enjoyed some each day, along with cool drinks on the ship's deck with her new friends. She felt so spoiled she thought she could never go back to being a housemaid and cook. Of course, being first a good wife and mother, she gradually resumed her busy work schedule after relaxing a few days at home.

The highlight of the trip for Daikichi was the last night aboard the liner at the captain's party. Daikichi was overcome with joy and happily chatted all night with the captain. He had the ship's photographer snap many photos of him with the captain. He, too, was in heaven. Regrettably, none of the many photos taken on that memorable cruise can be found.

SECOND RETIREMENT

Daikichi loved his new life after retirement from the plantation. He opened his stand daily, including Sundays. Finally, after seven years, he gave in to advancing age and began his second retirement. He was not a man of wealth, since the fruit was inexpensive. But he was definitely rich in many happy memories. The seven years of hard work also entitled him to benefits from the Social Security Administration. The business was taken over in 1957 by Mrs. Taniguchi, an issei woman who lived in the plantation village of Whitmore. Eventually the little pineapple stand was torn down, and the current Pineapple Plantation was established. It is now a popular attraction, and people from all over the world come to taste the delicious golden fruit and the fresh pineapple sherbet.

Every year for New Year's, even after the children were married, the Sawais all gathered to pound *mochi* (rice cakes). After pounding the *mochi,* Fuyuno always had dinner for her large family. They all feasted and brought home the *mochi* to decorate the Shinto shrine to pray for another year of good fortune and happiness. Mr. Pratt's son, Dickson, who now lives in Portland, Oregon, still remembers how the Sawai girls were dressed in their beautiful silk kimonos and colorful sashes, sewn by Fuyuno, to formally wish the Pratt family a happy new year. They always brought over New Year's *mochi*. And when Boys' Day came, on May 5, they brought *mochi* and paper carps to fly over the rooftop because Dickson was the only son. In Japanese tradition, the Sawais wanted to wish him well by presenting him with the colorful carp, though Daikichi couldn't explain the symbolism. Giving carp streamers to the firstborn began during the Edo period (1600–1868). Carp are traditionally thought to symbolize success, courage, virility, and strength. I remember how at Japanese school the teachers emphasized in the *shushin* (moral ethics) class how the carp's strength gave them the ability to swim upstream against strong currents to reach their spawning ground. The teachers reminded us that we should keep that vision in our mind always. The issei parents displayed the paper carps on Boys' Day because they wanted their sons to grow up like the carp—brave and strong, able to overcome life's obstacles. It is likely that Daikichi, being a faithful servant to Mr. Pratt, wished this for his friend's son but didn't know how to explain the significance of the paper carp. However, they seemed to have enjoyed the pleasant cultural exchanges. After I heard these stories, I contacted the younger Mr. Pratt, who now lives in Oregon, and learned that, even after many years, he still had fond memories of the Sawai family.

THIRD TRIP

Years later, in 1961, the Sawais went on their last trip together to their homeland. Again they joined a tour group and ended with a visit to relatives. They had planned on a leisurely six-month stay in Hiroshima. At this time Fuyuno was quite a "devoted health addict," according to her children, and became a member of the well-known Nishishiki health organization. The group met monthly, practiced difficult physical exercises, and maintained a vegetarian diet. Fuyuno was patient and diligently learned to do the many exercises. Daikichi, on the other hand, was a bit less disciplined than his wife, claiming his body was too old and stiff to participate in such strict and severe training.

In Japan, Fuyuno was referred to as a "health master" with the Nishishiki organization, and signed up for a month's stay there. Participants were fed nutritious food, mostly vegetables—no meat, no desserts, and no medication. The portions were small. They did a lot of rigorous exercises, making her hungry all day. In spite of some weight loss, she enrolled in a week of fasting. Daikichi was reluctant to undergo such rigid practices and did not join her. He roomed at the inn with Fuyuno, but he took his meals out. Fuyuno was hungry but determined to complete the program. Weekends were "free time," and Fuyuno eagerly joined Daikichi and feasted on delicious Japanese cuisine at nearby restaurants.

At this time, one of their neighbors in Wahiawa, Mrs. Yoshika, was also in Japan visiting her brother, who owned and operated an inn in Fukuoka prefecture. Knowing this, one day Fuyuno convinced Daikichi to get on a bus heading toward Fukuoka from Hiroshima, which is quite a distance. With no map or itinerary, they boarded the bus early in the morning. Late in the afternoon, they asked the bus driver to direct them to an inn. It took them days, but eventually they safely arrived at their destination. They quietly registered at their friend's brother's inn, got a room to relax, and finally looked for Mrs. Yoshika. What an unexpected surprise for their neighbor! After a joyful short visit, Daikichi and Fuyuno again boarded the bus and safely returned to Hiroshima. Fuyuno surprised everyone with her daring and adventurous spirit.

U.S. CITIZENSHIP: SUMAKO'S RECOLLECTIONS

For many years after arriving in Hawaii, Daikichi remained a Japanese citizen, making him an alien in the United States of America. Long after his retirement, Daikichi, along with Fuyuno, attended night classes at nearby Leilehua High School in Wahiawa. They studied American history offered in the Japanese language. They both successfully passed the citizenship test and became proud naturalized American citizens on September 5, 1962.

Daikichi Sawai   World War II alien registration no. 5031321
                     Naturalized as an American citizen on September 5, 1962,
                     at age seventy-nine
Fuyuno Sawai   World War II alien registration no. 4806694
                     Naturalized as an American citizen on September 5, 1962,
                     at age sixty-seven

One day in the 1960s, while Daikichi and Fuyuno were at home, they observed a taxicab letting off an elderly couple outside their house. They watched the couple approach. When the guests reached the door, Daikichi recognized them as old plantation friends and asked, "What are they doing here?" It had been many, many years since they'd last said goodbye. The couple, with tears in their eyes, explained the purpose of their visit. Long ago, they had gotten a $100 loan from Daikichi. They had been extremely poor, and with a big family to feed, they were not able to save from their small monthly wages. Now their children were all doing well. However, they decided to keep the debt a secret from their children. Through all the years, Fuyuno would encounter the lady at the Hongwanji temple every Sunday, but she would avoid Fuyuno's eyes. How she must have suffered all those years trying to keep it to herself. In recent years this couple had saved some money from their Social Security checks and were finally able to repay the debt.

In addition to bringing the money, the couple came with gifts: a large bottle of sake for Daikichi and some yardage for a dress for Fuyuno. Daikichi accepted the gifts but declined the money. He said the loan had been a lifetime ago and should be forgotten. The couple insisted on repayment, and repeated their gratitude, bowing their heads over and over. In the end, Daikichi reluctantly accepted the money. However, Fuyuno insisted that the couple accept $40 as reimbursement for their taxi fare. When everything was settled, they all cried and laughed over the past. This couple was so proud they had outlived their poverty and hard times and felt a great sense of relief. Soon Daikichi's second son, who lived next door, returned home from work. As usual, he came over to check on his parents. Satoru happily offered to drive the couple home to spare them the taxi fare.

Daikichi and Fuyuno felt sad as they realized how many years the couple must have endured the guilty feelings of not being able to repay their debt. Then they felt deep joy, knowing that finally the burden of guilt and shame had been lifted from the elderly couple. Daikichi and Fuyuno stood in front of the altar in their living room. They clasped their hands in prayer and gave thanks to the Shinto Kami-sama (God) and asked the O-Kami to bless the couple so that they could now enjoy their twilight years in peace and happiness. I could sense the pride Sumako felt about her parents' empathy and how they forgave the elderly couple.

REFLECTING ON A LONG LIFE

Daikichi was a true Meiji man, but not domineering like some issei husbands. Fuyuno truly represented the Meiji woman of that period, always obedient, never talking back to her husband, putting his interests and concerns first and finding joy in raising her large family. Yet in her own way, she was also very independent. They both lived long and productive lives, and were loved and respected by their children, their grandchildren, and the people in the community.

Daikichi Sawai died on November 19, 1974, in Wahiawa at the age of ninety-eight. His wife, Fuyuno Tani Sawai, died on June 28, 1991, at ninety-six. They left a living legacy of twenty-three grandchildren and seven great-grandchildren.

Kishi Oki Tsujimura
GAMBARE SPIRIT (NEVER GIVE UP)
January 4, 1896–May 1, 2002
Born in Kabe-mura, Asa-gun, Hiroshima-ken
Arrived in Hawaii November 17, 1915

Kishi Oki Tsujimura came to Hawaii as the nineteen-year-old picture bride of Keiji Tsujimura on November 17, 1915, on the USS *Seattle*. Her life spanned three centuries, as she was born in 1896 and passed away in 2002, at the age of 106. Her remarkable longevity was not just a matter of good genes, discipline, and healthy diet; other factors were her embrace of strong Confucian ethics and values, a positive attitude toward life and people, and her Buddhist faith, all of which had been strongly instilled in her since childhood, and which had a profound influence on the way she lived her life.

When I was shown the photo taken on her 106th birthday, I noticed the sparkle in her brown eyes and the happiness on her face that seemed to come from within. It made me wonder what her journey had been like, having been raised in a village in Hiroshima, Japan, then married to an issei man who worked on the historic Waiahole water tunnel project on Oahu before moving to Wahiawa. Kishi's experiences coping with new challenges as her husband transferred from one place to another formed an amazing story. Until then, the majority of picture brides I had interviewed had all come to Hawaii to marry contract laborers on the plantations and had lived most of their lives in one location. After retirement and in widowhood, they all stayed close to each other, as each plantation provided retirement homes where these senior citizens could live comfortably for the rest of their lives. Kishi, however, followed her husband, Keiji, wherever his dreams led him as she persevered in accepting new challenges, learning new things while moving from place to place. She never once mentioned the word *kuro* (suffering) in her interviews.

When I first met Kishi Tsujimura on March 20, 2001, she was already 105 years old. Most of the picture brides I had interviewed up to this point were in their mid-eighties to mid-nineties. Kishi, her silver-gray hair neatly combed back in a bun, was a picture of good health. She was still very sharp in mind, and her lovely face was a healthy tan from doing lots of gardening. She appeared to be about five feet

Kishi Tsujimura, blessed with good health, spry and beautiful, celebrating her 106th birthday with family. Photo courtesy of Koji Tsujimura.

tall. Osteoporosis had curved her spine, which was the only physical trait that might give away her age. Her sons thought she used to be about five foot three or so in her younger days. Kishi wore a simple three-quarter-sleeved blouse in a tiny floral print on a gray background and long pants. Over that she wore a long white canvas apron. I sensed her pride and joy as she showed me her garden.

"I plant all these vegetables we use every day for cooking—see, here's carrots, turnips, eggplant, cabbage, and string beans. I give to my children and grand-children and friends when they come by to visit. I put up the poles for the string beans to crawl up, then it's easy for me to pick them," she said.

In one corner she had asters, stately Easter lilies in bloom, and gladiolas in a lovely array of colors. In a shadier part of the yard near the tool shed, I was amazed to see bright red anthuriums and rare, exotic orchids. I wondered whether these orchid plants were gifts from her children and grandchildren, given to her on special occasions. Kishi nurtured them with love and affection, remarkably doing all the planting and digging herself. She said she sat on the ground to do her weeding, and when she was not able to stand, she crawled on her belly and dug furrows with a short hoe to plant the seeds. This was done when she thought no one was around, but friends who had dropped in unexpectedly and seen this were impressed by her strength and determination to be independent, keep busy, and lead a productive life.

After a pleasant tour of her garden, Kishi invited me into her home. She took off her white canvas apron smudged with red dirt and hung it on the hook by the kitchen door. Before we sat down on the sofa, Kishi opened the fridge and offered me a drink and a snack.

She said, "Look at all the cooked food, fruits, and snacks all my sons bring for me every day. I cannot eat them all. When Keiso, my oldest son, comes in with fresh food prepared by his wife, Yukie, he tells me to throw away the old ones, even the rice brought the day before. He wants me to eat the fresh cooked rice that he brought. I say no, you cannot waste food. Kazuto, my second son, brings more food that his wife, Mary, cooked for me. Then Koji [third son] and Masato [fourth son] bring me more food and fresh eggs, so that my *aisu boxu* [refrigerator] is always full. I can only eat so much, you know. So when friends come visit, I tell them to take some food home. I have four sons and good daughters-in-law. They take good care of me. After my husband, Keiji, died in 1980, when he was eighty-seven years old, my boys come to see me every day. I want you to take some food and eggs home."

I quickly responded, "I can't take home what your sons kindly brought for you. They want you to stay healthy."

We finally sat down on the comfortable rattan furniture in the living room, with the cushions upholstered in colorful Hawaiian foliage designs that brightened up the room. Next to the sofa I noticed a Singer sewing machine that seemed like an early 1900s model. To the right I saw a tall Buddhist altar lined with memorial tablets of her ancestors and family and holding a vase filled with sweet-scented flowers from her garden.

CHILDHOOD MEMORIES

Kishi began her story. "Kabe-mura, where I was born and raised, was known as Sengan-mura because it comprised a thousand homes. It was considered quite a large village during that time. Today, it is part of Hiroshima city and is called Kabe-machi [Kabe city]. Imagine, among these thousand homes, the Tsujimura and Oki families lived only three houses apart." It seemed strange that during their growing-up years Kimi Oki (Kimi was her given name at birth; I will explain later how she came to be known as Kishi) hardly knew Keiji Tsujimura.

Kishi spoke in a soft Hiroshima dialect, but she included some Hawaiian words and some Pidgin. She told me, "My father's name was Masakichi Oki. My mother's name was Tomo. She died when I was six years old. I can't remember my mother because I was too young. Those days, people didn't take photos, so I had no way of remembering my mother's face. The only thing that remained in my memory was the *aza* [birthmark] on her face. Funny, that is the only thing I can remember about my mother. After a while, my father remarried and more children arrived from the second marriage.

"My *mamahaha* [stepmother], Mina, was not good-looking but a very kind person and had a good heart. In those days, children died so young—so my parents worry about me to make sure I stay healthy. I was pampered and fed only good things like *iriko* [parched small sardines] and eggs. I never had to eat *tsuke mono* [pickled vegetables]. Most poor families, that's all they had most of the time besides *miso shiru* [soybean soup] every day. My sister and younger brother died young. Toshiko, my half sister, survived and lived to be about ninety years old, dying in 1986. I was about ninety years old then.

"I attended Kabe *sho gakko* [elementary school], Koto *sho gakko* [intermediate school], and continued to *hoshuko* [ninth grade]. In those days some of the *hoshuko* graduates taught at the elementary schools. It was impossible for me to commute to high school in the city. I had to help my parents in their tofu and *aburage* [fried tofu] shop. I'm glad I learned the technique of making good tofu and *aburage* from them. That knowledge came in handy when I came to Hawaii and needed to supplement the family income when we were going through hard times," Kishi recalled.

Kishi reminisced about the ancient Hongwanji temple grounds where the ancestral tombstones of the Oki family, weather-beaten from age, were still standing. "Since my half sister Toshiko is gone now, there's no one to inform me of the latest news from home. See, I have Toshiko's letters from Japan, all kept in this *kyodai* [dressing stand] drawer. Oh, here it is with her new address in Hiroshima city. There had been many changes since I left the village in 1915. . . . Toshiko had two boys and one daughter. Both sons died young. One died of cancer. I heard he was very bright and graduated from Tendai. Too bad . . . he could have done some worthwhile things. The older son went off to war and died. I know during World War II when the atom bomb was dropped in Hiroshima, the entire city burned down. It was awful. Kabe-mura is in the suburbs, so we were spared. It was so sad for the people of Hiroshima city. The Hiroshima-ken people in Hawaii sent whatever kimonos, casual clothing, and foodstuffs they had to relatives. That's the reason I don't have any kimonos to show you," Kishi said sadly.

"My childhood wasn't anything eventful. My father worked as a *nakagai* [middleman or broker] for *aizome* [indigo dye business]. One of his co-workers came as a *yoshi* [adopted son-in-law] into the family. People wondered why he came as a *yoshi* when his family had fine family status in Kabe-mura. Even in the Oki family, one son went as a *yoshi*. For that reason, *keizu* [family history] is valuable because it records the true family line. The status of the *yoshi* is clearly stated and included as part of the genealogy. This *yoshi* wasn't able to help with the business and the family went bankrupt. Because my father was the *hoshonin* [witness] in co-signing the loan when the owner borrowed money to start the indigo dye business, he lost everything. To survive, he had to think of an easy way to make money right away, so he started the tofu business. Japanese people used tofu a lot for their everyday diet. He thought tofu was an easy way to make money, but it was hard work and time-consuming. I used to watch my father make tofu. You have to be patient and stir the ingredients slowly to produce a good-textured, solid tofu. Since tofu making turned out to be a success, Father started making *aburage*. Masakichi learned all he could about the business. He got so good in making *aburage* it became a good seller. *Aburage* is made from sliced tofu and fried in hot oil until it gets brown and crisp. If rancid oil is used, the *aburage* does not get crispy and results in a soggy *aburage*. These cannot be sold, so the family used it for their meals, and yet it was delicious," Kishi said with a smile, adding, "Nothing was wasted." At a young age, Kishi learned to be frugal.

KEIJI TSUJIMURA

Keiji Tsujimura was born on February 13, 1893, in the same village as Kishi. During the early immigration period, the greatest number of immigrants came from the southwestern prefectures of Japan, especially from Hiroshima and Yamaguchi. Those regions were hardest hit with famine and poor economic conditions and many young farmers eagerly responded to the recruiting efforts of the Hawaiian sugar planters. Keiji was barely fourteen years old, but since his older brother, Koichi, had left for Hawaii in 1903 during the *jiyu imin jidai* (free immigration period, 1900–1907) to work at the Koloa sugar plantation on Kauai, he also wanted to follow in his brother's footsteps. His dream finally came true. Keiji bade a sad farewell to his parents and promised to return after the three-year contract was completed, confident that he would strike it rich by then. Keiji boarded the ship USS *Siberia* in Kobe and after a rough ten-day voyage arrived in Honolulu on September 20, 1907.

He came during the *yobi-yose* period (1907–1924), known as the "summoning of relatives" period, so he must have been summoned by his older brother, Koichi. According to the U.S. Census report, he headed for the Mountain View and Glenwood area of Puna district, Hawaii, about twenty-two miles from Hilo at the Volcano Road camp. The third son, Koji, learned that his father had worked at the Mountain View Puna plantation on the Big Island in the *mokuzai ko jyo* (lumber mill). The lumber mill made railroad ties that were used by various sugar plantations for their trains to haul sugarcane from distant fields. Today, koa wood is a luxury item, but in those days, koa trees grew wild on the Big Island and were used for railroad ties. They were much stronger than ordinary lumber so they must have made sturdy tracks.

Keiji told Kishi how difficult it was at that young age to work among the older men who were so much stronger and could lift the heavy ties. He had to do everything on his own. The living conditions were very poor, and the kitchen had an earthen floor. Later, when Kishi came as a young bride and had to go through so many hardships, Keiji told her about this early period when he first worked for the Puna sugar plantation. The hardships he endured as a young boy were so difficult that he could barely talk about that time. The pay was so little, but everyone worked hard. He ate simple food, such as canned deviled ham, which he packed with his rice for lunch along with pickled turnips, dried fish, or canned sardines cooked over a small kerosene stove. Often, though, it was only rice, pickled vegetables, and miso soup.

PICTURE BRIDE TO HAWAII

After Keiji completed his three-year contract at Puna plantation, his older brother, Koichi, encouraged him to come to Honolulu instead of renewing his contract. Koichi managed a taxi business in Aala Park, which was good business in those days when the immigrant families did not own cars. When Koichi felt that Keiji was earning a good income and ready to settle down, he wrote home and asked his parents to find a bride for him. Keiji's parents immediately thought of their neighbor Kimi. Both families had known each other for many years, and they had watched Kimi grow up to be a lovely young lady, hardworking and efficient. Keiji and Kimi, however, had hardly known each other while they were growing up. Her stepmother had sent her to kimono sewing class, etiquette training, and tea ceremony school in preparation for marriage.

"For my dowry, my father wanted to buy me a special silk fabric for a dressy kimono. He went himself to the kimono fabric shop across the street. It was very expensive and my father told me not to mention the price to my stepmother. I guess father was *kitsukau* [sensitive] about hurting my stepmother's feelings. Father must have felt that if my mother had lived long enough to see me get married, she would have made something special for my dowry. In a way, I felt happy to come to Hawaii; it would be easier for my father now. I didn't realize until then how difficult it must have been for him. My stepmother was very good to me and I felt so *arigatai* [grateful] for her help and guidance . . . all those years. There must have been lots of things she wanted to teach me, but she held back too, not being my real mother. While crossing the Pacific, I made friends with other picture brides. It made me aware of a great many things.

"Our *baishaku nin* was our next-door neighbor. He owned a candy store and knew both families well. He acted as the intermediary and wrote letters back and forth to the family friend who was handling arrangements in Hawaii. Even though they were old friends and close neighbors, the exchange of photos, the *miai,* had to be formally done to show respect to both families.

"Although I heard many stories about Hawaii, I never imagined that someday I would be traveling 4,000 miles across the Pacific Ocean to become a picture bride of a man who left the village in 1907. He was fifteen years old at that time. We were married by proxy. Someone took the place of my husband when the marriage ceremony was performed with the *san san kudo* exchange of cups of sake. In those days, that was how you were considered officially married, according to traditional Japanese custom. The most important thing was to register my name into the Tsujimura *koseki* [family register] at the *yakuba* [village office]. I think that was when the clerk at the village office registered my name as Kishi instead of Kimi. I didn't notice the mistake at that time. When I arrived in Hawaii and had to go through immigration inspection, I noticed my name was registered as Kishi Oki Tsujimura. After that I used the name Kishi, and I learned to like it," said Kishi, breaking out in laughter.

"I lived with my in-laws for six months, waiting for my visa to be processed. I think I was spoiled, and I'm embarrassed when I think about it now. Because my home was nearby, whenever I was unhappy about something I used to run back to my home," she laughed.

"The sea was rough during the ten-day voyage. I got so seasick, no appetite. I threw up everything. I was relieved to see land again. We arrived in Honolulu harbor on November 17, 1915. I wondered if there would be someone to meet me. I could not speak English or Hawaiian, only my Hiroshima dialect. After we got off the ship, we followed everybody into the huge room in the immigration station . . . there were many other picture brides, and we all seemed scared and nervous to be in strange, unfamiliar surroundings. I remember taking brief examinations and comprehensive tests before we were allowed to go out. I felt a sense of relief when my husband, Keiji, identified me by the picture he had. He came with Giichi Saji, who was also from our village. He was a small man but very smart. He later worked as a radio announcer for a Japanese radio station. This was the first time I met my husband formally. When he left the village in 1907, I hardly knew him. In those days, boys and girls were not allowed to talk to each other in school or even sit next to each other," Kishi explained, chuckling as she recalled those days. Keiji and Kishi were married en masse at the immigration station with other picture brides and spouses by Rev. Yemyo Imamura, who later became the first bishop at the Honpa Hongwanji Mission in Honolulu.

According to Koji, Keiji and Kishi started their married life in Honolulu. They resided at Dowsett Lane in Palama, where their first and second sons, Keiso and Kazuto, were born, and where Keiji first worked as a driver for his brother's taxi stand, after completing his plantation contract and moving to Honolulu from the Big Island. Today it would be near the Tamashiro seafood market.

Kishi arrived at a very interesting time in Hawaii's history. Waiahole Water Company, with the cooperation of Oahu Sugar Company, was building the Waiahole water tunnel to send water through the Koolau Range from windward Oahu to leeward Oahu, where large fields of sugarcane were being cultivated. They had a workforce of about nine hundred people, and Keiji worked on the tunnel project from about 1910 to 1916.

"The tunnel was big. Because it was so long they had to cut it and make an exit so people could get out from in between, and the main tunnel had many shops outside," Kishi described. Keiji was a man of many talents, as he proved with his construction and technical skills. He was eventually selected as one of the first issei engineers for the water tunnel project, and he was the first issei to drive the locomotive in Kaneohe. The young family moved from Palama to the windward side.

Kishi remembered what a lonely and isolated place Kaneohe was back then. "There must have been about a hundred workers of many ethnic groups. There were three other issei families, the Uratas, Haradas, and Mizunos, whose husbands also worked on the water tunnel project. We lived in tents made of canvas. The Haradas lived in the largest tent by the tunnel entrance. Not many houses in Waiahole in those days. Water for cooking was taken from the higher place, upstream. It rained all the time, and we felt miserable.

"There was only one big wooden *furo* [bath] outdoors, shared by the three families. There was only one outhouse, so that too, we had to stand in line. When women had menses, with long line waiting, no privacy. It very hard to imagine the hardships we endured. The women all helped each other; we became like one big family."

The couple's third son, Koji, was born in Waiahole, and Keiji worked there until the tunnel project was completed. Koji remembered living in a house stained green, using an outhouse, and bathing in a *furo*.

Kishi continued, "When the tunnel project was *pau* [finished], we all moved to Wahiawa, which was between the Waianae and Koolau ranges and known for its cool climate and lush tropical forests. It's famous for its delicious pineapples and *aka deppo* [red dirt]. The Harada family's oldest daughter, Marian, started Dot's Drive-Inn, which later became Dot's Restaurant and Marian's Catering. To this day, we are still good friends, and our children are good friends, too. We had many friends from Hiroshima doing business in Wahiawa."

Keiji and Kishi made many wonderful friends in windy and rainy Kaneohe, but after the tunnel project was completed, the family was happy to move to Wahiawa, where Masato, the fourth son, was born. Keiji had a good friend, Mr. Sunahara, a nisei who was born in Honohina, Kauai. Their parents came from the same village in Hiroshima, and the children became good friends. It was Mr. Sunahara who encouraged Keiji to move to Wahiawa and join him in the taxi business. Wahiawa was

Kishi Tsujimura in her younger days with her pet dog Bear, in Wahiawa. Photo courtesy of Koji Tsujimura.

located next to the Schofield Barracks, and soldiers frequently needed a ride to town. During World War II, however, Keiji, an alien, was banned from entering Schofield Barracks. Losing the soldiers as passengers made a great difference.

They also offered taxi service from Wahiawa to Honolulu about every hour, or when they had enough passengers. The fare was 50 cents one way, and the trip took one and a half hours. The taxi stand was across from the Shibuya restaurant, where Jiffy Lube stands today. They eventually had ten issei men who provided daily transportation to Honolulu. It was interesting to hear from Tajiro Uranaka that these two good friends were also good *shakuhachi* (bamboo flute) players, and while waiting for passengers they would play the *shakuhachi* to pass the time. How beautiful the strains of the *shakuhachi* must have sounded in those peaceful prewar days!

Masato said, "In the early days, Mother raised chickens. She sold the eggs and vegetables from her garden to the Nakai grocery store on Kilani Avenue. We would eat chicken once a year. She used whatever means to make extra money to supplement the family income."

During high school, Koji remembers delivering the gerbera daisies his mother raised to Endo Florist, located in the first building coming into Wahiawa. She also grew gladiolas. Keiji made sake out of rice to sell to Narusawa Restaurant. Since it was illegal, he had to hide it to bring it to the restaurant.

In the 1950s, Kishi began raising anthuriums in red, orange, and white. She didn't have the fancy ones yet. They would get dry taro husks from the Waiahole poi factory to use as the planting medium. She bought anthurium plants from various people in Wahiawa and from her daughter-in-law Yukie's father, who also raised anthuriums in Kaneohe. Kishi was never idle.

DECISION TO REMAIN IN HAWAII

In 1926, when Keiji finally made up his mind not to return to Japan but to settle permanently in Hawaii, he purchased a lot for $200 from Mr. Seichi Nakagawa, also from Hiroshima. According to Koji, the lot was approximately 9,000 square feet and was located at 244 Muliwai Avenue in the lower part of Wahiawa. At that time, land could be purchased for 10 cents per square foot.

Keiji was very *oyakoko* (observant of filial piety). He never forgot the promise he had made to his parents to return someday to take care of them, but now, with four sons, he decided to make Hawaii his permanent home. Keiji and Kishi were glad they took their four boys several times to visit both families in Japan while their parents were still healthy and able to enjoy their grandchildren.

Kishi recalled, "A railroad track ran alongside our property at the end of Muliwai Avenue. At one time, it was owned by the Dillingham family and later sold to the Kaneohe Ranch Company. The Oahu Sugar Company and Dole Pineapple Company used the tracks daily to haul the sugarcane and pineapples. Every time the trains passed, it made a lot of noise, but for my boys and their friends, it was exciting to watch the trains go by."

Keiji, with his carpentry skills and great ideas, built a nice three-bedroom, single-bath home on the newly acquired lot on Muliwai Avenue. The cost to build the house was $1,500. At that time, the front entrance faced Muliwai Avenue. Old friends know the entrance facing Muliwai Avenue is the front entrance to the original structure of the duplex, where Keiji and Kishi resided.

A most interesting attraction at Kishi's front entrance was the black mynah bird that perched on the sill when it was let out of its cage. This was Kishi's pet. It was an unusual mynah bird who imitated Kishi when she sneezed in the morning; the bird's "Hakshu!" sounded exactly like hers! That was the first sound the mynah learned to imitate. The first name he learned to call was Ko-chan, Kishi's affectionate name for her third son, Koji. It was Koji who had found the mynah at the Wahiawa Hongwanji temple grounds while volunteering to help out with the year-round construction work being done at the temple. He thought the baby mynah could have fallen off a tree branch, so he brought it home to his mother. He thought she would enjoy having the mynah for a pet. It turned out to be a wonderful companion. She adored the baby bird and took good care of it, feeding and nurturing it. Kishi enjoyed talking to it for many years.

The mynah's name was Mano, and Kishi told how Masato, her fourth and youngest son, would catch grasshoppers for its food every day, much to her delight.

Masato came in the mornings to check on his mother. He brought cooked food for her, fresh eggs, and helped her with her morning bath. The mynah would call, *"Ma-chan, Ma-chan,"* exactly the way Kishi sounded. Kishi also had an adorable black *poi* (mixed-breed) dog named Bear. Kishi would prepare his food by cooking scraps of food in a small pot. When she brought the food outside for Bear to eat, she would tap the spoon on the pot and call out, "Bear, *kau kau.*" Mano would imitate Kishi's voice exactly, and the sound of the spoon as well: *"Clink, clink, clink, clink! Bear, kau kau."* Mano would even imitate the sound of Kishi walking in her *geta* (wooden clogs) on the concrete walkway: *"Kalan koron, kalan koron."* Kishi would sometimes take the bird out of its cage, but it never flew away, and would nip at her

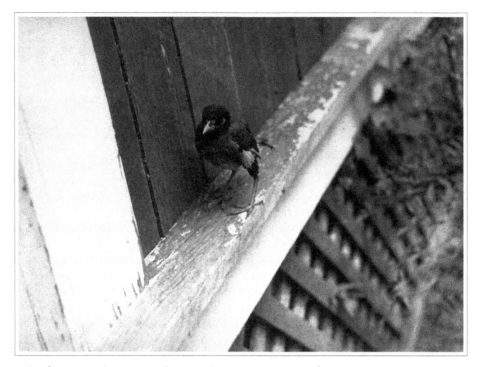

Kishi's favorite pet, the amazing talking mynah bird. Photo courtesy of Koji Tsujimura.

legs in a playful way. As time went by, the bird became old, and one day they found it lying on the bottom of the cage. It was a sad day when the family buried the loving mynah bird in the garden. Koji, Masato, and Kishi's granddaughter Carolyn shared this delightful story about the talented Mano.

WHEN SONS MARRIED, KISHI GAINED FOUR DAUGHTERS

Although Kishi didn't have any daughters, she found the joy of sharing and teaching traditional Japanese cooking, sewing, and other things, like any mother and daughter would do, with her daughters-in-law. She was a very wise and loving mother to her four sons, and as each son got married, the couples lived with Keiji and Kishi in their house, which they expanded into a duplex (which explains why there were two front entryways to the Tsujimura residence). Keiso and his wife, Yukie, stayed with the family for about three years; the younger brothers each stayed for a year or so.

When I asked her, "Didn't you miss not having a daughter?" she replied, "Well, when I was raising the boys and saw my friends with their daughters, I used to envy them. But after my boys were grown up and became of marrying age, they all brought home lovely wives, so I felt that I had gained four wonderful daughters. Having raised four boys, I found girls are so *yasashi* [sweet]. I regarded them like my own daughters. I may have been too strict at times without being aware of their feelings, but I taught them how to sew aloha shirts and men's trousers, cook traditional Japanese dishes, and we did craft work together."

FIRST SON, KEISO, AND HIS FAMILY ON MULIWAI

Kishi recollected, "Keiso got married to Yukie Yamashiro through matchmaking. We had our meals together and shared the housework and cooking. Yukie was a hard worker and an excellent cook. She had worked as a domestic for a Caucasian family in Honolulu when she was young, so we enjoyed the food she prepared." Kishi was delighted to taste the special dishes Yukie prepared. She said, "Yukie's stuffed green peppers was something new that everyone enjoyed." Kishi excelled in traditional Japanese cooking, so trying American dishes for the first time was a delight. Also, to have her oldest son's wife doing the cooking and to see her boys enjoying the American dishes made her happy. Yukie was a devoted daughter-in-law. Even after they moved to a place nearby when their daughter, Carolyn, was three years old, Yukie came all the time to help Kishi with cooking and cleaning.

TEACHING SEWING

Kishi taught Yukie how to sew aloha shirts. She showed her how to cut the patterns so that the designs would match and face the right way. Kishi was very exact in teaching the young bride how to line up the design on the pocket of the aloha shirt with the design on the bodice. Kishi even taught Yukie to sew men's trousers and how to do the set-in pockets, which was a very complicated step. Yukie had to rip the pocket off and redo it many times until Kishi was satisfied. Kishi had sewn military uniforms, so she was an expert in men's tailoring.

Kishi learned just as much from Yukie about gardening and raising anthuriums. Yukie's family had been in the anthurium business in the Kaneohe/Waikane area on the island of Oahu for many years. When their first granddaughter, Carolyn, arrived, Keiji and Kishi were thrilled, and of course they pampered her and never let her out of their sight.

Eventually Keiso, Yukie, and Carolyn moved behind the Service Motors Company at the corner of Ohai and Olive Avenue. Later they moved to their residence on Glen Avenue, in the cool upper highlands of Wahiawa. Keiji helped to build their home. As Carolyn explained, "We were fortunate that Mrs. Kimie Matsuda, owner of Omochaya, sold half of her property of 10,000 square feet on Glen Avenue to my parents. Mrs. Matsuda knew they would be good neighbors." Yukie continued to raise her anthuriums, expanding to include variations of *obake* (flowers with multiple colors). Yukie sold her flowers at Big Way Market. During the busy spring season of Easter, Mother's Day, and Memorial Day, Kishi would help Yukie clean and bundle the statice, button daisies, and marguerites.

SECOND SON, KAZUTO (GEORGE), AND HIS WIFE, MARY

When Kazuto, who was known as George, and his wife, Mary, first moved in, Keiso, Yukie, and their baby daughter, Carolyn, were still living with Keiji and Kishi. With his carpentry skills, Keiji built an extension to the house on Muliwai Avenue and added a bedroom and bath. George and Mary lived there for one year. Mary remembers her mother-in-law as a smart and hardworking lady. She was always neatly dressed, kind of *oshare* (fancy), and had her hair done by Mrs. Murakoshi, who did beauty work at her home. One of the first things Kishi taught Mary as a new bride was how to be frugal, not by lecturing but by demonstrating it, holding up a paper bag with holes on the bottom. Mary wondered what her mother-in-law was trying to show her. Kishi explained that putting a penny into the bag is like spending, spending, spending, because the money cannot stay in the bag. But if you close the bottom, even a penny dropped into the bag every day will amount to something by the end of the year. You need to close the bottom of the bag by placing a can in it, or you will become poor. To this day, Mary never forgot the valuable lesson Kishi taught her: *"Issen ni warau mono wa, issen ni naku"* (those who laugh at a penny will someday cry over a penny). Kishi never forgot the days of struggle during her childhood in Hiroshima, and passed on the valuable lessons she had learned to her daughters-in-law and grandchildren.

Kishi also taught Mary how to sew aloha shirts, as she had taught Yukie. Mary, however, didn't have the patience to learn how to sew men's trousers. Sewing the set-in pocket was just too difficult. Kishi was very understanding and didn't force her to do it. To this day, Mary is grateful to her mother-in-law for teaching her to be a good seamstress.

According to Mary, living together in the duplex during the early part of her marriage was a wonderful learning experience. She was born and raised in Honolulu and had enjoyed a carefree existence as a young girl, and had to adjust to country living. Mary's mother thought she was too young to get married and wouldn't be able to cope with a strict mother-in-law. Contrary to Mary's mother's concerns, however, Kishi cherished her sons' wives as the daughters she'd never had, and enjoyed sharing things with them. It made her life richer.

Granddaughter Carolyn learned a lot about her *obaachan*'s (grandmother's) generosity. "Obaachan grew tender green beans, and I always wondered why she gave me only five string beans in a paper bag. When I heard Aunty Mary talk about the generosity of Obaachan, it dawned on me that she wanted to give equally to Yukie, Mary, Amy [Masato's wife], Grace [Koji's wife], and the neighbors too." Carolyn was grateful to learn from her grandmother at a very young age the wonderful sense of sharing something that she had grown herself. "Obaachan's string beans always tasted so tender and so good!"

Mary mentioned during her interview, "I am happy I married into the Tsujimura family. All the brothers always helped each other in time of need. I guess it's the way the parents had set an example for the boys to follow ever since they were young."

KOJI, LAST TO GET MARRIED

With his skills in machine work and welding, Koji, the third son, initially went to work for a construction company to help build Tripler Hospital. In 1948, he was drafted into the army and went for basic training at Schofield. One of the officers asked him if he wanted to be in the infantry and go to war. Koji decided to heed the officer's implication and transferred to the Air Force, which stationed him at Hickam

Air Force Base. He later transferred to the Hawaii Air National Guard, serving for eleven years.

Around the 1950s he became a very successful contractor and started Wahiawa Builders Inc. He built a large number of the important buildings in Wahiawa and some in Mililani town. I said to Koji, "I bet your mother must have been very proud to see all the wonderful buildings that sprang up in Wahiawa and Mililani."

"I don't know how she felt," he replied. "She was probably too busy."

Koji married Grace Yamaki on July 3, 1951. He built another duplex with a second story on the east side of the house built by his father in 1926. They lived there and had their meals together with his parents every day. When asked what kind of food Kishi prepared, Grace replied, "She cooked Japanese dishes, so most of the food was seasoned with a little sugar and shoyu, like *nishime* and different types of fish." Keiji loved fresh sashimi, so Kishi always bought fresh fish. Granddaughter Carolyn gave a good description of how her grandfather prepared the sashimi with much ceremony. "He would sharpen his special knife, then carefully slice the sashimi into thin slices," she said. "The sashimi prepared by Grandfather was so delicious that today when I eat sashimi at the Japanese restaurant, they are cut too thick. You really have to chew on it or bite it into several pieces. Ojichan's sashimi was easier to eat and tasted better." Grace said it was wonderful learning new things from her mother-in-law.

Koji later turned the duplex over to his parents for a rental after he built his and Grace's own home on Glen Avenue. Keiji and Kishi rented the duplex to people they would enjoy having as neighbors.

After Grace had her first child, she quit her job and helped her husband's business with the paperwork and running errands to military establishments. One day Grace took her mother-in-law to Barber's Point in Ewa district to deliver some contract papers from Wahiawa Builders. She wanted Kishi's help in taking care of her little girl while she ran into the military base office. It caught her by surprise when the security guard would not let Kishi in with her because she was an alien. Grace felt so bad leaving her mother-in-law alone with the security guard. But that was following World War II, and Grace hadn't realized the restrictions imposed by the military establishment. Kishi didn't complain and wasn't afraid. She quietly waited for Grace to finish her business at the base.

Koji recalled the day a letter came from Hiroshima notifying Kishi that her half sister Toshiko had passed away. He happened to walk in on one of his daily visits when he saw his mother sitting in front of her Singer sewing machine, trying to sew, and crying her heart out. Kishi had the Buddhist altar right next to the sewing machine, and she had immediately lit the *senko* (stick of incense) for Toshiko's soul to enter nirvana. They had been very close and Toshiko was like a real sister to Kishi. Since Kishi had come to Hawaii in 1915, Toshiko was her only link to their village after her parents were gone.

No matter how busy he was, Koji visited his mother daily during lunch hour. Kishi enjoyed fixing lunch for him and sometimes opened a can of crab for lunch, which was quite a treat in those days. Koji gave his parents part-time jobs at his business, wanting to make sure they could claim Social Security benefits when they retired. Keiji, with his expertise in carpentry, added a lot of improvements around the shop and office, which Kishi cleaned daily—even at age 103.

FOURTH SON, MASATO

Masato, the youngest son, married a woman named Amy, and the newlyweds lived with Kishi and Keiji for a few years. They spent many happy times together, cooking Japanese food and doing crafts. Kishi fondly remembered how Amy always assured her, "Please don't worry, I'm going to take care of you when you get old." "But Amy died so young, at age sixty-three," Kishi quietly told me as tears filled her eyes. Masato later married a second time, to a woman named Gladys. When my book *Japanese Immigrants' Clothing in Hawaii, 1885–1941* was translated into Japanese and the Shirokiya store arranged to have book signings at Ala Moana and Pearl Ridge, Masato and Gladys brought Kishi to the Pearl Ridge branch. At 104, Kishi turned out to be quite the celebrity.

DECEMBER 7, 1941

World War II caught everyone by surprise. When the 442nd Regiment Combat Team was organized on March 23, 1943, the War Department called for volunteers to form an all-Japanese American army combat unit. Koji and George volunteered for the 442nd and went together to the Schofield dispensary to have their physical exam. This was a very uncertain time, especially for their parents, who were considered enemy aliens, and no one knew what would happen to the boys who volunteered for the U.S. armed forces. Kishi was proud the boys wanted to serve the country of their birth but was afraid for them. Koji recalled that day and how sad it was to see his mother crying because she thought she was never going to see her two boys again. However, the recruiting official unexpectedly said the army could take only one son from each family, so George, being the older son, got inducted. He was sent to Camp Shelby, Mississippi, for training. From October through November 1944, the 442nd served in northeastern France and fought in the bitter-cold forests of the Vosges Mountains. George's company was involved with the other units that rescued the Texas "Lost Battalion" near Bruyeres; he also fought in Italy. George was wounded in France and awarded the Purple Heart and the Bronze Star. On his return, he applied for work at the Pearl Harbor shipyard as a machinist, and was hired in part because of his service during the war. Later on he went to work with Koji at what by then had become Wahiawa Builders.

RELIGION

Kishi belonged to the Wahiawa Hongwanji Mission and was a member of the *fujinkai* (women's association) there, but she did not have time to attend church services regularly. Although she did not attend services, Kishi chanted the *shoshinge* (Buddhist sutra) every morning. During those sessions she would ask for everyone's well-being. When asked how she could remember the sutra, she said, "I chanted it with my mother as a young child and over the course of the years had memorized it. I also listened to the Japanese radio station on Saturdays and Sundays when they had good sermons. I enjoyed listening to that. In Japan, on special occasions, the priests went house to house. We always made *orei* [offerings of gratitude] besides letting him take some food."

Keiso's wife, Yukie, was a Christian and had attended church as a young girl. But to Kishi, it didn't matter what religion people belonged to. "I believed that all religion never taught anything bad and always taught good things to help people. If no religion, then not good."

Carolyn admired Kishi's openness and understanding about religion. Carolyn's own mother was a Christian, and not all of Kishi's children were Buddhist, but that did not bother Kishi, who believed that there were many roads that led to heaven, each one with its own faith, and that in the end, all converge together. "She was quite happy when I joined the Wahiawa Hongwanji, and told me that when she died, she wanted me to take the *butsudan* [Buddhist family altar, also referred to as *obutsudan*] that sat next to her sewing machine." Today, Carolyn Uchiyama is in charge of the Dharma School at Wahiawa Honwanji and takes care of the family's Buddhist altar.

Kishi mentioned that when she first came to Hawaii she had wanted to learn the art of *ikebana* (flower arrangement), but she became pregnant with her first child, Keiso, so she gave up on the idea. After moving to Wahiawa, she finally had the opportunity to take formal lessons from Reverend Hino's wife at Wahiawa Hongwanji through the *fujinkai*.

KISHI AND HER 1927 SINGER SEWING MACHINE

Carolyn remembered her grandmother sewing on the Singer machine she had bought back in 1927. She was amazed to see how meticulously Kishi sewed despite having never taken sewing classes. In Hiroshima they only wore kimonos, which were hand-sewn. But when Kishi came to Hawaii she met a kindly issei woman who showed her how to sew Western-type clothing. She shared some patterns with Kishi, who, being a smart, industrious woman with a curiosity to learn new things, learned all the tricks of the trade in no time. By trial and error she learned to sew her husband's work clothes and the school clothes for her four sons. She even sewed sailor hats for her boys.

Mrs. Haruno Uranaka, a kind and wonderful neighbor, also shared many intricate sewing techniques. Mrs. Uranaka sewed military uniforms and did alterations for the soldiers stationed in nearby Schofield Barracks. She also sewed on the stripes for the soldiers' uniforms. Mrs. Uranaka couldn't keep up with the heavy demand and asked Kishi to help her. It was a wonderful opportunity to supplement the family income at a time when many issei men's income was insufficient to support a growing family. So Kishi began sewing her own *kanaka-gi* (Hawaiian-style dress) on her sewing machine. She was an expert in sewing kimonos by hand, but she found it much more fun to make clothes with the machine.

Koji's secretary, Hiroko Yamaki (Grace's sister-in-law), remembered, "Mrs. Tsujimura worked for the Hayashi family tailor shop and sewed pants and shirts. Later she worked for Aloha Tailor. She was a fine seamstress and did very neat sewing. With scraps that she brought home from the tailor shop, she made shorts and aloha shirts for my sons. My oldest son, Evan [born in 1952], was four years old then."

Masato added, "Mother sewed GI clothes for Hayashi Tailor on Kam Highway. She would take the clothing apart, make patterns from the pieces, and sew it back together again. That's how she learned."

Masato's daughters, Lois, Merle, and Edean, also had fond remembrances of their *obaachan*. "She was an expert seamstress, and lovingly sewed numerous *chanchankos* [vests] for her great-grandchildren. The fabric for the girls was pink with flowers or cranes, and blue or brown for the boys. Each of these *chanchankos* was lined with flannel, with meticulously hand-stitched pleats, and designed to be secured with ties or single-buttoned button loops." Lois still has some of her grandmother's *chanchankos*.

The sisters noted that "Obaachan's Singer sewing machine cabinet drawers held evidence of an organized, meticulous, and thrifty individual. There were sharpened, one-and-a-half-inch stubs of pencils; matchbox-size boxes of buttons, sorted by color and size; screwdrivers of all sizes and shapes; buttonhole blades; safety pins of all sizes; sewing machine parts carefully packed in a box with cloth remnants, or in cloth bags sewn from fabric scraps; and a pocket-sized memo book filled with numerous scraps of paper and pages with scribbled measurements in *katakana* [the Japanese writing system]."

Carolyn remembered how Grandma Kishi walked all over Wahiawa town, from the Castner store on Kamehameha Highway to the Cornet and Ben Franklin stores on California Avenue, looking for fabrics to sew for her family. Kishi enjoyed buying fabrics for her four daughters-in-law. As Mary pointed out, "She never gave to only one. She gave equally the same amount of yardage but selected the color and print to fit the age. She had pretty good taste. For the oldest daughter-in-law, she would pick something appropriate for her age, for the second one, maybe a little brighter, and for the third and fourth, the designs were bolder and more colorful." The daughters-in-law were equally wise and appreciative: they happily sewed the blouses and proudly wore them around. As for herself, Kishi bought conservative fabrics of gray, blue, and dull colors in small floral prints and paisley designs. Once in a while she bought black fabric to make something she could wear to a funeral. She sewed all her dresses almost till the end, and her vision was still sharp enough to thread the needle on the sewing machine.

In those days, peddlers came around from town. They carried Japanese fabrics to make kimonos for adults and children. They also had everything from groceries, vegetables, candies, and medicines to a variety of American fabrics and notions. It was convenient for the issei who didn't have cars. Carolyn remembered, "While living with Grandma, every time the peddler came around, Grandma would let me select the fabric I wanted for my dress. It was such a delightful time for us. I remember the peddler coming in his truck into Obaachan's driveway and dropping the wide side window to reveal all the array of goods neatly displayed inside. It was like a miniature store."

GARDENING

Besides going in to clean the office and workroom of Wahiawa Builders, Kishi spent time in her garden and planted all kinds of vegetables and flowers. She wanted to be comfortable working in her garden, so she wore pants and a jacket. She took in Carolyn's old pants to fit her. She usually wore a heavy canvas apron to protect her clothing and wore *jika tabi* (rubber-soled footwear) in the garden.

Granddaughter Lois and her sisters enjoyed the bounty from their *obaachan*'s vegetable garden, which she tended daily. "She grew string beans, eggplant, lettuce, and other vegetables that she always wrapped in newspaper for us whenever we visited. Her garden thrived, as she used scraps from her morning papaya, apple, or orange skins to make her compost. Obaachan also had a huge hothouse of beautiful pink, red, and white anthuriums that she generously shared with family and friends."

Carolyn remembered, "As she got older and even into her hundreds, Obaachan continued to go into her garden. The only problem was that she would stumble and instead of falling forward, she would fall backward. She would be stuck there for hours until someone found her. You see, Obaachan had osteoporosis and with a curved back, falling backward was like putting a turtle on its back. I was often surprised that she did not get dehydrated. She did not let her condition stop her from doing anything. Friends saw her crawling on her stomach, digging and planting seeds, or digging weeds. They admired her *gambare* [never give up] spirit. She never complained about the pain because, as she explained, *'Shikata ga nai'* [can't help it]. Obaachan would always have a smile on her face to family and visitors alike."

Carolyn was fortunate to enjoy Kishi's cooking. "Obaachan made *takuan* with her daikon. She would cut the daikon into bite-size pieces, marinate it with the sauce, and leave it in the white enamel container under the dining table."

KEIJI: MAN OF ALL TRADES

While Kishi kept busy with her many activities and hobbies, Keiji was equally as busy. When he worked for the Waiahole water tunnel project, he acquired valuable experience and technical skills repairing locomotive engines. In those days, there was no one to train him, so he taught himself by taking the engine apart to see how it functioned, then putting it back together. By repeating this a few times, he learned the mechanics of what made the engine run efficiently. He was very intelligent and mechanically inclined, and he was self-taught, as were many issei men during the early immigration period who had incentive to improve their working skills. Keiji was good with his hands in whatever he did. People referred to him as a jack-of-all-trades.

Carolyn had delightful memories of her *ojichan*. "His favorite time was when he came home from a day's work. He would pour himself one cup of sake, according to Obaachan's instructions, but he would drink half and pour himself another cupful. Then he would sit down and roll his own cigarette using the tobacco in the Bull Durham bag. One bag used to cost 25 cents. After that he would relax by playing the *shakuhachi*. Grandma Kishi mentioned how good he was with the *shakuhachi* and she enjoyed the beautiful music in the quiet of the evening."

Carolyn recalled, "One day while Ojichan was working on his car, the jack slipped and smashed his finger. I remember he walked all the way to the doctor's office. His finger was amputated at the middle knuckle and after that he could not play the *shakuhachi*. It was sad not to hear Ojichan play the *shakuhachi* anymore."

NEVER WASTEFUL

Carolyn continued, "Talk about meticulous and orderly! Obaachan would sit on the floor in the kitchen, open the drawers, and put the packages together by size. The containers for food were stored in the same way.

Keiji and Kishi Tsujimura with nine-year-old granddaughter Gayle when she won Radio KOHO's song contest. Photo courtesy of Koji Tsujimura.

"As Obaachan got older she did not sew as much, but her friends got her to crochet *fuikin,* or washcloths, that she made out of cotton yarn. She would make solid or multicolored ones with the variegated yarn. The Japanese tradition of always having something to give someone when they visited was not a problem for her because she always had washcloths handy.

"Being frugal and meticulous, she would use all the scrap pieces of yarn and make a washcloth that was colorful! She even knew how many yards of yarn it took to make one washcloth. That meant she would crochet it, then take it apart to measure how much yarn she had used."

After Carolyn got married, she rented the bottom floor of the house that Koji had built and that he and his wife, Grace, had lived in. "Obaachan gave me some dishes that I still use today. It's hard to give them away even though they are old and I could get new dishes that all match. She even gave me a pot that I still use even though the bottom of it is out of shape. I use it to cook the bigger dishes like corned beef and cabbage. I bought new cookware but it's still sitting in the box. Sounds silly, yeah?"

RAISING A FAMILY

All of Kishi's sons graduated from Leilehua High School and attended vocational school, where the curriculum included training in mechanical work, welding, and electrical work. Masato mentioned, "The rest we learned on our own. We learned by doing and by talking to others."

Kishi became a loving grandmother to eight grandchildren: Carolyn (Keiso's daughter); Joanne (George's daughter); Gayle, Lori, and Lester (Koji's children); and Lois, Merle, and Edean (Masato's daughters). Koji's son is the only one to carry the Tsujimura name. These eight grandchildren gave her twelve great-grandchildren.

"Grandma Kishi had a fantastic memory. Much to the delight of the grand-children and great-grandchildren, she always remembered their birthdays and would have an envelope with money in it. She gave everyone the same amount of $5, no more, no less, and of course, some special goodies to eat!"

Lois remembers "a little memo book in which Obaachan had a page where she wrote down all her grandchildren's and great-grandchildren's birthdays. She gave the girls pieces of fabric for our birthdays and Christmas. We never went home empty-handed. Besides vegetables from her garden and anthuriums, we also took home cookies, crackers, or candy that she received as gifts or purchased from the Naka-mura vendor truck which visited the neighborhood weekly. On numerous occasions she gave us $5 that she took out from an envelope she had tucked in the kitchen drawer or from her purse. She remembered how to sign her name on the envelope by saying out loud, 'Up-u down, up-down' for each letter."

Carolyn was impressed at the way her *obaachan* was able to adapt to technologi-cal advances. Many elderly Japanese people might shy away from leaving a message on a telephone answering machine, either because they were hard of hearing or they did not understand the English language heard on the machine. "Not my grand-mother," Carolyn recalled. "She would call me on the phone, but if I was not home, she would go right along and leave a message. Isn't it amazing for someone at her age that she was not afraid to learn and keep up with the times!" Carolyn said proudly.

Kishi lived to the ripe old age of 106, cared for and loved by her four sons and loving daughters-in-law; she was indeed very blessed that her life was rich and fulfill-ing all the way to the final stages of her wonderful journey. After her two older sons passed away, Koji and Masato came in every day, brought her cooked food, fresh eggs, and fresh vegetables that she might need, and took turns bathing her every day.

At her passing, Rev. Kevin Kuniyuki came to Wahiawa General Hospital for the *makuragyo* (bedside service). He asked Mary what she'd like to say to her mother-in-law, and she responded, *"Obaachan, imamade kawaigatte kudasatte arigato kozaimashita* [Grandmother, thank you very much for being so good to me]." Yukie added, "Now you are in *gokuraku* [heaven]."

Kikuyo Fujimoto

FROM WASHINGTON PLACE
TO THE ROYAL HAWAIIAN HOTEL

October 16, 1898–May 14, 2008
Born in Iwakuni-shi, Yamaguchi-ken
Arrived in Hawaii November 16, 1916

My interview with Kikuyo Fujimoto took place in 1988, when she was ninety years old. Her oldest son, Kunio, and his wife, Morran, joined us for the interview. A number of years later, in 2004, I interviewed Mrs. Fujimoto's oldest daughter, Thelma Chiyomi Onogi, and her second daughter, Edna Nakamoto. Thelma was the first and only nisei to be born at Washington Place in Honolulu, on the grounds of Queen Liliuokalani's palace (which later became the governor's mansion). They helped to clarify some of the historical points in their mother's remarkable life story.

Kikuyo Fujimoto came to Hawaii at the age of nineteen to become the wife of Hikosuke Fujimoto, who served as a steward to Queen Liliuokalani, the last monarch of the Kingdom of Hawaii. It is a unique story because it provides a rare glimpse into the life of a picture bride who, unlike the majority of picture brides of that period, did not come from a farming village. Instead, she found herself living among Hawaiian royalty as she began her married life in Hawaii.

Kikuyo, like most of the other twenty thousand picture brides who came to Hawaii during the restricted immigration period (1908–1924), did not meet her husband until she arrived in Hawaii aboard the *Nippon Maru,* on November 16, 1916. Until then, she had only seen his face in an exchange of photographs.

Hikosuke Fujimoto had come to Hawaii ten years earlier, in 1906. He was from Iwakuni city in Yamaguchi prefecture and was born in 1886, the year after the first *kanyaku imin* [Japanese contract immigrants] began arriving in the islands. After completing his three-year contract with the Hakalau sugar plantation on the Big Island's Hamakua coast, Hikosuke was encouraged by his friend Mr. Morisato to move to Honolulu because job opportunities were better. Mr. Morisato had been working at Washington Place, at the residence of Queen Liliuokalani.

Hikosuke followed his friend's advice and went to Honolulu. His first job was on Beretania Street at the residence of Lilly Wilkenson. From there, he was hired to work at Washington Place.

Exchange photo of Kikuyo Murashige from Yamaguchi prefecture. Photo courtesy of Kikuyo Fujimoto.

Like her husband, Kikuyo was born in Iwakuni city, on October 16, 1898. Her father was a well-educated master craftsman who made a variety of sacred orna-ments and streamers, *shikishi* (poetry cards), and other handicrafts associated with special Shinto ceremonies—just as his father, grandfather, and many generations before them had done. Seven hired assistants and apprentices helped him. Kikuyo recalled that he even made a *torii* (shrine archway). Concrete slabs are now used for shrine structures, but in her father's day, she said, very particular types of stones were used to construct the shrine's foundation.

Kikuyo came from a large family of five girls and four boys. She said her mother was a housewife who was kept busy taking care of her children. She also prepared meals for her husband's workers.

In spite of being brought up in a large family, Kikuyo was able to attend school until tenth grade. In *kootooka* (senior high school), she studied history, music, mathematics, geography, composition, calligraphy, and other subjects. At the higher level, girls were taught kimono sewing, handicrafts, and etiquette to prepare them for marriage. Singing was also taught at school, but Kikuyo said her voice was so bad that instead she learned to play the *shamisen* (three-stringed instrument) and sing *nagauta* (long epic songs) from the time she was ten years old. One would think that it would be much more difficult for a child of ten to learn *nagauta* because the lyrics were written in calligraphy and were hard to read. While she was singing and playing the *shamisen,* the pauses had to be timed perfectly, so it required lots of practice. Still, she said, she enjoyed singing *nagauta.*

When asked what her childhood was like, Kikuyo smiled, recalling that she played games like *ojyame* (tossing the bean bags) and *nawatobi* (jump rope). Her eyes twinkled as she described how she made dolls out of cornhusks and the silk tassels from the corn. At the age of ninety, she still remembered how she crimped the silk tassel fibers for the doll's hair, made the face, and fashioned the layers of kimono from the husk. She said the dolls didn't take very long to make and were usually done as she talked with her girlfriends. I asked if her grandchildren might enjoy the dolls. She said they probably would, but noted that today's children have lots of other toys and might not appreciate homemade toys. Even at age ninety, she still participated in the arts and crafts program at the Lanakila Senior Center, making many intricate projects and works of art, which her family has carefully preserved.

While she was growing up, she said, her grandmother constantly reminded her to "learn whatever you can, and learn everything well. 'The only thing I don't want you to learn is how to steal from others,' she told me." Because her grandmother encouraged her to continue learning, Kikuyo never had to help with household chores or cooking.

After graduating from *kootooka,* she attended sewing school with about thirty students. She learned how to sew a basic kimono for children, and then moved on to adult sizes. She eventually continued to the higher level, which involved sewing dressy silk kimonos, formal *montsuki,* short *haori,* obis, and *hakama.* After she became proficient in the intricate art of cutting and sewing a formal kimono, her teacher waived her tuition and allowed her to teach the other students.

MARRIAGE PLANS

Hikosuke's sister went to the same sewing school as Kikuyo, and when Hikosuke's mother was looking for a wife for her son, Kikuyo was recommended.

"Someone suggested that I would make a good match for him. His family asked a *nakoodo* to investigate my family background and genealogy. They were pleased with the findings and sent the *nakoodo* to ask my parents for my hand in marriage for their son. Since they checked our background, my family got someone to do the same. My parents said his family and siblings were all nice people, so even if we stayed in Japan after our marriage, it would be pleasant for me. His parents said the same thing about our family. From ancient times, the Japanese have that saying: 'When you select a bride, judge the parents' character first.'"

Kikuyo was reluctant to leave her family and friends to marry someone she had never seen except in a photo, and to live in a place she knew nothing about. Her mother, however, thought going to Hawaii was a wonderful opportunity for her daughter. Kikuyo begged her grandmother to dissuade her mother, but parents with large families were anxious for their daughters to marry because it meant there would be one less child to support.

"Once my marriage was decided by my parents, I was married by proxy at my husband's village home in Iwakuni. His younger brother acted as his proxy. I went through the formality of the *san san kudo,* but did not exchange sake cups with his brother, because he was not the one I was marrying. Then my name was registered in the Fujimoto *koseki* in the *yakuba* [village office]. I returned to my parents' home after that and waited six months before I was legally allowed to come to Hawaii as his wife."

The customary dowry was prepared by Kikuyo's mother. She filled a large *yanagi gori*, a trunk woven from willow, with a formal *montsuki*, the five-crested kimono with a handwoven silk obi. Kikuyo's *montsuki* bore her mother's *mon* (crest), a *mitsu wari kikyo* (tri-divided Chinese bellflower). Kikuyo explained that in her area of Yamaguchi-ken, a daughter's *montsuki* bore her mother's crest. Her husband's family crest was the *maruni kikyo* (Chinese bellflower with a white circle). She also packed several *yukata* (cotton kimonos), *meisen* (silk) kimonos, and *komon chirimen* (silk crepe) kimonos with an allover pattern and several obis. "My kimonos were unlined, to suit the warm weather in Hawaii," she noted.

"My mother didn't think a futon was necessary for the tropical climate in Hawaii. However, when my mother's older brother came from Kamakura and found out I didn't have one, he said no bride should get married without a futon, so he rushed to order one for me. I don't remember how I packed the bulky futon into the willow trunk," Kikuyo said.

Kikuyo still remembered the last words from her father as they parted. "He said, 'Remember, once you get married, you can never come home again.' I felt so sad, I cried all the way. I can't even remember passing the Hiroshima train station or seeing any of the scenic countryside along the way because I was crying all the way." Her parents told her that if she had gotten married in Japan at that time, it would have cost them 2,000 yen to prepare her dowry, money they could have used for her brother's education.

JOURNEY TO HAWAII

"I was too seasick to hardly eat anything during the ten-day voyage. As the ship approached the port of Honolulu, I was filled with anxiety. A couple from Saitoku who had come to Hawaii before were very kind and helpful. Another friend who was in my sewing class also came as a picture bride. She went to the Big Island of Hawaii to marry someone there, but I never saw her again. One thing I remember vividly is meeting Katsunuma-san, the inspector. He was a very funny man."

Hikosuke met her at the immigration station. When I asked what their first words to each other were, Kikuyo replied, "I forgot, it's too long ago. We must have at least said 'Hello.'" She smiled and chuckled.

Hikosuke hired a *hakku* to take them to the Izumo Taisha Shinto shrine, where they were married in person. Hikosuke was eleven years older than his wife. "I didn't have time to change into my *montsuki*, so I got married in the dressy *komon chirimen* that I had worn on arrival." Rev. Shigemaru Miyao performed the brief marriage ceremony, including the exchange of nuptial cups. "Now we truly sipped the sake to formalize our marriage."

Although exhausted after not having eaten much during the voyage, Kikuyo recalled how quiet and beautiful Honolulu seemed to her. As Hikosuke led her through the streets of the city, she was fascinated by the open streetcars, which then cost a nickel to ride.

When the *hakku* stopped at Washington Place, Kikuyo thought, "So this is the place I'm going to live."

NEW HOME

"Washington Place hasn't changed much," Kikuyo said when I interviewed her in 1988. "It's almost exactly the way it was when I first saw it in 1916. The backyard of Washington Place was very big, and our cottage was way in the back. We lived downstairs in the back cottage, which included a big washhouse. In Japan, I always slept on a futon spread on the floor, but here, for the first time, I slept on a bed."

Lodgings were provided for those working in the palace. The *hakku* stable was in the downstairs quarters of another building. Two other Japanese couples lived upstairs. "Mr. Monji Watanabe was the cook; he got paid $8 a week. Mr. Okihiro, from Hiroshima, and Mr. Sato, from Takayama, were the yardmen; they got paid $6 a week," she recalled.

"My husband was the steward and attended to the personal needs of the queen. He served three meals a day to the queen and ran errands for her until she died on November 11, 1917. He got paid $7 a week. Mrs. Okihiro and Mrs. Watanabe did all the laundry and housecleaning for the royal family. Both wore their *yukata* while working."

Friends of the queen visited every Sunday, Kikuyo said, and she recalled that they addressed Liliuokalani as *alii* (chief).

"There was a bachelor by the name of Kaipo, seems like he was related to the queen. Kaipo lived on one side, and the garage was on the other side. Now it's a tennis court," she said.

"When I came here as a young bride, Queen Liliuokalani was not feeling well, and she hardly came out, although my husband saw her every day. She used to ask my husband to bring fresh flowers to Iolani Palace every day. The flowers were placed at someone's photograph at the palace. The doctor came often to check on her.

"Living in our own cottage on the grounds of Washington Place was pleasant and comfortable. An office boy by the name of Miyake-san took care of things," Kikuyo said.

The Washington Place staff also included a driver who Kikuyo thought was a *poroki* (Portuguese) man. The Japanese servants ate their meals in one large room. "The *cooku-san* was Japanese, Monji Watanabe, so we all ate Japanese food: rice, miso soup, *tsukemono*. The *cooku-san* used to go marketing every morning to buy fresh food. We had fresh fish often," she said. "The Hawaiian servants ate separately. A man named Malo used to pound the poi [made from the corm of the taro plant] every day. He and his wife lived in a cottage right below us. The Hawaiian people had poi and *opihi* [Hawaiian limpet]. I used to see them cleaning *opihi* all the time. They bought the *opihi* from the market."

QUEEN LILIUOKALANI

Kikuyo's son Kunio recalled his father telling him as a youngster how nice the queen was to her servants. "When the queen was going for a buggy ride, she would sometimes invite my father to go riding with her. My father refused, because he was afraid of what the Hawaiian people might think," she said.

In fact, Hikosuke became fluent in Hawaiian and easily communicated in that language with other servants who worked at Washington Place. Kunio recalled watching his father and his friend Mr. Nakata conversing in Hawaiian while drinking sake.

Kikuyo has only fond memories of Queen Liliuokalani. "The queen was a very gentle and kind person. She used to tell my husband, 'I'll teach you Hawaiian, so you teach me Japanese.' This was when she was well. That was before I came to Hawaii and she was still healthy.

"Sometimes she would drop her ring and my husband would pick it up and return it to her. Then she would say, 'Thank you for finding it for me. I would give this to you, but this ring was given to me by Queen Victoria of England, so I cannot give it to you.' The queen must have received it when she went to England for a visit," she said.

Kikuyo recalled that when the queen was in better health, she often asked Hikosuke to go out and buy cigars for her. Kikuyo thought the queen wanted to give the cigars to her friends and relatives who visited her. However, Kunio recalled reading somewhere that the queen enjoyed smoking cigars. "The queen used to give my husband money to buy cigars; then, after he came back, she forgot and wanted to pay him again."

Kikuyo did not have to work since Hikosuke was kept busy serving the queen. A year after arriving in Hawaii, she gave birth to a baby girl, Thelma Chiyomi, on September 1, 1917. She was the first and only nisei to have been born at historic Washington Place. Kikuyo gave birth with the assistance of a Japanese midwife, to whom she paid $50. She remembered that everyone felt it was too much to pay, but the midwife was a big help to Kikuyo. She came every day for a week to bathe Chiyomi and helped with other things that Kikuyo was not familiar with as a new mother. "Everybody was so happy. They say, *Hanau, hanau'* [Hawaiian for "birth"]." Everyone congratulated Kikuyo and Hikosuke and brought many gifts for the new baby.

When asked what the queen gave to the new baby, Kikuyo replied, "She was not feeling well by then . . . but she gave my baby a Hawaiian name. That was a precious gift." Kikuyo said that Queen Liliuokalani gave her daughter the Hawaiian name Kealohilani, which meant "the shining heaven" or "the brightness of heaven." During my interview with Kikuyo Fujimoto, her son Kunio mentioned that Kealohilani is also the name of a street in Waikiki. It is located a block after Ohua Avenue and Paoakalani Street, where the queen's summer home was located. Chiyomi explained that her father did not want the Hawaiian name on the birth certificate, because at that time non-Hawaiians did not give their children Hawaiian names and people could have misunderstood and thought she was part Hawaiian. Unfortunately, the name was never recorded on the baby's birth certificate. However, the registrar, a Mrs. Lyman, did list Thelma Chiyomi's birthplace as Washington Place.

Queen Liliuokalani died two months later, on November 11, 1917, at Washington Place.

THE QUEEN'S PASSING

"When the queen died, my father said there was a beautiful rainbow and that was a good omen," Kunio recalled. "My father felt badly that he couldn't attend the queen's funeral. He didn't have the money to buy a suit. At that time, there was a belief that two *haole* guys had forged her will and left it under the queen's pillow, so all payments stopped. My father and the other servants didn't get paid, so he didn't have any money. Since he didn't have a black suit, he stood on the sidewalk to watch the funeral procession as it passed along Nuuanu Avenue to the Royal Mausoleum. When the Hawaiian people saw my father, they yelled, 'Fuji, Fuji, come in,' but he didn't have a suit, so he felt ashamed. He later followed in the back," Kunio told us.

I asked Kikuyo whether her husband had received a keepsake of any kind from the queen. "*Kanaka* style, they don't give anything for keepsake," she replied.

She remembered the day the queen died at the age of seventy-nine. "As soon as she died, they took her body to Kawaiahao Church. So *cooku-san*, my husband, and all the servants helped make coffee and fried things to take to the mourners at the church."

Kunio said his father had mentioned that there was a special visitor from Japan: an *ishii taishi*, or plenipotentiary—similar to an ambassador. "When the Hawaiian people saw my father, they took him way in front during the funeral service at Kawaiahao Church."

"One of the queen's servants, or perhaps her friend Mrs. Kuhio, burned everything in a big hole dug out in the palace backyard," Kikuyo remembered. "Many of the queen's things were burned. Mr. Kuhio, her husband, was there. Yes, I saw all those things burned."

MOVE TO WAIKIKI SUMMER HOME

The passing of the beloved queen also changed the Fujimoto family's life. They had lived in a stable and friendly environment where they were trusted and treated kindly by the queen and all the Hawaiian people who lived and worked at Washington Place. The aftermath of the queen's death was a difficult period. However, the family was fortunate to be offered a new home at the queen's summer cottage in Waikiki because of the kindness of Mr. Iaukea, a supervisor who served the queen. Mr. Iaukea continued to look after the Fujimoto family's needs for many years.

"It had one large living room and a big veranda about eight feet wide which encircled the entire house," recalled Kunio. This home was his birthplace. "As the family expanded, we needed an extra room, so we enclosed the front veranda," he added.

"Kunio was born there on June 11, 1919, Kamehameha Day," said Kikuyo. "If the queen had lived, she might have given him a Hawaiian name, too."

Kikuyo vividly recalled the old Waikiki, with its the banana patches and rice paddies. "It was like swampland where plenty of ducks were swimming around," she said.

Kunio fondly recalled his boyhood in Waikiki. He remembered the Hawaiian man who lived in a grass shack near their home, and described the many streams that flowed leisurely on both sides of the queen's summer cottage. The streams took their natural course—half flowing in the area where the Moana Hotel stands now and the other half flowing just behind the Moana, where the Royal Hawaiian Hotel now stands—out to Waikiki Beach. He lamented the disappearance of the old and tranquil Waikiki.

"The summer cottage had an outhouse, just like a plantation house," Kunio remembers. "Because we lived at the end of the road on Ohua and Kuhio, isolated

Hikosuke and Kikuyo Fujimoto were allowed to live at the queen's summer cottage in Waikiki for many years after the queen died. Photo courtesy of Kikuyo Fujimoto.

from the other homes, we didn't have any electricity. To install it, the family had to pull the electric wiring from that corner to our house, setting up three posts in between, costing about $25 each."

There was also a large concrete swimming pool on the *makai,* or ocean side, of the property. "Mr. Iaukea paid for everything, including the electric posts and the cesspool. In those days, it cost $200 to dig the cesspool. The rental for the summer home was $15, but he paid *us* that much for watching the place, so rental was free. I guess he did that to make it legal, to balance the books," Kunio reasoned.

"Ours was the only house. The other houses were located two blocks away on Kaneloa Street. At night, the kiawe trees made such a big noise, *gii . . . gii . . . gii . . .* a weird sound when the wind blew. We got really scared!"

Kikuyo took out a family photo that was taken at Queen Liliuokalani's summer cottage. The children were well dressed and were all wearing shoes. I asked her if she had sewn the children's clothing. "Oh no, I ordered everything," she replied. "There was a dressmaker nearby. Mrs. Morisato, whose husband also worked at Washington Place, was from Iwakuni. She was a talented seamstress who dressed the women in that area in fashionable dresses and gowns for special occasions. When Chiyomi was a little older, she herself started sewing for the entire family. My husband bought those shoes from the McInerny store, downtown."

Thelma said her father was a wonderful provider and that she and her siblings were never in need of anything. "My father raised chickens in the backyard and he made the best chicken *hekka*. In the 1930s, he even ran a small restaurant in Waikiki, at the corner of Ohua Street, on one side of St. Augustine Church.

"We lived in the summer cottage for almost thirty years when my father took the advice of Mr. Iaukea and leased the land for $99 a year. Before the lease was up, we were paying more than $500 a year in lease rent. In 1937, my father built a three-bedroom house for $3,000. I remember Mr. Iaukea was still living at that time in Manoa Valley. Every Christmas, my father used to bring him a gift and took me along. My father never forgot how kind Mr. Iaukea was to our family after the queen passed away."

FINDING WORK AFTER LEAVING THE PALACE

Upon leaving Washington Place, the former palace servants had to find work elsewhere. To support their growing family, Kikuyo and Hikosuke eventually started a laundry business at home. With that, Kikuyo joined the other Japanese working housewives in Waikiki. About two hundred Japanese families lived in nearby camps; many of them took in the laundry of the rich *haole* families. The women who had children couldn't go out to work, so they took in laundry, while those without children worked as maids for rich *haole* families.

"After I got settled, I began doing laundry for the rich ladies who came from the Diamond Head area. They brought their laundry in on Monday, and I finished it by Wednesday. One household alone had many sheets and bedspreads. I made $120 a month. One rich man used to tell me, 'You go overseas, you can make double.' I had so much ironing, I used two charcoal-heated irons. They were very heavy, and I had to make charcoal on the hibachi to keep the iron hot. I used to boil all the laundry outdoors in large cans over an open fire.

"The women learned that there was ozone present in the air, which acted like a bleaching agent and made the sheets very white. We spread the sheets on the grass to dry; they really turned white without bleaching," she said.

By then, her daughter Thelma was nine years old. She helped her mother wash, scrub, and boil the laundry, and then helped with the ironing. At night she neatly folded the linens. Thelma also helped deliver the clean laundry, walking as far as where the Moana Hotel now stands. Across was the Seaside Hotel, a bungalow-type hotel. During the interview, Thelma marveled at how she used to walk long distances, about a half mile, from their home on Paoakalani Avenue, carrying a heavy load of linens without a cart. When she delivered the linens, the proprietor kindly gave her ten cents to take the streetcar home. But by then, she would be so thirsty that she instead treated herself to a cup of fresh pineapple juice. Thelma said she still remembers how delicious the juice tasted. She said it was well worth sacrificing the ride home.

Her mother depended on Thelma, as the oldest child, to help care for her younger siblings and to help with the household chores, leaving her with little time to play with her own friends. If she went to a friend's house, she had to bring her two sisters along in a buggy. Although she was busy with her family, Thelma did well in school and excelled in typing. Her teacher encouraged her to continue on to high school, but Thelma was forced to leave school after the ninth grade.

In the afternoon, she attended the Jodo Mission Japanese-language school, where she earned a *kootooka* certificate. Thelma later attended Tachikawa *jyo gakko*, a girls' Japanese-language school, which she thoroughly enjoyed because she learned so much. "In those days, we obeyed whatever our parents wanted us to do. We never talked back to our parents or to the teachers."

In 1918, Hikosuke began working as a butcher at the Moana Hotel. While in training, he was paid $50 a month. Meanwhile, Kikuyo continued the laundry work, earning quite a bit of money to supplement the family's income.

Hikosuke also started attending night school, learning English from Rev. Takie Okumura, to help him at work. Besides placing his daily orders in English for items such as fresh fish from the Otani fish market, he had to keep records in English. By the time Hikosuke left the Moana Hotel, he was earning $90 a month.

When the Royal Hawaiian Hotel opened in 1927, Hikosuke took a job there and trained under the hotel's chief butcher. When he completed his training, his pay increased by $50. Later, another *haole* man came in and took over as chief butcher. Kunio remembered his father saying that the position of chief butcher was considered a high position and difficult for a Japanese person to attain.

Meanwhile, Kikuyo had become quite an entrepreneur with her laundry business and opened a laundry shop in Waikiki, across from the Aoki store. With a service station next door, it turned out to be a good location. When Kikuyo got busy, she hired people to help with the ironing. By then, Hikosuke had purchased a Model T Ford. Among other things, he used it to drive Thelma around, delivering the laundry to her mother's customers. At the time, Thelma was sixteen. She remembered the long hours her mother worked, from early in the morning to late at night. Oftentimes her mother had already left for work by the time Thelma awoke in the morning. And yet, she said, her mother never complained about the hard work.

DEATH OF KIKUYO'S MOTHER

In the midst of all the problems she was facing, Kikuyo received a letter from her family in Iwakuni telling her that her mother was gravely ill. "At first, I was reluctant to go home because I still felt bitter about the fact that my mother had forced me to come to Hawaii. I was deciding whether to go home or not. It was my husband who persuaded me to return home so I would not have any regrets later. He promised to take care of everything and reminded me not to worry. I finally decided to go. In the early 1930s, the only way to travel to Japan was by ship. I immediately left by ship, but before I reached Japan, my mother had died."

Kikuyo was heartbroken that she couldn't have been at her mother's bedside before she died. She had been so busy struggling to raise her growing family that she hadn't been able to return home since leaving in 1916. Overcome with grief, Kikuyo fell ill and could not return to Hawaii for a few months. Thelma took care of her siblings while she and her father managed to keep things going.

HOTEL MAID

Finally, at age fifty-one, Kikuyo gave up her laundry business, only to begin working as a room maid at the Royal Hawaiian Hotel. "There was a *haole* housekeeper,

Mrs. Anderson, who was my boss. I worked until I was sixty-three years old. The *haole* housekeeper wanted me to continue working. She said, 'Japanese are neat and honest and never talk back. Young people talk back, but Japanese cannot speak English so cannot talk back.'

"Those days, hotel maids got $1.70 an hour; now it's $6.00. The Filipino *wahines* were smart; they worked on a daily basis and made better money. My husband didn't want me to work, so I used to sneak to work at 3:00 p.m. and work until 11:00 p.m. Chiyomi used to pick me up, take me to work, and bring me home at night.

"There were two or three room maids," she remembered. "On the night shift, two other friends and I cleaned one floor. The night shift people hardly had tips. When people left a tip, I gave it to the housekeeper. My husband said if I worked as a maid, I'd get bad *konjo* [character], so he was opposed to my working. Because I went to Japan, I had to make up the time to get my pension money, so I worked eleven more years. Mrs. Anderson advised me to work longer, even on a part-time basis, so that I could benefit in retirement. She was right. I am so thankful for the Social Security benefits I receive today."

Kikuyo reminisced about the trip she and Hikosuke took to Japan for his father's memorial service. "We had joined a tour group. After the tour, we went to Iwakuni, our birthplace, and stayed there for six weeks. After we returned, my husband wanted to keep on working, but Thelma felt that at age seventy, he should retire." Hikosuke, a devoted husband and father who had worked hard and gave of himself selflessly in whatever he did, died of a heart attack on September 9, 1959, at the age of seventy-two, leaving Kikuyo a widow at the age of sixty-one.

THE CHILDREN

When I interviewed Kikuyo at age ninety, she recounted to me the birthdates of her five children. Besides Thelma Chiyomi, there was Kunio, who was born at the summer cottage on June 11, 1919; her second son, Hikoso, born May 30, 1921; Edna Junko Nakamoto, born March 12, 1925; and her youngest child, Dorothy Aiko, who was born September 16, 1927.

"Today, I feel differently; I'm glad I came to Hawaii," she told me in 1988. "My children are all doing well and they are good to me, so I can enjoy myself in retirement. I live with my oldest son, Kunio, and his wife. I have a wonderful daughter-in-law who takes good care of me," she said. "I take the bus from Pearl City to Ala Moana. Every day I go to Liberty House to learn knitting on the second floor. I'm knitting my own vest now. I made things for each of my children. My eyesight has not been as good lately, but I still have my own teeth."

I was curious to find out what had become of her firstborn, Thelma Chiyomi, who was born at Washington Place and had been given a beautiful Hawaiian name by Queen Liliuokalani. The queen would have been proud of what Thelma Chiyomi Kealohilani made of her life. She completed the ninth grade at an English-language school, helped her mother with the laundry business, took care of her siblings, and did all of the family's sewing during her teen years. She became a self-made businesswoman who helped build up her husband's business, Auto Parts Service.

Like most issei parents, Hikosuke and Kikuyo were very strict with Thelma. They didn't allow her to go out by herself. One day a family friend, Dr. Kaneshige, invited Thelma's family and three boys to dinner at a restaurant. He was probably trying to do some matchmaking. He purposely seated Wallace Onogi next to Thelma. After dinner, Dr. Kaneshige suggested that Wallace take Thelma home, but she declined and returned home with her parents.

Wallace, who lived in Kalihi, was the sixth child in a family of ten. His parents worked at the pineapple cannery, and Wallace worked with his older brother in his auto parts shop. For Wallace, the dinner proved to be love at first sight.

Three years passed before Wallace, a nice but shy guy, finally met Thelma again, this time at a *hana matsuri* (Buddha Day festival) at Kapiolani Park in 1938. Thelma was about twenty-one years old then. He thought she was so beautiful and wanted to ask her out on a date, but he also knew how strict her parents were. Finally after three more years of waiting, he asked Thelma out on a date. After a few years of dating, he proposed to her.

Theirs was an unusual courtship: Wallace's mother accompanied them on dates, although Thelma didn't mind. Whenever there was a Japanese movie showing in town, Wallace's mother would purchase three tickets. They all went together and had a good time. Hikosuke and Kikuyo gave their blessing to the couple. Thelma had been a wonderful, obedient daughter, and they knew they could never have survived the hard times without her sacrifice. Thelma and Wallace had an elaborate traditional Japanese wedding, a ceremony called *oiro-naoshi*. She wore a formal Japanese wedding costume and changed her kimono three times. The celebration gave Hikosuke and Kikuyo the happiness and fulfillment of seeing their daughter married in elegant formal tradition, something they had not had in 1916 when Kikuyo arrived in Hawaii to become Hikosuke's wife.

Thelma and Wallace Onogi on their wedding day, March 31, 1941. Photo courtesy of Thelma Onogi.

Thelma, with her strict upbringing and training, was a wonderful wife to Wallace. Wallace's mother was also very happy with her new daughter-in-law, and all three continued to enjoy their outings together.

Kikuyo also had another reason to be proud: two of her sons served their country in World War II. Kunio, who earned a Bronze Star, fought with the 100th Infantry Battalion in Europe and was wounded in Italy, an injury that earned him a Purple Heart. He was sent home in June 1944. Kikuyo's second son, Hikoso, later volunteered for the 442nd Regimental Combat Team. While he was in training on Oahu, Kikuyo prepared *bento* for him and visited him every week. Although Hikoso was not involved in combat, since the war was nearing its end, he was nevertheless proud to have been part of the 442nd. He passed away in November 2004.

"It was difficult to send my two sons to war, but I was proud that they willingly wanted to fight for the country of their birth. Of course, I did worry like all the other mothers who sent their sons off to war, and prayed morning and night in front of our *obutsudan* [family shrine] for their health and safety. It was our religious faith and spiritual guidance that helped us through difficult times during World War II." In July 1982, at the fortieth-anniversary banquet of the 100th Battalion, Kikuyo Fujimoto was asked to represent the issei parents who had sent sons off to war. She delivered an eloquent and moving tribute to the men of the 100th and their families. It was an honor for her, she said.

Kikuyo Fujimoto at age eighty-four speaking at the 100th Infantry Battalion banquet, celebrating the unit's fortieth anniversary, 1982. Photo courtesy of Kunio Fujimoto.

Kikuyo's 107th birthday with son Kunio and his wife, Morran. Photo courtesy of Kunio Fujimoto.

With Hikosuke's passing in 1959, Kikuyo had to be the pillar of strength for her family, setting an example of hard work and perseverance. In doing so, she also provided a solid education for her three younger children.

KIKUYO'S 107TH BIRTHDAY

On October 16, 2005, Kikuyo Fujimoto reached yet another milestone in her very long and successful journey through life when she celebrated her 107th birthday with her family. Her children shared in the blessings of their mother's long life. Kikuyo was thankful to have lived such a unique life. She had led a rather sheltered existence until she left her home in Iwakuni city. But she persevered in a new world of challenges—struggling, surviving, learning, and earning the respect of people of other ethnicities as she ventured into the work world. And it is remarkable how two strangers, Hikosuke and Kikuyo, managed to build a strong and happy life together and raise a wonderful family.

Although Kikuyo became more tired as she grew older, her bright smile and the sparkle in her eyes were ever-present. As she shared with me the photo from her 107th birthday party, she thanked me many times, bowing her head in gratitude—but it is I who wanted to thank her and say, "*Omedeto gozaimasu* [congratulations] on your 107th birthday! *Arigato* [thank you] for sharing your remarkable story."

Shizu Kaigo
THE SPIRIT OF SHO-CHIKU-BAI

August 20, 1896–October 30, 1998
Born in Ikochi-mura, Yamaguchi-ken
Arrived in Hawaii December 5, 1916

I first heard about Shizu Kaigo in Lihue, Kauai, on January 9, 1986. At that time, I was participating in "Picture Brides: Lives of Hawaii's Early Immigrant Women from Japan, Okinawa, and Korea," a series of presentations funded by the Hawaii Committee for the Humanities, and co-sponsored by the Women's Studies and Ethnic Studies Programs at the University of Hawaii, Manoa.

When I heard that Shizu Kaigo had moved from Kauai to Molokai to be near her adopted daughter, Leslie, and son-in-law, George Hideo Tamura, I made a special effort to contact her. Having heard about her extensive knowledge of traditional Japanese bridal costumes and kimono dressing, I felt she was just the person I had been searching for to expand my research on Japanese immigrant clothing. In April 1987, I finally had the opportunity to make a special trip to Molokai to interview her and several other issei women at the Kaunakakai Senior Center.

It was a pleasant surprise to meet Shizu Kaigo for the first time. She was very petite, about four feet ten inches tall, and had a lovely face that matched her soft-spoken voice and gentle manners. We sat across from each other at a long wooden table with the tape recorder placed between us.

On Kauai, I had heard, Shizu had been very active at the Lihue Hongwanji Mission and served as president of the Lihue Hongwanji Fujinkai for twenty-six years. She also served for nine years as vice president of the Kauai Rengo Fujinkai (United Women's Club). She taught *ikebana,* the art of flower arrangement; *chado,* or tea ceremony; kimono sewing; *nihon shishu,* Japanese hand embroidery similar to satin stitch; and other craftworks to the issei and nisei women in the community. She was also well known and respected for her expertise in the intricate art of bonsai, the cultivation of dwarf trees.

When I was growing up on a plantation, I thought of bonsai as a hobby of issei men in their *pau hana* (retirement) years. Bonsai is a unique art whose goal is to produce a natural scenic landscape in an ornamental tray or pot, and it requires a lot of patience, skill, and creativity. It takes talent and imagination to plant one or more trees in a container and keep them only a few inches high. The branches and roots of the tree have to be constantly and carefully pruned and the soil has to be changed often. If they are well shaped and sculpted, they can be a symbol of nature. They are often used as a decorative element to enhance indoor settings.*

During my dressmaking days in Wahiawa, in the 1950s, a man named Mr. Akiyoshi was well known for his bonsai collection. His backyard was filled with fascinating bonsai plants. Most people use pine trees for bonsai, but Mr. Akiyoshi had an unusual pomegranate tree bonsai that was colorful and ornamental. I was surprised to learn that Shizu Kaigo, an issei woman, was an enthusiastic lover of bonsai. I wondered how this frail-looking, gentle person could have managed the difficult and time-consuming task of pruning and sculpting the branches and roots of the trees. Once I got to know her, however, I was not surprised to learn that she had been awarded a special medal from Emperor Hirohito of Japan for her outstanding achievements.

CHILDHOOD IN THE VILLAGE

Shizu's four brothers, as she related to me, worked hard on the farm, helping their father maintain the large parcels of rice-producing land. "My mother died very young, when I was only three and a half years old, so Father remarried the following year. My stepmother was very good, *yasashi* [sweet]. Most people don't speak highly of their stepmothers, but I was blessed to have one so loving. Thanks to her, I never had to work on the farm. Instead, she sent me to a reputable sewing school in the village when I was nine years old. I continued taking sewing classes after school hours and on weekends until I graduated from the eighth grade at fourteen years old. Shimada *sensei,* my teacher, took in about ten students, many from wealthy families. My teacher was well respected and highly regarded for her outstanding knowledge of sewing traditional men's and women's formal attire."

She continued, "How fortunate I was to be able to master the sewing of every type of kimono, from casual to formal wear; the formal men's *hakama* [pleated divided skirt], *haori* [coat], formal *montsuki* [men's and women's kimono with five crests], and *maru* obi [wide sash made of stiff brocade with exquisite designs woven into the fabric, usually worn with a bridal costume or dressy kimono]. Most difficult to learn was the elegant *hiyoku,* a dressy undergarment. Special sewing techniques were used to create a double-layered look at the sleeves and hemline. Few women learned to sew this *hiyoku*-style kimono. It's too complicated and requires a lot of patience. It was considered a luxury item in those days." Her soft face beamed with pride as she continued, "Also, from the same teacher, I learned *nihon shishu* [Japanese embroidery] and *ikebana*. She even taught *reigi saho* [etiquette] on weekends. I loved kimono sewing and the *shugei* [handicrafts] that I was able to learn from *sensei* before I came to Hawaii."

Shizu let out a sigh of gratefulness as she continued, "Little did I realize in my youth that someday the valuable things I learned from *sensei* would be my treasure to keep with me throughout my life. Who would ever have thought those valuable

---

* Mock Joya, *Things Japanese* (Tokyo, 1971), 395, 448; Takeshi Fujimori, "Bonsai: Dwarf Trees," in *Japan Color,* ed. Ikko Tanaka and Kazuko Koike (Tokyo, 1982), print 22.

sewing skills, the cultural ethics, and knowledge that *sensei* had instilled in me over the years would someday be a great asset for me to survive in a foreign country? There were about ten girls in the sewing class, and we all got along well. *Sensei* taught me everything I needed to know as a young girl, as the issei mothers used to say, 'in preparation for marriage.' It was during one of these sessions that *sensei* had asked me if I would be interested to go to this *Hawaii no rakuen* [Hawaiian paradise] across the Pacific Ocean."

Shizu's face lit up a bit as she recalled that day many years ago. "I was about nineteen years old. Yes, I did hear about the Hawaii *netsu* [fever]. Everybody had the yearning to go to the golden paradise. *Sensei* showed me her nephew's picture one day and asked me if I would be interested in going to Hawaii as his picture bride." Shyly taking a quick glance at his picture, Shizu thought that he seemed to be a very nice person. "I figured if I stayed in Japan, I wouldn't be able to go to school anymore. My knowledge of the outside world would be limited. So when my sewing teacher asked me, I thought it would be fun to go to a foreign country to learn new things." She said it was her adventurous spirit and curiosity to learn new things that helped her make the decision to come as Tomoji Kaigo's picture bride. As her case demonstrates, this initial photo exchange was done in a casual manner, without causing any embarrassment to either party. Depending on the skill of the *nakoodo,* picture bride marriages were arranged in a variety of ways, often in a humorous fashion.

PICTURE BRIDE MARRIAGE

Until then, Shizu had led a happy and carefree existence in a farming village amid a loving environment, learning the things that mattered most to her. Because she grew up as the only daughter among four brothers, it was surprising that she had the courage and spirit to challenge her future by marrying a young man unknown to her. She said thoughtfully, "Of course, once I made the decision to go to Hawaii, I was concerned about marrying someone I had never met. So I inquired here and there around the villages with families who had been to the islands. Then I came to the conclusion that I should go. After all, he's the nephew of my sewing teacher, whom I respected and was very fond of. Even his younger brother and all his relatives in nearby villages seemed like very nice people. His older sister was also my elementary school teacher and was married to someone in our village. She was a fine teacher. They all urged me to go to Hawaii. I felt confident that he must be a nice person. In those days, no one could get married without parental consent. My parents knew all his relatives and thought he was a good prospect as my husband. They must have discussed it among themselves." Shizu smiled as she recalled the anxiety and concern she had felt at the time.

"My husband, Tomoji, came to this island of Kauai about ten years ahead of me. He was working at the Lihue plantation sugar mill as a supervisor. That was considered a good position for an issei from Japan. He started as a contract laborer and within ten years he must have proved to be a trustworthy person to be given a high-status position." Her expression reflected the pride she felt at his achievement.

Once the matchmaking was arranged through the exchange of photos, Shizu said, "Yes, we started writing friendly letters back and forth. Both of us were mutually so-so in writing. I wrote him asking, 'What kind of clothes should I bring?' He wrote back, 'Bring whatever you have.' So I even brought my kimono worn during winter, since I would be coming in December. From the time the matchmaking began, it took about a year before I finally was able to come. The wedding ceremony was performed by proxy since the prospective groom was in Hawaii. His family then had to register my name into the Kaigo *koseki* [family register] at the village office so the Japanese government could officially recognize the marriage. According to Japanese tradition, both families had separate receptions. My family gave a farewell reception for me. The groom's family gave a more elaborate one with a close family friend acting as proxy for the *san san kudo* ritual. For the solemn ceremony that showed respect and acceptance of the bride into the groom's family, I wore the *san-mai gasane,* a three-layer kimono, all at once, to both receptions for the families to see and remember," she said.

Shizu's description of how she wore her wedding kimono was slightly different from others. The customs, values, and beliefs handed down through the generations varied by prefecture, by social status, and with each individual family. As she said, "On my wedding day in the village, I first wore the five-crested red kimono with a hand-drawn bamboo design on the hemline. Everything worn for the first entrance was red, even the long underkimono, to show that I was going to be reborn into the Kaigo family. Most brides wore the white *montsuki* first. For the village wedding, underneath my formal kimono, I wore a *hiyoku,* an underkimono that is single and unlined but made to appear like a double- or triple-layered kimono because of the color contrast added at the sleeve opening and at the hemline. Few issei women possessed such an elegant undergarment. I later sent this *hiyoku*-style kimono back to Japan. It was too dressy and I didn't see any need for that in Hawaii. The last layer I wore was the *kuro tome sode* [five-crested black *montsuki*] with the pine design. The obi I wore was handwoven of pure gold thread. To think that I loaned these elegant kimonos to dress the young girls for the Japanese festivals on Kauai! They walked in the parade along that dirt road, and, oh my, Hakuyosha Cleaners could never remove the red dirt from the hemline. How little I knew about the care and preservation of fine kimonos," Shizu sighed, wishing she had been more careful.

CRANES FLYING ABOVE: A GOOD OMEN

Shizu left her village home on November 19, 1916, accompanied by relatives and friends. Her husband's younger brother took her to the train station. "I had a large *yanagi gori* [trunk woven from willow vine] that I had filled with both summer and winter kimonos. When we were about halfway between my village and the train station, someone spotted two *tsuru* [cranes] flying above in a place called Tsuga in Yamaguchi prefecture. There were hundreds of cranes that migrated from Siberia during winter, and that's where they must have come from. This pair must have wandered off and flew to that spot. Everybody thought it was a good omen and was so happy for me." Shizu smiled as she recalled the incident. "As you know, the *tsuru* is a symbol of long life, fidelity, and monogamy and is often used for wedding decorations. They say that once they become a pair they never leave each other. If one gets sick or gets injured, the mate never leaves. That's the reason why the crane design is commonly used for auspicious occasions." It was fascinating to hear Shizu talk about the cranes, and then she added excitedly, "You know, we were standing there, watching the graceful pair of cranes . . . when an airplane flew right above us! That was indeed a historic event, because that's the first time an airplane had flown over the skies of Japan!" Shizu's soft brown eyes opened wider as she tried to recapture the excitement she had felt the day she left her village.

ARRIVAL IN HAWAII

Shizu finally reached Yokohama, the departure point for Hawaii. The *Persia Maru* was a small ship, and Shizu wasn't used to sea travel. She recalled, "In December, the sea was extremely rough. On the third day we got tossed around like a *buranko* [swing]. The huge waves even washed fishes on board! The boat rocked like this," she said, swinging her hands back and forth. "Many of the passengers got so seasick, we could hardly eat or keep any food down. As the sea finally calmed down—much to our relief—I was anxious to see this paradise island I had heard so much about. We arrived on December 5, 1916. As the ship slowly approached Honolulu harbor, there were throngs of beautiful dark-skinned natives in colorful muumuus waving at us. I was shocked to see naked boys swimming and diving for coins. Some passengers who were coming here for the second time showed me how to throw the coins in the water. I had heard rumors that it was warm in Hawaii, but in Japan it was still winter and very cold in December. People wouldn't think of going in the water!" she chuckled.

"After we disembarked from the ship, all the picture brides were put on a *tsurakku* [truck], like a rubbish truck, with benches made of plain wood placed here and there for us to sit on. We wondered where we were being taken. Somebody said, 'Probably to the quarantine.' They called it the *senningoya* [hut of thousand people]. In a large room there were many shelves, one above the other. This was our bed. It reminded me of silkworm shelves back in my village. Yes, I had heard about the Chinese man who died of bad illness, the fourth day of our voyage. This was the reason we were held back in quarantine. We also had to take tests for pinkeye and hookworm. They asked us some questions, too. I passed all these. I think we were held there for ten days," she said.

TOMOJI COMES FROM KAUAI

"My husband, Tomoji, came over on the ship from Kauai to get me. There were no interisland planes in those days. At the immigration station, all the picture brides were lined up on one side; the grooms were coming in from the other side. Right away, I recognized my husband because my *sensei* had shown me his picture. He also looked like his brothers in Japan. Reverend Motoyama of the River Street Church married all the ten couples in a single ceremony. He gave a brief prayer, raised his hand, and that was all. Yes, a Christian ceremony. I can't remember if we said anything to each other," she chuckled. "We were probably too dazed and confused with what was going on, too shy to say anything. Reverend Motoyama charged each couple $5," she said.

Shizu pointed to the muumuu she was wearing during the interview and said, "This was the summer kimono I brought in 1916. Rather than storing it away in the chest of drawers, I took apart the kimono and made it into a casual muumuu in 1985. Imagine the durability of the handwoven fabric that was part of my dowry in 1916. Aside from the many kimonos I brought in my *kori,* I packed a bag of roasted chestnuts for my husband. He was very happy with that."

SETTLING ON KAUAI, THE GARDEN ISLE

Shizu resumed her story. "After spending one night at the Kobayashi Hotel in Honolulu, my husband took me on an interisland ship to Kauai, today known as the Garden Island. It was harvesting season at the time, and the burnt sugarcane was being hauled on cane cars to the mill to be washed and crushed to make raw sugar. Tomoji was a supervisor at the sugar mill and had to rush back to work.

"Everything was strange and new to me. I followed Tomoji as he walked down the steep slope, quite a ways downhill from the sugar mill. Dressed in my snug wrap-around kimono and obi, and walking with slippers, it was a bit difficult to follow my husband's brisk steps. I felt grateful he carried my heavy *kori* all the way, until he came to an abrupt stop in front of a long bungalow-type house with whitewash paint. My, that was my first plantation home. It took me by surprise. It wasn't what I had envisioned! Even if I came from a farming village, we lived in a comfortable home. I don't think there are any more shabby houses like that now on Kauai. There was a bachelor living next door at that time. Until I came, my husband lived in that long house, only one room, just to sleep in. We had our meals in the boardinghouse kitchen with the other bachelors. The older couple that ran the boardinghouse was very kind. The woman did the cooking and laundry for the bachelors. The boardinghouse lady taught me how to do the laundry the way it was done in camp." Shizu was very observant and quick to learn the new ways.

"I had only heard good things about Tomoji when I inquired about his character back in the village. But of course, as a bride, marrying someone I had never met, there were many things we had to learn about each other. He had been a carefree bachelor for a long time. He loved his sake and gambled like all the single men, so he had some debts I didn't know about."

PLANTATION WEDDING ON KAUAI

"In those days, in 1916, there wasn't anything exciting happening in a sleepy plantation community, so when a bachelor's picture bride arrived, it was a big event. The plantation bosses gave everybody a few days off to prepare a wedding reception for us. The men folks opened up the three partitions of the single men's quarters in the long house, which became one spacious party room. They had straw mats on the bare wooden floor, and the men had set up long temporary tables. Neighbors loaned their *zabutons* [cushions] so everybody could be comfortable. Today, the young people spend a fortune for wedding banquets at plush hotels, but back in those days, all the wedding parties were held at home. Everybody chipped in and helped prepare the feast, mostly Japanese food: lots of fresh fish for sashimi caught in Kauai's deep waters. The table was laden with *gochiso* [festive food], but I didn't eat anything. I was too excited to even nibble on the delicious-looking food. Kimura-san, who was the chief cook at the Wilcox home, was hired to plan the wedding feast. He supervised the preparation of the food for the wedding reception, and was assisted by the wives of the laborers in the camp. The huge red sea bream someone had caught offshore was made into a spectacular *ikizukuri.*" She was describing a centerpiece where a live red fish is artistically shaped in a curved position, the tail turned upward as if it is ready to leap. Then a "fish net" carved out of fresh white turnip is draped over the fish. It is truly a work of art. Shizu went on, "No matter how difficult it was for the issei families during their early years of struggle, they always had one *ikizukuri* for a centerpiece, as a good-luck symbol for the bride and groom. Everybody had a grand time, especially the men, who feasted and drank to their heart's content and often fell asleep on the floor." Shizu chuckled as she remembered the funny incidents.

SANMAI GASANE: A THREE-LAYERED KIMONO ON KAUAI

Shizu continued, "On the island of Kauai no one had ever seen a *sanmai gasane,* the three-layered bridal kimono, with the traditional symbols of pine, bamboo, and plum blossom, or *sho-chiku-bai,* separately hand-drawn on each kimono. The black *montsuki* had the pine design, the red *montsuki* the bamboo design, and the white *montsuki* the plum blossoms. The issei women were fascinated with the elegant hand-drawn designs, embellished with gold and silver coil couching, that stood out on the lower front of each kimono. Each had the Kaigo family crest: *agehanocho* [a design featuring a butterfly with raised wings]. I decided to wear the three layers of kimono together. The front bottom layers of the kimono were carefully spread to give a striking effect of the black, red, and white. The back hemline of the kimono was left in a train, to create a graceful look as I walked slowly into the reception room. My *maru* obi, woven of *kinran* [pure gold thread], was tied into a fluted butterfly design in the back. It took hours for the women to dress me. The obi is the most decorative element of the formal kimono dressing. Sadly, there was no one who owned a camera to take my pictures. Because I came in December and it was Christmas, the three-layered kimono created a festive mood and gave elegance to the occasion." Those years still remained vivid in Shizu's memory.

SHO-CHIKU-BAI SYMBOLISM: PINE, BAMBOO, AND PLUM

Shizu explained the meaning of *sho-chiku-bai:* "Most *montsuki* or *kuro* [black] *tome sode,* the basic set of formal kimonos worn by a bride for her wedding, have the *sho-chiku-bai* theme combined in one kimono. The basic black *montsuki* displayed the pine, which stays green throughout the year and symbolizes strength. The red *montsuki* had the bamboo design: bamboo branches bend under heavy snow but never break, springing right back when the snow melts, symbolizing resilience and endurance. The white *montsuki* had the plum blossoms: the bud of the plum survives the harsh winter under the snow, and is the first flower to bloom in February, symbolizing perseverance and bravery."

Collectively called by the Chinese name *sho-chiku-bai,* these three symbols of congratulations signify virtues of physical and spiritual discipline and stamina, and are sometimes known as the "three companions of the cold." These same virtues were passed on to the nisei generation. For Shizu and many picture brides who came during the 1908–1924 period to marry plantation laborers, these virtues were deeply embedded in their upbringing and helped these young women tremendously in overcoming the many adversities encountered in a strange new land.

Shizu had many fond memories of her wedding. "At the reception, Mr. and Mrs. Tamura sat next to us. They must have acted as our *nakoodo*. My husband must have become good friends with them since he was there for ten years. They were like family. They were to be our lifelong friends."

ADAPTING TO LIFE ON A SUGAR PLANTATION

"After a few days of celebration," Shizu continued, "everybody had to go back to work. I was busy trying to learn new ways and adapting to a new way of life. For a month, we lived in the one-room bachelor's quarters. A couple that recently completed their three-year contract had returned to Japan, so we moved into their house on Mokoluhe Street. It was strictly a Japanese camp when I came, but now it's a Filipino camp. Never having done any farm work back in the village, physically I wasn't in condition to even handle a hoe in the cane field. So I took the job held by the issei lady who returned to Japan. I began work with the *haole* family right away."

Shizu couldn't anticipate how difficult it would be to adapt to plantation life, as Japan is a homogeneous society. "We grew up speaking the same language and we did the same things culturally. Here in a new land, there were so many new faces, and names I could not learn to pronounce. I suffered most from the language barrier. To work, you have to communicate: you have to understand what the boss lady wanted. So sad . . . many times I wanted to cry. No matter how hard I tried, I couldn't learn to communicate, except get by with gestures.

"My husband worked twelve hours, from 4:30 in the morning until 4:30 p.m. Our camp was all Japanese, but the Filipinos lived on the other side of the camp. The people who lived in that camp were mostly mill workers. I walked to the *haole* house, did the wash and the housecleaning. The husband was an Englishman and the wife was part Hawaiian, born in Kohala, on the Big Island of Hawaii, and they had an adopted child. The man, Mr. Stewart, worked for the Wilcox family as a bookkeeper. The Wilcox family had about thirty people working for them. I went to work from 8:00 a.m. until 4:00 p.m., sometimes finishing earlier and sometimes later. Two Japanese people from Lihue who did the laundry for the Wilcox family sometimes picked me up in their *basha* [horse and buggy]. Yes, those *haole* families had a cook. I had to learn to speak English from the Japanese laundry lady. Ooh, how I suffered. I did not understand a word the *haole* people said. I could not communicate in English. It was so frustrating. I was lonely, too, not being able to talk to anyone. But, you know, I felt that the other picture brides who came before me must have learned to endure, so I should, too. How miserable I felt for not being able to know the names of articles or objects; I felt so stupid. The other side seemed as lost, not knowing how to explain the way to get things done. Sometimes I wondered why I ever came to Hawaii. I was so frustrated. Every night, I cried myself to sleep." Shizu continued, "I had to keep reminding myself, 'Gambare, gambare! Have courage! Don't give up!' That's what all the other picture brides did, too. No matter how miserable I felt, well, there was no money to go home, so I had to persevere.

"Although I never did work in the cane fields, I used to see the young mothers go to work early in the morning, clad in their *kasuri* work clothes. They had babies strapped to their backs, a banana placed in the baby's hand, and carried a heavy bag and tools in one hand. They reminded me of the *mono morai* [beggars] in the villages in Japan. I really felt sorry for them," she said sadly.

Shizu recalled, "I could have gotten a job working at the sugar mill, sewing up the top of burlap bags packed with raw sugar. That paid $13 a month. If I worked there I didn't have to worry about struggling to speak English. But people told me I'd be better off to take the woman's job at the *haole* home. I myself wanted to learn, so that's why I chose to go there. I worked as a maid for the Stewarts during the day, and when I had orders for kimonos, I sewed late at night. As soon as I got home, I started cooking dinner for my husband so he could eat as soon as he came home. Then, after cleaning up the kitchen, I would hand-sew the kimonos at night for others. I sewed, crocheted, and knitted. My teacher in Japan had a niece who had taught me to crochet and knit. Yes, in those days, I charged only 50 cents for one *yukata*. Both men and women wore them to the bathhouse and wore them at home to relax. The dressy *yukata* was worn during the Obon [festival when the souls of the deceased return to their homes] dancing. So orders kept coming in. Today [1985] people charge $15!

"When I came here in 1916, there really weren't many activities. The men used to get together for sumo wrestling. My husband was crazy about sumo. When we lived down below the mill camp, yeah, he dug one arena right next to our house and everybody got together for sumo. That was one source of relaxation for the hardworking laborers. Once a week we had Japanese movies. No talkie, it was silent movies from Japan. Nakamura-san was the *benshi* [the narrator who accompanied the silent movie]. A lot depended on the talent and skill of the *benshi*. He had to impersonate the men's and women's voices back and forth, which requires a lot of skill and timing to match the actors' movement on the screen. Some *benshi* were so good! When the stories were tragic, he put so much emotion in his voice and got the audience crying. It was surprising to find out that Nakamura-san was from the same village in Japan. The big stars those days were Kurishima Sumiko and Satsuki Nobuko. I didn't have time to go to the movies the first three years. I stayed home and did the sewing to help pay my husband's gambling debts. All the men, especially the single men, gambled. You can't blame them. I can't say how much, but he earned $35 a month and I earned $15. It seemed like a lot of money in those days," Shizu recalled.

"We were married fifty-nine years. . . . In ten months it would have been sixty years, but Tomoji died before that. No, no children. But we adopted Leslie and she was like a real daughter to us. We didn't have that much trouble raising her. My husband and I differed about eight years in age, not bad. Some men were ten years, twenty years older than their wives or even more. There were many brides in that situation, but once they came here, there wasn't much choice. Somehow they managed to overcome the obstacles for the sake of the children. Being a mother helped them to be stronger." She said, "I consider myself very lucky. Tomoji was a good man. He stopped gambling after we got married, not too much drinking, and he never fooled around with other women. *Ichiban arigatai kotowa* [the deepest appreciation I feel toward him] was the fact that not once did he make me feel that I was a useless wife because I couldn't bear him any children. In those days, many issei women who were barren were sent home by their husbands or in-laws. Tomoji

Unidentified wedding photo of nisei bride
dressed in a traditional kimono by Shizu
Kaigo, Lihue, Kauai, mid-1930s. Barbara
Kawakami Collection.

allowed me to adopt Leslie, and he was a loving father. Unlike most issei men, he
gave me the freedom to pursue whatever interest or goal I had, as long as I kept up
with my domestic duties. Tomoji even allowed me to buy a new car when I got busier
and busier as more nisei girls became of marrying age. You see, the issei mothers
were willing to sacrifice some necessities to give their daughters the type of weddings
their own parents could never afford. The demands on me as a bridal consultant and
kimono dresser became too busy. People were so surprised to see a petite, frail-
looking issei woman driving this gray Chevy coupe all around the island of Kauai.
Leslie always squeezed into the backseat of the car. She seemed quite happy."

RETURN TO JAPAN AND SPECIAL TRAINING

"In 1926 I returned alone to Japan to visit my mother, who was ill. I stayed for two
or three months until she was well," Shizu recalled. "Then, in 1930, my husband's
mother became ill, so we both had to return to Japan. She died soon after. One
thing followed another. I became sick and had to undergo surgery. Also, I wanted to
have children, so I had an operation at a leading medical hospital in Hiroshima.
Sadly, the doctor told me I could never have any children. The doctor removed everything, a hysterectomy. My body became lighter. That was when I made up my mind
to learn whatever I could during the two years I remained under his care. It was
during this time I saw the elegant *takashimada,* the bridal coiffure, and decided to
take up the intricate art of learning this bridal hairdo."

Smiling, Shizu recalled, "As well as taking an interest in bridal attire, I noticed the many interesting and beautiful decorations associated with the marriage custom that had been handed down since ancient times. The origin of *mizuhiki* [an art form that uses a special cord made from rice paper] is very old. It was always made in two colors, red-white, gold-silver, or red-gold." Shizu learned to make wedding table decorations with the colorful *mizuhiki*. She made a complete set of auspicious table decorations that was displayed at many weddings on the island of Kauai. Her collection of decorations is presently stored at Hawaii's Plantation Village, in Waipahu, Hawaii. "I also took an interest in drawing the family crest. It usually took ten years to master this time-consuming skill. Since I spent almost two years in Japan having one surgery after another, I made use of the waiting period to learn whatever I could. One of the most valuable trainings I received was the art of dressing a bride in traditional wedding attire. When I got married on the island of Kauai, in 1916, there were no professional bridal dressers or consultants. The issei women who had watched the brides being dressed back in the village did their best to help. The intensive training I went through to learn the traditional bridal costume proved to be worthwhile when I returned to Hawaii in 1932."

Shizu had the foresight to see that there was a need for a professional bridal kimono dresser and hairdresser in the plantation community. By this time, most of the issei parents with their ever-expanding families had given up the idea of one day going back to their homeland. Their nisei offspring were fast approaching marrying age, and the issei mothers wanted to give their daughters the weddings they

Shizu Kaigo showed the author the *mizuhiki* that she made for weddings. Barbara Kawakami Collection.

Nisei bride dressed by Shizu Kaigo in full
traditional wedding attire, ca. 1934.
Barbara Kawakami Collection.

had never had because of the circumstances of their marriages. Shizu's timing was
perfect. Soon after she returned from Japan, she was in such great demand that she
was compelled to learn to drive, and that's when she bought the car. She was the
first issei woman to drive around Kauai. There were times when she had to dress
five brides in different locations, and she couldn't have done it without her car. According to her daughter, Leslie, her father never learned to drive. It was Shizu who
drove him around, and no matter how busy she was, she would drive him to his favorite fishing spot on the other side of the island.

  Shizu continued the bridal consultant business until the outbreak of World War II,
when everything Japanese was banned. "Actually, in the olden days in Japan, being a
hairdresser was not considered a respectable profession. However, for me, while having surgery and recuperating, I kept busy with something I enjoyed doing. The fact
that I could never have any children, I thought, I should be prepared with some kind
of skill to support myself."

ADOPTING A DAUGHTER

"Leslie was a little girl who lived next door to us. When I came back to Hawaii in
March, 1932, Leslie's mother was very sick. She came with her father early in the

morning to greet me. She started calling me *fune no obachan* [boat lady], because I came home on a boat. Her mother was so ill that a nurse took care of her. Leslie must have felt uncomfortable, so she came to stay with me. A year later, her mother died. Leslie didn't want to go home. Her father felt that he was imposing on us too much and came with her older sister to get her. He would carry Leslie home, put her in bed, and then she would burst out crying. She said she would pretend to be asleep when her father carried her home, then she'd cry when she was put into her own bed, so he brought her back to me. Leslie's father couldn't do anything and he'd say, 'Oh, this girl is impossible!' This went on for quite a while until she finally just stayed at our house and went home only on weekends. I felt so much for that girl, to think that she'd rather stay with me. At the time I was teaching kimono sewing to three girls and couldn't go anywhere anyway, so I took care of Leslie on the side. She was only three and a half years old, and even now she still remembers and talks about it." Shizu's eyes filled with tears just thinking of the little girl who wanted to stay with her rather than go back to her father. Shizu loved Leslie like she was her own.

"Yes, she lived with me continually. When I dressed the brides for Saturday weddings, I stayed overnight at the bride's home, so Leslie stayed with her grandmother, her father's mother. That way I never worried. In the beginning, when I wanted to adopt her, I gave it serious thought. I knew of cases when the baby was given away and the child later resented the parents for giving them away. So I told her father, 'I'll wait until she's old enough to understand and she says okay.' After Leslie graduated from eighth grade, we sent her to Mid-Pacific Institute, the private school in Honolulu, thinking that someday she'll be our own. When she was in the third year of high school, we realized we couldn't claim the tuition expenses for our tax exemption because she wasn't legally ours. That's when we decided to adopt her. Her father had accepted the fact that she would be ours someday. She used the Kaigo name during her year at Mid-Pacific and during the four years in college at the University of Hawaii. She got married soon after she graduated, but she used the Kaigo name for maybe five or six years." Shizu seemed happy about that.

"After college, Leslie got a teaching job, and soon married George. They didn't have children for eight years. We were still on Kauai then. When my first grandchild came, they needed a babysitter. My husband was retired and I had just returned from a trip to Japan and wasn't working, so we moved to the island of Molokai to live with Leslie and George. Molokai is a wonderful place to live. People are so friendly. I feel very fortunate! I don't think there's anyone as happy as I am. I'm very lucky. Leslie is good to me and so is her husband, George."

TRADITIONAL WEDDINGS

"The two years of training and study I did in Japan was well worth it. I came back from Japan with all this knowledge. The timing was right and everything went very well. I sewed the bridal kimono, dressed the bride, then did the bridal hair. I drew the crests on the kimono, and I could do the *mizuhiki* tying for the *yuino* [betrothal gifts]. I even sewed the covers and stenciled the crests on all the covers for the bride's dowry furniture. There were other hairdressers and bridal consultants, but I was fortunate to have many people come to me. When I returned from Japan, I needed a model to advertise my business in the Japanese newspaper. Here's the photo. She was a friend of mine, a very sweet person, and so beautiful. Her husband was a newspaperman. Yes, she made a perfect model. I remember she had a permanent wave. Her hair was so short. It was difficult to comb the bridal coiffure. I had to start early in the morning. I combed her hair once, then recombed it again. Later, I started using a wig for girls with a permanent. This simplified the process and saved time. I must have done hundreds of brides. I received $25 each from the bride's and groom's families, so I made a total of $50 from each wedding. I never had a set price, but they gave me that much in gratuity," she said smilingly.

"For casual kimonos, I used to dress four or five girls in no time, sometimes ten girls. During the Obon, the young girls would come over and beg, 'Obasan [auntie], please dress me in my kimono.' During the Obon I dressed from forty to fifty girls in one night. I had a friend assist me in handing over the little sashes to speed up the job."

"For weddings, it's more complicated. On the average, for the bride, I handled at most about five or six people. I had to dress the attendants, too. Now I don't have the strength in my hands anymore to tie the obi like I did when I was younger. Once I dressed three brides in one Sunday. I drove around in my car. I would dress the bride, take her picture, then hurry to the next one, and then the next. When I dressed the bride, the front parts of the three kimonos had to be layered exactly and not show the underlayer. But when the bride begins to walk slowly, the front part of the kimono skirt will open and show the contrasting colors of the underkimono. The three layers in the front part of the kimono had to be perfectly aligned. You have to be very careful in folding the kimono so that when you wear it the next time the fold will be in the right place.

"When I went to Japan the second time in 1930, the women in Japan used to wear the traditional bridal coiffure. It was beginning to gain popularity in Hawaii, and on Kauai, too. Of course, the weddings were much simpler here. It was impossible to follow the traditional marriage ceremony as it was held in Japan. The issei could not have been able to afford it. I still have the formal sake cups for the *san san kudo* exchange of nuptial cups. People used to come over to borrow them for their weddings."

In the nuptial ceremony, *san san kudo,* a young girl serves sake to the groom, who drinks it in three sips. Then more sake is poured into the same cup and the bride takes three sips. The second cup is then offered to the groom, who drinks the sake in three sips, and then to the bride, who takes three more sips. The groom and bride then do this a third time. Because three cups are filled with three pouring motions, and the sake is taken in three sips, the marriage ceremony is called *san san kudo* (three, three, nine times). In Japan, when a couple goes through this ritual, they are declared legally married.

The highlight of the marriage celebration was the *utai* (chanting) of the Takasago, a Noh drama text, a very difficult piece to sing. A long time ago, a poem was written about the grandeur and beauty of two pine trees on the shores of Takasago on Kyushu. The ancient black and red pines stood with their branches entwined together and appeared like a single tree. They were widely worshiped as a symbol of long life and wedded bliss.*

"I also decorated the bride's table with the *takasago* [good-luck symbol of the old man and old lady]. It's decorated with the pine, crane, turtle, barley, soybean, and rice. The Japanese always use the *tsuru-kame* [crane and turtle] because they have long life spans. I had them stored under the house and the bugs ruined the pine tree. You can never see these things in Hawaii. I also have the treasure boat, and I wanted so badly to show them to you, but I was so tired I couldn't walk downstairs to get them. Everything is stored under the house. So many of my things are ruined, because the bugs ate them all. I may only have the platform left." Shizu felt sad about not being able to show them to me.

Shizu talked about the many items she had kept all those years: "The treasure boat is used for weddings and to celebrate happy occasions. It represents the bride entering the home. It symbolizes wealth because the bride is expected to contribute whatever she can to her new family. The *sho-chiku-bai* symbolizes strength, endurance, and good health. *Chocho* [butterflies] always fly in pairs, and this shows compatibility. Red coral is also used, because it multiplies. This is the lobster, which is always used for auspicious occasions like weddings and New Year's. This turtle on a decorative container was used for the bride's engagement ring. Yes, I made them all. There is a *gosan no kiri* [five and three paulownia] crest. There's a *goshi chi no kiri* [five and seven paulownia] crest. This is used to wrap the bride's obi when the groom's family brings the *yuino* to her home. This is a ceremonial wrapping." At age ninety, Shizu remembered the valuable meanings of each one.

"These wedding photos are from 1932 to the outbreak of World War II. I cannot remember all the names. I really dressed a lot of brides. You can see that. I had to work real fast. I could dress one person in twenty minutes. The bride's mother, relatives, and about six people all at one time. I took my time with the bride and dressed her carefully. I also wanted to take pictures, so that took extra time. Sometimes when the bride had to change kimonos at the reception, I had someone to help with the dressing part. But having a car really made a difference, to rush from one place to the next. There was one incident, this girl lived near Lihue. I forgot her first name. She was *hapai* [pregnant]. The food was prepared for the reception when she gave birth that day!" Shizu pointed at the photos. "These were her dowry, all given her by friends and relatives. That's a *tansu* [chest of drawers] and *toronko* [trunk]. Parents buy some things for their daughter. Some relatives and friends give generously, too. Actually, the parents are supposed to provide those; however, brothers and sisters chip in on the gifts, too. This is a *sugatami* [full-length mirror]. Some brides were lucky enough to have this." Shizu vividly remembered every detail.

"For the men, it was much simpler," she told me. "The groom usually wore a black or dark navy blue wool suit. Nothing fancy because they were too poor. Usually a dark suit cost about $20, a month's pay if you worked in the fields. In Japan, they probably would have worn the traditional black *montsuki, hakama,* and *haori* to match the bride's formal attire. They didn't wear tuxedos like today's grooms. In the old photos where couples took group pictures in matching outfits, I'm sure they were borrowed. By the time I started my business in 1932, most men owned their own suits."

---

* Mock Joya, *Things Japanese* (Tokyo, 1971), 498–499.

Shizu Kaigo on the left and her assistant
on the right, dressing a bride in Lihue,
Kauai. Barbara Kawakami Collection.

PEARL HARBOR ATTACK, 1941

"I dressed a bride on December 6, 1941, the day before the attack, a girl from Hanamaulu. That very next morning, everything was set for the wedding and reception at the Hanamaulu Café later that day. I went to Kapaa early in the morning to buy *tako* [octopus] for the wedding table without knowing about the attack. I didn't have time to turn on the radio that morning. The man at the market said, 'How can you be so *nonkina* [nonchalant] when Japan attacked Pearl Harbor this morning?' I shuddered at the thought. I rushed home and turned on the radio. I used to get direct broadcasts from Japan and they were blasting the news on shortwave radio. What a dreadful thing Japan did, I thought. After that, the shortwave radios were taken away. I had appointments scheduled for three more weddings on every Sunday in December, but they were all cancelled," Shizu recalled.

FAMILY CREST

"The bride usually takes her mother's family crest, because when the mother dies the *montsuki* customarily goes to the daughter. That's my assumption. The groom takes his father's family crest for his *montsuki,*" Shizu commented.

Nisei bride dressed by Shizu Kaigo with gifts from the groom. Barbara Kawakami Collection.

"This is called the *fusencho;* it is my mother's crest. *Fuse* means 'lying down'; *cho* means 'butterfly.' This is the *hanabishi* [a flower-shaped rhombus]. The flower is added within the space of the diamond shape to make it more decorative. There is also the *agehanocho* crest. That is the Kaigo family crest that I have on my *montsuki.*

"Nowadays people are not as particular as in the past. People used to ask me to select a design for them from the book of crests to put on their daughter's *montsuki.* They did not know their ancestor's crests because their mothers did not bring their *montsuki* to Hawaii, or they didn't care for the design. On Kauai, the Okinawan people often asked me to select a popular pattern for their *mon* [crest]. They wanted it on their formal kimonos. I thought that was unusual, because family crests in Japan are usually handed down through the generations. In ancient Okinawan history, the court people and the warrior class did have their family crests; however, ordinary people did not have a family crest, except on their furniture. On Kauai, before the war, a *naichi* bride usually brought a *montsuki* [with the family crest drawn in] as part of her dowry. Everything was done more formally in those days. The *yuino* for the bride was elaborately decorated with the *mizuhiki* and placed on a specially made wooden platform. That was the proper way. I loaned out the red lacquer sake cups, the *horai* [festival ornaments], and *shimadai* [Isle of Eternal Youth symbolic ornaments]. I loaned them out free; I never charged money for it," she said.

DRAWING THE CREST

"Originally, the silk crepe for the kimono was white, dyed a solid black. The part where the crest is to be drawn is left white. When you bring it to the dyers to have it completely done, the black background within the crest is expertly *somekomi* [dyed together] with the rest of the cloth. If the crest is drawn after, that small area has to be filled in with a tiny brush. That's very difficult to do. With black, it's easier to match, but in the case of the colored *montsuki,* the color used in the tiny space in the crest design has to match perfectly with the rest of the dyed color of the kimono. Otherwise it wouldn't look right. So to draw the crest afterward requires lots of skill and you have to know how to mix the colors to match the rest of the kimono. See? This moon crest here is drawn in later. See, if they bring me purple or blue *montsuki* with the crest to be drawn afterward, when I fill in the background of the crest design, purple or blue, the color has to match exactly with the rest of the dyed color. That is quite a task."

Shizu explained in detail how to draw a *mon* on a kimono. "The *kimono* is dyed at the dyers and the area for the crest is left white. On a table on a flat surface, I put a thick cut board of paulownia wood underneath. I place a paper on the surface, then heat the small iron and place it over the crest design to flatten the pebble of the crepe silk, being cautious not to burn the fabric. Then I trace a pattern of the crest with *shibugami* [paper treated with the astringent juice of persimmon]. I use the dressmaker's compass to draw the fine lines. After I draw the pattern, I apply a special kind of wax that won't smear or rub off. Then, with the knife, I cut away the area that I don't need. Once the pattern is neatly cut, I place it over the exact position of the crest, press the paper firmly down and then apply the color with a fine brush. The cut-out area becomes the colored background for the white crest. With the fine brush, I paint in the color, being careful not to let any color run into the pure white of the crest design. I also have to make sure the color is well set. It's very delicate work. With these hands, it's impossible to do it right now. When the dyers do the crest there's no problem, but when I draw the crest afterward, no matter how careful I am in matching the background color of the crest to that of the kimono, it doesn't always turn out perfect. I learned to mix colors and practiced a lot. If it's an easy pattern, I can draw the crests for five kimonos in a day.

"Each kimono has five crests," she explained. "Yes, 50 cents for each crest. I got $2.50 for each kimono, very profitable. I could draw the crests for five kimonos in a day and it took the same amount of time to sew a single kimono. If the pattern was already made or they used the same crest, the work went faster. See, to make the pattern took time because I cut the design out with a fine knife first."

In my many years of research on Japanese immigrant clothing, Shizu Kaigo was one of only four individuals I encountered who were masters of this unique art of drawing the family crest in prewar Hawaii.

MATCHMAKING IN HAWAII

"The idea of matchmaking nisei couples came naturally to me," Shizu explained. "Whenever I was asked to dress the bride, the bride usually asked her best friend to be the maid of honor. She also wore a beautiful kimono and obi. In the process of dressing her, I had the opportunity to get to know her in a friendly and casual manner. If I thought the bridesmaid seemed like a nice girl, I would try to find a nice young man who would be a good match for her. Mainly I observed the person and tried to get to know their attitude in life, whether they were hardworking and well liked by others. I would sort of figure out if they would be a compatible couple. That's how I did it. I made a point of investigating how much the man made. I tried to match a couple with equal backgrounds. Too much difference in social status is not good. I couldn't investigate their family background in Japan, so I checked their educational level and what type of family he or she had. When I found a couple most suited for each other, I approached the family. I have matched many young couples successfully. Most nisei girls here find their own husbands," she chuckled. Shizu was ideally suited for the role of *nakoodo* because everyone liked her and found her very trustworthy. She was highly respected in the community and had tremendous knowledge and understanding of the traditional culture and practices.

AWARD

Shizu never mentioned the award she had received from Emperor Hirohito of Japan until I asked her about it. "I am embarrassed to think a person like me who has never done anything special should receive such an honor! I really don't know who selected me, but I suddenly had a call from the Japanese consulate in Nuuanu [Honolulu] that I was to receive the Order of the Sacred Treasure, Silver Rays Award for my outstanding contributions to the community. I was very surprised. The call came on April 29, 1975, on the emperor's birthday. Then in May, the consulate official called me to come to Honolulu to receive the award, so I did. I think there were nine people receiving the awards. I was almost eighty years old! I really don't know what I did to deserve this. I can only say that I've always had a curious mind to want to learn new things, and wanted to learn everything."

When I asked her to show me the award, Shizu replied, "You're not supposed to show off these things." I got in touch with her daughter, Leslie, on Molokai and inquired about Emperor Hirohito's award and the souvenir photo taken at the consulate, but she didn't remember what became of either the medal or the photo.

IN RETROSPECT

Shizu got emotional as her thoughts flashed back to the early days when she first set foot on the island of Kauai. "In the beginning, I suffered because of the language barrier. Everything was so different from what I had expected. I cried and cried, and wondered why I ever came to Hawaii. I guess the other picture brides felt that way, too. I kept reminding myself, 'Gambare! Gambare! Have courage. Don't give up!' Now I'm so happy I came. I'm moved to tears with gratitude. I have gained a loving, wonderful daughter, a great son-in-law, and also grandchildren who take good care of me," she said with tears streaming down her cheeks. Anyone could see there is a special bond between them.

Leslie added, "She has been a real mother to me, and now it's my turn to take good care of her." I could not help but feel the warmth and sincerity of the expression of love and appreciation she had for her remarkable mother.

When my book *Japanese Immigrant Clothing in Hawaii, 1885–1941* was published in 1993, I sent Shizu Kaigo a copy because I wasn't able to deliver it personally. She was 97 years old then, and not doing too well. According to Leslie, she was so happy to receive my book and recognized the rare photos she had contributed of the nisei brides she had dressed. "Every night, Mother would hold your book against her heart, close her eyes, and utter a prayer. Then she tucked it under her pillow before she went to sleep." I was overwhelmed to hear these words from Leslie. How fortunate I was to have had the privilege to document the life of this remarkable woman.

Shizu Kaigo's achievements were phenomenal for a woman with only an eighth-grade education. In the beginning she suffered because of her limited ability to speak English. In spite of that, she became a leading bridal consultant, dressing hundreds of nisei brides in the traditional wedding costumes and bridal hairdo. She taught many nisei girls the art of traditional Japanese kimono sewing. She was an expert in bonsai. She also held an instructor's certificate in *ikebana*. Shizu became a naturalized citizen on December 16, 1953. In 1975, her remarkable achievements culminated with the Emperor of Japan recognizing her many contributions to perpetuate the rich Japanese heritage and culture in Hawaii. Shizu truly lived the life of *sho-chiku-bai,* the embodiment of the Japanese spirit, symbolizing physical and spiritual discipline. It was this *gambare* spirit that kept her going.

In 2009, the Japanese Overseas Museum in Yokohama, Japan, borrowed Shizu's three-layered kimono for its "History of Picture Brides" exhibition. Empress Michiko and her entourage of court ladies came to see the exhibit. They were very impressed to learn that a picture bride was able to bring such an elegant wedding costume to Hawaii in 1916.

In 2010, Shizu's three-layered wedding kimono was the highlight of "Textured Lives: Japanese Immigrant Clothing from the Plantations of Hawaii," an exhibit at the Japanese American National Museum in Los Angeles that displayed many of the kimonos I collected in my years of research. It was exciting to see so many people admiring the beauty and elegance of her *sho-chiku-bai* kimono.

On August 18, 2012, Shizu Kaigo's elegant *sanmai gasane* wedding kimono and gold-brocaded obi were the highlight of JANM's "Textured Lives" traveling exhibit at the Bishop Museum in Honolulu.

Shizu lived to be 102 years old. She passed away on October 30, 1998.

Haruno Tazawa

INSPIRATION FROM TATTERED CLOTHING

February 2, 1897–June 7, 1994
Born in Adachi-machi, Fukushima-ken
Arrived in Hawaii July 17, 1917

Among the many people I interviewed over the years, Haruno Tazawa, at age eighty-seven, was the most reluctant to grant an interview. You know there's something amiss when a person shies away from sharing stories about her past. That aroused my curiosity and spurred me to try harder to interview her.

I was very grateful when, in 1984, after my third phone call, she finally consented to see me. When she finally agreed, she shared a most extraordinary story that was worth the patience. Perhaps she agreed because I mentioned that my mother also had been a young widow, left at age thirty-nine with eight children to support.

Haruno was delighted to hear that my mother was also from Fukushima prefecture, a few villages away from her childhood home. I described things that I had heard from my mother as a young child—how, during the winter months, snow fell eleven feet deep and covered their thatched roofs, so everyone was confined indoors. I told Haruno that my mother spoke fondly about her three sisters and how they spent time together weaving striped cotton cloth and *kasuri* (ikat) fabrics for their kimonos, doing quilting, patchwork, and embroidery, and became adept with various kinds of crafts. The men did wooden craftwork, too, and did lots of reading during the cold winter months. Although they were farmers, many of them were self-educated and very scholarly.

I shared with Haruno my first impression of my mother's quaint village, set against beautiful lush mountains. The autumn landscape was spectacular, a breathtaking collage of brilliant colors, exactly the way my mother had described it. I told Haruno how, during my growing-up years on the plantation in Waipahu, my mother would join her children on the spacious veranda in the evenings to "talk story." While mending our clothes, she reminisced about her childhood in her beloved village home, which she had left in 1912. My mother was never able to return there. Haruno, however, had been able to make a visit to Fukushima before the outbreak of World War II.

Maybe this sharing of my mother's story formed that special connection that brought us together. There were so many similarities in the things they both had to endure to survive as widows on the plantation, with only a small pension.

Before Haruno could change her mind, I quickly arranged to meet with her at her plantation home. She lived on Bond Street, within walking distance of the old, dilapidated sugar mill, once the bustling center of the Ewa sugar plantation in its heyday. Now only the dry, deserted cane fields remained in the area, overrun by koa trees and weeds.

It was a small house with slightly faded green paint, a couple of bedrooms, and a cozy kitchen. A huge mango tree provided nice shade for the house and produced the most luscious Hayden mangoes, according to Haruno. It was here where Haruno, a pretty young picture bride, began her life in Hawaii in 1917. As the interview progressed, I wondered how she had managed to raise her four children in this tiny space.

THE INTERVIEW

Haruno greeted me at the front door of her modest home as I walked up the narrow wooden steps. She was still spry and as sharp as could be, with a twinkle in her eyes, and her warm, friendly smile was contagious as she welcomed me in her Fukushima dialect. It immediately reminded me of my mother, who also spoke *zu zu ben*—an onomatopoeic name for what the Fukushima dialect sounded like to people of other prefectures. It's very difficult to understand unless one is accustomed to hearing it, as I was.

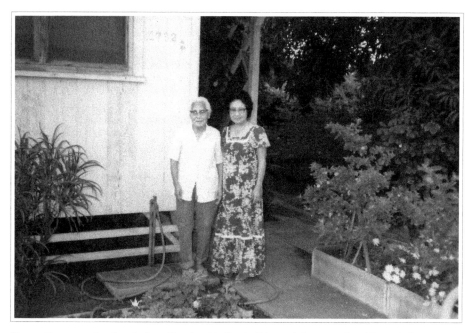

Haruno Tazawa and author Barbara Kawakami in front of Haruna's home on Bond Street in Ewa.
Barbara Kawakami Collection.

After retiring from working in the cane fields for ten hours a day at the Ewa plantation, Haruno began a new career at the Tenney Center restaurant, a popular gathering place for people in the community. She assisted in the kitchen with preparation of food and doing the dishes until she was seventy-eight years old. When she wasn't needed in the restaurant, she would go into the yard outside to do some weeding. Most young people would rest during a break, but Haruno never stayed idle. The boss was impressed with her diligent work ethic and gave her a raise immediately. Now finally retired, and even though her spine was bent with osteoporosis, she still kept busy, raising orange ilima flowers to sell to the lei makers. Getting up early and picking the tiny blossoms is quite a task, and Haruno takes joy in making the Hawaiian lei sellers happy. Besides the beautiful ilima, Haruno nurtured a bed of white iris in one corner of her yard, and graceful purple iris with long sword-shaped leaves grew near the front walk. When I admired the rare white iris, she generously shared one of the plants with me. I placed it in my rock garden in the backyard, among the purple iris plants. When the flowers bloom in profusion, I enjoy their beauty and think of the remarkable stories she shared with me.

As soon as she invited me into her neat, cozy-looking home, she immediately offered me a comfortable *zabuton* so I could sit on the mat-covered floor in Japanese fashion. Since I had explained about my research on plantation work clothing and about the kimonos brought from Japan by the issei, she had everything ready for me. Much to my surprise, there were two *kori,* bamboo wicker trunks, filled with a treasure trove of old clothing that dated back to 1917 or even earlier. As she carefully took out the garments, she began telling her story as it related to each garment. She was an amazing storyteller! As she slowly unfolded her life's story, quite literally, it seemed as though she had been waiting for the right moment to share what she had kept deep within her heart for so many years. I could now understand why she had kept the story to herself all these years. It was just too painful for her to recall. It seemed like a miracle that this issei woman whom I was meeting for the first time trusted me and shared with me the most intimate, memorable experiences of her life, secrets that she had never even revealed to her children.

PICTURE BRIDE MARRIAGE

"I was twenty years old when I came from Fukushima as the picture bride of Chozo Tazawa," she began. "It was unusual that my marriage was arranged by a sister. My older sister had gone a few years earlier as a picture bride to marry a plantation laborer at the Ewa sugar plantation on Oahu. She wrote to my parents about a bachelor from Niigata, Japan, who had a prestigious position as a *luna* at Ewa plantation. She sent my parents a photo of a distinguished-looking young man with a mustache, dressed in *kasuri* kimono and *haori.* I thought he was nice-looking, and I didn't mind going to the island paradise I had heard so much about. Although there had been several proposals of marriage from the village families, I didn't relish the thought of spending the rest of my life as a farmer's wife, working knee deep in the rice paddies. I was anxious to escape the drudgery of farm life."

"Once my marriage was decided, I went from Fukushima to Niigata to live with my future parents-in-law for six months. They were wonderful and I had the happiest time of my life, although I couldn't understand their Niigata dialect at all. People

Haruno's exchange photo.
Barbara Kawakami Collection.

Chozo's exchange photo.
Barbara Kawakami Collection.

say the Fukushima dialect is difficult to understand, but the Niigata dialect is even harder to comprehend," Haruno said with laughter. This was sort of a trial period for the bride to gain approval by her in-laws. If they didn't approve of her, they had the right to not enter her name in the family register in the village office and the marriage would not take place.

Before leaving for Hawaii, Haruno stopped in Fukushima to see her family. In spite of the excitement she felt about traveling to a foreign country, saying goodbye to her family, especially to her mother, was most difficult.

"To this day, I can never forget the sad expression on my mother's face as she held back her tears and told me to hurry up and leave before she broke down and cried. My mother must have known that we would never see each other again. It certainly turned out to be true."

ARRIVAL IN HAWAII

Haruno arrived in Hawaii on the *Shinyo Maru* on July 17, 1917. "As I disembarked from the ship, I wore the purple cotton *kasuri* kimono that I had woven on my own handloom and hand-sewed myself. My hair was done in the pompadour hairdo, adorned with a lacquered hair comb that my mother bought for me. I didn't even have a handbag. I don't think any of the other brides had one. We tucked most of our valuables in our obi. We certainly must have looked like *inakappe* [country bumpkins]." She broke out in laughter. "It had been many years since my older sister left for Hawaii, so I was looking forward to seeing her again."

Haruno smiled and her eyes lit up as she recalled the first encounter at the immigration station. "My husband, Chozo, recognized me immediately from the photo my family had sent him. I thought he looked so handsome, dressed in his dark suit and white shirt with high debonair collar and bow tie. However, he didn't have a mustache like he did in the photo of him in his kimono. I was a bit apprehensive about whether he was the right person or not. Finding myself in a strange place and not being able to communicate other than in my native dialect, I had no choice but to follow him," she explained with a chuckle.

Haruno's physical checkup and required exams went smoothly. Chozo hailed a *hakku* to take them to the Yamashiro Hotel. Then, as if waiting for the right moment, Haruno quietly handed Chozo the money that was carefully tucked in her obi. He seemed puzzled, so Haruno explained. "'This is the leftover money from the *yuino-kin* you sent to my parents in preparation for my dowry. With that money, they bought me a set of *kuro tome sode* and accessories. Because I wove my own fabrics and sewed my three kimonos, there was some leftover money that my mother told me to return to you.' Chozo quickly replied, 'Why didn't you give this to your mother? I wanted her to accept all of it as a gift.' He was surprised at my mother's honesty. Imagine, that was the only conversation we had the first day after we got married," she said.

Haruno mentioned other incidents that seemed funny now. "I was probably the only picture bride who came with two large *kori*. In one *kori*, I packed all my clothing, while the other *kori* included a large futon and a *tanzen* [cotton-padded kimono]. Fukushima is known as snow country and my mother, not knowing about Hawaii's tropical climate, had included these items as part of my dowry." Haruno's eyes got a bit misty as she spread the garments before me. She must have thought about her mother's love and concern for her and about the sad expression on her mother's face the day Haruno left her village.

Haruno was married in absentia in Japan and her name was registered in her husband's family *koseki* in the village office; according to Japanese law, she and her husband were then legally married. However, Chozo had a Buddhist priest perform a marriage ceremony at the Yamashiro Hotel, to conform to the laws of the Territory of Hawaii. The next day, her husband hired a taxi and they headed toward a mountainous region, passing through miles and miles of vast sugarcane fields. Suddenly the taxi came to a stop at an isolated house surrounded by tall cane fields. Haruno was devastated at the sight of her new home, which reminded her of their horse barn back in the village.

PLANTATION WEDDING

Haruno was caught by surprise the day after her arrival at the Ewa plantation. When she awoke early in the morning, Chozo's friends and neighbors had pitched huge tents in the yard, while the women were busy with preparations for the wedding feast. The entire community was invited to the reception to honor the newlyweds. Chozo's high status in the community was evident. There was plenty of food spread on a long table, such as sushi, sashimi made from fish caught in the nearby sea, *nishime,* red fish, *morimono* (an assortment of food served on happy occasions), and lots of sake. The party continued for a few days, and everybody had a good time.

At the reception, Haruno wore her *kuro tome sode,* the black formal kimono with five crests, though without any *suso-moyo* (design at the hemline). She said her family couldn't afford such luxury for her. However, had they utilized Chozo's generous monetary gift for her dowry, Haruno's mother could have bought her a bridal kimono featuring an elaborate hand-drawn design on the hemline. Chozo would have preferred that instead of having the leftover money returned to him.

Haruno had never seen so many strange faces. "This was the first time I had ever laid eyes on a *gaijin* [foreigner], and I was scared. I came face-to-face with the *gaijin* as I poured sake into their cups to greet them. They had such big eyes and tall noses. Some of them shook my hands and said something like *nisu girlu* [nice girl]. There were all kinds of *gaijin—poroki* [Portuguese], Puerto Ricans, Spanish, Filipinos, a few Koreans, and some Okinawan people. The Portuguese and Spanish were referred to as *haole* in those days because they closely resembled the Caucasians. The most difficult thing to cope with was learning to communicate with people of other ethnic groups." Haruno's initial culture shock slowly wore off as she gradually acculturated into the melting pot of races in Hawaii.

LIFE ON A PLANTATION

"My husband was a *luna* at the Ewa plantation and made a salary of $80 a month. That was considered a good salary when the ordinary field worker was paid $20 a month for ten hours of hard work every day. So I didn't have to work in the fields like the other picture brides. I stayed home for six months doing household chores and working in the garden all day. Housecleaning was difficult. The plantation used rough lumber for the construction of the homes. If I accidentally touched the walls, it really hurt my hands, so I pasted newspapers all over the walls. Although the floor was covered with straw matting, it was so *zara zara* [messy] with *ishibai* [lime] constantly falling all over the floor. I can't even describe how dirty the house was! It needed cleaning all the time. The *benjo* [outhouse], without any running water, was built a short distance away from the house.

"Ewa plantation still did not have electricity installed in the homes in 1917, so we used kerosene lamps. We carried them around as needed, even to the outhouse at night. The kitchen was partly an earthen floor and some of the cooking was done over an open fire using kiawe wood. As a young bride, learning to cook only a cup of rice for the two of us was not an easy task. Back in the village, rice was cooked for eleven people in a large *kama* over an open fire, so the rice tasted better." Haruno had to learn to improvise and adjust to local ways of cooking with whatever was available.

DIET ON THE PLANTATION

Haruno recalled bleakly, "The food in those days was not what we have today. The menu consisted mostly of vegetarian dishes; most families couldn't afford to buy meat. Most of the vegetables were home-grown, and we often traded with our neighbors whatever we had in abundance. In Japan, we had only *mugi-gohan* [barley rice], miso soup, and *tsukemono* [pickled vegetables]. In Hawaii, we ate polished rice every day, a luxury back in my home village. Ewa is located near the seashore, and the peddler came around with a fresh catch of fish. We bought *akule* [aji] for 10 cents a pound—when fried to a crisp, they were delicious. Other sources of protein were tofu, *iriko* [parched small sardines] used for *dashi* [soup stock], *natto* [fermented soybeans], and a variety of dried beans from Japan. We also had *tara* [dried codfish] cooked in sugar and *shoyu*, and dried *shio-shake* [salted salmon], which were considered a *gochiso* [feast] in those days. Any leftovers we packed for the next day's lunch in a double-decker lunch pail. We always stuck an *ume* in the rice. *Ume* keeps you healthy. Actually, this simple food we ate kept us in better health than the luxury food we are enjoying today." Haruno smiled, and I could see the pride in her face.

WORKING ON THE PLANTATION

After six months of being idle at home, Haruno decided to work in the sugarcane fields like the other picture brides.

"I would get up at 4:00 a.m. to prepare breakfast and pack lunch for my husband and myself. I washed the rice the night before so I could cook it first thing in the morning. The *bento* I packed for lunch was fairly simple, with cooked vegetables and pickled vegetables. At times I could add leftover salted salmon or codfish for lunch, and that was quite a treat. When I think of the simple food we used to eat— the young people today live like a *tonosama* [lord]," she said laughingly.

Working for the plantation was a new experience, not at all like the easygoing working conditions in the village, where the entire family worked together. During the planting and harvesting seasons in Japan, everyone worked very hard, but there was still time to relax after that. "In Hawaii, from the early morning whistle to *pau hana* time [the end of the workday], we really worked hard in backbreaking labor. In the morning as soon as we finished breakfast, I hurriedly dressed in my *kasuri* work clothes and left for work at 4:30 a.m. It was a ten-minute walk to the train station. The train took an hour and fifteen minutes to reach our destination, and we started work at 6:00 a.m. In those days, Ewa sugar plantation extended as far as Nanakuli.

"I had my first child two years after we were married. With each baby I carried, I worked until the last minute to earn the bonus. Usually, when the time was near, we were allowed to work in the nearby fields. As soon as the abdominal pain started, I rushed home and called the midwife, Mrs. Maki Igarashi. In those days, the midwife charged $5 for delivering the baby. She continued to help for two weeks, to bathe the baby and help with washing diapers. I was fortunate to have an easy delivery. After the baby came, my husband helped me for a while, but soon after, he began sneaking out at night, to gamble and to fool around," she said.

HUSBAND'S DEATH

In 1928, eleven years later, Chozo suddenly died, leaving Haruno a widow at thirty-one years of age, with the responsibility of raising four children. It was an earth-shattering experience for her. Her oldest daughter was only nine years old; the youngest was two. Her second son was born handicapped and needed extra care.

"My husband had gambled away all the money he made. All I had was 35 cents in my coin purse." Because her husband had been a *luna,* she had to give him a funeral appropriate to his status in the community. "The girls needed white dresses for the funeral, so I begged the village seamstress to please make any kind of dress, even with bleached rice bags, anything, so they can put their head and hands through. And that's what they wore to their father's funeral. People were so kind in those days. They all *dashi dashi* [chipped in] and helped pay for the *osenbei* [tea cookies] to serve with tea to the guests when they came to offer their condolences. I had to borrow $5 to give the *orei* [offering of gratitude] to the priest. How thankful I was to have so many people help me. Yet I feel so much shame when I think about those days," she acknowledged.

She closed her eyes against the tears that streamed down her cheeks, and tried to wipe them away with her fragile work-worn hands. She was eighty-seven years old when I interviewed her, and she still hadn't forgotten the kindness and generosity she had received from neighbors and friends so long ago.

Haruno Tazawa donated her two *kori* full of her kimonos, plantation work clothes, accessories, and the *kakocho* (family death register). This is a valuable document in which all the condolences that were presented, such as monetary offerings, rolls of incense, candles, and flowers, were carefully recorded in calligraphy by the minister who performed the funeral service. The *kakocho*'s list of the small offerings given by friends, relatives, and members of community reflects a time of poor economic conditions, when everybody was struggling to survive. The *kakocho* is preserved at the Japanese American National Museum in Los Angeles along with all her plantation clothing and artifacts.

Haruno with her four children in 1928, about a year after her husband passed away. The girls are dressed in the bleached rice bag dresses they wore for their father's funeral. Barbara Kawakami Collection.

WIDOWHOOD

After her husband's death, Haruno immediately went back to work in the sugarcane fields. She worked ten hours a day, toiling in the hot sun, and also did laundry for the plantation bachelors. She kept her nine-year-old daughter home from school to care for the younger siblings. The Ewa camp police often arrived at their home to try to force her to send her daughter to school, but Haruno had no choice but to prevent this from happening, as she did not have any relatives to help her. Her oldest daughter assumed a lot of responsibilities as a young child and suffered, too. She not only did the household chores but took care of her siblings while her mother worked in the fields, and she also helped with the laundry for the bachelors.

To supplement her meager income, Haruno did sewing for the plantation bachelors. The Ewa plantation didn't have electricity until the early 1930s. After working ten hours in the cane fields, she sewed *tabi* by hand late at night under the dim light of the kerosene lamp. Sewing the three layers of heavy denim for the *tabi* sole was very difficult; at times the needle pricked her finger instead of penetrating through the thick layers of cloth. "A Chinese lady gave me a mold of wax she brought from China. She taught me how to slide the sewing needle into the wax. It would make it easier to penetrate the thick layers of cloth. Times like this, I felt the utter hopelessness of my endless struggles. How many times I thought of dying—yet when I saw the peaceful, innocent faces of my four children sleeping on the futon on the floor, I wondered who would take care of my children after I was gone. How often I thought that if there was a way to walk across the ocean to Japan, I would have done so. I think the children gave me the strength and hope to persevere.

"In 1939, eleven years after my husband's death, I was able to return to Japan for the first time, but both my parents were deceased by then. I guess my mother must have had the premonition that we would never see each other again. The round-trip fare in those days was $65—I scrimped and scrimped on everything. I don't know how I saved the money, but I wanted to go *hakamairi* [visit a parent's grave] at the ancient village temple. On the way, I decided to stop over in Tokyo to visit my niece, and there I noticed the square box wrapped in white cloth, placed high on the Shinto shrine in the living room. My niece's husband told a story of many hardships he had endured working on a coffee plantation in Brazil. He said the pay was so small, he barely made a living, and it took him a long time to return to Japan. With just one set of work clothes, he survived the long years of struggles. He brought them home in this box as a reminder of the heartbreak and prejudice he had suffered in Brazil. He felt that after that experience, there was nothing he couldn't overcome in this life. His story made such a profound and lasting impression on me that it inspired me to save my own tattered *kasuri* work clothes," which she then showed to me. They were so threadbare that you could barely see the original *kasuri* design.

Haruno had come to Hawaii as a carefree young bride to escape the boredom of being a farmer's wife. She never dreamed that life could be so harsh in this place she had envisioned as paradise. It was a shock when she first met people from so many

Haruno being filmed by the Japanese American National Museum for a documentary, *Textured Lives: Stories from the Plantations of Hawaii*. Barbara Kawakami Collection.

different ethnic backgrounds, but when she began working alongside these people, she was amazed at how much she could learn by observing the methods they had brought from their own countries. She even learned to speak Pidgin English and overcame the language barrier. However, it was her spiritual faith, hard work, and determination that helped her survive and keep her family together. She enjoyed a fruitful life until the age of ninety-seven.

Perhaps Haruno's crowning glory was the tribute given to her as an example of an issei woman in the NHK centennial documentary film shown in 1985 throughout Japan and Hawaii. She was the first picture bride to appear on the screen, with that beautiful smile and the twinkle in her eyes. She even received a fan letter from her village priest, along with full-page coverage of her story by the local newspaper. Haruno was overwhelmed with joy when she received so many congratulatory messages. After she saw that film, she told me with tears in her eyes, "Now I can die anytime. I'm glad I stayed in Hawaii. All the suffering and pain I went through seemed worthwhile. It's such an honor for a nobody like me to be considered for the centennial celebration. Now I can finally hold my head high and walk on Bond Street near the old sugar mill. Thank you for making this happen!"

The pale, ethereal blossom does not last very long; still, when the iris plant Haruno gave to me blooms in my yard, I take the flowers to her grave in Mililani Cemetery to express my gratitude for sharing her remarkable story, and for giving me the inspiration to carry on my work.

Taga and Kamezo Toki

"TWO PICTURES GOT MARRIED TO EACH OTHER"

September 24, 1901–April 2, 1991
Born in Hayao-machi, Yatsushiro-gun, Kumamoto-ken
Arrived in Hawaii November 22, 1918

Taga Hiraki grew up in a farming family in Kumamoto, Japan, at the beginning of the new century. She was a middle child, bright and inquisitive, and did exceptionally well in school. During the Meiji era, however, girls in farming villages usually went only as far as the third or fourth grade, though later compulsory education was extended to the sixth grade. That Taga was the valedictorian of her sixth-grade class was an achievement well beyond the dreams of most young girls of that time. Still, Taga recalled, it was a bitter experience to learn that she would not be allowed to go further. Even though her homeroom teacher and the school principal came to their house to try to persuade her brother to allow Taga to continue to high school in the city, he stood firm. She still remembers her older brother's harsh words: "If a girl has too much education, no man is going to marry her." She couldn't hide her disappointment over not being able to continue to high school. She pouted for three days and did not talk to anyone. As time went by, she thought of Hatsuko-san, the girl next door, who always had to babysit her younger siblings while her parents were busy working on the farm and peddling vegetables. She never went to school at all. At times she would come to school with her youngest sibling strapped on her back and stand on the porch listening to the teacher's lecture. How she must have longed to study and play with her friends. Thinking of Hatsuko-san somewhat lessened the pain she felt. Taga felt blessed that at least she had been able to finish the sixth grade with high honors.

After graduation, Taga kept busy learning all the things that young girls were supposed to know in preparation for marriage—especially the intricate art of kimono sewing. She had advanced to the point where she could sew the women's formal ceremonial type of kimono, as well as the men's traditional formal kimono and *hakama*. That alone was quite an accomplishment.

Meanwhile, halfway across the Pacific Ocean, Kamezo Toki was a young, carefree bachelor who worked on the Lihue sugar plantation on the island of Kauai. His was kind of an unusual story. He was born in Japan, and when he was very young, his parents went to Hawaii. Kamezo remained in Japan in the care of his grandparents in Yatsushiro, Kumamoto. Yatsushiro is a small city two hours south of Kumamoto city, in a mountainous region in southwestern Japan with rich forests filled with valuable lumber. The train to Yatsushiro runs along the edge of Kuma River, allowing passengers to enjoy the breathtaking view of the deep gorge below. That train runs as far as Hitoyoshi, capital city of Kuma county.

When I interviewed him for my book on plantation clothing, Kamezo was thrilled to hear that I had been born in Kumamoto and brought to Hawaii when I was three months old. He was also born in Kumamoto. During World War II, we were both considered enemy aliens by the United States. Kamezo had lived there until he was fifteen years old but had never heard of Suye-mura, located in Kuma county, next to Hitoyoshi. There were no automobiles while he was growing up in the isolated mountains, not even roads to travel on. Nevertheless, he was raised with all the love and affection of his grandparents and relatives. He was well disciplined and completed his required compulsory education. During his formative years as a teenager he was very fortunate to be trained by his uncle, a skilled stonemason. In later years in Hawaii, this valuable skill he had learned from his uncle turned out to be a great advantage for him. On Kauai he observed how the natives made many stone implements using the dense basalt rock. Kamezo used his hammer and chisel to carve poi pounders, also the small stone lantern used with kukui nut oil, and many other tools. His Hawaiian friends were fascinated with Kamezo's skill in carving the lava rock, and often depended on him to make their stone implements.

When Kamezo was fifteen, his father sent for him to work with him at the Rice Estate at Kipu Kai, on Kauai, the "Garden Island." There he had many Hawaiian neighbors, and most of his friends were Hawaiian boys and girls. It was no surprise that this Japanese boy quickly learned to speak fluent Hawaiian, play the ukulele, sing Hawaiian songs, and fish like any native Hawaiian. While I was interviewing him, he sang a few Hawaiian songs for me.

Kamezo started taking notice of the exotic-looking, pretty Hawaiian maidens on the island. Over time, the father of one of the girls took a liking to him. One day he told Kamezo, "Hey, Kamezo, you go climb the highest coconut tree on my land and look as far as your eyes can see—I give you all that land if you marry my daughter." Of course, Kamezo was too young to take the offer seriously; he realized later that had he married that Hawaiian *wahine,* he would have been a wealthy man indeed.

Kamezo soon enrolled in night school to learn English. He had a young Hawaiian teacher who dazzled him with her beauty. He couldn't take his eyes off her in class and admitted that this was why he never could learn any English. Wilfred, Kamezo's son, remembers fishing with his father one day on the North Shore, and his father telling him this story. "So he said, 'You know, it was quite some years after we left Kauai and moved to Honolulu. One day while riding a *den-sha* [trolley] I met one of the pretty Hawaiian maidens whom I used to know on Kauai during my youthful days.' My dad was so surprised to see how much she had changed. He opened his eyes wide with a surprised expression, spread out both hands wide, and exclaimed, 'That pretty *wahine* now *konna-ni momona ni nato-ta* [has gotten this big]!' He did not mention if it was the girl he could have married or his Hawaiian teacher."

By this time Kamezo's father had become concerned about his son's future. Marriage between members of different ethnic groups was unheard of in those days, so his father sent a letter to his uncle in Japan, who was a *kendo* (fencing) instructor at the police station in the village, and asked for assistance in finding Kamezo a suitable bride. His uncle immediately found a very good possibility in seventeen-year-old Taga Hiraki, who had graduated from sixth grade as the valedictorian.

PICTURE BRIDE MARRIAGE

When the unexpected marriage proposal occurred, Taga could barely hide the excitement she felt at being able to travel to a foreign country. With her adventurous spirit and the curiosity to want to learn new things, she was more than willing to go. Her older sister was already married to an issei plantation laborer on the island of Kauai. She often sent money home and wrote exciting tales about life on a *tengoku* (paradise) island. So Taga yearned all the more to travel to this paradise, work hard, and make lots of money like the other immigrants.

Since Taga's father had retired a few years earlier, her oldest brother now acted as head of the household, so Kamezo's uncle asked for her hand in marriage through

Kamezo Toki's exchange photo.
Barbara Kawakami Collection.

her brother. Her brother knew that his younger sister showed some interest in this matter and consented to the marriage.

Kamezo's uncle then served as the intermediary, and began sending letters and photos of the prospective bride and groom to both sides of the families.

When Taga was asked, "What was the first impression you had when you saw his picture?" she chuckled and explained, "Well, when his picture arrived in our village home, the family made a big fuss over it. I was only seventeen and too shy to look, so I ran into the bedroom. That night someone placed his photo beside my pillow, so when no one was around, I took a good look at it. My, he was *hansamu,* not *bolo* head like he is now!" Everyone broke out in laughter as Kamezo rubbed his bald head.

On the other hand, when Kamezo was asked about his reaction to her photo when he received it, he replied, "Well, I felt that I'm twenty-two years old now, I guess it's about time I settle down." With a twinkle in his eyes, Kamezo said, "In our case, two pictures got married to each other, not the romantic *lavu lavu* [hugs and kisses] kind you see today."

MARRIED IN ABSENTIA

A *kari-shugan*—a temporary marriage ceremony, or marriage in absentia—was held at the uncle's home in the village, since he was the go-between for their marriage. The bride wore her formal purple five-crested *montsuki* kimono with delicate hand-drawn designs on the hemline. Instead of the traditional bridal coiffure, called the *takashimada,* Taga had her hair fashioned in the stylish pompadour hairdo, which had originated in France during the 1890s and become popular in Japan at the turn of the century. Taga said it was called *nihyaku sankochi* or "203 Meter Hill." This odd name refers to a hill that was the object of a fierce battle between Japanese and Russian troops in Port Arthur, Manchuria, in 1905, during the Russo-Japanese War. The hill was rounded like the pompadour hairdo. It was the soldiers returning home from the war who gave it that name.

Since the groom was in Hawaii, Kamezo's picture was placed on a high shelf to show honor and respect to the bride's future husband. Then the ritual of *san san kudo,* the three-times-three exchange of nuptial cups of sake to seal their marriage vows, was held between the bride's and groom's pictures. The bride's name was then entered into the Toki family register in the village office. The marriage was now official according to Japanese law; however, the bride had to wait six months before joining her husband in Hawaii. She finally left her village to begin the long journey on October 11, 1918, via the port of Nagasaki.

For the first time, Taga left her remote mountain village, walking through deep valleys and rough terrain to reach the train station. As Taga left on her journey to a foreign country to marry a man she had never met, her mother's last words were, "Taga, do the best you can, and take good care of yourself."

On the other hand, her father's last words were, "Taga, you're not a raving beauty, but you've got brains. Use them wisely, cater to your husband, and work hard so he won't send you back!"

Taga recalled, "My father, brothers, and sisters saw me off at the train depot, but my mother couldn't bear to be there. Saying goodbye to my family was very hard. I had to fight back tears. . . . I still remember my mother wiping her tears with her apron at the gateway. That . . . I can't forget even to this day." Taga's eyes filled with tears as she reminisced about the last time she had seen her parents, more than sixty-eight years earlier.

"I felt so helpless as the train started moving and the lush valleys and hills of Yatsushiro faded from view. That was the first time I ever took a train to go to a far place." The train was headed toward Nagasaki. There Kamezo's aunt, who taught classical Japanese dancing, met Taga. They had prepared a feast and celebration for the young bride. It was a brief encounter but a happy one. Then they saw her off as the ship set sail for Hawaii.

ARRIVAL IN HONOLULU

Taga was seasick throughout the voyage across the Pacific Ocean. She recalled, "The *pake san* [Chinese cook] served *moyashi* [bean sprout] dishes every day. It was so smelly, it made me sick. They didn't serve Japanese meals, but I was able to buy boiled eggs, which I ate with rice. At least I was able to eat a little."

After the long sea voyage across the Pacific, Taga arrived at the port of Honolulu on November 22, 1918. She remembered bringing five or six kimonos in her *yanagi gori,* which was made of sturdy willow vine. On arrival, she wore the silk *kasuri* kimono that her mother had woven on her handloom and sewn for her. The group of picture brides was taken into the immigration station's spacious room, lined with what appeared to be wooden shelves. Taga was surprised when she saw the many berths, one built on top of the other. She remarked to someone that she felt like she was being placed on a silkworm shelf back home in the village.

Soon after the brief physical exam was over, the twenty or thirty picture brides who had come on the voyage all had to line up before the inspectors, Dr. Katsunuma and a *haole* man, to take the competency test. Katsunuma-san spoke first, saying, "You people do not understand English, but this *haole* man is going to do some testing, so I'll translate to Japanese, so listen carefully. Then you answer, make gestures with your hands."

"My question for the competency test was '*Te de anata no tsuma wo tsumami-nasai,*' which literally meant 'With your hand, grab the front upper layer of your kimono skirt.' The *haole* man nodded with approval, which meant that I had passed the test. Some brides were asked to hold up the right sleeve of their kimono, which was simple. But no matter how many times Dr. Katsunuma repeated the question, they couldn't understand, and some took forever to answer by gesture. I felt like helping them. There were some who never had any schooling at all. In those days in farming villages, most women only went as far as the third or fourth grade. They knew only their regional dialect and didn't understand the standard Japanese spoken by Dr. Katsunuma."

Meanwhile, on the day of the ship's arrival in Honolulu, Kamezo's father told his son that morning, "Kamezo, you go pick up your *wahine* today." So Kamezo took the steamboat *Kinau* from Kauai, which took about five hours, to come to the island of Oahu. By the time he got to Honolulu, Taga, his bride, was already there.

Kamezo was dressed up rather fancy in a dark suit, a white long-sleeved shirt, and a necktie that he had bought from a Chinese store on King Street. The shirt cost

30 cents, and the Chinese proprietor even sold him gold cuff links. He matched everything for the young man, as he knew this was a special occasion. Kamezo, who had never worn a necktie before, struggled and twisted his body trying to tie the knot. The only thing he lacked was a pair of shoes, so someone gave him a pair of old shoes that were a bit oversized. When he walked along the street of Honolulu, "it went *pakka, pakka, pakka, pakka*—how unsightly and noisy they were!" he chuckled.

When he finally arrived at the immigration station, he noticed the other grooms anxiously waiting for their brides. They all seemed sort of in a daze; no one uttered a word. They were probably worried about what sort of bride would appear before them. Kamezo kept reminding himself, "'Well, no matter what she looks like, *shikata ganai* [can't help it]. It's too late to do anything.' I never complained one bit." At the station, the picture brides were standing behind a curtain and only their feet were visible. Then one woman who had become friends with Taga while they were on the boat moved forward ahead of the others. She whispered into Kamezo's ear, "You want to find your bride, you look for the feet with the largest-size *tabi*." Sure enough, Kamezo said, when he lifted the curtain, he spotted them right away. He thought, "My, what big feet this *wahine* has!"

The picture brides were all lined up as Dr. Tomizo Katsunuma called out the names. When her name was called loud and clear, "Taga Toki, wife of Kamezo Toki," she answered, "*Hai* [yes]!" and stepped forward, dragging her willow-vine trunk and bag with her. Kamezo went immediately to claim her.

At sight of Kamezo, Taga's first impression was, "*Ya re! Ya re!* What a relief! He looks like a nice quiet man." At that moment, she vowed to work hard for him. Kamezo, too, felt relieved to see his bride. They quickly got a *hakku* and headed toward the Kyushu-Ya Hotel. Kamezo explained, "There were no cars in those days in 1917. You can hear the horses' hoofs go *poka, poka, poka, poka* as the horses trotted along the streets of Honolulu and deposited large-size dungs. In those days, there were many farmers from Manoa Valley who followed the *hakku* and picked up the manure to use on their farm."

Their son Wilfred recalled fondly, "Upon arrival at the hotel, Kamezo asked his new wife, '*Bota-mochi tabe-tai-ka* [would you care for some rice cake]?' She replied softly, '*Hai.*' So he walked far into the night on King Street. After a long wait, he returned with the *bota-mochi*. This reminded her of the *bota-mochi* her parents made on her departure from Kumamoto, and homesickness engulfed her. '*Oishii-ka* [is it delicious]?' she heard in a soft gentle voice. '*Yasashi-hito* [what a kind person],' she thought. 'I can come to like him.'" So Taga's arrival turned out to be very pleasant.

The next day, Kamezo and Taga boarded the boat *Kinau* to get to the island of Kauai. On board the boat, they had to lie down on the straw-matted floor on deck, right below the poi (taro) bags. There were many Hawaiian people on board. When the boat rocked back and forth the bags of poi fell and rolled on her. Taga recalled, "That was the first time I overheard the Hawaiian women talking to each other. I was impressed by the sound of their melodious voices speaking in a lovely rhythm. Even now, I love to listen to Hawaiian songs."

Taga, as a young picture bride, had a great perspective about her new surroundings. She described how beautiful the Hawaiian women looked in their *holoku*, the muumuu with a train, and how gracefully they held the long train by a loop at the end of their fingertip. She thought, "Although the Hawaiian women were chubby, they looked very nice in their costumes. After all, their clothing was made to fit the body." The Hawaiian women would have been happy if they knew what this Japanese bride was thinking.

SETTLING DOWN ON THE GARDEN ISLAND

When they arrived on Kauai, Kamezo's family and friends had a big reception in honor of the newlyweds. The bride did not know about this and did not have time to change. She appeared at the reception with the kimono she had been wearing on arrival. How she wished she could have worn the beautiful *montsuki,* the traditional five-crested purple wedding kimono, for Kamezo to see. That was the kimono she had worn when she exchanged the sake cups with Kamezo's picture back in the village.

The next day, when Kamezo mentioned that they were going to his mother's grave to pay their respects and notify her spirit of the auspicious event, Kamezo's father thought, "How happy Mother would have been to see Kamezo and his lovely bride get married. *Okaa san ga kusaba no kage kara yoro kon de iru daro* [her spirit must be overjoyed in her grave to learn of his marriage]." She had died seven years ago when Kamezo was sailing to Hawaii from Japan. For Kamezo and Taga, this was a special moment to kneel in front of her grave, to offer incense, clasp their hands, and recite *namu amida butsu* together. Taga felt deep gratitude to Kamezo for bringing her to his mother's grave.

Taga, thinking they would be going only to the gravesite, wore the dressy white muumuu with lace trimmings that her older sister had made for her. Her sister had sewn the fancy garment out of cotton fabric and trimmed it with ruffled lacings on the bodice and sleeves. In all the excitement of being a newlywed, Kamezo had forgotten to let his bride know that on the way to the cemetery, they were to stop at the photographer's studio to have their formal wedding picture taken. Had Taga known that, she certainly would have dressed in the purple traditional *montsuki* that she had worn back in the village. She deeply regretted that Kamezo had never seen her in her wedding kimono. Wilfred recalled, "Little did she know that many years later, when the children celebrated their fiftieth anniversary, she would finally get to wear her purple *montsuki* for Kamezo!" Her children had seen to it so she wouldn't feel any regrets.

"I barely had time to settle down in my new home," Taga recalled. "Kamezo's father had remarried while he was being taken care of in Japan. A second mama was there, a young mama. She had already made for me a set of work clothes out of *kasuri* fabric to wear in the sugarcane fields. Although I had vowed to be a good wife and work hard for Kamezo, I had never worked on the farm back in the village. That created a lot of anxiety for me. I had to start working in a few days. The women in the neighborhood came over every morning so we could go to work together to cut the grass in the fields. They were dressed identically in their *kasuri* work clothes and wore a straw *papale* [hat] with *tenugui* [towel] wrapped around their head. This was an entirely new experience for me. To think that I had such a carefree life to be sent to kimono sewing school and creative art classes for my enjoyment!

"Now I had to get up at 3:30 every morning to cook the rice in a *hagama* [cooking pot] outdoors, over an open fire, then rush to make breakfast, make *bento* for my husband and myself. Sometimes I bought *akule* for only 15 cents a bucket. I

Wedding photo of Kamezo and Taga Toki
with a friend's daughter, 1918. Barbara
Kawakami Collection.

would salt each fish, then fry it until it was crispy. It was so delicious. In those days
they didn't have an icebox, so when the fish was kept for a few days, it would begin
to smell, but I fried it and used it anyway. We didn't waste anything."

At night, if Taga was a bit worried, she would ask her husband, "Papa, today's
fish tasted a little funny, didn't it?" He would reply, "It was okay, even if it tasted
funny on the tongue. I was hungry, I ate it anyway." Kamezo was very kind and
thoughtful and never complained.

Taga explained that when fish gets spoiled, the tongue begins to hurt after eating
it. "You can tell. If I was smart, I would have dried it the way the *kanakas* did. I worried too much about my fieldwork, so I didn't have time to think about those things.
Our daily diet was so simple. I don't think today's young people can stand the type of
food we ate. That is how we were able to survive on our meager earnings. Sometimes,
for the *bento,* I opened a can of deviled ham, split it with my husband. For breakfast
and supper, we had *miso* soup and pickled vegetables every day with rice."

Taga said sadly, "One unhappy experience I could never forget was when Kamezo and I did *hapai ko* [carrying cane] together. It required good teamwork. I was
just no good at working in the fields. I got nothing but scoldings from my husband.
My body was big, but was good for nothing. When the pin marking was up, I was
supposed to follow the line straight down, to unload the cane, but I could not understand that. The other *wahines* took the work within easy reach; the far places were
left for me to do. I was so naive. So when my husband got angry, he would sit down

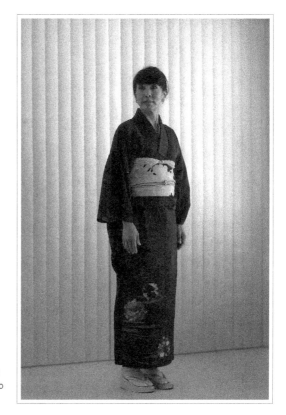

Granddaughter Linda Wijaya is wearing
Taga Toki's wedding kimono, 2004. Photo
courtesy of Wilfred Toki Collection.

on a plank. He wouldn't move. That was because I didn't have the know-how to work fast. That made the other people happy. The more bundles of sugarcane a couple made, they made extra money. There was a picture bride who did farming back in the village. She was small, but she was a fast worker. Everybody praised that *wahine*. My husband used to say, 'My *wahine* only body big but cannot work.' That made me feel miserable."

Wilfred remembers, "My father always addressed my mother as *wahine*. Although it might seem disrespectful to today's generation, I have never heard Mother complain. In fact, I think she felt complimented when it was spoken in a soft, gentle tone. *Wahine* sounded more endearing and feminine than 'Taga.' Maybe it was his way for Mother to feel comfortable and included in this new and foreign land."

Following one miscarriage, Taga had her first child after four years. There were no relatives to babysit, so all the young mothers strapped their babies onto their backs with a sash and went to work in the fields. They would pitch a tent to protect the child from the hot sun, and the baby would sleep on straw matting.

Giving birth in those days was very difficult for the young mothers, who were still adjusting to life on foreign soil. Taga often thought of her mother and sisters and wished they were nearby to give her moral support.

Taga recalled, "When I gave birth, I had to depend on my husband. Unless Kamezo held my hand, the baby wouldn't come, even if the midwife was present.

Kamezo and Taga Toki with their two
older children. Photo courtesy of Wilfred
Toki Collection.

In those days, the neighbors all helped each other. Papa helped a lot when the new baby came. He helped with the laundry and household chores. But once the family got larger, he didn't help as much and spent more time drinking sake."

The most exciting thing that happened during their entire life in Hawaii was when Kamezo was hired to dig a tunnel in Kokee, on the island of Kauai. The goal was to make an irrigation ditch adjacent to the Kekaha sugar plantation. However, the entrance of the tunnel was solid basalt. The contract workers hired for that project had tried for months to remove it. Finally, Kamezo, an experienced stonemason, was hired for the job. Within three days of hard work, he and his men were able to penetrate the wall of basalt.

Wilfred recalls, "An incident occurred during the digging of the tunnel that could have turned tragic for our family. On a Sunday morning while everyone was home from work, Father decided to work on the tunnel by himself. He was alone and carrying only a kerosene lantern when the tunnel suddenly caved in on him. Half buried in stone and dirt, with the lantern out, he wondered if he would be rescued in time. Using his hands, he dug frantically in the pitch-black darkness for hours, not knowing if he would start to suffocate as the oxygen ran out. Eventually a bright light and fresh air gushed through a tiny opening. He emerged from the tunnel covered in dirt and grime. Although he felt no pain, as he looked down he saw both his hands were bloody with several fingernails missing. He felt thankful to be alive." What an ordeal to go through alone! It showed his outstanding character, his courage, and his determination to never give up.

Kamezo's success in moving the boulder made the front page of the Japanese newspaper on the island of Kauai. Because he had proved his skill as a stonemason and performed an impossible task, he got paid a large sum of money. That attracted many gamblers, who came to borrow money. Taga, being an intelligent woman, knew what the consequences would be and cautioned Kamezo to be careful. Each time a gambler came and told a sad story, Taga would give him the eye, but Kamezo was so good-natured that he couldn't say no. Soon the money he had earned was gone.

During that time, there were twenty bachelors who worked on the tunnel project, for whom Taga did all the cooking. Every morning she got up at 3:00 to cook the rice outdoors in a big *kama* over an open fire of kiawe wood. While she did the cooking, she carried the baby on her back, so his crying wouldn't wake Kamezo from his much-needed rest. Often the baby would cough from inhaling too much smoke, and Taga would feel sorry for the child.

Later the couple moved to Honolulu and then finally settled in Waialua, near the North Shore. They both kept on working until their seventies. Kamezo was well known for his finely carved Hawaiian poi pounders and other useful Hawaiian implements, many of which were exhibited at community art shows.

When World War II came, the Waialua sugar plantation contributed to the war effort by cooperating with the military in providing nine acres of land to grow bush beans and tomatoes. The plantation was banned from growing sugarcane any taller than three feet in height along the coastal area—the military was taking precautions

Charcoal sketch of Taga Toki with a baby strapped to her back while cooking outdoors, as remembered by her son. Artwork by Wilfred Toki.

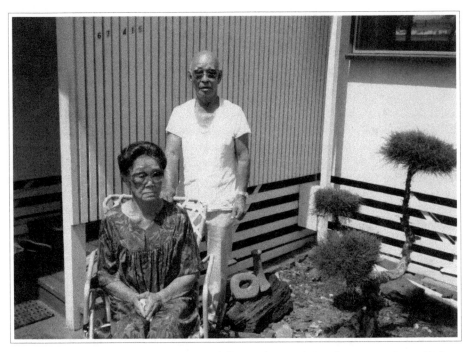

Kamezo and Taga Toki at their Waialua home with bonsai plants and Hawaiian stone sculpture. Barbara Kawakami Collection.

to ensure that any invading Japanese soldiers would have no place to hide. Most of the cane along the coastline was cut down and replaced by vegetable gardens.

At that time, Taga was working at the experiment station for Waialua Sugar Company. The boss was impressed by her intelligence, efficiency, and work speed. The fact that she could communicate in Pidgin English with military men as well as schoolchildren made a great difference. After taking some brief training in judging the grades and quality of the beans, Taga was promoted to a supervisory role for the bean-picking group. She also supervised the schoolchildren who contributed to the war effort by working part-time to grow vegetables for the military. Very few women who came as picture brides accomplished the many things Taga did as she grew more confident and experienced through the years.

When asked to share thoughts on the picture bride marriage, Kamezo replied, "We've been married more than sixty-eight years now. When we think of the long years we shared our joys and hardships together, life has been good to us. There isn't anything we would change now. Our love for each other grew gradually over the years. While bringing up the children, you learn to respect each other. It's a different kind of love than what today's young people feel."

When Taga was asked if she was glad she came as Kamezo's picture bride, her face lit up with a warm smile. She bowed her head, looked toward Kamezo, and replied, "I want to say to Papa, *arigato!* We attend the Waialua Senior Citizens Club together, and I teach people of other ethnic groups how to do the Japanese folk dances. When I start dancing, the Filipino, *haole*, Portuguese, *kanaka*, and Japanese all follow me and dance. There's a lot of cultural exchanges, and we all have a good time. I teach Japanese dance to the Waialua Elementary School children for their May Day programs. Every year, I dance at our Kumamoto-ken *shinnenkai* [New Year party] at Dot's Restaurant. All the people who perform are outstanding singers and dancers—I'm the only one who is so awkward and stiff that I can't even keep the rhythm to the music—but because I love to dance, I participate every year." Taga continued, "There is an old Japanese saying that applies to me: *heta no yokozuki.*" *Heta* means "awkward, unskillful," and *yokozuki* means "love it anyway." I attended the Kumamoto-ken New Year party every year and watched Taga, in her late eighties, as she danced. It is true what she said about herself; the audience can see and feel the joy she feels going onstage before a couple of hundred people and doing something that she really loves. She always received great applause. Kamezo and Taga kept busy even in their retirement and lived life to the fullest until the end.

As Kamezo pointed out, "Not bad, for two pictures getting married and making a lifelong journey, achieving many successes along the way in their adopted land."

Ayako Kikugawa
THE UNSUSPECTING PICTURE BRIDE

November 1, 1899–June 6, 1997
Born in Meno Dake-mura, Kamoto-gun, Kumamoto-ken
Arrived in Hawaii August 6, 1918

I remember meeting Ayako Kikugawa for the first time in the winter of 1985 at Dot's Restaurant in Wahiawa, Oahu. It was at the annual Kumamoto *kenjinkai* (prefectural club) for the Wahiawa/Waialua district *shinnenkai* (New Year celebration). The club was reactivated after World War II, in about 1955, after the nisei sons returned home from serving on the European battlefields. My husband, Douglas, was president of the Waialua/Wahiawa area club for ten years. So I was fortunate to meet some of the issei women who had come as picture brides from Kumamoto. Many of their issei husbands had once been leaders of the club but had since passed on. Some of these wives were still in good health and looked forward to the celebration each year. One such wife was Ayako Kikugawa. She came as a picture bride in 1918 on the *Shinyo Maru* when she was eighteen years old. At eighty-seven, she was still beautiful and very graceful. Her delicate features, dark brown eyes, and fair complexion matched her soft-spoken, gentle manner. It was difficult to imagine that she was once one of the many picture brides who were forced to toil away in Wahiawa's pineapple fields under the scorching sun to make a living.

After retiring from the pineapple plantation, Ayako settled down with her husband, Shitoku, and her third son, Akimi, in Wahiawa. Akimi had invested in the new land after World War II. Wahiawa was often referred to as "Pineapple Town" because it was surrounded by acres and acres of rich pineapple fields.

Their home was located in a peaceful setting of tall eucalyptus trees along the Kakunahoa River, which flows lazily into tranquil Lake Wilson, the largest freshwater lake on Oahu. The Waialua Sugar Company first built this reservoir to irrigate the sugarcane fields all the way to Waimea Bay. Some people called it the Wahiawa Reservoir, but today it is better known as Lake Wilson. It is a popular year-round fishing spot for tilapia, catfish, bluegill, and other varieties of fish. The river also has green turtles. The front lawn of Ayako's single-story home was beautifully landscaped with a Japanese rock garden, shapely pine bonsai, and red camellia plants. Akimi, his lovely wife, Reiko, their sansei (third-generation) daughter, her husband,

Ayako at her home. Barbara
Kawakami Collection.

and their adorable yonsei (fourth-generation) grandchildren all lived happily under
one roof.

When I visited Ayako on August 11, 1987, she greeted me with a warm smile and
bowed her head a few times at the door. I responded with a bow, just as my mother
had taught me when I was very young. Ayako, like many other issei women, dressed
conservatively, in a simple blue cotton dress covered in a floral pattern. Her silver-
gray hair was set into a chignon on the back of her head and held in place with an
olive-green lacquer comb. She sat comfortably on the sofa with her hands folded
on her lap. I noticed that her hands were covered in scars from stripping the spiny,
razor-sharp leaves from the crown of the pineapple plant. They were the only tell-
tale signs left of the years she had worked on the plantation. As she began unfolding
her past, her voice faltered a bit with emotion. She paused, and gradually regained
her composure.

She was the embodiment of a typical woman from the Meiji era: strong-willed,
independent, and hardworking. Surprisingly, in her two-hour interview she did not
use much of her Kumamoto dialect. She used standard Japanese with some dialect
and very little Pidgin or English.

I began to wonder about the way she spoke. Over the course of my interviews
with many issei throughout the islands, I realized that those who kept in close touch
with other villagers from the same regions retained their dialects and village customs. It was easier to communicate with each other in their familiar language. The

kimonos they wore displayed the handwoven ikat designs that could be identified with their home region.

As I had grown up on a plantation camp in Waipahu, I was quite familiar with the various types of Japanese dialects, though to me they always sounded a little funny and were difficult to understand. Issei men and women developed their own Pidgin English while working alongside people of other ethnic groups, including Hawaiians, Chinese, Portuguese, Spanish, Puerto Ricans, and Filipinos. By combining foreign words with their own dialect and borrowing some gestures, Pidgin became a very effective and friendly way of communicating within the diverse plantation community. Because their nisei offspring grew up speaking this, for them it was a creole language, rather than Pidgin.

Since Ayako did not use much of the Kumamoto dialect, I surmised that she must have associated more with friends from other regions of Japan who used standard Japanese. During the early periods of immigration to Hawaii, the largest group of immigrants came from Hiroshima. Although the people from Hiroshima do have a dialect of their own, their manner of speaking is closest to the standard spoken Japanese. Immigrants from less well-represented regions began using the Hiroshima dialect to be able to communicate with each other.

MEMORIES OF CHILDHOOD IN KUMAMOTO

Ayako Maruyama Kikugawa began by recalling her life back in the village as a young girl. "I was born in Meno Dake-mura, Kamoto-gun, Kumamoto-ken, on November 1, 1899, to Takasugi and Yuki (Watanabe) Maruyama. Our home was located on the outskirts of the village. It was close enough to shop in the nearby towns and enjoy the many village activities, yet we were distant enough to see breathtaking views of the mountains with stately cypress, cedar trees, and bamboo groves. I still remember going to the mountain to gather shiitake mushrooms and *warabi* [young fern shoots]. My family lived in a fairly comfortable farmhouse with a straw-thatched roof surrounded by a silkworm farm."

Ayako was six years old when her mother suddenly passed away on September 15, 1906, at the age of thirty-seven. She still remembered how a kindhearted relative carried her up close enough to have a final look at her mother's face at the funeral. After her mother died, her father had trouble managing the silkworm farm while also raising three children. Eventually a female relative arranged for Ayako's father to wed one of her father's nieces, Kamo Nakayama, who became his second wife. As a result of the marriage, Ayako gained half brothers and half sisters. In a family of seven, she was the middle child.

"My stepmother was very *yasashi* [gentle and kind] and the siblings all got along so well. Maybe she felt sorry for me, losing a mother at such a young age," Ayako recalled sadly. "I will refer to my stepmother, Kamo, as 'Mother' from here on.

"She would often *oppa* me [carry on her back] and whisper to me, 'Do not fall asleep, you'll be heavier when you fall asleep.' I remembered that so well. My friends used to ask me, 'How is your *mamahaha*? Is she mean to you?' I always responded, 'I never felt she was a stepmother. She is like a real mother to me!'"

In Japan, children entered first grade at eight years of age. Ayako handed me a class photo taken when she was twelve years old and in the fifth grade. In the photo,

Ayako Maruyama's fifth-grade class photo, taken in Meno Dake-mura, Kamoto-gun, Kumamoto-ken. Ayako is third from the right in the front row. Barbara Kawakami Collection.

the principal and faculty members were all seated rigidly in the front row. The boys were dressed in black uniforms and caps, while the girls were wearing kimonos tucked into *hakama* (long pleated skirts).

Ayako resumed, "No matter how busy she was, my mother would comb my long hair into a *momo ware* [split peach] hairdo every morning. That was the fashion in the early 1900s. That's me, here, with the hairdo," she said, pointing with her index finger. "We usually wore striped cotton kimonos or *kasuri*-design kimonos to school.

"My father and mother were busy raising silkworms with some hired help. Father also worked at the village *yakuba* [office]. He was well educated. He excelled in math and was an accomplished calligrapher. After I graduated from eighth grade, I began helping my parents on the silk farm, picking mulberry leaves and feeding the silkworms. It was quite a task. Silk culture went hand in hand with silk weaving, so I learned to weave from a young age.

"During the off-season from farming and silkworm raising, girls were sent to the Montokuji Buddhist temple in the village to learn to sew kimonos, *haori* [coats], and *hakama* from the minister's wife.

"My mother was skilled in spinning the silk thread and was an expert in weaving the various types of cloth. She wove sturdy striped cotton for casual wear and for work clothing. Her intricately woven *kasuri* cloth was much admired. The fine silk fabrics she wove were sent to Kyoto to be hand-dyed and made into beautiful designs by skilled artisans. I was fortunate to have beautiful silk kimonos, some of them which I brought to Hawaii." (Ayako's kimonos are now in the permanent collection at the Japanese American National Museum in Los Angeles.)

"Since our village was nearer to the city, we were advanced in many school activities, especially in sports. The boys played football in grade school. I participated in tennis matches, three girls against three boys. I loved to play tennis and did well in matches. I was *otemba* [a tomboy]. Although we competed in sports with boys, we never dated or socialized outside of school.

"My father was very kind to me, but my older brother was strict and *gankona* [stubborn]. He used to whack me on my buttocks for staying late at my girlfriend's house. On the other hand, I was so mean to my older sister. She hated *miso* [bean paste], and I often threatened to put that in her mouth at night. I was really naughty, wasn't I? Poor thing!"

UNEXPECTED HAPPENING

When I asked Ayako how her marriage to Shitoku Kikugawa was arranged, her eyes lit up and she burst out laughing.

"Oh, so funny how it happened. My aunt, who is my father's first cousin, who later became my mother-in-law, had a problem. The woman who was intended to be the picture bride for her oldest son, Shitoku, in Hawaii, had eloped with her boyfriend just before she was supposed to depart for Hawaii. Yes, she was quite a beauty, as seen in the formal photo taken of her in elegant white bridal costume and coiffure. The photo had already been sent to Shitoku in Hawaii.

"It so happened that the man she ran away with was a *yoshi* and he was supposed to marry someone his adoptive parents had chosen for him. So the parents disowned him and chased both of them out. They encountered many problems, and he divorced her! She couldn't return to her parental home, because it would be a disgrace to her family, so she wanted to go to Hawaii to be Shitoku's wife. That was when I overheard my aunt and my father discussing all this and whether to take her back. It was a delicate situation, because they were all related. Oh, I was so angry at that girl for doing such a terrible thing to my aunt. I told my aunt, 'Don't you ever let that woman go to Hawaii!'"

Ayako felt the woman's selfish actions had caused her dear aunt undue pain. "So that is how I volunteered to go to Hawaii to bring her son back to Japan. Can you believe it? I only wanted to keep that woman from going to Hawaii. Oh, when I think about it now," she chuckled, "I sure had some nerve to react in such a bold manner!

"Of course, my aunt exclaimed, 'Ayako, you can't do such things in one or two months.' So I replied, 'Obachan, don't worry, I will go to Hawaii, bring Shitoku back, and hand him over to you.' I didn't even know how far Hawaii was! I thought it was like going to another village. I sure had the *dokyo* [guts] to say such a thing, don't you think so?" She broke out in laughter. "You know, years later, when my husband and I returned to Kumamoto for a visit, we found out that Shitoku's first intended picture bride never got married, and we felt so bad.

"Oh, such an innocent gesture by a young girl. At that time, I never even thought about marriage. I didn't even know what marriage was about!" We all laughed at her honesty. Her son Akimi and daughter-in-law Reiko were also there at the interview, hearing all this for the first time, and they thought it was really funny, too.

"Yes, that's how I happened to come to Hawaii under those unusual circumstances. Sure enough, as my auntie said, once I got here, I could not go back to Japan

Ayako Maruyama's exchange photo.
Barbara Kawakami Collection.

for a long time. I had no idea that my father and my aunt had made the decision that since I was so eager to come to Hawaii, they might as well arrange to have *me* become Shitoku's picture bride! I didn't know it then, but my photo must have been sent to Shitoku." Her photo was taken six months before she left Japan, and her name was listed in Shitoku's family register in the village office without her knowledge.

Interestingly, the photo of Ayako that was sent to Shitoku in 1918 was used to publicize the 1993 movie *Picture Bride,* by director/producer Kayo Hata. It appeared in the *New York Times* along with her story. At that time, I was assisting with the production of the movie as a historian and fashion consultant on Japanese immigrant clothing. Some of the original plantation clothing, kimonos, and artifacts were used for the production. The female star, Riyo, wore Ayako's cotton *yukata* in an early scene.

As Ayako continued, "When I came to the immigration station in Honolulu on August 16, 1918, I thought, 'My, I've never seen his picture! How will I recognize him?' Back in the village, people had told me he was a nice person, had a good disposition, so they called him 'smiley face.' He never made a cross face. I think I'm the one with the bad temper. So we all stood in a line. Other picture brides had photos of their *muko-san* [husbands] clutched in their hands. Then the men slowly filed in, all anxious and concerned, trying to match the *hanayome* [bride] photo in their hands. The young brides stood behind their *kori,* studying each face, wondering which one would be her husband. I stood behind my *yanagi gori,* too, waiting, wondering.

Picture brides at the immigration station in Honolulu, Hawaii. Hawaii State Archive Collection.

"Then I saw a kindly, smiling face. He paused in front of my trunk to read the name written in calligraphy on the *kori*. As I stood watching, I thought, 'That must be the man!' He looked up and asked, 'Are you Ayako?' I replied, '*Hai* [Yes].' Then he said, 'Oh, that's good.' That was all he said. He always was a man of few words. Then he quietly carried my *kori*. That was my first entry into a foreign country—everything seemed so strange. Not knowing what to do, and not knowing how to communicate in English, I wasn't even sure what I was supposed to do. I just quietly followed my trunk and got out of the immigration station. There was a sense of relief that he seemed to have recognized me. My father and aunt, his mother, must have sent him the date of my arrival with my photo. I didn't know a single soul in Hawaii. When I think about it now, I sure had the nerve to come."

Ayako seemed still to be amazed by her bold and spirited actions in her youth. She certainly gave me the impression of a spunky, adorable *obaachan,* a true woman of the Meiji-Taisho era.

Shitoku hired a *hakku* that took them to the Saikai-Ya Hotel, where they had their first dinner together. The next day, instead of taking the train, he hired a *hakku* again to take them to a place called Haleiwa. "It was a long, bumpy ride along the picturesque but rugged coastline," Ayako recalled. Today, Haleiwa is the heart of the area known as the North Shore, whose beaches are famous for spectacular waves that attract the world's best surfers. Nowadays it struggles to retain the charm and beauty of old Hawaii and is resisting large developments.

"On the way to Haleiwa, it suddenly started to *para para* [rain], and that surprised me. I thought this tropical island never had rain. So I said, 'My, it rains in Hawaii, too?' Then Shitoku replied, '*Baka jya* [you fool], of course it rains in Hawaii!'

That was our first conversation. Yes, that's right. I always got scolded for making foolish remarks like that," she said with a slight grin.

SURPRISE WEDDING RECEPTION IN HALEIWA

"Funny, I can't remember ever having a marriage ceremony, nor the exchange of sake cups to solemnize our marriage." Ayako looked at me in a surprised sort of way and said, "Maybe I wasn't legally married?" I thought she was kidding, but she was quite serious.

Mr. and Mrs. Yoshida operated a small store stocked with imported Japanese merchandise, dry goods, and so forth for the issei families in the community. Shitoku Kikugawa worked there as a sales clerk.

"When we arrived at the Yoshida residence in Haleiwa, which was behind the store, they had a reception ready for us, plenty of *gochiso* [festive food]. This was a surprise. I had come to Hawaii with the intention of bringing Shitoku home to his mother. I didn't expect to get married. I was so young, I didn't realize that my father and aunt had arranged the marriage without consulting me or explaining to me why they allowed me to come. I guess Shitoku must have known all along," she said with a whimsical smile.

After conducting many interviews, I learned that there were all kinds of arrangements made for picture bride marriages. Some photo exchanges took place between the parents of the intended bride and groom back in the villages, and the parents were the ones who made the decisions. It is quite unique that Ayako's naive volunteering to do an act of goodwill for her beloved aunt resulted in a happy marriage that lasted for decades.

"At the Yoshida residence," Ayako continued, "there were many men and women rushing around, helping with food preparation, and setting the long table on the straw-matted floor for the reception. I wore the striped *meisen* silk kimono I arrived in, but Mrs. Yoshida quickly changed that and dressed me in a *montsuki* for formal picture taking. I realized later that it was supposed to be our formal wedding photo. She also loaned me a lovely Western-type dress."

Ayako was not familiar with Western fashion, but judging by the wedding photo taken in 1918 (as well as other early issei picture bride marriage photos), the dress was made in the Gibson Girl look of the 1890s, which, along with the pompadour hairdo that originated in France, was introduced to the Japanese elite of the urban areas during the industrial beginnings of the Meiji period. The Gay Nineties fashion with the pompadour hairdo was also seen in photos of the early missionary women who accompanied their husbands to Hawaii from the East Coast of the mainland.

"Mrs. Yoshida, the proprietor's wife, also loaned me her shoes and lovely hat. See, this photo? Doesn't the hat and shoes look too large for me? I took pretty pictures at that time, don't you think?" Ayako smiled as she showed me the photo that had been taken more than sixty-seven years previously. She chuckled, "Mrs. Yoshida had kindly loaned me the dress she had worn for her own wedding. She, too, had come as a picture bride a few years before. The photographer, Mr. Tanji, noticed a ring on my finger and asked me to turn my hand so it would show in the formal photo. It must have been unusual for an issei picture bride to be wearing one.

Formal wedding photo of Shitotoku and
Ayako Kikugawa. Barbara Kawakami
Collection.

Most issei men were too poor to afford a ring for their bride, or never even thought
of one. It was not a Japanese custom to give the bride a ring." Ayako may have been
one of the few picture brides who received a ring from her husband.

NICE DETAIL

"When I mailed the wedding photo to my father in Kumamoto, he thought I had
married a wealthy man, not knowing the fancy dress was borrowed. He wrote back,
'You must be living quite well in Hawaii!' Of course, I didn't dress like that, you
know. I only wore kimonos then. That was the only time I ever wore a dress like
that." Ayako was fortunate to have so many wonderful photos from her 1918 wedding. Many picture brides did not have any souvenir photos taken.

  As Ayako showed me the photos, I asked her, "Who was your *baishaku nin?*"
She replied, "Oh, it was Maruyama Kiyoshi, Father's cousin from his village in
Kumamoto. They went together to Victoria, British Columbia, in Canada, in Meiji
26, 1893." Ayako's father became ill in Victoria and returned directly to Japan.
However, his cousin, Maruyama Kiyoshi, stopped in Hawaii. Since he was visiting
friends in Haleiwa, he became the go-between for Ayako and Shitoku. "My husband worked for the Yoshida Store another year after we were married. Then he
wanted to save money faster to return to Japan, so he switched to pineapple fieldwork." The Yoshida Store building is still standing in Haleiwa and will be preserved as a historical landmark. It is now rented to people who specialize in

Ayako in borrowed Western clothing.
Barbara Kawakami Collection.

Hawaiian beachwear. The original "Yoshida Store" sign is still there, dated 1923; however, according to North Shore historian Barbara Ritchie, it was actually built around 1916.

WORKING IN THE PINEAPPLE FIELDS

When Ayako came to Hawaii in 1918, she didn't know that her husband had a large debt. Soon after the wedding festivities were over, the first thing he told her was not to ask him for money to buy anything. Then he told her the reason for it.

As Ayako recalls his words: "I borrowed $400 from friends to build a fishing boat, so I could earn money faster and return to Japan. My boat was finally finished, and I was eager to go out to sea. There was a storm warning, and my friends tried to stop me, but I thought, 'How can I be a good fisherman if I'm afraid of a little storm?' True to my friends' warnings, the storm came. My small boat got thrashed around by the huge waves and sank. I didn't think I had a chance of surviving, but I started to swim against the strong waves in deep water. Then came the miracle. When the wave drew back, I saw a huge rock before me. I clung to it for dear life. The strong waves hit me and pounded me about ten times, and I knew I would be washed away, so I tried to swim ashore. I kept on swimming until I got so exhausted, I felt I couldn't go on. I thought, 'This is the end for me!' Then I thought of Konpira-san [god of the sea] and prayed and prayed with all my heart!

The wave seemed to subside, and somehow I was able to ride a wave and swim to shore."

Shitoku told Ayako that it truly was a miracle that he had been able to make it back to land. He was totally exhausted. Ayako recalled, "He was anxious to get home, and somehow he trudged slowly along the railroad tracks to Haleiwa. A Chinese rice farmer saw him, took pity on him, and brought Shitoku to his shack. He served Shitoku some rice gruel, cooked pork, and cabbage. As exhausted as Shitoku was, he could see that this kindly Chinese rice farmer was barely surviving on his own. Shitoku's clothing was torn to shreds, and the Chinese man insisted on giving him his own tattered and faded jacket and pants to wear. Shitoku never forgot the kindness of the Chinese rice farmer. Shitoku soon regained his strength and finally headed home, following the railway track. Midway, he was met by his friends who were searching for him, thinking he had perished in the storm. Shitoku never forgot the miracle of Konpira-san and always prayed in gratitude to the god of the sea. Years later, on his return to Kumamoto, he went to the Konpira shrine in the village to offer a special prayer in gratitude."

After listening to Shitoku's account of the harrowing experience, Ayako vowed to work hard to help pay the $400 debt. "I never did farming in Japan, except for helping in raising the silkworms. I applied for a job at Dole Company to work in the pineapple fields. We lived in Ondo Camp, located deep in the valley where Helemano is today. The next-door *obasan* [lady] sewed a work outfit for me: a jacket and skirt made of *kasuri* fabric and accessories. She taught me how to wrap the kerchief around my face so I would not get sunburned. Everyone was so helpful in getting me ready for fieldwork. I never thought work was terrible."

FATHER'S LETTERS WRITTEN IN CALLIGRAPHY

Ayako showed me a box filled with the fragile letters her father sent after she came to Hawaii in 1918. They were written on *hanshi* (rice paper) in calligraphic brush and ink, in a style known as *soro bun* (epistolary style). By the time of our interview in 1985, the rice paper had turned yellow, but the brushstrokes were beautifully done. I asked Ayako if she could read one of them, sent in 1918 and addressed to Shitoku, and I was able to record her reading on tape.

> Shitoku *dono* [Dear Shitoku],
> My daughter Ayako does not have a good education and, being raised in a
> country environment, she may not be able to fulfill her role as a good wife.
> I truly hope you will be patient until she learns to be an efficient and dutiful wife.
> I pray that both of you will have a long and happy life together.
> Dozo yoro shiku [please take good care of my daughter].
> Sincerely,
> Father Maruyama

It should be noted that it is a Japanese custom not to praise one's own daughter, no matter how brilliant or beautiful she is. This is the ideal of *kenjo no bitoku*, which roughly translates to "Humble is beautiful."

Another letter she pulled out was written by Ayako's father when she and Shitoku were able to visit Japan after World War II with their children. This letter was
written after they left Japan.

> Dear Shitoku and Ayako,
> It's autumn now, and it's getting cooler. The mountains are covered with autumn
> foliage in brilliant colors. I hope all of you are fine and have had a safe voyage
> back to Hawaii. It touched my heart deeply to see my adorable grandchildren and
> to see how well you and Shitoku have raised them. By now, you must have left
> Nagasaki and stopped over in Kobe, as you are on the way to Hawaii, or may
> have reached there by now. With deep appreciation, I thank you for coming home
> to Kumamoto with your family. Please take good care of yourself and family.
> Sincerely,
> Father Maruyama

Ayako read the brief letter in tears, then explained that it had taken fifteen days
for them to travel via Kobe and Nagasaki. "Father must have written that letter a
few days after we bade farewell to him. I can still see my aged father running after
the boat at the pier. He wanted to see the children once more, and I could see his
lone figure waving to us. He must have been lonely because my older brother and
sister had died before him. So sad, that's the last time we saw my father."

Ayako mentioned that now and then when she felt lonely, she would take out her
father's old letters and look them over. She found so much love and comfort in reading her father's words that she often didn't realize how long she had been looking at
the letters and that it had already become dark outside. "Father was a kind and good
man, and he wrote often. During my early years, it was difficult to keep up with him,
but every once in a while I would write to him just to let him know I was fine." I was
honored and so fortunate that Ayako shared this beautifully intimate and enduring
expression of love between a father and his daughter.

"As a young bride, the first time I made miso soup, I bragged to my father in a
letter. That made him very happy. We were struggling, paying the debt on the lost
fishing boat by working in the fields. I gathered the young shoots of the Spanish
needle [a weed] that grew wild in the pineapple fields. The other issei women taught
me that the green leaves were edible, and tasted better than some vegetables. They
told me the *kanakas* used it for medicine. But I didn't like the *konpeito* [black sticky
needles] that clung to my pants.

"After working ten hours in the pine fields, I went home and prepared supper for
Shitoku while he took a hot bath. I washed the young leaves, boiled them slightly,
seasoned them with *shoyu* and sesame oil. My husband would say, 'Oh, this is *oishii*
[delicious]. What is this?' That made me happy. Imagine, that was our main dish
with miso soup and *tsukemono* [pickled vegetables]. Those days, we didn't eat anything fancy, but we were healthy. Even our bedding, I sewed the outer cover of heavy
muslin and stuffed it with dried grass from the fields. I used it in place of a mattress.
Now I wonder how I did it. I give myself credit." She smiled as she thought of those
clever ideas that saved her money. The Japanese call it *seikatsu no chie* (wisdom of
living). Aside from doing fieldwork, Ayako made extra money sewing *tabi* and *bento*

bags for the single workers and charged only 50 cents for each item. She would sew late at night, after washing the dishes, by the dim light of a kerosene lamp.

"In the beginning, it was very lonely living in a small isolated camp, near the mountains. How often I regretted coming to Hawaii! I asked my husband, 'Which side faces Japan?' Then he would point to one direction and say, 'That side is where Japan is.' Every night, I would always turn in that direction, clasp my hands, and pray to Hotokesama [Buddha]."

With tears in her eyes, Ayako continued, "One day, Shitoku surprised me with a Buddhist altar. He said, 'Oh, *ka wai so ni* [you poor thing]. Every day, I see you pray at nothing, so I bought you a *butsudan*.'" Ayako said it was a small, simple Buddhist altar, but now that she had something to pray to, it became more meaningful. "My husband was very *yasashi* [sweet]. We returned to Japan twice after we paid up the debt and the children were old enough to travel. On the first trip to Kumamoto, I took the altar with me to give to my father. At that time, my father said, 'That altar has a special meaning to you, so you should bring it home to Hawaii.' I still have that *butsudan* in my bedroom. The termites haven't gotten to it yet. It's still in good condition." Many years later I called Reiko, Ayako's devoted daughter-in-law, and although they had since bought a larger and more ornate *butsudan,* she still has the original one in her home.

RAISING A FAMILY

"The first place we lived after our marriage was at Ondo Camp, near the mountains in Helemano. At that time, it was still a wilderness. There I had my first baby girl, Michiko, born May 27, 1922. Those days there were no midwives nearby, so Mrs. Igarashi came from Ewa and delivered my firstborn. There were no doctors, so she handled many of the births for the issei families in the Leeward area and pineapple camps nearby.

"When I had my second baby, my oldest son, Toshinori, on May 25, 1925, the midwife was away on a trip to Japan and my husband was busy working in the pine field, so I gave birth myself! One day while working in the pine fields, my stomach went *kiri kiri* [birth pain], so I gathered my things and rushed home. I didn't give much thought to giving birth. I put down the futon myself, spread the newspapers on the floor, and boiled the water to bathe the baby in. I not only gave birth all by myself, but I also cut the umbilical cord and cleaned up everything. Giving birth was so easy. When I hear the ladies say giving birth is hard, I can't believe it. Back in the village, when my mother gave birth, the midwife used to come over, and I watched her, so I knew what giving birth was like. I did everything and never had anything bad happen. I even took care of the placenta, the afterbirth. I put it into an empty tea can and covered it. Then I dug a hole under the house and buried it. If I dug there again today, it might still be there. Yeah, I was healthy and strong, I cannot believe I did all those things!" She said this smiling with pride. Most women say giving birth is one of the most painful experiences of their life. Ayako was indeed unique.

"Later, the plantation doctors were available and urged the women to have their babies in the hospital, but I didn't want to leave my husband and children behind, so I gave birth all by myself. I was never afraid of giving birth.

"As soon as the baby was old enough to carry on my back, about forty-eight days later, I returned to fieldwork. I would get up at 4:00 a.m., make breakfast for my husband and me, pack two *bento* bags with tea, and carry the heavy equipment and diapers for the baby! I strapped my baby on my back. My job was *tane-mushiri* [strip the crowns] of pineapple. First I trimmed the top with a knife, stripped some of the spiny leaves, then cleaned and dried the tops for planting as seedlings. The *luna* praised me. I was very neat! I never did farming in Japan, but I guess I did okay. I'm glad the baby was all right, since there was always plenty of dust and insects all around. I gave my breast milk whenever the baby was hungry. One older woman told me I should give some water in between, but I didn't know that. I sure worked hard! Poor baby had to stay in the hot sun and his skin was burnt, but he always smiled when I looked at him. In the olden days, I took an empty cracker box to place the baby in. I covered the box with a flour bag to give him some shade." Ayako's eyes were getting misty.

NO PLACE LIKE LANAI

From Helemano, Wahiawa, Shitoku and Ayako were transferred to another island, to Lanai City, where they worked for the same company, Dole Pineapple. The manager, a Mr. Frazier, was a nice man.

"Oh, Lanai was a wonderful place to live. The nicest place we've ever been. No danger, only three or four cars were on the island. The rest was only company trucks. It was like *hanare jima* [isolated island], peaceful, friendly people, everybody was so nice!" Ayako had fallen in love with Lanai.

The Kikugawa family in front of their Lanai home. Photo courtesy of Patricia Takahashi.

"In Lanai, the camp houses were all alike, lined up in a row. One day, when I returned home, I saw a man sitting down at our kitchen table, eating our food. I said, 'What happened?' Then he asked me, 'Where is the sugar?' I replied, 'It's supposed to be there.' Because the houses were all alike, somebody's husband came to eat our food! Yeah, at night some of the husbands made mistakes, and entered the wrong house!" She chuckled.

Ayako said, "The most enjoyable time we had after working hard in the field all day was going to the big *furo* [community bath]. After supper, we called out to each other, 'Come on, let's go *furo*.' We grabbed our *tarai* [pail], towels, soaps, and children and walked together to the bathhouse!"

Ayako explained, "There was a wooden partition in the middle of the *furo*. Men stayed on one side, women, on the other. However, there were Filipino men on the men's side and somehow the Japanese men preferred bathing together with the women and children on one side. Men, women, and children all went *hadaka* [naked] and bathed together like in Japan. Nobody stared. Now maybe they would stare." She laughed. "I washed my children first, then helped to scrub our friends' children. How soothing it was to soak in the steaming hot *furo* to ease our aches and pains. Going home after the *furo*, the ladies stood outside and 'talked story' for hours, ending up getting chills!"

Having just discussed these pleasant memories, Ayako paused for a moment. Then she said, "All we did was work, work, work. We endured many hardships."

The next two children were born on Lanai. Tadaaki, the second son, was born on March 31, 1928, and Akimi, the third son, was born on October 30, 1931. Kiyomi, the fourth son and fifth child, was born on November 27, 1940, after they returned to Oahu.

"Shitoku was a good man. I had a bad temper, but he never scolded his children. He was such a loving father. In the olden days, we had no money to buy toys, and my husband used to make all kinds of toys from wood he found along the shore and in the forests. He carved swords out of wood and polished the surface real nice! The boys enjoyed playing samurai. The manager, Mr. Frazier, liked Shitoku, and he would have been promoted to *luna*, but Shitoku worried that if he accepted the promotion, he would be there for a long time. He was concerned that the children would be deprived of a good education if we stayed in Lanai. Education was limited to the eighth grade. We hated to leave our friends, so we moved very quietly back to Oahu and started all over again. My husband made a wise decision. The children all turned out well.

"After we moved to Wahiawa and settled near the Wahiawa Hongwanji temple, I became a member of the temple. Shitoku continued working for Dole Company until his retirement, but I stopped working in the fields then. I started making tofu at home to make extra income.

"When we finally paid the $400 debt on the boat, we used to put the paycheck on the *kami dana* [Shinto shrine]. From then on, we started putting money aside for Shitoku to go home to his mother. He was making 80 cents for ten hours of work a day! I made much less for the same hours of work. We lived frugally and really worked hard to pay that debt."

When Ayako and Shitoku returned to Kumamoto to visit her parents and relatives, it was a happy homecoming. Her old classmates were full of envy when they heard the stories of the good life she was enjoying in Hawaii. Her friends had endured so much hardship during World War II that Ayako felt sorry for them and was now happy that she had gone to Hawaii.

Ayako was fifty years old and still in good health when she retired from the pineapple fields. She wanted to keep busy and began working at a Japanese restaurant in the Seto Chang building on Kamehameha Highway. She gained a lot of experience while working at the restaurant. Then one day she met an old friend, Mrs. Saku Sekiya, who had just retired from working with her husband, Genpachi, at the tailor shop on Cane Street in Wahiawa. Ayako and Mrs. Sekiya were both looking for something to keep busy, and since they both loved to cook, they began to talk about opening an *okazuya* (Japanese delicatessen) together. They soon began preparing tasty foods and *bento* lunches at reasonable prices and met with instant success. Word spread quickly and people stood in line to buy Ayako's *makizushi* (rice rolled in seaweed) and *inarizushi* (cone sushi). When people complimented Ayako's tasty food, she humbly replied that it was the customers who gave her ideas and taught her how to cook good food. One day a young man asked her to cook a simple dish that his mother used to cook for him. That *okazu* (side dish) became an instant hit.

Ayako kept busy with her newfound career, while her husband also kept busy running a taxi business from 1937 to 1941. Wahiawa town was located next to Schofield Barracks, the military post. There were no bus routes at that time, so taxi drivers were very much in demand among officers and enlisted men who commuted to town. Shitoku could not speak or read English, so Akimi, who was in grade school, sat beside his father, read the street signs, and directed the way.

"When Akimi, our third son, was almost ten years old, we were blessed with another son, Kiyomi, who was born on November 27, 1940. I was forty years old. Shitoku was overjoyed over gaining another son at this late stage in our lives. He decided they would send Kiyomi to medical school to become a doctor. Sadly, that dream never materialized.

"One day when Kiyomi went on a school excursion with his sixth-grade class, he came home feeling sick with fever and severe rashes all over his body. He didn't have any appetite, so we took him to the doctor. The doctor gave Kiyomi an injection and kept him at the hospital for one night. Kiyomi was only twelve years old, and I didn't want to leave him alone. I reassured him, 'I'll come early next morning.' I tucked him into bed and went home.

"The phone rang early the next morning, and we were told to come to the hospital. My husband was shaving, so I told him to hurry, and we rushed to the hospital. The moment we entered his room, my husband knew Kiyomi was already lifeless. That was a shocking experience. I wondered how in the world such a terrible thing could happen to us. Shitoku uttered a gasp, 'Ahhh!' and just collapsed. It was like a *kami nari* [thunderbolt] had struck him. He never recovered after that, and he grew lifeless like a zombie and never cared to do anything. I told him, 'I'm the mother who gave birth to him, I feel as much pain. I cry every day, but I have to go back to open the *okazuya* because people miss our food and encourage us to stay open.' In a way, our friends were trying to help us get back on our feet, to keep busy so we could forget our pain. My husband never recovered from the shock of losing Kiyomi. He was at such an adorable age and was a good boy.

"Shitoku died on July 8, 1954, on his birthday. My daughter, Michiko, had brought a fresh peach for him. She peeled it and took it to his bedside. After he enjoyed the delicious peach, he died peacefully at the age of seventy-two. Shitoku was a good husband, a good father, and the children all turned out so well."

Ayako fondly spoke about her daughter. She was kind to her younger siblings and always gave spending money to her brothers. Michiko had a successful career as a nurse. She graduated from Leilehua High School in Wahiawa and later from Kuakini General Hospital School of Nursing in Honolulu. She later attended Cornell University/New York Hospital School of Nursing, taking an advanced course in obstetrics. After completing her studies, she returned to Kuakini Hospital to become the head of the obstetrical department. She married Teiji Chinna, who was a demolition specialist in the U.S. Army. He was a private first class, served in Europe during World War II, and received several medals. It was their eldest daughter, Patricia, who provided many of the early photos of the Kikugawas.

Ayako's eldest son, Toshinori (Reggie), who was born on May 25, 1925, was a good student. He went on to study architecture under Frank Lloyd Wright. During World War II, at the age of eighteen, he volunteered and served in the military intelligence unit. Because of his knowledge of the Japanese language, he was eventually assigned to General MacArthur's Eighth Army headquarters in Tokyo, Japan. Having completed his military service with distinction, he went on to earn his master's degree in civil engineering at the University of Oklahoma. He started a partnership with a friend, and the business venture went so well that he traveled around the world to meet his clients. He married Patricia Ann Wilson, whom he met at the University of Oklahoma. He never came back home to live in Hawaii. After thirty-seven years he decided to retire. His wife passed away in 2007; Reggie himself died a few years after that.

Tadaaki, the second son, graduated from Hardin-Simmons College and taught math at De Anza High School in El Sobrata, California, for twenty-seven years. He married Elinor Kuboyama of Wahiawa and settled on the mainland.

The third son, Akimi, stayed behind to take care of his parents. After he graduated from Leilehua High School, he became a commercial fisherman and helped his older brothers with college expenses. He was drafted into the army on March 24, 1953, three years after his high school graduation. He served in Korea and was discharged on August 20, 1957. He later worked as a U.S. postal carrier.*

Ayako Kikugawa told me in her original interview that she went to Japan to find Akimi a wife. Twenty-five years later, that wife, Reiko, told me exactly how it happened. After Akimi finished his military commitment in Korea, he stopped over in Kumamoto to visit Ayako's older brother. Her older brother took Akimi to Kagoshima prefecture, which is next to Kumamoto, to visit a relative with the purpose of matchmaking Akimi and Reiko. Akimi and Reiko corresponded with each other and the relationship steadily blossomed into a romance. They were married a year later in 1958 in Hawaii. Apparently Ayako and her older brother had this planned all along to coincide with Akimi's visit to Kumamoto.

"Akimi's wife, Reiko, was a great daughter-in-law and took good care of us. She helped at the *okazuya* part-time while her children were young and later took over the business." Ayako retired at age seventy-two, and Reiko turned out to be as good a cook as Ayako was.

---

* Information about Akimi's military career was provided in a telephone interview by Diane, Ayako's granddaughter, on September 9, 2011.

RETIREMENT

During her retirement, Ayako was happy to be surrounded by her grandchildren. They didn't speak much Japanese, so whenever they spoke to Grandma Ayako, it was all in English. Ayako would say, "You speak Japanese!" Then the grandchildren said, "Grandma, why you don't speak in English? How long have you lived in Hawaii?" She broke out in laughter, and said, "Yeah, when I think about it, my, it's been sixty-seven years and I still can't speak English, ho, ho, ho. My grandchildren are so right." She chuckled.

Ayako also told me that whenever the grandchildren threw good things in the rubbish bin, she would think of the days when they were so poor, when Shitoku had to make all the toys for the children. She didn't have the heart to be so wasteful. Ayako would go to the bin each time and pick out the discarded things. The grandchildren took photos of Ayako doing that.

She continued, "I attend the Wahiawa Hongwanji Buddhist temple regularly, since I joined in 1936 after we moved here from Lanai. Rev. Hino was the minister then. I enjoy the friendship of the *fujinkai* ladies, who were all issei. I served as treasurer and secretary for many years. I'm hard of hearing, so I go together with Mrs. Hirai and Mrs. Mochizuki. We go to *oasaji* [morning service] and help clean the temple and columbarium. Mrs. Kakazu and I used to clean the *benjo* [lavatory], but now the younger *fujinkai* members have taken over. We still help with the preparation of food for special occasions and the New Year *mochi-tsuki* [making rice cakes]. Then we go at 5:00 a.m. As we get older, we do get tired, but we enjoy talking about our early days and reminisce about Japan." She attended the seniors club at church, and she enjoyed the singing and dancing.

Ayako rarely got sick. She would say, "I never worry about my health." One morning she didn't have much appetite, and by lunchtime she still didn't care to eat anything. When she became incoherent and unsteady, her daughter-in-law Reiko got worried and rushed her to the doctor. At the hospital, she died peacefully in her sleep.

Few people are so fortunate to live a life like that of Ayako Kikugawa. She happily volunteered to come to Hawaii with an adventurous spirit. The harsh living and working conditions on the plantations were difficult, but Ayako never complained. She didn't think the fieldwork was that hard. She brought four of her babies into this world by herself, claiming it was easy, when for many women it is one of the most painful ordeals a human being can endure. Ayako was a typical example of a lady who showed the spirit of the Meiji women. They were raised in a very traditional culture where men were the central figures and the women endured. By her sheer determination to survive and to make a better life for her husband and children, Ayako displayed a unique feminism. Through the spirit of *gaman* (perseverance), Ayako helped pay her husband's debt while carrying the same workload as he did. After retiring from fieldwork, she kept herself busy operating a popular delicatessen with the help of her good friend and her daughter-in-law. Surrounded by her loving family, Ayako worked very hard, enjoyed good health, and remained mentally alert until the very end. What a glorious and remarkable journey Ayako had, compared to many of the other picture brides who were not as fortunate. Her story is unique in this collection, as she was an unsuspecting picture bride who came to Hawaii not realizing that she was in fact to be married.

Kama Asato
SHOULDERING HUNDRED-POUND BAGS OF *PULA PULA*

March 5, 1904–August 14, 1989
Born in Ginowan-shi, Aza Futenma, Okinawa
Arrived in Hawaii July 31, 1920

I had interviewed Kaku Kumasaka about plantation clothing in 1979 while working on a class project at the University of Hawaii, Manoa. Being a picture bride herself, Kaku shared exciting stories about her friend Kama Asato, a hardworking Okinawan woman who could lift a hundred-pound bag full of *pula pula* (cut cane seedlings) on her shoulder as well as anybody. Mr. Ernest Malterre, a well-respected *luna,* mentioned that even the average issei man, who was short in stature, sometimes had trouble lifting a hundred-pound bag on his shoulder. So Kama Asato stood out as a woman of tremendous strength, known to outdo the issei men at heavy work in the fields. "Yeah, but her pay was more small than the men," said Kaku. "You go talk to her, yeah, she tell you all about those early days we come Hawaii as picture brides!"

Years passed before I finally interviewed Kama Asato in her modern home in a new subdivision in Waipahu. Her home was located near the August Ahrens Elementary School, where I started the first grade in 1929. Driving there brought back many fond memories, yes, but so much was gone, too. There was no trace of the old Spanish camp, which once was filled with lively music and pretty girls dancing the tango and flamenco. The Filipino camp, where the cockfights were held, was not there, either. Gone were the Portuguese camp, the Puerto Rican camp, and Japanese Camp One, located across from the sugar mill where I grew up. All the camp houses were completely demolished a few years after the mill closed down. Only the old Manager's Road remained, which once led to the plantation manager's mansion, the spacious home of Mr. Hans L'Orange at the top of the hill.

Visiting Kama that day in old Waipahu ignited images of my childhood, such as the Rizal Day parade, when the hardworking Filipino men, dressed in snappy white uniforms, played their loud instruments and proudly marched down Manager's Road. People of all ethnic groups stood by the roadside to watch the band go by. The entire plantation closed down to celebrate Rizal Day. Now, new homes have replaced the camp houses. Even the fields of tall, swaying sugarcane, our old playground where we would play hide-and-seek, have disappeared from the landscape.

After working for Oahu Sugar Company for many, many years and living in a dark-stained plantation home, Kama and her husband moved into a new housing area for retired plantation workers. They bought their new home for $11,000, a single-walled house built with modern features and an indoor bathroom.

This was quite an improvement from the old Waipahu house, with its *furo* (bath) that had to be heated with an open fire from the outside, a tedious job that Kama would tackle the moment she returned from her ten-hour day in the cane fields. To heat the water for the *furo,* she chopped kiawe wood to start the fire. No matter how tired she was, she always thought of her husband first. She made sure he could soak in a hot tub to relax and relieve the aches and pains of the day. While he soaked in the steaming tub, Kama rushed into the kitchen to start dinner for her husband while keeping watch over the children. The rice was also cooked outdoors, in a heavy cast-iron *kama* (pot) placed over an open fire of kiawe wood.

In the old place, the outhouse was located quite a distance from the main house. It was shared with the neighbors and didn't have running water. Occasionally, laundry water was run through the pipeline to prevent an unpleasant odor. Everyone feared the hideous cockroaches that were crawling around the outhouse!

Aside from hearing about Kama from Mrs. Kumasaka, Kama's daughter and my younger sister were best friends and classmates in English school. They both left together for the mainland after graduating from Waipahu High School. I felt as though I was meeting an old friend, and she seemed happy to see me. If we hadn't had these relationships, I don't know that she would have shared her life so intimately with me.

Kama greeted me with a warm smile. She was dressed in comfortable blue cotton pants and a dressy white shirt with a tie at the waist front, very up to date. For an issei woman, she certainly kept in step with fashion. She had sewn both garments herself. I didn't realize how tall she was: about five feet five inches in height. Most issei women were between four feet ten inches and five feet tall. Occasionally I met some *naichi* (main-island Japanese) women who were as tall as Kama.

Her living room was arranged with a matching set of chairs with cushion covers in a Hawaiian design. Kama sat in one of the chairs that she seemed to favor. She chose to sit in a certain position, as if to relieve the sharp pain caused by arthritis in both legs. Despite the pain, she still kept busy raising her own vegetables and flowers. The sweet fragrance of fresh lilies on the Buddhist altar reminded her of her deceased husband, who had passed away at eighty-two years of age, several years before our interview. "I hate to stay idle," Kama told me. She was happy to be useful doing the household chores, laundry, and cooking for her oldest son, his second wife, and their children. When her son's first wife died of illness, Kama returned to Okinawa by herself to search for a new wife for him to help raise his one-year-old baby girl and five-year-old son. "My daughter-in-law works as a domestic housekeeper at the condominiums in nearby Pearl Ridge. She does the grocery shopping," Kama said. "I look in the fridge to see what she bought. I plan the meals from what she brings home." Kama made it sound so easy.

Everything was quiet and relaxed when I set the tape recorder on the table near her. Later, I would discover that her voice was hardly audible, which was really

Kama Asato at her home in 1985 when
she was interviewed by the author.
Barbara Kawakami Collection.

disappointing. This had occasionally happened in previous interviews, but because of the pain from her arthritis, I hesitated to move her closer to the microphone. She still used a lot of archaic Okinawan dialect, which sounds a little like Chinese. She also used some honorific Japanese, Pidgin English, Portuguese, Hawaiian, *pake* (Chinese), and Filipino words and phrases. A clearer tape would have been a valuable tool for students who specialize in linguistics. Fortunately, as I have done in every interview, I transcribed everything on paper, the responses verbatim, with all the mixed dialects she learned while working with many ethnic groups on the plantation. Here, however, I have modified the Pidgin and mixed language to make it understandable for the reader.

Kama retraced her eighty-one years of life. At the age of sixteen, more than sixty-seven years earlier, she had come to Hawaii from Okinawa as a picture bride. She raised a family while working a major part of her life in the sugarcane fields. She was one of the last issei woman fieldworkers to retire from Oahu Sugar Company. She wistfully glanced at the old photos spread on the round coffee table, her eyes coming to rest on a photo of her and Kaku Kumasaka in their *palaka* outfits, standing in the cane field, smiling at us from the newsletter article announcing the retirement of the last two issei women from Oahu sugar plantation. Kaku was from Fukushima prefecture, but she and Kama were longtime best friends. She quietly began to unfold her fascinating story, pausing now and then in thoughtful recollection.

CHILDHOOD

Kama was born on March 5, 1904, to Kama and Usa Tamashiro in Ginowan-shi, Aza Futenma, Okinawa. "Our village was well known because of Futenma, a small farming village located near the sea with shapely old pine trees near the shoreline. Futenma is the home of the Gongen Shrine, where people came from distant villages and towns to worship. It was very popular and everybody knew the place. We're thankful Gongen Shrine was not destroyed during World War II. It's still standing there today. There was also a Shinshu Hongwanji temple where my parents worshipped. In Okinawan tradition, everyone believes in ancestral worship, which has been faithfully carried down through the generations."

Kama's father, like the rest of the village people, was a farmer. He raised sweet potatoes to feed his family and the animals. He also raised sugarcane. The neighbors took turns harvesting the cane so they could help each other and not have to hire outside labor. They cut the cane and took it to the factory to make into sugar. This factory had big 130-gallon tubs—that was how much sugar was produced in one day. From the money made from sugar, Kama and her sisters would get an allowance. They also sold sweet potatoes for extra income.

The people in Futenma used a lot of raw sugar. The sugar was extracted by using a special wheel harnessed to an ox. "Ox is very strong animal," Kama said. The animals pushed this device round and round to extract the sugar. Farmers depended on oxen and horses to do the heavy work in the fields. The ox pushed the sugar-pressing device from early morning until three in the afternoon in the three *satogoya* (sugar production sheds) in the village. The sugar was then sent to mainland Japan, and thus it provided the people of the village with an annual income used for

Ox and the sugar-pressing device in Okinawa. Photo courtesy of Amy Murayama.

living expenses, the purchase of fertilizer, and household necessities. Many Oki-nawan people brought back the molasses cakes made from raw sugar as gifts to friends in Hawaii. We were fortunate to be able to enjoy these treats occasionally.

Kama continued, "Because my grandfather died at very young age, my father took care of work on farm. My father not too strong . . . he need someone to drive the horses and the ox in the fields. My parents had no son, only us three girls, so they adopted a son, a *yoshi*, so he can take care the property and ancestral grave. Then eventually, his children took over the work on the farm and take care the an-cestral graves.

"I found out later that during World War II when Okinawa became a battle-ground between the Japanese and the U.S. Army, this adopted son and his family were hiding from the enemy soldiers in the large family tomb. One night, they were at a point of starvation, so this *yoshi* cautiously ventured after dark to look for food, but he never came back. The family assumed that he was killed by American sol-diers." Kama had heard this from surviving relatives after returning to Okinawa long after the war was over.

"Grandmother took care of us when we were small. After she got old, cannot do any work. She died in her seventies. My mother, I don't think she suffer too much from lack of money. She worked hard raising *soyu* beans for income. With those earnings, she made tofu to sell. She died during wartime of illness, must have been in her eighties. It was sad. We lost contact with relatives in Okinawa during World War II and didn't know anything. So many of them passed away during the war.

"I graduated eighth grade in village school. That was good education for girls in those days. Many families cannot send children beyond sixth grade, you know. We learn to speak *naichi* [honorific Japanese] at school but at home we talk Okinawan dialect. Our parents and elderly Okinawans, no understand the *naichi* way of speak-ing. Even now, I try not use Okinawan dialect at home. Oh, my nisei children and sansei grandchildren, get hard time, no understand me." Kama sighed.

Kama talked about her education. "I never care for school. I had to weave hats to help with family income. I made better money weaving straw hats than working on the farm. Two *naichi* salesmen come from city to sell thread [fiber] to weave hats. My sisters and I, we usually make two, three hats a week. For the large-size hats, we earned $2.50. The fancy boys' hats, we got paid $1.50 to $1.65. Some of the girls real fast, you know, they get more money. We make about $5 or $6 per week and give all that to our mother. She used to say, 'You girls keep on weaving hats, and you don't have to work on the farm.' She felt that it was wiser to hire men at 50 cents a day for farm work and let the girls earn a higher income by weaving hats. With that profit, she could buy farm supplies. It really make sense, no? I used to get up 7:00 a.m. an' work all day until 9:00 p.m. My mother give us allowance whenever we got paid. If I wove one hat, my parents could hire two or three men to do the field work! The only time my mother asked us to work in the fields was in time of heavy rain and extra help was needed.

"Us girls not allowed to play with boys when we were young. Girls played among themselves and made *temari* balls with colorful thread, bouncing it high into the air. By the age of ten, we learned to weave narrow obi from *basho* [plantain banana fiber]. During the summer, we wore kimonos made from *basho*, so cool and light for the warm weather in Okinawa. When I began making money weaving straw hats, instead of doing the intricate weaving of the *bashofu* [cloth made from *basho*] my-self, I began buying my kimono fabrics with my allowance money. A few months before coming to Hawaii, I stopped weaving hats to rest my eyes, to make sure I can pass the eye exam at the immigration station. Many picture brides were turned back at Yokohama because of pinkeye infection," Kama said.

MARRIAGE ARRANGEMENTS

Kama leaned forward and reached for an old photo on the coffee table in front of her, showing a handsome young boy dressed in a kimono. This was Kamei Asato.

"See, this my husband's picture when he come Hawaii. He was sixteen or seven-teen years old, was taken 1919. He kept it all these years. It's one funny story, you know. My aunt in Okinawa let me take pictures about the same time, and sent my photo to him in Hawaii." She smiled as she recalled the day the photo was taken. She had not known why someone was taking a formal portrait of her.

Kama was barely sixteen when her parents sent her to a photo studio in Oki-nawa. Her parents were trying to arrange a picture bride marriage between Kama and the twenty-one-year-old Kamei Asato, who had left for Hawaii in 1919 at the age of seventeen. He was working on a sugar plantation in Waiakea, on the Big Island.

Kamei Asato's exchange photo.
Barbara Kawakami Collection.

Friends and relatives tried finding him a bride, but women were scarce in Hawaii, so his parents started looking for a bride in their village in Okinawa. They contacted Kama's parents.

"This is my photo. I am wearing the handwoven *kasuri* kimono. That day, I went with my girlfriend to the photo studio and I decided to have my photo taken, too. I didn't know that it was all planned ahead of time. Little did I know then, during that innocent picture taking, the many hardships awaiting me in Hawaii." As Kama slowly reached out for another photo, I couldn't help but notice the deep scars and bruise marks on her hands—an indelible reminder of the tough years of hard work in the cane fields. To think, a long time ago, these two strong hands had been able to lift a hundred-pound bag of *pula pula* on one shoulder!

Kama continued her story of how their marriage was arranged. "When I became full sixteen, his parents and my parents talk it over and made arrangement for marriage. We had no *nakoodo* because the parents on both sides made the decision. They didn't even ask me! My husband was twenty-two years old and I was seventeen years old by Japanese age. [In Japan, an infant is considered a year old at birth.] In my younger days, we did exactly what our parents told us to do. I had no choice. I did not even know what kind of place I was going to, or what kind of man I was going to marry. I only saw his picture. Living in a small village where everyone knew each other, I remember little bit what he looked like when he left for Hawaii, but of course we didn't know at that time how we felt about each other. He was older. I was just a kid!"

The issei woman of the Meiji period, raised according to Confucian ethics, was brought up to serve her father in youth, to serve her husband as an adult, and then

Kama's exchange photo, 1920. She wears an intricately woven *kasuri* kimono with white underkimono. Barbara Kawakami Collection.

to serve her sons in old age. As Kama often said in her interview, "We were trained to be quiet, subservient women and were taught to listen to our parents and elders, even in the decision making regarding our marriage."

JOURNEY ACROSS THE PACIFIC

Kama recalled the last words her mother said when she left Okinawa: "She told me, 'No matter how many children you have, don't ever come home without your husband.' In those days, many men sent their wives and children back to the village and didn't send any money back to support them. My mother watched these women suffer! That's really true. When wife and children not around, husbands get loose with their money. That much, men are *asamashi* [despicable] when they are left alone. For the wife also, once she's sent back to the village and has to live under the watchful eyes of her mother-in-law, she loses her independence. She's regarded more as a servant, given endless chores besides working on the farm." Kama appreciated her mother's concern. Her parents were quite old, and despite the fact that they had planned this marriage without consulting her, they were worried about her future. They may have been carried away when they heard glowing reports that in "paradise" the streets were paved with gold and "money grows on trees."

Her mother-in-law's expectations were different. She told Kama, "When you have three children, you come home." Maybe she was more concerned about the continuity of the family tradition. "And there was my girlfriend. In parting, she held me tightly and tearfully told me, 'Kama, you save your money quickly and come home.'

"The sea voyage up to Yokohama was not as lonely as I thought. There were many other picture brides like myself whose parents had arranged their marriage." They too were filled with anxiety and fear of the unknown. Kama was glad she didn't get seasick like so many of the others. At the port of Yokohama, many *naichi* picture brides came on board. Immediately Kama noticed the differences in their manner of wearing the kimono and their hairdo. The *naichi* brides wouldn't speak to the Okinawan brides but openly stared at them. Some of the *naichi* brides admired the beautiful *kasuri* kimonos with bright splashes of red and yellow worn by the Okinawan brides. They thought it strange, however, that the Okinawan girls' kimonos stopped above the ankles, and that the Okinawans tied their obi draped in the front like a courtesan in mainland Japan. The *naichi* brides wore their kimonos full length and did not expose the ankles, and had their obis tied in a drum shape at the back of their waist. The most obvious difference was that Okinawan brides had their hands tattooed in indigo to symbolize their married status. In Japan, only people who were sent into exile were branded with tattoo marks. Of course, a majority of these *naichi* brides came from rural farming villages, and meeting the Okinawan picture brides was altogether a new experience for them. They just couldn't comprehend the great differences in their cultural upbringing.

ARRIVAL AT IMMIGRATION STATION

The *Siberia Maru* docked in Honolulu on July 31, 1920. All the picture brides were gathered on deck, anxious to see what their husbands looked like. It may seem funny to us, but not one of the picture brides I interviewed talked of the enchanting view of Diamond Head or the beauty of the shoreline as seen from the ship. Their first concern was to identify the man who would match the photo carefully tucked into their obi. Kama had noticed that none of the brides came with a purse.

"At the immigration station, after the examination and tests were done, I waited and waited for my husband. I got scared! I began worrying that he may not come to claim me at all." Kama vaguely remembered what her new husband, Kamei, looked like. "I knew him by face only in Okinawa, and from that photo sent to me. He may not have been able to identify me," she thought. He didn't show up for two weeks! Kama did not know that he lived on the Big Island, Hawaii, and that he had to travel by boat to come to claim her.

Some picture brides waited forever. Dr. Tomizo Katsunuma, the inspector at the immigration station, empathized with the predicament of these poor stranded women. They had nowhere to go, and often could not communicate other than in their native dialect. Dr. Katsunuma was the only one who could understand the various dialects spoken by the newly arrived issei immigrants. Often the first thing the issei women noticed about Dr. Katsunuma was that his face was all *puka puka* (pockmarked) from smallpox, but they all remembered him as a nice and compassionate man.

Of course, Kama didn't want to be one of the unclaimed brides. Day by day, her anxiety grew worse. She didn't know a soul. She could not find anyone who understood her Okinawan dialect. Finally, after two weeks, Kamei showed up and explained the reason for the delay. In those days, passengers who traveled interisland were put on the cattle ship. It was his first time traveling interisland since he had come as a young man of seventeen. He hadn't realized that the cattle ship would take that long, and there was no way for him to contact her.

SETTLING ON THE BIG ISLAND OF HAWAII

After the long wait at the immigration station and the rough ride on the cattle ship back to the Big Island, Kama was in for more surprises. "We had no ceremony, no party to celebrate our marriage. Kamei took me to a lonely, desolate-looking camp surrounded by sugarcane fields in Waiakea. Ohhh, I was so dismayed at the sight of my first home! Not fit for human being to live! The lumber for house, not smooth kind, very rough, you know. You lean on, you get splinters in your hands!" Kama talked about the first night. "We having supper, an' the white sand from the white-wash paint come fall on the floor, on the table, on the food. I had to spread old Japanese newspapers on the floor. I come from small village, used to simple life, but Waiakea was really horrible." She was near to tears as she told her story.

Kama was happy to meet a woman who came from her home village in Okinawa. "She was very kind to me. She would ask me to her house and invite me for meals. There were three other women from our village. When I was ready to go to work, one of the women sewed my fieldwork clothing and accessories out of Okinawan *kasuri* fabric. She had learned to use the Singer sewing machine. I was so homesick and lonely. Their kindness really touched my heart," she said.

"In Waiakea, it rain and rain and rain—no matter how much it rained, we had to keep on working. Even while eating our *bento*, we had to cover our *bento* with our straw *papale* [hat]. Never have I seen so much rain, from morning till night—just rain, rain! I feel miserable, I cry all the time. In the beginning, I used to tell my husband, 'I want to go back to Okinawa,' but there was no money to go home. I had to get up at four each morning, make *bento* for my husband and myself. Really hard. Life so much better back in the village." Kama told me about the famous phrase heard on the Big Island that every issei learned because of the constant heavy rain. "Yeah, even if you forget your *bento,* don't forget your *kappa* [raincoat]!" she chuckled.

"I barely had time to settle down as a young bride, still trying to adjust to a new life, when a terrible thing happened! My husband's cousin, who came a few years ahead of him from Okinawa, was already married and had four children. This cousin had invested in large acres of land to raise sugarcane and had borrowed $500 from a friend. He asked my husband to be his witness. Being a close village friend, Kamei was glad to help out. That was before I came to Hawaii. Well, one day, this cousin came running into our house and said, 'My wife, she run away with single man!' She left their four children behind. Now this cousin wanted us to take care of his children so he could work in the fields—meaning me! It seemed an impossible task. Me, a young bride, I dunno how take care of little children! I was weaving straw hats at home, dunno house kind things." But her husband, Kamei, said yes, and Kama suddenly was forced to cook for and feed the four little children and keep up with the laundry. "Oh, how hard it was, me being so young, and not use to living in this strange place." Things got worse after that. All the stress and responsibility was too much for her husband's cousin. From the burden of working long hours in the cane fields and staying awake at night to tend to the children, he finally collapsed. He died six months after his wife ran away. "Real pity, you know," Kama said, breaking into tears as she told the story about this poor man.

Kama and Kamei searched for his runaway wife and her new husband. With the neighbors around the camp helping, they finally found her and begged her to take her children back. The mother refused. "Her new husband didn't want those children. Even our friends tried to convince them to take the four children." Kama was disgusted with the mother's attitude and told her, "If you, the real mother, don't want to take care of your own children, what stranger going to take care of them, huh?" It's amazing to me that this young woman, living an uncharted life in a strange country with a man she hardly knew, revealed her strength and determination when a crisis arose. She wasn't afraid to voice her opinion and insisted on what she believed was the right thing to do. This must have stunned the children's mother into facing reality. Reluctantly, she and her husband took the children back.

"The *wahine* not even pretty, you know. But too many single men in Waiakea those days. I heard he make her *hapai* [pregnant], so when her husband find out, he chase his wife out, tell her to live with this man! I guess that's the real reason why she ran away one day with her boyfriend." In those days, many Japanese women ran away with single men. The abandoned husband would demand that the new husband reimburse him for the *ryohi kin,* the remittance fee, about $400, that he had paid to bring her to Hawaii from Japan. "So, this woman's new husband said, 'I already pay that husband $400 for the fee, so I don't have to take care his children, too.'" Kama finished by saying that the runaway wife and her husband didn't live a long life. Also, three of the four children died very young. Sadly, only one child had survived to old age at the time of our interview (1985).

MOVE TO OAHU

"In Waiakea, my husband and I worked hard together in the sugarcane fields. Everybody had many acres of land and we worked for independent owners. They paid us by *hiyaku,* by the day, so pay was little higher than for regular plantation workers. We made $1.50 to $1.75 each day. That was good pay because my woman friend who came in 1922 [Kaku Kumasaka] and worked for Waipahu sugar plantation got paid 75 cents for ten hours of work a day. My husband made about $2 a day, but no matter how hard we worked, it was never enough. We still had to pay the $500 debt left by his cousin. It seemed as though we had to work forever to pay off that big debt. How often I yearned for the life I had back in Okinawa."

They stayed in Waiakea for two or three years, until their oldest daughter was born; then they moved to the island of Oahu. "It was my husband's other cousin who encouraged us to move to Oahu. We moved across from his home in Waipahu, to Oahu Sugar Company plantation camp. We had a mean, cruel *naichi* neighbor. Because we were Okinawan she went out of the way to hurt us, but we never fought back. We had to use the same passageway to go to the kitchen to do the cooking, and she would say cruel things, but I never said one word. We then moved to another camp called Nishi [West] Camp, to a single-dwelling house. There were many *naichi* people there, too, but they were all very nice people. They treated us really well, and we had many *naichi* friends." Kama mentioned her neighbor Yayoe Suzuki, who happened to be my older sister, and how nice she was to her. Our

Kama Asato (left) and Kaku Kumasaka (right) were the last two issei women employed in the cane fields of Oahu Sugar Company. Kaku Kumasaka took early retirement in 1964, after working for the company for nearly thirty-two years. Hawaii's Plantation Village Collection.

mother always taught us to be kind to Okinawan people, insisting that they are the same as the *naichi* people. It made me happy to know that Kama found many *naichi* friends in her new neighborhood.

"I worked for Oahu sugar plantation until I retired at age sixty-two and started getting my pension. Kaku Kumasaka and I were the last two issei women left in the regular *hapai ko* [carry-cane] gang. When cut-cane season was over, there were only two of us old-timers left from the original *ho hana* [weeding] gang. Oh, let me tell you, we had all kind of *lunas*. At Waiakea, we work for *konpan* [self-formed group working an area of land]. That was good, made better money. When we came to Waipahu, few *poroki* [Portuguese] *luna,* some good, some bad. Then, we move to this side camp, we had Filipino *luna,* he call me, 'Wahine! Wahine!' Real nice, you know. Then there was a *kanaka* [Hawaiian] *luna.* He was a huge man, oh, so mean! All the time he say, 'Hey you Japanee, too muchi *pilau* [dirty, greedy], you, only think money, money, money!' He scold us all the time, everybody scared of him!"

BABY HOME FOR WORKING MOTHERS

"Before, when I work cane fields, when children small, no more relatives like in Okinawa to help babysit, so I take my children to baby home," Kama recalled, describing the service provided by the plantation for working mothers. From her $20 monthly pay, she paid $2.50 for each child per month to be looked after from 5:00 a.m. to 3:30 or 4:00 p.m. "Sometime, I take two kids when I work *hapai ko,* because the pay good. But sometime, if pay by day, I make only $1 one day, better for me to stay home with children. Oh, so sad, you know, when I drop them off at baby home when still dark. The babies cry and cry when I hand them over. When they scream and cry after me, it make me feel like a bad mother to leave them behind with strangers. It tear my heart, make me feel bad inside. After, babies get used to the mama-san, it became easier. They gladly reached out their hands to them. The two issei women who took care of the many children were paid $1 a day, just like the field workers," Kama explained.

PREGNANCY, CHILDBIRTH, AND CHILD-REARING

"I did not have too much trouble with pregnancy. Of course, it was tiring to work in fields, but most issei women work until the seventh or eighth month, sometimes, until ready to give birth! All my children I give birth at home. I had six. We call Ishikawa *sanba-san* [midwife], who came to the house to deliver. She drove a Model T Ford all around the plantation camps, even to distant isolated camps. Mrs. Ishikawa trained in midwifery school in Niigata prefecture. She was a good midwife, make me feel very comfortable. She massage my belly to ease the pain. Everybody liked her and respected her. Sometimes, when the midwife don't arrive on time, neighbor woman deliver the baby. Issei women all helped each other.

"In Waiakea there was no midwife. A neighbor lady from Okinawa deliver my first baby. When we moved to Oahu, we always call midwife. They charged $14 or $15, help bathe the baby, some wash diapers and help. Those days, nobody went to the hospital.

"In child-rearing, usually the oldest daughter sacrifice the most, no time to play with friends. She cannot go to school, had to take care of the kids too while the mama work in the fields."

BIRTH CONTROL

"In my day, issei women no talk about birth control. When I had my sixth child, I say that enough. All *pau* [finished], I don't want no more, too hard for me to work and take care children. I go see Dr. Uyehara, who had private practice. He was Okinawan doctor. His wife was *naichi* from good family. He was well liked and respected by the issei people. Many issei prefer him than go to plantation doctor. He understood trouble I get with my big family, so he put some kind birth control device [IUD] inside and I never have any more babies. I think I was in my late forties then. Later, after I was about fifty-five, I went back and had it removed. So far I'm okay. Those days, nobody know about birth control. No issei women want to ask doctor. I guess, me the only one who had courage to ask for help. Otherwise, I would suffer more."

MENSTRUATION

"Today, women and young girls lucky, have good protection to wear when the bleeding come. In the early days, women had none of that. Issei women working in the fields had rough time doing all that heavy work dressed in layers of clothing, during the bleeding." Because of an assignment I was doing for a women's studies project at the time, in some interviews I included some very personal questions that ordinarily I would not have asked. Surprisingly, the issei women were very open and frank. The issei women usually either used soft rags, such as old worn-out *yukata,* for pads, or old bleached rice bags. Some who could afford it bought gauze-like fabric or the commercial pads sold at stores. I asked how they changed the pads in the fields. "Well," Kama chuckled, "that was hard. No toilets in the fields, yeah? We look for a thick brush or go deep in the cane fields to make sure no men around. Of course, there's centipedes and scorpions, so we had to be careful! We bury the rag in the ground. Hard for the women on those days, you know, to do the same work as the men. I wonder how we managed." Kama shook her head, remembering those difficult times.

HUSBAND'S FAMILY AND DEMAND FOR MONEY

"Since I came to Hawaii, I really did lots for my husband's family in Okinawa. My father-in-law, every time he ask for money, we send and send. We struggle to raise our big family, but he don't worry. He never satisfied, he want more. Look at my children, here in America now, they don't send me money! No, and I don't expect them to help me!" Kama laughed. "I don't expect them to help me, because I don't want them to suffer. But my husband and me, every time his parents write us that they want money, we say, 'All right,' and send right away. The pay was so cheap in those days, $20 for women, $30 for men a month. My father-in-law wrote back that he bought land, so he needed more money. On and on, it was endless.

"I complain to my husband, 'We send them money but we need money for our children, too.' We argue sometimes, but as long as they keep asking for money, my husband feels obligated to send. You see, my in-laws buy land, thinking someday my husband go live in Okinawa. My husband send back half of his hard-earned money, but he die here in Hawaii. No make sense! Today, his relative own the land an' lease to the government, get paid $10,000 a year in American money! To think, all come from our blood an' sweat, money we send every month." Kama let out a deep sigh. "My *ji-san* [husband] so good-natured. When he finally go back to Okinawa and see the poor living an' the lease money so low, only $400 to $500 a year, he feel sorry for them. At that time, I tell him, 'Keep the lease money,' but he said, 'What can you do with so little money?' I told him, 'How can you say that? Did you ever get one penny from your children?' From his parents' estate, he only get $200 or $300."

Kama's son, Yuki, understood his mother's feelings and frustrations, and elaborated upon them some years after my talk with her: "After World War II the Asato land was taken over by USA as a small portion in building the U.S. Marine base. In time, that portion of the land was returned, in a settlement, to the rightful owner, the Asato family. After the death of my grandfather, the land was deeded to my father. Some years later, my parents were both retired and went to Okinawa for a visit. During that visit my father transferred the land to his sister. My mother objected to his decision, but to no avail.

"My mother was crushed by my father's decision. She had sacrificed a lot in sending money that could have been used for her children's needs in Hawaii. I can relate to her frustration. When I was a young child, one afternoon I took a $5 bill from my mother's safekeeping place to buy a loaf of bread at my neighborhood candy shop. The lady proprietor asked me where I got the money, and I replied that I found it. The shop owner gave me the bread and returned the rest of the money to my mother. My mother did not say anything about the incident, nor did she scold me for taking the money. I have come to understand, in time, her deep feeling of frustration, despair, and anguish to see her son hungry enough to take money from her. This event is one illustration of the remarkable strength of character of a remarkable woman! She was truly an inspirational mother."

"After Okinawa came under the Japanese government, the lease value went up, almost *ichiman doru* [$10,000]," Kama recalled, continuing on with her story. "At that time, my husband was making $30 a month and I was making $20 a month. However, during cut-cane and *hapai ko,* we *hanahana* [work] on contract basis. Between both of us, we make $100 to $130 a month. That was good money. When finally things seem to be looking toward a brighter side, the unexpected happened."

HUSBAND'S ACCIDENT

"One day, when working with heavy equipment in the fields, my husband's shirt-sleeve on the left arm catch on the wheel. It hurt his left arm pretty bad. They rush him to the hospital and operate, but there was a deep gash on the arm. Later it got infected and more complications. He no can work for a year. Oh, I really had hard time without my husband pay. My oldest daughter just graduate eighth grade at Waipahu Intermediate School. She just thirteen years old. I feel sorry for her but no can help. I have to let her take husband place. We work together, to make the $100. She still too young, not strong enough for heavy work, so I help her a lot. Somehow, she keep up working with adults for one year and we make quota. Thanks to my oldest daughter, we somehow survive the crisis. I feel sorry for her. After that, she get domestic job for naval officer family on Ford Island, that part of Pearl Harbor.

Then come December 7, 1941. Japan bomb Pearl Harbor. Everything turn to chaos, many wives go back to mainland. My girl lose her job. Meantime, oldest boy finish ninth grade. He start working on plantation, at least some income for family to survive."

Kama hesitated for a while, looked out the window quietly for a moment, then continued softly, "My husband, he drink too much, so I suffer. He use to beat me when he get drunk. The children used to be so afraid. They run out to the outhouse an' hide, till the beating stop. Sometimes, they wait in dark outhouse long time. Children suffer, too.

"Times like that, I think how different my life would be if I stay back in Okinawa. I think my life may be happier, yeah? Don't have to slave too much. When my husband sick for a long time, I wish I was in Okinawa, where all the relatives would have come to help!"

Several years after Kama's death, one of Kama's daughters confirmed the beatings. "He was a nice quiet man, a good father when he was sober, but when he drank too much, that's when he'd get out of hand. He beat my mom and sometimes beat us, too. Yeah, we'd hide in the outhouse. It was cold out there sometimes, too, but we waited in the dark until 11:00 p.m. until the beating stopped." She understands now that her father's drinking was likely a result of his frustration because he couldn't go to work. These situations were common during the Depression years for plantation families.

EDUCATION FOR CHILDREN

"Because I work hard for cheap pay all my life," Kama continued, "I want my kids get good education. Out of the six children, two boys sacrifice and work in cane fields after they graduate from eighth grade. The rest graduate high school." Takashi, the oldest son, graduated from Waipahu High School and was inducted into the U.S. Army. He was stationed at Fort Lewis, near Seattle, Washington.

"Yukio, my second boy, graduate Waipahu High in 1957, wanted to go college. He know we cannot pay high tuition money, so he join the army. One day, next-door neighbor's son went University of Hawaii to take entrance exam, so Yukio went too. They both passed.

"Yukio get baseball scholarship to pay for tuition. He graduate in four years in microbiology. After that, he enlisted in the U.S. Army since he volunteer before. He served in army three years. He came home, and work at University of Hawaii, Manoa. One professor, impressed with him, told him, 'This job pays you $500. You get higher degree, you find better job later.' Yukio work as teacher's assistant, did all kind of jobs. He earn master's degree in microbiology in 1966." Further encouraged by this mentor, Yukio earned a Ph.D. in microbiology in 1969. Yukio found a permanent position with the University of Massachusetts as a professor of biology. His research area was genetic regulation of the cell division cycle.

Kama did not fully understand the complexities of Yukio's scientific research, but she knew it was special, and she couldn't be any prouder. She was even more impressed because he did all this on his own without her help. I could feel Kama's heart swell with pride as she told me about Yukio's accomplishments with a big smile. "He teach in Massachusetts and he come home every year with wife and two girls for a nice long visit with us." Nothing could be more rewarding for Kama. All the years of hard work, tears, and sweat seemed like a distant dream.

RELIGION

"My parents belong to Jodo Shinshu Hongwanji temple in Futenma. The Shinshu temple was different, not like here in Hawaii, where we sit and listen to a sermon given by priest. Nope. In the village, there is no priest to be seen, so we just make offerings, bow our heads, and say our prayers. Only when someone die, priest come to the home, with assistant, to offer prayer. I belong to the Jodo Shinshu sect in Waipahu. It is a Hongwanji sect. The main temple on the Pali Highway. When I younger, I go church for special occasions and help the *fujinkai* [women's club]. Now that I'm *makule* [too old], hard for walk that far. I no go out night time for so long time, *no go yo* [Pidgin, "don't go"]. The church tell us, no worry about dues no more. Nobody come around to collect."

RETURN TO OKINAWA AFTER WORLD WAR II

Kama suffered along with other issei after the surprise attack on Pearl Harbor. It was difficult being regarded as enemy aliens, restricted from participating and helping in the war efforts. The issei women wanted to help the Red Cross roll bandages and send packages to the soldiers, but for security reasons issei were not allowed to work in any military establishments, even for janitorial or domestic work. It was heartbreaking to hear the devastating news about the heavy casualties suffered by Okinawans caught between the United States and Japan. Never a day went by that Kama did not pray for the safety of her family and friends.

After World War II, the situation in Okinawa became stabilized and Kama had the opportunity to return to her village. She was now retired, and with her pension money from the plantation, she could afford to travel. So much had changed since Kama left her beloved village in 1920. During World War II, Okinawa was Japan's final battleground. Many precious documents, art treasures, valuable textiles, and ancestral graves were destroyed, along with so much of the civilian population. Futenma, once the peaceful fertile farmland where she was born and raised, had been transformed into a U.S. Marine Corps base, the center of a conflict among Japan, Okinawa, and the U.S. government.

"When I went home in 1983," Kama related, "I climb up the hill to search for my younger sister's grave. I search and search in the mountain but could not find any trace of her grave. So I built a nice tombstone for her, it cost $400 American money. I felt so much better. That the picture I show you, yeah? I put one orchid lei that somebody gave me when I left Hawaii. That sister died right after she give birth to her baby. She only twenty years old. Child die later, when a few years old. I want to put her husband ashes with hers, but his grave was gone in war, too. At least I have peace of mind that my sister has nice resting place now. I always worry about that. I send money home all that time and I don't know why nobody build her one decent resting place. So I put one up for her." People in Okinawa believe in ancestral worship and make it a priority to take care of the tombs of the ancestors. Even the people of Okinawan descent who now live in Hawaii follow this tradition.

RETIREMENT/REFLECTION

"Though I retired now, I more busy than before! I take care of house, I cook, do laundry, garden. I don't have time for senior program. Sometimes I travel to mainland to see my children and grandchildren. They come to visit me often. My children very independent, and never ask for money. Yes, I see my other friends. I feel lucky."

I asked Kama about her friend from the fields, Kaku Kumasaka. Kama sighed and told me, "Her two children stay far away; so lonely for her. I still remember when she and I work together. Sometimes we get so tired, you know. So during thirty-minute lunch, we say, 'Let's rest little bit.' But the *luna* come an' yell, 'Hey you! Go *hanahana!*' Ho, no can talk about those days, too sad, really hard."

"I think back sometimes to girlhood days in village. There was one boy I like. We met at *moashibi* [night play] where young people got together. We played games, sang, and danced. But we never dated . . . I too young. Such a long time ago . . . but I keep these thoughts deep inside my heart, no say nothing and come to Hawaii, have to obey parents, you know. See? How pitiful. I use to wonder why I ever come to islands. That boy I remember, he marry some girl in village, but he die during World War II. His children, they all grow up an' working now. I visit them when I go back to Okinawa. Yeah, make me happy to see them, and they all doing well." Kama's thoughts seemed to wander off to the quaint little village she had left behind so many years ago.

After the endless years of backbreaking toil under the scorching tropical sun, Kamei Asato, Kama's husband, died at the age of eighty-three, on February 28, 1983. Six years later, Kama passed away, on August 14, 1989.

Kana Higa

GOMEN YO (FORGIVE ME), IT WAS THE SAKE

June 20, 1901–May 11, 2001
Born in Aza Kawakami, Haneji-mura, Kunigami-gun, Okinawa
Arrived in Hawaii June 1922

When I learned that Kana Nakao was born in a place called Aza Kawakami in Okinawa, I was surprised, because I thought that "Kawakami" seemed more like a *naichi,* or mainland Japanese, word, and that it was unusual for it to be used as a place name in Okinawa. Kana explained that her village was located above the river, so it was named *kawa* (river) *kami* (above). Above this river on one side of the hill were rows of cherry trees. The blossoms of Okinawan cherry trees are dark pink with double petals. When in full bloom, the trees are a spectacular sight to behold. "At a distance from our village, we could see the rolling hills—the lush, green forest where we gathered tender ferns, edible roots, and bamboo shoots. How delicious those fresh bamboo shoots were. The forest was our favorite place to play, to relax from farm work," Kana fondly recalled.

Kana Nakao Higa was one of twenty thousand picture brides who came to Hawaii during the restricted immigration period, 1908–1924. Kana's picture bride marriage was unusual. When she was twenty-one years old, her relatives arranged her marriage in absentia to Koho Higa, who was working on a sugar plantation in the islands. "My husband was second time to marry, so I worry if he was legally divorced from first wife! Someone tell me, she cannot have baby so he sent her back to Okinawa. So at first I didn't want to come . . . took me long time to make up my mind."

"I was willing to marry a man sight unseen. When I look at his photo, looks like nice man." Other than that, Kana's young heart and spirit held a romantic notion about beginning a new life with this nice-looking man in the photo.

When I first encountered her, Kana Higa was among a large group of Okinawan men and women who gathered daily at the Waipahu Senior Center to play the *shamisen,* the three-stringed Japanese instrument, and sing some Okinawan *minyo,* or folksongs. Some of the younger seniors practiced the lively *paranku,* hitting the small drum, so that whenever there was a festival or parade, they could march in unison with good timing and rhythm. They looked forward to getting together for

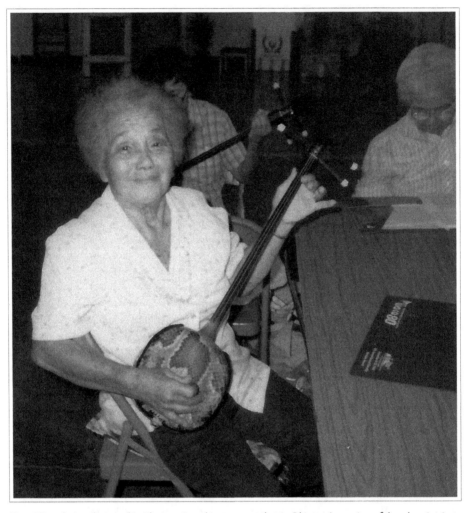

Kana Higa playing the *sanshin* (three-stringed instrument that is Okinawa's version of the *shamisen*) at the Waipahu Senior Center in 1985. Barbara Kawakami Collection.

merrymaking, karaoke, and folk dancing. After long years of toiling in the sugarcane and pineapple fields, raising large families, and providing a good education for their children, this finally was a time for them to relax and enjoy themselves. They lived within walking distance from this center, and enjoyed having the lunch provided for a reasonable fee.

Kana remembered, "In Okinawa, men, women, and children all enjoy *odori* [dancing]. It just comes naturally whenever we get together for some kind of celebration. When I was young, I was so busy working on the farm that there wasn't enough time to learn Okinawan dancing. I finally started taking an interest in it here in my eighties, after I retired from working on the plantation. Yeah, I became a pretty good dancer once I got started. I made good use of the many kimonos I brought from Okinawa. My friends used to borrow from me, too," she said.

When you're with a group of Okinawan women, their warmth and friendliness make you feel as though you are with a group of old friends. Some of the issei women still use their Okinawan dialect, but it is not too hard to understand. Kana was exceptional, and she captured my attention immediately. At age eighty-seven, five foot two, with large brown eyes and a fair complexion, she was the picture of good health, still very spry. Her wavy silvery-gray hair was partially combed back, revealing a gentle face that reflected a keen and alert mind. She was a striking, exotic-looking beauty, and some people might have thought she was Spanish. She had a remarkable way of telling stories in a mixture of her native dialect, some *naichi* words, and Pidgin. She wasn't afraid to be honest, telling it the way it happened, and at times she became so emotional that the sequence of events in the stories got mixed up. I had to backtrack at times to get the timeline of events correct.

Our initial interview was done in 1985, with additional meetings in 1987, 1988, and 1990, when I was working on clothing brought to Hawaii by the early Japanese immigrants. I later interviewed her nisei children to complete her life story. Through the help of Ruth and Grace, Kana's eldest daughters, we found some missing links.

Kana lived with her married daughter, Ruth Yukie Oshiro, in Waipahu. This land was formerly the property of Oahu Sugar Company, and once had been surrounded by acres and acres of lush sugarcane fields. As I walked up the steps, memories from my childhood sprang vividly to mind, of the silver tassels at the top of the sugarcane swaying gently in the tropical breeze.

Kana appeared at the front door with a cheerful smile. I bowed my head and greeted her, "Kana-san, *konichiwa, doozo yoroshiku* [good afternoon, thank you for allowing me to interview you]."

Still in a reflective mood, I started to share with Kana some of my own memories from childhood. During the early 1930s, this Camp Nine area was one of our favorite playgrounds. It was near Camp One, where we grew up, right near the sugar mill. There were hardly any cars in those days, so the boys played baseball on the dirt road. We flew our fancy homemade kites, made from colorful wrappings and newspapers, dashing back and forth along the dusty road. We used to play hide-and-seek among the tall, razor-sharp cane stalks, except during the harvest season, when it was dangerous for the children, with all the heavy trucks driving back and forth. This area was almost on the outskirts of the plantation town known as Waipahu Junction, the intersection where Pearl City, Waipahu, and Waikele converge. Today, Waikele is a town by itself, with beautiful homes and an upscale shopping center designed to attract the tourists. Kana Higa lived a few blocks from this intersection.

I told Kana that back in the 1930s, there were no street names. In 1934 the whole bunch of us kids walked *hadashi* (barefoot) from Camp One to Waipahu Junction to catch a glimpse of President Franklin Delano Roosevelt, who passed by in an open car. The plantation children were out of school that day, so we all lined up along the dirt road. As young as I was, I have a vivid picture of the president dressed in a white linen suit as he waved his white Panama hat to the excited onlookers. Kana had lived at the other end of Waipahu, in Kunia, during that period, so she had not known this.

Kana's daughter, Ruth, and I thought that their house must have been situated in the area that was once called Camp Nine, where the Spanish, Puerto Rican, Filipino, and Portuguese families all used to live. After the plantation closed down, these former employees, who had devoted the best years of their lives to work for the plantation, were finally rewarded by being given the opportunity to purchase land at a special price to build their own homes. Today there's no trace of the dusty, sleepy old plantation town where we grew up. The diverse ethnic groups of people who once lived in segregated camps are all good friends and neighbors living next door to each other. Many of the new homes look alike. I learned to identify Ruth's home by the bright yellow hibiscus with red stems that bloomed in abundance all year round in her front yard.

The minute I entered the living room, I immediately took notice of the unusual artifacts from Okinawa, as well as the photos of three generations of family on both sides. Some of the photographs had faded. Kana couldn't remember all their names or how they were related, but the clothing worn by those distant relatives made me take a second look. They were wearing the Ryukyu *gasuri*. Today, those exquisite handwoven *kasuri* are rarely seen. Most of the early treasured *kasuri* fabrics were destroyed during World War II.

CHILDHOOD IN OKINAWA

Kana spoke of her mother, Kamado Higa, and her father, Jiro Nakao. "My mother was much older than my father, thirteen years older—he had no choice. My *baban* [Kana's grandmother, her father's mother] Matsu made the decision to select a wife for him. The focus of the matchmaking was mainly to find a hardworking woman to work on the farm, raising sugarcane, vegetables, and hogs. A great portion of work was done by the women, so they had to be good and healthy," Kana added.

"My father was twenty-four years old when I was born. I had one baby sister. I was only three years old when my father died at age twenty-seven. I heard he got bitten by a poisonous snake on his right hand while working in the fields. We always had to be cautious and protect ourselves against snakes when working in the fields in Okinawa. I don't remember anything about my father. After he died, my mother was sent back to her natal home, taking my baby sister, Nae 'Nabe' Nakao, with her. She was barely one year old. So sad, we never lived together as sisters, and I hardly got to know her. She later married a man from her village, named Kinjo. I don't know whether it was my grandparents who sent Mother home to her parents," Kana said uncertainly. "How lonely it was, living away from my mother and the only sister I had.

"Soon after that, Baban decided to bring a *yoshi*, an adopted son, to help with work on the farm. She never told me about adopting a *yoshi*. I was very hurt that she didn't let me know. Maybe I was too young to understand. Until then, the young man she adopted had been working with one of the relatives in a nearby village. I guess it was too much for Baban to take care of the farm after my father died, so an uncle brought the young man to our house. They even arranged a marriage for him, with a girl from a poor family. Usually the wife of the *yoshi* is supposed to help on the farm, but instead she worked for someone else, and our family paid her money, too. Because he was a *yoshi*, he was *waga mama* [spoiled] and took advantage of his position in the family. He drank sake and hardly worked on the farm. So, when I was thirteen, I had to cut all the grass in the fields, to feed the cows and goats. Every day I cried and cried while cutting grass. That was hard work on a huge farm, and the *yoshi* was supposed to do all that work! I told Matsu *baban,* 'How come you adopted such a good-for-nothing like him?'" Even after all these years, Kana still felt anger toward him.

The villagers all raised sugarcane on their land, besides sweet potatoes, which was a staple. Kana recalled with pride, "Yeah, the village people all helped each other when come time to harvest sugarcane. Women cut and clean the cane leaves, to feed the cows. Men cut the tough cane stalks, then carry to factory in neighboring village where the juice was extracted and made into raw sugar. Then it was made into different grades of *kuro sato* [black sugar]. Black sugar was made in a *kame no naka* [pottery jar]. For snacks we ate *kuro sato* made in size of rice bowl. We store the black sugar for one year," she said. The Okinawan people were known to be good workers on the plantations in Hawaii because of their experience in raising sugarcane in Okinawa.

"Matsu *baban* was very affectionate and took good care of me after my father died, but she couldn't afford to send me to school beyond the fifth grade, even though I loved to study. My teacher was so kind. She gave me a short pencil and tablet, and helped with schoolwork until she was transferred to another district." Kana also loved to practice her calligraphy. With the ink and brush her teacher had given her, she practiced on old newspapers whenever she could. Ruth added, "Even now, she loves to read and keeps up with historical events, and never fails to read the local Japanese newspaper. Her mind is still sharp."

Kana had fond memories about the village school. "I attended Hanechi Ko, an elementary school located between Aza Nako Shi and Kawakami. We attended classes from 8:00 a.m. to 2:00 p.m. and studied *shushin* [moral ethics], *tsuzurikata* [composition], *sanjitsu* [arithmetic], *chiri* [geography], *rekishi* [history]. We studied the same subjects as the students in mainland Japan. Our principal was *naichi* [from mainland Japan]. Most of the teachers were young Okinawan teachers with *koko* [high school] or *hoshukka* [continuation school]. I had Miyashiro Gyosei *sensei.* She was a good teacher. My cousins and girlfriends all continued to high school. That's the reason why I encourage my children to have a good education. All my girls graduated from high school; my eldest daughter graduated from junior college. They worked their way through high school working for a *haole* family as maids. They also worked at a pineapple cannery during summer. My three sons all worked their way through college doing all kinds of tough jobs. In the summer, they worked in the cane fields or pineapple fields." Kana smiled with pride. In spite of the hard times they all had to endure, the children were good and never complained.

"In Okinawa, we had a fairly nice home, very spacious with many rooms. It wasn't thatched roof like other village homes. We had a big *kura,* the warehouse where the bags of *ine* [rice] and plenty of sweet potato were stored for one year. *Naichi* people loved the Okinawan sweet potato, the purple-color one. When we bring white rice for lunch, people laughed at us, because most of the Okinawan children ate sweet potatoes three times a day. Family too poor to afford white rice. Our family, we lucky to have white rice every day. In the morning when I pack my school lunch, I spread miso on top the rice. Oh, it tasted so good at lunchtime. *Katsuo musubi* [smoked tuna flakes in rice balls] was good, too. *Kandaba sushi* [rice with vinegar and sweet potato leaves] had many vegetables inside, very healthy and delicious." Kana couldn't hold back a few tears as she thought of her childhood days.

I asked, "What did you do as a child for fun?"

"Of course, the *buranko,* a swing we had strung to the strong branch of the sturdy pine tree, was our favorite pastime. We played jump rope, hitting the *temari* ball, and *ojyame* [tossing the bean bags]. It took some skill to toss three bean bags at once." Kana described how they filled the bean bags with *shi shi dama,* seeds from the plant called Job's tears. This plant also grows wild in Hawaii, and kids there used its seeds to make *ojyame,* too, as it made a nice sound when you tossed it around.

"You can see here," Kana said while reaching toward a stack of old pictures, "when we had special functions at school, we dressed more formally. This picture was taken during winter. Even in Okinawa, it gets cold. We wear double-layer kimonos during cold weather. For summer, we wore *kunji,* an unlined kimono. That is a kind of sheer fabric that kept us cool."

"Matsu *baban* had been trained and taught special weaving and dyeing techniques since she was a young girl. She wove the most beautiful Okinawan kimono fabrics and obis. She was very skilled with her hands. She spun the thread and tied the thread to make *kasuri* fabric. She also bought the silk threads, tie-dyed the thread herself, and wove the most exquisite *kasuri* silk fabric that everyone admired. She was always accurate in tie-dying the thread in creating the complex *kasuri* [splash pattern] designs. We had a big house, and the women in the village all gathered at our house to watch Grandma sit on the *takabata* [handloom] weaving her magic. Not too many people in the village owned a handloom. Grandmother

Kana Nakao with friends in Okinawa.
Barbara Kawakami Collection.

supervised the work. Everybody trusted her. Sad to say, I didn't inherit her talent. I never made an effort to learn. The kimonos that I had learned to tie-dye and weave on our own handloom from Baban—I left those in the village when I came to Hawaii. Baban felt that I would surely come home someday, so she kept the ones I made. She used to write to me, kept telling me to come back to Okinawa. It was sad to find out that those precious handwoven kimonos were destroyed during World War II, with all the battles on Okinawa." Kana sighed as she thought of all the kimonos she had made as a young girl and which were now lost.

Kana took out her kimonos and demonstrated how she wore the *ushinchi* for dressy occasions. She explained that "*ushinchi* means 'to insert or tuck in.' See, first a sturdy *himo* [narrow cord] is tied very firmly around the waist and over the *jiban* [short blouse] and *suteteko* [long pants]. Then the right front of the kimono is first tucked into the waist at the left side, and the left front side of the kimono is tucked into the right waistband. When the upper part of the kimono is loosely draped over the waist it gives a blouson look, very dressy. It's comfortable and ideal for summer wear." It seemed complicated to understand, so I took photos of Kana showing the various steps.

PICTURE BRIDE MARRIAGE

Kana's picture bride marriage had an unusual start. Koho Higa had gone to Hawaii in 1913, joining his village friends to work at the Ewa sugar plantation on Oahu. He had high hopes of making a "pocketful of money" and then returning to his village a wealthy man. Things did not turn out as favorably as he expected. There was a major strike throughout the sugar plantations on Oahu in 1920, and he decided to move to the island of Kauai. He settled on a sugar plantation in Wahiawa, Kauai. There a friend had arranged a marriage for Koho to a young girl with the family name Kaneshiro (first name unknown). After two years, she had not borne any children, so Koho divorced her.

Several years after that, a relative in Kana's village had a request from Koho's family to act as intermediary and arrange a picture bride marriage between Koho Higa and Kana Nakao. Pictures were exchanged between the prospective families. Koho received Kana's photo through his parents. As noted earlier, Kana was hesitant to come at first because she worried whether he was legally divorced.

On the other hand, Kana, who had never ventured beyond the boundaries of the neighboring villages, had a romantic notion about beginning a new life in so-called paradise with the nice-looking man in the photo. She thought that anything would be better than the miserable existence she had to bear with the *yoshi* her *baban* had adopted. In 1922, after two years, she finally decided to come to Hawaii.

"In Okinawa, before I left for Yokohama, I didn't pass the 'stool test' for the physical exam, so I stayed behind in Naha for a few days. From Naha I took the small boat to Kagoshima. Ah! The sea was so rough, and the small boat made big noise, I couldn't eat anything for three days, until we reached Kagoshima. From there, the other picture brides and I took the train to Yokohama and waited to transfer to another ship to go to Hawaii. There, I met a nice *naichi* woman. She said she was from Fukushima, northern part of Japan. I could see she was feeling a bit sad. Her husband had gone to Hawaii earlier and had left her and a child behind. This time she wanted to take her little child with her, but her mother-in-law was concerned about the child's safety and insisted on keeping the child. So she gave me the extra pillow that was meant for her child," Kana related sadly.

Kana left Yokohama on the steamship *Korea Maru* on June 4, 1922. She was seasick all the way to Hawaii. "One *naichi* lady combed my hair for me. She was also a picture bride going to meet a Hawaii-born nisei named Machida. We never saw each other again," Kana said wistfully. She wondered what had happened to her. Was she able to find happiness with her nisei husband?

ARRIVAL IN PARADISE

The *Korea Maru* docked in Honolulu harbor in June 1922. At the sight of beautiful Diamond Head from a distance, Kana and the other picture brides grew excited, knowing they would be meeting their husbands soon for the first time. "We were too nervous to talk." With mixed emotions, the picture brides rushed to their places to get dressed, trying to look their best. "Of course, we never used any makeup, no lipstick. Just applied some face cream to look pretty," Kana said. "The other girls from the villages wore their colorful *kasuri* kimonos with splashes of red and yellow designs against their indigo blue cloth. Some wore their *bashofu* kimonos [made of plantain banana fiber]. I couldn't decide which kimono to wear. Then the kind *naichi* lady from Fukushima prefecture helped me get dressed in a wide obi, like the *naichi* women.

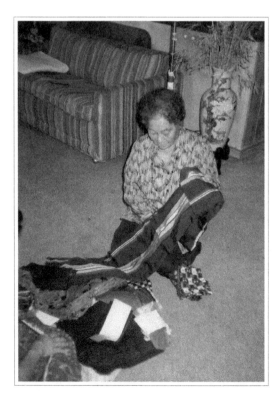

Kana showing the kimono she brought with her in 1922. Barbara Kawakami Collection.

"When I disembarked from the ship with other picture brides from the village, I probably stood out because the woman from Fukushima prefecture was kind enough to dress me the *naichi* way. Baban must have heard about the difference in the way the *naichi* women wore their kimonos. That explains why she took me to the special store in Naha where the kimonos were imported from mainland Japan. It was a beautiful striped *meisen* silk kimono, with a *haori* made of *habutai* [fine silk]. It was very expensive. Can you believe that I even brought my *shikibuto,* my heavy comforter to sleep on, as part of my dowry?

"The majority of the Okinawan brides had their obi tied and draped down the front, the way the courtesans dress in mainland Japan. That's the reason why *naichi* picture brides misunderstood them as courtesans and ridiculed them." Kana chuckled at the memory.

As the group of bewildered picture brides finally passed through the various exams and tests, they were led into a huge reception room. "We were required to take written exams as well as physical exams. It was so sad—one girl from Okinawa had leprosy and was sent back. We felt so badly for her. The rest of us passed the exams," said Kana.

When Kana's group of Okinawans entered the immigration station, she said, "naturally we all felt strange and insecure in a unfamiliar foreign environment. None of us spoke English or Hawaiian. As we stood waiting, staring at other unfamiliar faces, a man dressed in a snappy dark uniform and white cap came toward our group. He took me by surprise when he stopped in front of me. He gently grabbed my hand and walked me across the room to where a large group of picture brides from mainland Japan were standing, looking just as bewildered as the rest of us! He was so funny as he called everyone to attention, and said, 'Mina-san [everybody], I want to introduce to you this tall, good-looking picture bride from Okinawa!'" To Kana's surprise, he even sang couple of *uchinanchu* (Okinawan) songs, much to the delight of the audience. This happened in 1922, more than sixty-seven years ago, and yet Kana vividly remembered it. Later, Kana found out that he was Dr. Tomizo Katsunuma, who was the inspector at the immigration station whom so many other picture brides remembered.

BEGINNING A NEW LIFE IN HAWAII

Kana arrived in Hawaii not knowing that Koho, her husband, had moved from the plantation on Kauai to Honolulu. "Our first home was on Aala Street, where Aala Park is located today. We lived in a small room upstairs with his brother and wife. Koho took a temporary job working for a lawyer, a judge living in Pacific Heights. When I first arrived in Hawaii, I was so naive, did not know anything. One time, I was so lonely, I hire taxi man to take me to see night-blooming cereus in Honolulu." (I thought she was referring to the ones blooming in Punahou.) "It was so beautiful. I have never seen anything like it in Okinawa. But I had scolding from my sister-in-law and her husband for being wasteful with my husband's money on taxi fare! I felt like running away. My sister-in-law said she'll kill me if I run away. I had no family here, not a single friend," Kana said. She had never felt so miserable.

"It was after I came to Hawaii that I found out that my husband's older sister controlled the purse strings in the family. My sister-in-law said she would give us a house on Kauai. They had a store there. Good thing we did not go. She told me Koho borrowed money from her to bring me to Hawaii, so I was indebted to her. My husband gave all his pay to her. She sent it to Okinawa and they bought house and land. That's the way it was in those days," Kana said sadly.

In the meantime, an old friend from the village had told Koho about working for a pineapple company in Poamoho, in Wahiawa. There he found steady work and the company provided them housing. It was also there that their first child, a daughter, was born. They named her Chieko (Grace).

Later, they heard that Oahu Sugar Company was hiring workers, including women. The family then moved to Camp Forty-eight in Waipahu, off Kunia Road. Today, it is known as Royal Kunia, where beautiful homes have sprung up, with a spectacular view of Pearl Harbor. As the family expanded, they moved to Camp Fifty-six.

While the Higa family lived at Camp Fifty-six in Waipahu, a second child, Yukie (Ruth), was born in 1924. Ruth noted how happy her father was when, after having two girls, Kana gave birth to a healthy baby boy, Sadamori (David), in 1926; Koho gave a big party for the firstborn son. A third daughter, Miyeko (Lillian), was born in 1928; Fujiko (Doris) was born in 1930; and Kana (Alice) was born in 1932. Later Kana would have three more children, Mitsuo (Alfred) in 1934, Takemi (Harry) in 1936, and her last child, Yoshinori (Reginald), in 1942.

Kana was assisted by midwife Mrs. Setsu Ishikawa, who had graduated from midwifery school in Niigata prefecture. She was a popular midwife during the prewar period and one of the few who had received formal training in midwifery. Mrs. Ishikawa had a special technique to ease the pain during delivery, soothingly massaging the woman's back and abdomen. Kana described how Mrs. Ishikawa made her hold firmly to both ends of a *monosashi,* a fifteen-inch-long, one-inch-wide Japanese ruler made of bamboo, placed under the pillow; holding it with all her might gave Kana the strength to push harder. Kana remembered the afterbirth was placed in a coffee can and buried behind the chicken coop.

Mrs. Ishikawa, the midwife, was very knowledgeable. When Kana didn't have breast milk immediately to give to one of her later newborn children, Mrs. Ishikawa, the midwife, would let Ruth prepare boiled water and sugar, apply it to sterilized gauze, and put it to the baby's mouth. The baby would suck the sugar water until Kana's milk came in. Kana's husband, Koho, helped Mrs. Ishikawa to deliver Fujiko.

Kana's husband, Koho, worked very hard, but with an ever-expanding family and endless debt, he became frustrated by financial worries and began drinking. Though he had wanted to come to Hawaii to make "a pocketful of money," he once told his daughter, instead "I made a pocketful of children." He became an alcoholic and hardly stayed home. When he didn't come home at night, Kana often went around the camps with a kerosene lamp, searching for him. When he came home really drunk, he often beat her brutally, even during her pregnancy. He would chase her out of the house and leave her to sleep outside on the veranda in the chill of the night. At times when he got violently drunk, even the veranda was not safe to avoid getting beaten. Kana had to escape to the cane fields and often spent the night there. Ruth felt sorry for her mother and would keep her company, with only one blanket to keep them warm. Ruth said it got so cold during the winter months in Kunia, and feeling the mongooses running over them was scary, not to mention the centipedes and scorpions.

Ruth said, "Sometimes, when Father got violently drunk, we were so scared. He swore that he would kill Mother and the kids as he held a kitchen knife at us! He was a completely different person. Once my brother threatened to call the police, then he stopped."

Kana was bitter when she talked about this part of her past. "My husband, he sick all the time. Too much drinking! Don't go to work. Oh, he beat me terribly, punch me with his fists, even while I was sleeping. When supper not ready, he used to turn over everything on the table. When my son asked, 'Why you beat Mother all the time?' Father yelled back, 'She always take children's side and take me cheap" (i.e., she embarrassed him in front of the children). Kana said, "It hurt the most when Koho used to hit me in front of people." Kana cried and cried. Many times she thought of running away, but she couldn't leave the children behind. "The funniest thing is, in spite of causing all that trouble and scaring everyone, he didn't remember what he did, and next day, he acted like nothing happened." Kana herself finds it hard to believe the nightmare Koho created.

According to the eldest daughter, Chieko, Koho treated others better than his own family, even when he himself was struggling and working so hard to make ends meet. He borrowed money to help a friend in need and co-signed loans for others. They did not always pay him back. At times when things became too difficult with Koho's constant drinking and no money to buy food, Chieko remembered going around with Kana to collect the IOUs. It was very difficult to get the money back. Everybody was suffering during the Depression.

Kana didn't have any family in Hawaii to depend on, to look to for comfort. She said, "Because of the children, I was able to bear the loneliness and hardships. They were the ones who gave me the strength and the will to live. Once, at the darkest moment when I couldn't take it anymore, I contemplated suicide. I thought of drowning myself in the nearby reservoir, which is very deep in the center. But then I wondered what would happen to my children when my husband got drunk and threatened to kill all of them. I kept reminding myself, 'Be strong, don't let him scare you!'"

Ruth explained, "Camp Twenty-four was about five miles from Waipahu Plantation Hospital. The reservoir nearby had plenty of fish. Besides Camp Twenty-four, there were Twenty-five, Twenty-eight, Thirty-seven, Thirty-eight, and Fifty-six. At Camp Thirty-seven, my mother raised potatoes and other vegetables. The plantation camps had no names, not even street names. So even the children learned to identify the houses by numbers. The camps were not as far apart and confusing as it may seem—whenever we had to run errands, our parents gave us the camp number and we found it."

Kana worked hard to earn extra money to help in raising her family. When they lived at Camp Fifty-six, she made *bento* lunches for the single men. She took in laundry from the single Filipino men at Camp Eight. "I used harsh red soap and scrub with stiff brush, then pound the clothes to remove the stubborn red dirt. Then I boil the clothing in a big drum can, outdoors, over an open fire, using kiawe wood. This was tough work. I lucky, all *guru* [good] children. They all help me, chop kiawe wood." Kana even made tofu, which was time-consuming and involved a lot of work. She also raised pigs, goats, rabbits, ducks, and chickens. Both Koho and Kana tended the fruit trees and vegetable gardens. Kana couldn't afford to buy candies for the children, so she made sweet treats from watermelon and orange rind. She sewed all of the clothes for the children out of flour bags. For the girls she sewed underwear from bleached rice bags. She had no time to rest.

When asked how the children had gotten their English names, Ruth answered, "The children did not have English names until World War II. After Pearl Harbor, they decided to adopt an English name. They dug a hole outside in the backyard, and on a piece of paper, they put whatever names they could think of that they liked, then each one picked up a paper, and that's how they got their English names."

Living in an isolated camp, the children had to get up early to go to public school. Kana would pack *bento* for all the children. Mr. Shinsato, the plantation truck driver, transported the kids back and forth from all the outlying camps. By the time Mr. Shinsato picked up the children from Japanese school, it was really dark and the children were hungry. The mothers were just as concerned, and every night they would be waiting on the roadside holding a kerosene lantern and sometimes snacks to help ease the children's hunger pangs. Despite how tough the commute was for the children, going first to English school and then to Japanese school, they managed to keep up with their schoolwork, and excelled in both schools.

Kana also worked in the sugarcane fields. "I did *ho hana* [weeding] in the pineapple field and *hole hole* [stripping cane leaves]. I had to get up early and make so many *bento*. Only with few hours of sleep I went to work. So many children, no choice. When you young we don't feel tired, no matter how hard you work. Sad thing, no matter how hard we worked, never had enough money to pay bills. We work in the pine field and get 75 cents a day. If you work with fertilizer team you get $1. We thought that was plenty money. When I was pregnant with my third girl, the *haole luna* told me to quit before I give birth in the pine field."

Whenever Koho received his paycheck from the plantation at the end of the month, he brought home an empty envelope because everything the family had charged at the plantation store was deducted from his pay before he received it. It was very frustrating. That was when he would start drinking nonstop and begin to get violent. He was a completely different person when he got drunk.

"My boy was weak, he had pleurisy, and had surgery. He almost died. He stayed in Kuakini Hospital one month. Those days, for serious illness, we were afraid to go to plantation hospital, even if it was free. No matter how difficult it was to pay the medical bills, we went to hospital in Honolulu." Kana made sake to keep from getting into further debt. "However, Koho drank more sake, so I tell him I no make any more sake. When war came I had to stop making sake." Though Koho had a bad temper when he was drunk, when he was sober, he was a good man and a hard worker. He even grew vegetables and potatoes in or around the cane fields. Daughter Ruth remembered, "He made his own cart to haul his harvest. He shared some with the neighbors, and the good ones he sold to the stores. He made sure it was the best ones. When he offered us some of his harvest, we better accept it whether we wanted to or not. Otherwise, he got very angry."

WORLD WAR II

On December 7, 1941, Japan dropped bombs on Pearl Harbor. This incident completely changed the lives of the Higa family and all the other Japanese families in

Hawaii. From their camps in Kunia, they could see the planes attacking the ships in Pearl Harbor and hear the explosions. Ruth attended Waipahu High School until tenth grade, but after the attack on Pearl Harbor, the schools were closed. The schoolchildren had to help with the war effort by working in the pineapple or sugarcane fields. When the schools reopened, Ruth transferred to and graduated from McKinley High School. After graduation, she worked for an optical company, later apprenticed at a beauty salon, and then worked in a restaurant. She gave her paycheck to her mother and kept only the tips.

Koho always complained to Kana, "Why you wanna send kids to high school?" Kana, who had been forced to quit after the fifth grade and had been deprived of a high school education, was determined to send the children to high school. Kana added, "I also sent my girls to learn sewing. Ruth is an excellent seamstress. Besides the Western type of clothing, she also sews the colorful kimonos and elaborate children's costumes for the Okinawan dances. She sewed her kimono made of *bashofu,* which is stiff and very difficult to sew."

In 1942, after World War II broke out, Kana became pregnant again, at age forty-one. When she told Koho she was pregnant, he yelled at her: *"Osumara you makure no shame ka* [what's the matter, you old lady, no shame at your age]?" Without much empathy from Koho, she kept herself busy and worked until the ninth month. When her birth pains started, Koho was nowhere to be found. As usual, he was drinking somewhere. There was no one around the camp who could help. Kana was getting desperate. All these years, the issei mothers had depended on the midwives; however, after the Pearl Harbor attack, things changed completely. The midwives, because they were aliens, were banned from entering certain areas near military installations, and had to obey 6:00 p.m. curfews. Kana tried to find someone to help her with the birth, but during the war, many young people had left their low-paying plantation jobs and switched to defense jobs that paid well, so there was no one around.

"Chieko and Ruth were working in Honolulu. The boys were working in the pineapple fields. No telephone. Baby coming, so I just grabbed a few things and started walking. I must have worn a cotton dress and slippers and started walking toward the Waipahu Plantation Hospital, near Pearl Harbor." Kana walked over five miles from Camp Twenty-four to Waipahu Plantation Hospital. The long walk must have done her a lot of good, she said, because she had an easy delivery and gave birth to the baby before the doctor arrived. She stayed for a few days at the hospital and then walked all the way home to Camp Twenty-four carrying the newborn baby. This was the first and only time Kana had given birth in the hospital.

Kana continued, "When my husband got TB, he went to Leahi Hospital one year. He was shocked. He cried and cried, '*Mo betta ma ke* [better that I die].' People were so afraid and stayed away." While Koho was sick and couldn't work for a year, Kana was surprised to find that the amount they owed on their grocery bill was over $1,000. "All the Japanese stores that we've been buying from for years now stopped selling to us, and would not let us charge. Even friends in camp never lend us even 5 cents." Kana could never forget Mr. Sanpei, who was from Fukushima prefecture. "He was the only salesman who was so kind to let us buy on credit from the plantation store. I never forgot his kindness," Kana said tearfully.

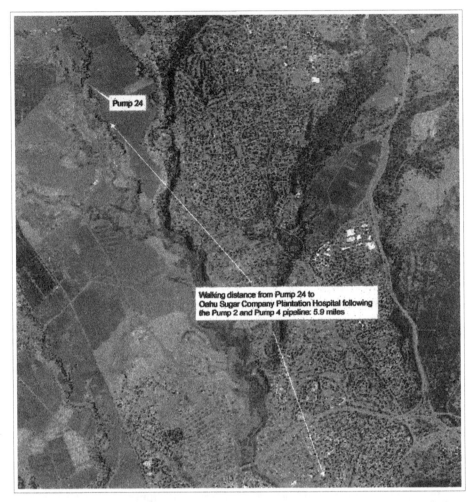

Pump 24

Walking distance from Pump 24 to
Oahu Sugar Company Plantation Hospital following
the Pump 2 and Pump 4 pipeline: 5.9 miles

An aerial photo of Royal Kunia subdivision in Waipahu today, which shows the distance Kana walked
from Camp Twenty-four, which was near Pump Twenty-four on the map, to the hospital when she went
into labor with her last child (5.9 miles). Photo courtesy of Glenn Oyama.

After Koho recovered from tuberculosis, he never touched sake again. He kept
on saying, "It wasn't me that was mean, it was the sake." For ten years Koho did not
drink. He realized that if he quit drinking and smoking, he could save some money.
He began cooking for the family, made coffee for breakfast, mopped, cleaned the
house, and treated Kana well. He kept apologizing to his family, "*Gomen nasai* [I'm
so sorry]." This was the beginning of many happy times visiting his children who
had moved away to the mainland. He enjoyed life with his wife and family. For
Kana, this was the start of a new life that she had never thought was possible.

When the last child was old enough, Kana started working in the pineapple cannery as a trimmer. "That was a tough job," she said. She would get up at 5:00 a.m.

and work eight hours a day for 17 cents an hour. She retired from that job at age sixty-five. Then she got a job as a janitor and worked four more years. After that she worked as a maid and took care of an invalid Chinese woman in Pearl City who lived until the age of 107. At that point Kana was seventy-three. She took care of her grandchildren for three years and enjoyed pampering them and teaching them the traditional Okinawan culture and values.

RETURN TO OKINAWA

In 1979, after retiring from their long years of hard work, Kana and Koho wanted to celebrate their fifty-seven years of marriage by taking a leisurely trip to visit their relatives and friends in Okinawa. One day Koho told Ruth, "Yukie, among the nine children, you have done the most for us. You were the most *oyakoko* [expressive of filial piety], so in gratitude I want to give you a trip to Japan." Ruth was ecstatic about this unexpected gift, for she had never been to mainland Japan or Okinawa. She contacted the Sus Tomita Travel Agency and they took care of all the travel arrangements. Ruth joined their deluxe tour to Japan, while Kana and Koho went directly to Okinawa. Ruth enjoyed an exquisite three weeks touring and then joined her parents. She couldn't wait to tell her father how much she had enjoyed visiting the fascinating and historical places in Japan.

When she arrived in Okinawa, however, she was shocked to find her father seriously ill in the hospital. Koho had duodenal ulcers with severe hemorrhaging that required ten blood transfusions. He had an operation. However, the doctor told Ruth that she should not worry, and that she could go home. Since her three-week tour was over, she returned to Hawaii with the tour group. As soon as she stepped into her house, the phone rang. The voice on the other end said, "Father died." She was shocked, because the doctor had said that her father was going to be all right! Without unpacking, she grabbed her luggage and took the next flight back to Okinawa.

FUNERAL IN OKINAWA

Ruth was still in shock and concerned about her mother. By the time she arrived, they had taken her father's body back to the house where he was born. "He was seated upright in a small coffin. The next day, they took him to be cremated in the mountains." The family then picked out the bones to put in the urn. The stress of Koho's unexpected passing must have been too much for Kana, for Ruth recalled, "Mother almost fainted at the crematorium."

Ruth said, "Father died when he was eighty-six years old. He probably knew that his time was near and wanted to go back to the place of his birth to enjoy his last days." When I asked Ruth what kind of memorial service he had in Okinawa, she replied, "It was my father's dying wish that, 'although I'm a Buddhist at heart, it is difficult for the children to keep up with the Buddhist tradition, so please have a Christian service for me.'" Since Kana had converted to the Christian faith earlier, she felt this meant that they would be together in paradise.

RETURN TO HAWAII

While they were in Okinawa, their home in Hawaii was burglarized and some of the money Koho had hidden was gone. The plantation wanted Kana to move now that she was alone. She refused; there were too many memories in that place. Ruth cooked for her and took her shopping. She wanted her mother to live with her, but Kana wanted to stay in her home. Then one day Kana walked to Ruth's house, and she lived with her after that.

Over the next two decades Kana was able to visit relatives in Peru and Brazil. She took several trips to Las Vegas and went to Bangkok. In 1982, Ruth, Grace, and Kana went back to Okinawa. Kana became an American citizen on February 9, 1983.

Kana loved to study. Years after she retired, she attended adult education classes to learn English. She practiced writing English words and was able to recognize written names. How proud she was to be sitting beside other senior citizens of various ethnic groups to study together.

Kana Higa died of cardiopulmonary arrest on May 11, 2001, at the age of ninety-nine years, five weeks, and six days. She had twenty-three grandchildren.

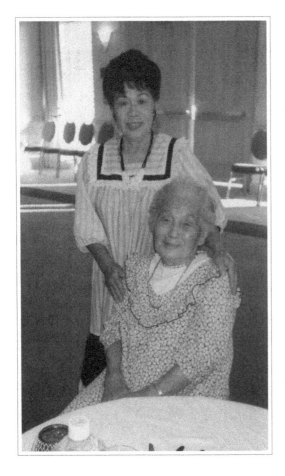

Kana Higa and daughter Ruth Oshiro at Kayo Hatta's *Picture Bride* film, 1994. Barbara Kawakami Collection.

Kana had lived a very productive life and finally found happiness in her twilight years. She was always surrounded and cared for by her loving family. Her later years were the happiest, after Koho, her husband, finally gave up drinking sake. Today, Koho and Kana rest side by side in the tranquil setting of the beautiful Byodoin Gardens in Nuuanu, where they have found eternal peace.

Ushi Tamashiro
IN SEARCH OF A FATHER'S BECKONING SPIRIT

September 26, 1902–May 5, 1986
Born in Kokuba, Naha-shi, Okinawa
Arrived in Hawaii February 18, 1923

Ushi Tamashiro was a born storyteller, with a soft-spoken and relaxed manner. Her large eyes sometimes twinkled with laughter when she recalled something funny about her childhood in a farming village in Okinawa, or at times filled with tears when she remembered something sad. Ushi's reason for wanting to come to Hawaii to marry a plantation laborer was quite unusual. Some time before, her father had gone to Hawaii, leaving behind his wife and their two children, with the thought of making big money there and later returning to Okinawa. He worked very hard but died within three years, before he could fulfill that dream. Although his ashes were brought back to Okinawa, his family believed that his spirit was still unsettled and had not reached nirvana, and that the spirit had been sending a message through Ushi's aunt in Okinawa. This was the determining factor that led to Ushi's decision to come to Hawaii as a picture bride to marry a man she had never met.

CHILDHOOD IN KOKUBA

Ushi Kakazu was born in a farming village on September 26, 1902. She described it as a fairly large village with about two hundred households. There were many Kakazus in the village, not necessarily related to each other despite the shared surname. This may have caused some confusion to an outsider in identifying a specific family. Another common name in that village was Kaneshiro. Although the home she grew up in was just average for a poor farming family, she felt it was nothing to be ashamed of. The walls of the house were built of sturdy bamboo, and it had a thatched roof that provided good ventilation in the warm, balmy climate of Okinawa.

"My grandparents were all farmers and owned their own land. Both my mother and father were born in the same village. In those days, marriages were arranged by parents because they preferred to have the bride from the same village for economic reasons. My father was four years younger than my mother. Both my parents, my

Ushi Tamashiro at home in Kalihi, 1985. Barbara Kawakami Collection.

brother, and grandparents worked very hard growing sugarcane, sweet potatoes, *gobo* [burdock], *araimo* [Japanese taro], and a variety of other vegetables on their own land."

Ushi described how the sweet potatoes and produce were taken to the market after they were harvested. By the time the produce was piled into a large *boki* (straw basket), it weighed about thirty to forty pounds. Everyone carried the heavy baskets on their heads as they headed toward the marketplace. It required some skill to balance the basket and to keep its contents from spilling.

Ushi said, "In Okinawa, the purple sweet potato is our staple food, and we ate it morning, noon, and night. We also ate the *kanda-ba* [green leaf of the sweet potato vine], which was sometimes added into *chuk* [rice gruel], which was very nutritious and kept us healthy. That is how the poor people were able to survive. We used to make our own green barley and *majin* [young sugarcane]."

Ushi chuckled as she recalled how, because she didn't have any younger brothers or sisters, she suckled at her mother's breast longer than most children. She hardly attended school, but even though she was absent a lot, somehow she was able to complete the sixth grade.

By the time Ushi was twelve, she was given the responsibility of caring for the horses, including cutting grass every morning to feed them. At age fourteen, she was sent into the field to do regular farming and worked from dawn to dusk. Ushi had only one older brother. He, too, worked on the farm, but eventually he emigrated to Brazil with other young men of the village. "I was very close to my brother and enjoyed visiting him in Brazil after World War I," Ushi recalled. Other than

doing heavy work on the farm, she spent part of her time weaving straw hats out of
areneba [palm leaf] to earn extra income. It was during this time that her father
emigrated to Hawaii as a contract laborer, thus leaving her mother completely under the dominance of her in-laws.

Her grandfather woke her mother up at four every morning to begin work in the
fields and to do all the domestic chores. Ushi did not cherish the idea of what life
would be like if she married a farmer's son in the village.

BECKONED BY HER FATHER'S UNSETTLED SPIRIT

Because of the difficult and demanding workload expected of her at home, Ushi was
happy to come to Hawaii as a picture bride. Many girls who went to Hawaii to marry
plantation laborers sent back pictures of themselves wearing dressy kimonos. Ushi
envisioned a life of luxury in a foreign land. She felt that she would not have to live a
boring existence as a farm wife, constantly being dominated by in-laws.

"I was about twenty years old when my mother's male cousin approached my
family to arrange a picture exchange marriage between a man in Hawaii and me,"
Ushi continued. "At first, my mother was opposed to the idea because my father had
died on foreign soil. I was close to my mother's cousin, and I felt he was more a
dear uncle to me. He and this man in Honolulu, Jintaro Tamashiro [who would

Ushi Tamashiro (1902–1986)

Ushi Kakazu's exchange photo when
arrangements were made to marry
Jintaro Tamashiro, 1923. The striped silk
kimono and *kasuri haori* were lent to her
by the photographer in Okinawa. Barbara
Kawakami Collection.

later become her husband], were close friends, more like brothers. Photos had been exchanged, which I wasn't aware of. When my grandparents and my mother saw the prospective groom's picture, they thought he looked like a nice man, and they trusted the judgment of my mother's cousin. Imagine the age difference . . . he was thirty-three years old, and I was twenty!"

Ushi later found out that her mother had already sent her photo to her cousin in Hawaii, asking his help to arrange the marriage with his friend. Now, gazing at this photo, she explained that the photographer in Okinawa had loaned her the exquisite, handwoven Ryukyu *gasuri* kimono, because her mother couldn't afford such a fine kimono. Ushi understood that her mother could not do much for her at all, since she had to live with her in-laws. "She really had a rough time after my father died, but she served her in-laws well until they died," said Ushi, remembering her mother's circumstances.

"It was during this time that my dead father's spirit kept sending messages through my aunt's body in Okinawa, saying, 'My spirit is still left in Hawaii, so please let me rest in peace.' There were repeated messages through my aunt's body because she talked about it all the time. She was like a shaman and could communicate with a deceased spirit. My uncle also became concerned about my father's restless spirit. I guess that was one of the reasons that motivated me to come here. I also heard exciting tales circulating around the village, and I used to daydream about going there someday. Yet on the other hand . . . there was that fear of venturing to an unknown destination."

Ushi explained, "My mother's cousin acted as the *nakoodo* for my marriage and also assisted me with the preparation of my simple dowry. I did bring a few fine kimonos with me at that time. However, after the outbreak of World War II, when Okinawa was turned into a battleground between American and Japanese forces, many of my relatives lost everything, especially their clothing, so I sent back whatever kimonos I had."

MARRIAGE IN ABSENTIA AT THE VILLAGE IN OKINAWA

Since the prospective groom was in Hawaii, Ushi did not have a formal wedding; however, her family, relatives, and close friends celebrated the occasion with a small party. She said she did not have a *montsuki* like the brides from the main island of Japan, but wore instead a dressy kimono with an obi and a simple hairdo.

Although her groom-to-be was not present, she made the pretense of entering his home as his bride. Her girlfriends formed a circle around the bride to shield her face and escorted her into the groom's home. According to tradition, the guests should not see the bride until she appeared at the party. The girls wore casual or dressy kimonos of handwoven, colorful *kasuri* cloth, *bashofu* (cloth made of plantain banana fiber), and *tsumugi* (striped pongee) cloth. Even without the groom, there was much feasting and drinking.

"At my in-laws' house, there was quite a feast prepared for the bridal party and guests. In those days in Okinawa, they did not make sushi as the *naichi* people did in Hawaii, but instead they served red rice [rice with *azuki* beans] to mark the festive occasion. Pork cooked in *shoyu* and tofu tempura were also served. Usually two slices of pork and two slices of *kamaboko* [fish cake] were placed on each plate. As *osonae-mon* [side dishes], *somen* and *namasu* were served."

VOYAGE ACROSS THE PACIFIC

After bidding farewell to family and friends in Naha, Ushi boarded the *Siberia Maru* and left for Hawaii via Kobe. In Kobe, she was detained for a month because of pinkeye. Ushi was relieved when the ship finally set sail.

"The voyage across the Pacific Ocean took ten days, but there were many other picture brides on board. That made the sea voyage exciting and fun! I became good friends with a girl who came from Tamagasuku village. Her father was the owner of Nakamura Mortuary on Maui. She came as a *yobi-yose*. We are still the best of friends. We used to meet at the Lanikila Senior Center often, until my legs started giving me trouble and I had trouble walking."

The *Siberia Maru* anchored in Honolulu harbor on February 18, 1923. "All the picture brides were so excited," said Ushi. "We applied face cream to pretty ourselves and dressed in our best kimonos to meet our husbands for the first time. In our village in Okinawa, we were never allowed to put on powder or lipstick. There were strict rules about girls using makeup."

ARRIVAL AND FIRST MEETING WITH HUSBAND

"As soon as we disembarked from the ship, all the women and young girls were put on a *tsuraka* [truck]—you know, the kind used to pick up *buta kau kau* [pig slop]. It was truly a funny sight. All the *naichi* and *uchinanchu* [Okinawan] brides, hanging on to their *kori,* were packed like horses into the truck. It was a rough ride standing in a crowded truck, until we reached the immigration station.

"At the immigration station, we were led into a large room and we were scared. We wondered where they were taking us. The place looked more like a *kara boshi* [jail], where we were detained for five days. In the meantime, we had to take the physical exams along with eye tests and written exams. The written test was quite simple. It was written in Japanese, so I read it aloud, 'You have a mole on your right eye,' and I passed."

Ushi was fortunate to have an old friend from her village who was living in Honolulu. "He had sent in food for me, and some navel oranges. That was the first time I had ever tasted one; it was so delicious. To this day, I cannot forget that taste. My husband had to come from the Big Island of Hawaii by boat, so I had a long wait. Some husbands never came to pick up their wives. It was so sad."

Ushi had begun to feel the anxiety of being an unclaimed bride when her husband, Jintaro, finally showed up. The first words he uttered were "*Genki de kitaka* [oh, you have arrived safely]." As soon as her husband cleared the official papers, he hired someone with a Model T Ford, the type with no roof, and drove them directly to a minister's home, where they were married in a brief ceremony. "The Christian minister must have prayed for us and mumbled some words, but of course, we couldn't understand a word of what he said. When the ceremony was over, he let my husband and me shake hands. The minister may have meant for us to hold hands. Then he congratulated us and someone took pictures. I kept the marriage certificate he had given us that day. Years later, to apply for my American citizenship, I had to show my marriage certificate, but the official never returned it to me. I don't know what happened to the photos taken at the wedding ceremony," Ushi mentioned regretfully, with a sad little smile.

SEARCH FOR HER FATHER'S RESTING PLACE

Right away, Ushi and her husband started searching for the home where she believed her father had lived until he died. Her mother's cousin, who was their go-between, had brought Ushi's father's ashes back to Okinawa, but Ushi wanted to purify the spot and ask forgiveness from his spirit so he could enter nirvana. The place where Ushi's father had lived was on Vineyard and River Streets. There, prayers were offered by a Buddhist priest. A few older fellow villagers and young men from Okinawa gathered to join them in prayer. After the blessing, a letter was sent to Okinawa, and the family seemed relieved.

FIRST HOME ON THE BIG ISLAND

Ushi was completely disillusioned when she and her husband arrived at Ninole, an isolated place in Hakalau, on the Big Island. It was a privately owned homestead and her new home stood in the middle of the sugarcane field. She said, "The house reminded me of the *yadegua* [outside playhouse] back in the village in Okinawa. It's hard to imagine how difficult life was for the early immigrants in those days. The one thing I felt better about was that I could eat white rice every day. In Okinawa, we grew up on sweet potatoes, so this was quite a change."

PREGNANCY AND CHILDBIRTH

As soon as Ushi settled in her new home, she started working in the sugarcane fields with her husband. When she became pregnant, she suffered severe morning sickness and couldn't continue to work. Once in a while, when she felt better, she helped with *ho hana* (weeding), until she gave birth to a baby girl in an easy delivery. Although there wasn't enough time to call a midwife, there was a lady in Ninole who was from her village in Okinawa and was skilled enough to deliver babies. "In those days, everybody was struggling on their meager earnings, so the midwife charged only $2 or $3 for a prenatal check-up, and $5 to deliver the baby. Even that amount was too difficult for some people. They gave whatever they could afford. Altogether, I gave birth to eight children. All of them I had at home, no trouble. Sometimes, if the midwife didn't arrive on time, neighbors pitched in to help. While the children were growing up, I was a full-time mother, sending the older ones to school, and my husband went out to work."

Ushi recalled, "In Okinawa, when a woman had a new baby, all the relatives and friends would gather to celebrate, drink up, play the *sanshin*, and be merry. Here in an isolated plantation camp, it was only my husband, the new baby, and me. The closest neighbor was quite a distance away, and fellow villagers from back home were too exhausted from working in the cane fields all day. They, too, were lonely, and would come for a brief visit at night to see the newborn baby, but they needed a good night's rest to get up early the next day, so there was no time to cele-brate. I didn't have the appetite to *kau kau* [eat]. The Big Island was a very lonely place and I used to cry myself to sleep at night. Never in my life did I realize the utter hopelessness of living in such an isolated place like Ninole."

Ushi's eyes filled with tears as she remembered that awful day when her four-year-old girl got sick with measles and then came down with diphtheria. There were no doctors in Ninole, so she would have to go to Hilo, and the only means to get there was by train, since no one owned a car in those days. "Sometimes we used the plantation cane car, loaded with the sugar cane, then transferred to a regular train to get to Hilo. I didn't know the train schedule and I missed the 7:00 a.m. train, so I had to wait until 4:30 in the afternoon. With that schedule, it was impossible to take my daughter to the doctor on time. She died on the train before we arrived in Hilo. It was too late to save my little girl. In those days, immunization for diphtheria was still unheard of. The grief of losing my first daughter was too much for me to bear. I was constantly reminded of her tragic death, and I decided to move from Ninole."

MOVE TO HONOLULU

Compared to most issei women of that period, Ushi considered herself very fortu-nate. Her husband, Jintaro, was a hard worker and he didn't expect her to go to work while the children were young. He always handed over his paycheck, from

Ushi with children at Hind-Clarke Dairy, where her husband worked, in east Honolulu. Barbara Kawakami Collection.

which she would give him a small allowance. He never took more than he needed. That was very unusual in those days, when most husbands went out to gamble or drink and never gave their wives any money. While in Ninole, he worked in the sugarcane fields, but after they moved to Honolulu, he began working for Hind-Clarke Dairy, a job he held for about six years.

She chuckled as she continued telling her story. "In Hakalau, on the Big Island, I had never seen issei women wearing shoes. No one could afford it. Women wore *geta* [clogs] all the time, everywhere. In Honolulu, for the first time, I noticed how nicely the issei women were dressed. It was a new experience to have a dress made for myself. I bought my first pair of shoes." Mr. Tsuha, a family friend, was anxious to try out his new camera and took pictures of Ushi and her children dressed in their new outfits, posed in front of a Model T Ford. He must have made a double exposure. "When I saw the pictures, I cut out the two halves and joined them together." Ushi was anxious to send that picture to her brother, whom she had not seen since he emigrated to Brazil, before she left for Hawaii.

The *haole* boss at Hind-Clarke Dairy paid Jintaro well, compared to the meager pay he had earned at Kohala sugar plantation. He worked seven days a week, for $75 a month. The only problem was the distance the children had to commute to school, so they moved to a place called Aina Kua, where the Star of the Sea School is standing today. At that time, it was nothing but a wilderness of kiawe trees.

At this new location, her husband worked as a stonecutter for a company. He also labored for the city and county as a maintenance man. Ushi was still not working during this time, because the older children were still going to school, but she began working after the children were all grown up.

WIDOWHOOD AND HARDSHIPS

Ushi thought she had left the hard life behind in Okinawa, but what she had to bear in Hawaii was even worse. Jintaro died in 1942, when he was fifty-two years old and Ushi was only thirty-nine. Her oldest son was sixteen years old, while her seventh child was barely two. While raising her first three children, she did not have to work in the sugarcane fields except to help Jintaro once in a while. However, after her husband died, she had to find a way to survive and keep the children together. "In those days, we had no knowledge of birth control and I had one child after another. During the Depression years the pay was so small, it was impossible to save any money.

"One thing my husband did for me, while he was still alive, really helped me to survive the crisis," Ushi said with tears of gratitude. "While I was staying home and raising the children, he built a hog pen and chicken coop to help me get started working on a part-time basis. After he died, I started raising hogs and chickens to make a living and support my children. I had three sows and about sixty or seventy red hens. The chickens were *tamago-dori* [egg-laying hens]. They laid red eggs [dark-colored eggs], which sold for a higher price. From then on, I bought chickens to raise and sell as fryers and broilers." When the laying hens could no longer produce eggs, Ushi used them to feed her family.

SUPPORT FROM THE CHILDREN

Her oldest girl, Chiyoko, had to quit school after ninth grade to help support the family. She worked as a domestic for a *haole* family. Their name was Rodrigues, but Japanese people regarded Portuguese people as *haole*. The family lived on Wilhelmina Rise, a very steep street going straight up a ridge. Chiyoko, at age fourteen, walked every day from Waialae Avenue to her workplace. However, when Pearl Harbor was attacked on December 7, 1941, the Rodrigueses were afraid to stay in Hawaii and decided to move back to the mainland.

"They were very nice people, you know. They told my daughter if she could find a better job, to go ahead. They paid her well. Before they left for the mainland, they did find a job for her at Kodak Hawaii. My oldest daughter really was a tremendous help in supporting her brothers and sisters. She began working at such a young age. So now all her brothers and sisters are good to her. I always taught my children, 'Your older sister sacrificed a lot to send you to high school when she herself had to quit school early, so be good to her.' She, too, became a young widow, thirteen years ago. She has four children. Her oldest son will graduate from college next year. My children are all good to their oldest sister, and they visit her often and help her whenever she needs help."

WORKING AT THE PINEAPPLE CANNERY

In addition to raising hogs and chickens, Ushi worked at the California Packing Corporation cannery as a pineapple trimmer. She also worked at the tuna packers for about two years. When her oldest daughter got the job with Kodak Hawaii, her second-oldest daughter took over the household chores and took care of the siblings. She was a big help, too. Ushi's face beamed with pride as she talked about her children. Ushi would prepare supper for the children before she left for the night shift at the cannery. "But I never got sick, even once!" she said. "The girls cleaned the dishes. I hardly had enough sleep during those days. During the daytime, I was busy taking care of the hogs and chickens, cleaning the pen and the coop, and feeding the animals. My second son, Kenneth, helped me a lot with this. Before and after school, he helped to pick up the slop for the hogs and cook it for a long time. At least the children were able to finish high school, except for the oldest girl.

"My deepest pleasure was in watching the children get along well together. They all helped in every way they could to ease my burden. They helped with many household chores, before going to school and after coming home from school. Those were my happiest moments. It helped to take away all the weariness I felt from the long hours of work, besides helping to forget the pain and loneliness. How happy I felt to be blessed with such loving and wonderful children."

WORKING SEVEN DAYS A WEEK

For Ushi there was never a day of rest. On Sundays she got up early to catch the 4:45 a.m. bus from Waialae to downtown Honolulu to sell eggs at the corner of River Street and Aala Park. "I used to wake up my number two boy, Kenneth, to help me carry the thirty dozen eggs. He was very small then. He must have been in the sixth grade, about eleven years old. I packed twenty dozen cartons in a box, and he carried this load on his shoulder. I carried the rest. All my children helped out. They never complained. With that money, I could buy better food for the children. That was always on my mind. Eggs cost $1.50 a dozen then. The red eggs sold out in no time, and we were back home in Waialae by 8:00 a.m. It was Sunday, so the neighbors were just getting up. So, once a week on Sundays, with Kenneth's help, I went to sell eggs. The rest of the week, I was busy raising hogs and chickens."

To raise the hogs involved a lot of work. Ushi described how her older sons got up at 4:00 a.m. and went around the neighborhood with a pickup truck to gather the slop from the neighbors before they went to English school. After her husband died, people felt sorry for her and brought their garbage to her place. Sometimes the slop was in a fifty-pound barrel. Her neighbors were very helpful, and the *naichi* people were nice, too. "When we lived in Wailupe [now Aina Haina], we had a nice *naichi* neighbor who was very kind to us. Even now, we live nearby each other, and we're still good friends. Since I moved to Honolulu, I made many *naichi* friends."

RELIGION: CHANGES

Ushi remembered going to an ancient shrine every March 29, in Naha, Suenaga, Okinawa, where she and her girlfriends attended a special festival. On the way home, they would stop to see a movie. The girls went in a large group, so they were never afraid of the dark. Also, in Okinawa, ancestral worship was very important. Once a year, all the relatives got together, packed lunches, and had a picnic at the ancestral grave. There was a big space in front of the tombstone where everyone spread their food and celebrated the ancestral spirits.

In Okinawa, Ushi didn't adhere to any specific religion except for her belief in ancestral worship. When she moved to Honolulu, she joined the Higashi Hongwanji Temple and attended regular services for ten years. She made many new friends. However, a few years ago, she became seriously ill and almost died. Ushi admired the life that her second son, Kenneth, his wife, and their three children led as Christians. She told him that when she died, she wanted a Christian funeral service. Kenneth then told her, "Mother, rather than becoming a Christian after you die, it's better to become one now . . . that might be better." Although she decided to become a Christian, she wasn't baptized. Ushi explained, "I can't attend services on Sundays anymore. My legs are real bad. I can't walk very far, but I read the Bible every day; it's written in Japanese. I strongly believe in that religion, so it's the same as going to church. You see, in Okinawan custom, the oldest son is supposed to take care of the ancestral shrine and memorial tablets, but his wife divorced him, and she remarried. My oldest son never remarried. So I worried about who's going to take care of the Buddhist altar in my home after I die. That's the reason why I converted to the Christian faith."

MOTHER'S GOOD HEALTH, LONG LIFE

When I interviewed her, Ushi said, "My mother died last year at the ripe old age of 106 years old. She was very healthy, so the health specialist in Okinawa visited her annually to document her report. Even at that age, she was never senile. She used to walk around the neighborhood to visit relatives. She was an *inkyo* [retired from active work], and played around with all the grandchildren and great-grandchildren. She ate whatever her grandchildren prepared for her, never anything special. She used to catch cold once in a while. My mother came to visit me in Hawaii when she was eighty-four years old, and stayed with me for six months. She was very spry and enjoyed herself. I think it was my mother's *shinko* [faith, belief] in ancestral worship that gave her such a long, happy life."

Ushi Tamashiro passed away in 1986 at the age of eighty-three. She was looking forward to attending the picture bride slide show that was to be presented at the Lanakila Senior Center, as she was one of the picture brides featured in the slide show. Regrettably, she passed away the day before the presentation. The program opened with a tribute to this exceptional wife, mother, and friend who had persevered through so much hardship with such an accepting and positive attitude.

E P I L O G U E

Dr. Tomizo Katsunuma

Almost every issei man and woman who entered the Territory of Hawaii as an immigrant between 1898 and 1924 met Dr. Tomizo Katsunuma, who worked as an inspector at the Hawaii immigration center during this time.

Dr. Tomizo Katsunuma had an illustrious background, and led an interesting life even before leaving Japan to study in the United States. He was born in Miharu town in Fukushima prefecture in 1863, the third son of a samurai family. After graduating from the boys's *chugakko* (middle school), he continued his studies at the prefectural Foreign Language School in Sendai. He later taught English at the *chugakko* in his hometown, Miharu.

Picture brides arriving at immigration station in Hawaii. Dr. Katsunuma is wearing a white cap.
Photo courtesy of Kiyomi Suzuki.

He excelled in his studies and received a four-year scholarship to the College of Veterinary Science of Tokyo. In 1889, just after marrying Mine Endo, he left for the United States to do further research in veterinary science in Utah and Idaho. There he took an interest in theology and continued to study English. While in Utah, he became a Mormon and a naturalized American citizen. (Mine would give birth to the couple's first child, a son named Katsumi, while Katsunuma was in the United States.)

In 1898, Katsunuma graduated from the University of Utah with a degree in veterinary medicine. I thought it was rather unusual for an issei to take an interest in being a veterinarian, so I asked Kiyomi, his daughter, about his education. She explained that Miharu, where Dr. Katsunuma was born and raised, was known for breeding the finest horses in Japan, dating back to the feudal period. During the warrior days, horses were used for battles and would need care, just like the warriors. So, according to Kiyomi, it was her father's lifelong dream to be a veterinarian when he returned to Japan.

But something unexpected happened when he stopped in Hawaii after his years in the United States. He was asked by the Kumamoto Emigration Company to help recruit immigrants in the Tohoku region. He agreed, returned to Japan, and solicited farmers to come to Hawaii. On July 26, 1898, the first group of a hundred or so immigrants from Fukushima, accompanied by Dr. Katsunuma, arrived in Hawaii. This was the turning point in his life. His wife, son, and newborn daughter, Kiyomi, would soon join him in Hawaii.

Because of his fluency in English and Japanese, his warm personality, and his sense of humor, he soon became an inspector to handle the arrival of immigrants from Japan coming to Hawaii. Katsunuma-san was well liked and respected, and he had a way of putting the newly arrived Japanese immigrants at ease. Japan is a homogenous society, so most of these new arrivals had never seen people from other ethnic groups. He understood the difficulties the newly arrived immigrants were facing in a strange new environment with so many strange faces. Every issei who met Katsunuma-san remembered him for his kindness and compassion in helping the poor and bewildered immigrants who had no one else to turn to. They only knew their own regional dialect, and most could not speak or understand a word of English. It was a terrifying experience for them to navigate the strict regulations and comprehensive examinations. If they did not pass these exams, they would be detained until they could pass the test. The test was in standard Japanese, which was taught in school, but many of these farmers were so poor that their schooling had ended in second or third grade. Katsunuma-san often helped the young brides so they could better understand the questions that were asked.

In 1990, when I interviewed Dr. Katsunuma's daughter, Kiyomi Suzuki, she was then ninety-one years old and still very sharp, witty, and knowledgeable about the many significant events that had taken place during that early period. "We lived on Metcalf and University Avenue. There was a constant flow of people from all walks of life, people bringing *omiyage,* large and small, to say thank you, whenever Father helped them with things they couldn't understand. Father was very fluent in English, so the early immigrants depended a lot on him." Her mother could not speak English, so when Kiyomi was a teenager she asked her daughter to accompany her father to social activities in her place. She said her father enjoyed social dancing and

Fushimi Taisho no Miya Denka (Prince Fushimi) and his retinue at the Japanese consulate in Honolulu were entertained with other foreign military dignitaries on November 3, 1904. Dr. Katsunuma is in the back row. Photo courtesy of Joseph Katsunuma.

danced with all the lovely ladies. He was very good at it, too. "During those days, whenever we would go to teahouse parties, my father never used chopsticks. The waitresses knew, and always prepared a knife and fork for him."

During the interview, she showed me photos of her wedding. Kiyomi and her husband were married at St. Andrew's Cathedral in Honolulu on September 6, 1923. Their marriage was arranged by a close family friend. She was dressed in a beautiful custom-made midcalf-length gown that was the fashion of that period, made from silk georgette, with an exquisite beaded bateau neckline. It was complemented with a long, flowing silk veil and a fluted net headpiece. Her two sisters, Yoshi and Yasu, served as maid of honor and bridesmaid and were also dressed in beautiful gowns. Keiji, the groom, was dressed in a swallowtail coat. Kiyomi said, "My father was planning a grand wedding with friends of various ethnic groups, many dignitaries, and all the consulate people. That would have been the social event of the year." However, something unexpected happened that changed everything. On September 1, 1923, a major earthquake struck Tokyo, centered in the Kanto area. More than ten thousand people were killed. "When my father heard of this great disaster, he decided to donate the money he had set aside for the lavish wedding reception to help the victims of the earthquake," said Kiyomi, her heart swelling with pride as she told me this story.

Mr. and Mrs. Keiji Suzuki were married at St. Andrew's Cathedral in Honolulu on September 6. 1923. Photo courtesy of Kiyomi Suzuki.

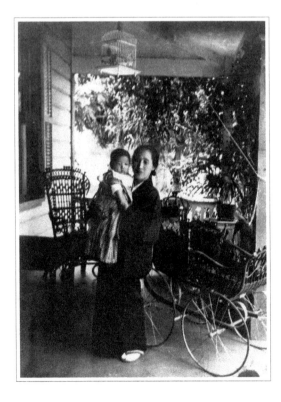

Mrs. Mine Katsunuma and her infant son Joseph, taken at their home on Metcalf Avenue. Dr. Katsunuma had bought the old Japanese consulate building and moved it to that location. Photo courtesy of Kiyomi Suzuki.

At the time, Kiyomi was twenty-four years old and Keiji Suzuki was twenty-seven. Kiyomi told me that when her husband had attended the Mid-Pacific Institute, he worked on campus as the yard man to finance his studies. Then he attended the University of Hawaii at Manoa and majored in civil engineering. He excelled in his studies and was one of the first issei to graduate with a degree in that field. Soon after graduating, he was hired by Castle & Cooke to work at the Ewa sugar plantation as an engineer. "It was his professor," she added, "who recommended him for the job. He worked there for fifty years."

Kiyomi had been an English teacher after graduating from normal school. After her marriage, though, she worked on the plantation as a clerk at the store. Later she worked as a dental hygienist and did a lot of volunteer work for the plantation community. She never returned to teaching after marriage and kept busy raising their three children. I truly respect and admire Kiyomi, who as a teenager had enjoyed a high-society lifestyle, wearing beautiful gowns and attending elegant functions in keeping with her father's high status, and then, when she married, went to live at the dusty, isolated Ewa sugar plantation for fifty years. "My lifestyle completely changed after moving out to Ewa plantation. Yet because my husband was an engineer and we lived on Manager's Circle, we were invited to dinner frequently by the manager and his wife," she explained.

In the 1980s, I was still doing some sewing while attending the University of Hawaii in Manoa. To keep up with my Japanese, I always listened to the Japanese-

Dr. Katsunuma with immigration station officials, ca. 1910–1915. Photo courtesy of Kiyomi Suzuki.

language radio broadcast. One day, I was listening to the daily talk show where people called in with whatever topic they wanted to discuss. An elderly issei woman began telling her story. I stopped my sewing to listen. She said, "I came as a picture bride in the early 1900s from a farming village with only a fourth-grade education. My family was struggling to make a living and arranged this marriage to a plantation laborer in Hawaii with the exchange of photos. I was afraid—I had never traveled outside of my prefecture until then.

"Finally the boat arrived in Hawaii. After the inspections and examination, I waited with the other picture brides. One by one, the other picture brides were claimed by husbands who held their photos. At the end, I was standing alone. No one came. I waited every day, hoping . . . I was beginning to panic, not knowing a soul in Hawaii. My husband-to-be had only sent a one-way fare and I had no money to return to Japan. After I had been waiting for two weeks, Dr. Katsunuma took pity on me and took me home. His wife, Mine-san, was kind and gracious and treated me warmly.

"After I had been staying with them for a while, Dr. Katsunuma acted as a go-between and found me a good husband." She continued amid sobs, "I can never forget the kindness of Katsunuma-san. Even if I myself had searched for a husband, I could never have found a man as wonderful, kind, and hardworking as the man who became my husband." They had a long and happy marriage. It touched me deeply that an issei woman would share such a personal story on a radio program.

Every man and woman I talked to for my research on plantation clothing mentioned Katsunuma-san's extraordinary kindness. He made them feel welcome. He showed them aloha. Eventually he became known as the "father of the issei pioneers." He is my hero. This collection of personal stories is thus a tribute to Dr. Tomizo Katsunuma, recognizing his outstanding work on behalf of the early Japanese immigrants. Katsunuma-san was truly a man filled with the aloha spirit.

GLOSSARY

ahina	[Hawaiian] blue denim cloth
bashofu	[Ryukyu] cloth made from plantain banana fiber
bento	packed lunch taken to work, school, picnics, etc.
bento bukuro	bento bag with long strap, made of denim, used to carry the double-decker lunch can to work in the fields
daikon	Japanese radish
fujinkai	women's association
furo	typical plantation-style Japanese bathtub, made of redwood with a copper bottom, all placed on a concrete foundation with an earthen furnace on the outside, fired with kiawe wood
futon	comforter, cotton-filled bedding; thin ones were used for coverlets, thick ones for mattresses
Gannen Mono	"first-year people," or Japanese who migrated in the first year of the Meiji Era, 1868; the first group of Japanese immigrants to Hawaii
geta	a wooden clog held on the foot by a thong that passes between the first and second toes
goza	straw matting
gun	district, county, subprefecture
hakama	divided ankle-length skirt with deep pleats at the waist, worn over the kimono; paired with *haori* for men's formal wear
hana	[Hawaiian] work, labor
hanahana	[Pidgin] work, labor
haole	[Hawaiian] Caucasian; foreigner
haori	short, medium, or three-quarter-length coat worn over a kimono
hapa haole	[Hawaiian] part Caucasian
hapai	[Hawaiian] to carry; pregnant
hapai ko	[Hawaiian] to carry bundles of sugarcane; laborers who did the heavy work of carrying cut sugarcane on their

	shoulders to the train cane cars were called *hapai ko* gangs
hiyoku	an underkimono that is single and unlined but looks like a double- or triple-layered kimono because of the color contrast added at the sleeve opening and at the hemline
ho hana	[Hawaiian] field work digging weeds with a hoe
holoku	[Hawaiian] a muumuu that features a train
hui	[Hawaiian] an association
issei	first-generation immigrant Japanese
jika tabi	thick, rubber-soled canvas footwear worn by field workers or fishermen
kaki	persimmon
kanaka	a Hawaiian
kasuri	cotton, silk, or linen fabric with a splash (ikat) pattern produced by tying and dyeing the yarn before weaving
katami	keepsakes; specifically, the belongings of a deceased person that are distributed to family members and close friends as a remembrance
ken	prefecture
kiawe	[Hawaiian] species of mesquite tree, with beans used as hog feed, flowers used for honey, wood used to make charcoal, and ashes used to scrub pots and pans
kimono	a long, loose, straight-cut garment with long sleeves (the word literally means "thing to wear")
koko	pickled vegetables
kompang	[Filipino] sugarcane or pineapple cultivation by a small group; see *konpan*
konpan	[Japanese] Japanese pronunciation of the English word "company," referring to a group of people who formed a partnership under the leadership of one person, worked a designated area of sugarcane or pineapple land, and shared the profits, with the group leader paid somewhat more than the others
kori	wicker trunk, woven of strips of willow vine or bamboo
koseki	family register
koshimaki	wraparound underskirt worn under the kimono by women and young girls
kumpang	[Filipino] Filipino equivalent of *konpan*
luna	[Hawaiian] foreman or overseer
manju	bun with azuki or lima bean filling
meisen	an especially fine silk, usually striped
miso	fermented soybean paste
mizuhiki	decorative paper cords; silver and gold or red and white are used for auspicious occasions, pure white and black cords are used for solemn events
mochi	rice cake
mon	family crest

montsuki	term used by issei women in Hawaii to refer to *kuro tome sode*, formal five-crested kimono
mori mono	an assortment of foods that include *kamaboko* (sliced fish cake), *yokan* (sweet azuki bean squares), sweet potato fritters, cluster of grapes, and other foods; an uneven number of foods is served for happy occasions, an even number for funerals
mura	village
muumuu	[Hawaiian] long, loose, flowing gown that originally the missionary wives taught the Hawaiian women to sew and wear
naichi	Japanese from the main islands of Japan
nakoodo	marriage go-between
namasu	a dish of vegetables seasoned in vinegar
nisei	child born to issei; second-generation Japanese American
nishime	a dish of meat or poultry with vegetables seasoned with sugar and *shoyu*
obi	wide sash worn with a kimono
maru-obi	a dressier silk or brocaded sash of double width, folded lengthwise with selvage sewn together, making both sides identical; brought by many issei as part of their dowry
Obon	Buddhist festival during which the souls of the deceased return to their homes
okai	rice gruel
okazuya	Japanese delicatessen
orei	gratuity
papale	[Hawaiian] hat
pake	[Hawaiian] referring to Chinese
pata-pata-pata	sound of pattering
pau	[Hawaiian] finished
puka	[Hawaiian] hole
pula pula	[Hawaiian] cutting sugarcane stalks to make seedlings
Ryukyu-gasuri	Okinawan silk or cotton *kasuri* (splashed pattern design)
sake	rice wine
samurai	Japanese warrior
-san	honorific term
san san kudo	the exchange of nuptial cups by the bride and groom to seal their marriage vows
sansei	child of nisei; third-generation Japanese American
sanshin	Okinawan version of *shamisen*; three-stringed instrument with a snakeskin sound box
sashimi	thinly sliced raw fish
sensei	teacher
shamisen	three-stringed Japanese musical instrument
shibori	a Japanese resist dyeing technique for textiles, involving folding, crumpling, stitching, plaiting, plucking and

	twisting fabric, which is then secured in place by binding and knotting to create interesting designs with blurred edges*
sushi	rice seasoned with vinegar, salt, and sugar
tabi	cotton socks that have a division between the big toe and the other toes and are closed at the ankle by a *kohaze* (oblong metal clasp) that fastens into a loop
Takasago	Noh song or ballad sung at weddings until World War II
takashimada	ornately styled formal bridal coiffure
tanomoshi	a mutual financing system commonly used by issei men and women to help each other in time of need
tatami	straw matting, about three feet by six feet
tokoromon	fellow villager; colloquial, affectionate shortening of *tokoro mono,* which means "a person from the same place"
udon	thick noodles
ume	pickled plum
wahine	[Hawaiian] woman
waraji	hand-woven straw sandals
-ya	[Japanese] used after the name of a store, shop, or other place
yanagi-gori	wicker trunk made of willow vine
yobi-yose	someone who was summoned to Hawaii by relatives during the restricted immigration period, 1908–1924
yobi-yose jidai	"summoning by relatives period," or restricted immigration period, 1908–1924
yoshi	son-in-law adopted into his wife's family
yukata	unlined kimono made of printed cotton, worn for casual wear or dancing
zabuton	square, cotton-filled floor cushion
zori	thonged sandals

---

* Yoshiko Wada, Mary Kellog Rice, and Jane Barton, *Shibori: The Inventive Art of Japanese Shaped Resist Dyeing: Tradition, Techniques, Innovation* (Tokyo, 1983), 17.

INDEX

Page numbers in boldface type refer to illustrations.

ABOUT THE AUTHOR

BARBARA F. (OYAMA) KAWAKAMI was born in Japan in 1921, and immigrated to Hawaii with her family when she was only three months old. Her father died when she was young, and her widowed mother raised eight children alone by doing laundry for Waipahu sugar plantation bachelors.

While she and her husband raised three children, Barbara also had her own business as a dressmaker. She earned her GED diploma and went on to Leeward Community College at age fifty-three to earn an associate's degree. She transferred to the University of Hawaii at Manoa to earn a BS in fashion design and merchandising, and then a master's degree in Asian studies. Barbara has been a researcher, writer, and consultant in a number of projects, such as the *Picture Bride* series for Hawaii Public Television as well as the film *Picture Bride*, released by Miramax Pictures in 1994. Her first book, *Japanese Immigrant Clothing in Hawaii, 1885–1941*, was published by the University of Hawaii Press in 1993, and received several awards. She has been a consultant and lecturer almost continuously since its publication, notably with the Japanese American National Museum (JANM) in Los Angeles, where a major part of her collection is on display; other parts of her collection are part of the Smithsonian Institution in Washington, D.C. In 2012, JANM and the Bishop Museum in Honolulu presented a special exhibition, "Textured Lives," that used clothing to tell the story of Japanese immigrants working on the plantations of Hawaii. Barbara was recognized in 2012 by the Honpa Hongwanji Mission of Hawaii as a Living Treasure of Hawaii.

Today, at age ninety-four, Barbara continues to work and write, and *Picture Bride Stories* is the result of oral interviews and follow-up research on these women, who represent another variation of the American immigrant experience.